CITY OF QUARTZ

Excavating the Future
in Los Angeles

MIKE DAVIS

Photographs by

Robert Morrow

VERSO

London • New York

for my sweet Roísín
to remember her grandmother by . . .

First published by Verso 1990
This edition published by Verso 2006
© Verso 1990
Preface © Mike Davis 2006
All rights reserved

5 7 9 10 8 6

Verso
UK: 6 Meard Street, London W1F 0EG
USA: 180 Varick Street, New York, NY 10014-4606
www.versobooks.com

Verso is the imprint of New Left Books

ISBN-13: 978-1-84467-568-5
ISBN-10: 1-84467-568-8

British Library Cataloguing in Publication Data
A catalogue record for this book is available from the British Library

Library of Congress Cataloging-in-Publication Data
A catalog record for this book is available from the Library of Congress

Printed and bound by CPI Group (UK) Ltd, Croydon, CR0 4YY

CONTENTS

ACKNOWLEDGEMENTS

There are no research grants, sabbaticals, teaching assistants or other fancy ingredients in this fare, just the love, patience and wit of Sophie Spalding, which I have attempted to return in kind. Anthony Barnett was the first to encourage me to try an L.A. recipe when I was still a homesick fugitive in England; Mike Sprinker kept me in the kitchen cooking. David Reid supplied an aqueduct of encouragement from Berkeley, as did Michael Sorkin from international air-space. David Diaz and Emma Hernandez were the salsa in our lives in El Sereno. Robert Morrow and I cruised the mean streets; his photographs speak for themselves. Roger Keil and Susan Ruddick kept me believing in the May Pole, as did Michael zinzun and Ntongela Masilela.

A primitive version of chapter three was read by Harvey Molotch, Eric Monkonnen, John Horton, Stephanie Pincetl, and the Berkeley collective of *Socialist Review*. I want to thank them for their invaluable advice and incisive criticism.

Roger Keil of Frankfurt University read and translated the German references quoted in chapter one. He also wrote the first draft of the 'Exiles' section and contributed several other allusions and ideas. I am deeply grateful to him.

In the course of writing this book I have felt the loss of my cousin Jim Stone and my mother Mary (Ryan) Davis. I want my daughter to know that their rebel spirits move this pen.

PREFACE

Authors are strange parents. Some never wean their offspring, preferring to keep them on their knee, forever close at hand. Others, like myself, punctually kick their progeny out the door, with orders never to call home. Apart from occasionally consulting a footnote or reference, I have not looked at *City of Quartz* since I sent the manuscript – the last relic of stone-age composition on an IBM typewriter – to my publisher in London in 1990.

Recently I skimmed through the bulk of this rather strange book, with its cryptic title and relentless black-and-white photographs taken by my friend and get-away-driver Robert Morrow. I was particularly nervous about re-encountering a sprawling chapter called 'Homegrown Revolutions'. This huge expanse of crabgrass, a discursion on homeowners' movements and the politics of NIMBYism, took centuries to research. It required reading, late at night on microform at the library of York University in Toronto where I was teaching political economy at the time, the various local editions of the *L.A. Times* for a thirty-year period.

As a result of these obscure labors, I became so attached to every sacred morsel of fact about picket fences and dog doo-doos that I failed to edit the chapter down to a reasonable length. I soon came to fear that I had made a suicidal mistake. 'No one,' I told myself, 'will ever read this.' Yet, some people obviously have; even a few who weren't coerced into doing so by their tyrannical Marxist professors.

In a meditation on the capriciousness of publishing and reputation, the philosopher Ernst Bloch once asked: 'Must books have fates?' The answer, of course, is yes, but not the ones chosen by their authors. The fate of *City of Quartz* was largely determined by events that followed its publication:

the explosive notoriety of L.A.-based gangster rap, the Rodney King atrocity, and, finally, the apocalyptic uprising that followed the acquittal of his assailants.

But the smell of smoke was already, so to speak, in the air by 1988 when I began writing the essays that constitute *City of Quartz* and which spilled over into several other, edited volumes. Although the owners of a certain graying newspaper on Spring Street may have missed the obvious omens, every eleven-year-old in the city knew that an explosion of some kind was coming. In a city tragically full of armed and angry teenagers, LAPD Chief Daryl Gates's 'Operation Hammer' – with its Vietnam-like neighborhood sweeps and indiscriminate nightly harassment – was universally viewed as a deliberate provocation to riot.

Indeed, this was the interpretation of the two rookie officers who arrested me after the LAPD's notorious attack on a peaceful Justice for Janitors demonstration in Century City in June 1990. I was in every sense a captive audience, cuffed in the back seat of their patrol car, as they launched into a hallucinatory rant about a coming Armageddon, LAPD versus Uzi-armed Crips and Bloods, on the streets of Southcentral. So, if there were premonitions of 1992 in *City of Quartz* they simply reflected anxieties visible on every graffiti-covered wall or, for that matter, every lawn sprouting a little 'Armed Response' sign.

City of Quartz, to use one of those Parisian terms that I usually try to run over with my pick-up truck, is the biography of a *conjoncture*: one of those moments, ripe with paradox and non-linearity, when previously separate currents of history suddenly converge with profoundly unpredictable results. *City of Quartz* – in a nutshell – is about the contradictory impact of economic globalization upon different segments of Los Angeles society.

In 1990, Los Angeles had been governed for almost a generation by a nationally unique coalition of downtown business interests, Westside entertainment-industry Democrats and Southside Black voters. After the helter-skelter of the 1960s, when the reactionary populism of rogue mayor Sam Yorty had come perilously close to wrecking the city, the administration of Mayor Tom Bradley, elected in 1973, represented the first sustained experiment in government by elite consensus. The long conflict between Westside and Downtown elites ended in a historic compromise that included Westside support for accelerated downtown redevelopment, and Downtown (especially Chandler-dynasty) support for a largely Democratic City Hall. Westside/Downtown cooperation under the honest brokerage of Tom Bradley made possible the most ambitious expansion of municipal infrastructure since William Mulholland built the original Aqueduct.

Indeed, the greatest single achievement of the Bradley era was the immense program of new investment in ports and airports that allowed L.A. to become a dominating hub of Pacific Rim commerce, and, thus, to survive the eventual post-Cold War downsizing of its aerospace economy. Bradley, moreover, was able to accomplish these Robert Moses-like feats despite a hostile environment of tax revolts, government downsizing and Reaganomics. His administration hewed to the conservative principle – pioneered by Mulholland and his fellow Progressives in the Department of Water and Power – that utilities should be self-financing and fiscally inviolable. In other words, any notional profits from the operation of the Port or LAX must be reinvested *in situ*.

Exploiting tax-increment financing, City Hall ratified the same principle for Downtown: fiscal windfalls from the appreciation of publicly-subsidized real-estate were ploughed right back into further redevelopment. These fiscal closed circuits sustained high levels of public investment in container docks, terminal buildings, and downtown bank skyscrapers that, in turn, kept happy a huge constituency of pro-globalization interests, including airlines, stevedoring companies, railroads, aerospace exporters, hotels, construction unions, downtown landowners, the *Los Angeles Times*, Japanese banks, Westside movie studios, big law firms, and the politicians dependent upon the largesse of all of the above.

But the city was subsidizing globalization without laying any claim on behalf of groups excluded from the direct benefits of international commerce. There was no mechanism to redistribute any share of additional city revenues to purposes other than infrastructure or Downtown renewal. There was no 'linkage', in other words, between corporate-oriented public investment and the social needs that desperately fought for attention in the rest of the city budget. Moreover, the dynamic leadership concentrated on improving the Harbor, LAX and

Downtown (and, later, organizing the Bradley *festschriften* of the 1984 Olympics) seemed directly subtracted from attention paid to the city's neighborhoods and their subsistence needs.

It is astonishing, in retrospect, how little heed City Hall paid to plant closure and redlining in the Southcentral neighborhoods that were Tom Bradley's original political base. Or, how little effort was made to redress the generation-long disfranchisement of the Eastside on the city council and the exclusion of Chicanos from significant leadership roles in the ruling coalition. Likewise, it is difficult to explain why the city council failed, despite innumerable warnings and protests, to downzone a city plan that was everywhere destabilizing residential quality of life with massive and irrational densities of permissible new development. Along Ventura Boulevard skyscrapers were literally sprouting from the front yards of single-family homes.

By the time I sat down to write *City of Quartz*, on the eve of Southern California's greatest postwar recession, Bradley's growth coalition was still intact, even triumphant, but it was fast losing control of its social landscape. From Porter Ranch to Watts, L.A.'s neighborhoods were ablaze with angry grievances and suburban *sans culottes* were threatening to overthrow the city's *ancien régime*.

In the Valley, a so-called 'slow-growth movement' had suddenly coalesced out of the molecular agitation of hundreds of local homeowners' associations. Although many of the movement's concerns about declining environmental quality, traffic and density were entirely legitimate, 'slow growth' also had ugly racial and ethnic overtones of an Anglo gerontocracy selfishly defending its privileges against the job and housing needs of young Latino and Asian populations. Indeed, many of the key leaders of the homeowners' revolt had originally won their stripes in opposition to school integration in the early 1970s (and they would continue in the 1990s to rail at new immigrants and unite with business interests to unsuccessfully promote the succession of the Valley).

Meanwhile, in the neglected flat lands of Mid-City and Southcentral Los Angeles, the invisible hand was wielding an Uzi, as crack cocaine sales – the local form of economic globalization – gave a terrible new economic impetus to gang warfare. The slaughter in the streets, three gang killings a day by 1990, also emboldened the LAPD to aggressively expand its power.

PREFACE

By 1988, Angelenos nervously wondered who really ran their city: Mayor Bradley or the megalomaniac Chief of Police, Daryl Gates? Meanwhile the very success of the Bradley coalition's program of globalization was transforming the composition of the regional elites who constituted its membership. Everything was up for sale and, against the background of the 'super-yen,' Japanese capital (with Canadian investors in a close second place) suddenly became the major stakeholder in both downtown real-estate and Westside movie studios. Editorial writers waxed hyperbolically about Downtown L.A.'s brilliant future as a command center of the Pacific Rim, while City Hall veterans wondered whether the city's new investors would become 'players' or not. Old elites, meanwhile, were disappearing into the darkness of their San Marino and Montecito mausoleums.

The social and politico-economic tectonic plates that underlay Los Angeles in 1989, in other words, had accumulated such impossible stress loads that you could almost hear the Hollywood Hills groaning. In a setting of increasing instability, only Tom Bradley seemed unchangeable, although his imposing gravitas – so reassuring in 1973 – now seemed tired and remote. (The mayor, in fact, was the silent prisoner of personal and political scandals, with the *Times* secretly holding the mortgage on his reputation.)

That was almost twenty years ago. And twenty years in the life of a metropolis as dynamic and unpredictable as Los Angeles is an entire historical epoch. The years of suspense, of the 'conjuncture,' became the years of crisis, a conjugation of social and natural disaster almost unprecedented in modern American history, followed by years of recuperation and, we are told, sunshine and prosperity, with nary a *noir*ish cloud on the horizon. After a municipal election (2005) sadly devoid of new concepts, genuine passions, or substantive debate, Los Angeles at last has a mayor – Antonio Villaraigosa – with a surname that resounds with the same accent as the majority of the population.

The election of Villaraigosa – once a fiery trade-union and civil-liberties activist – should have been Los Angeles's 'La Guardia moment,' an opportunity to sweep City Hall clean of its old scheming cabals with their monomaniac obsession with gentrifying Downtown at the expense

ix

of the city's blue-collar neighborhoods. Instead Villaraigosa, like Tom Bradley in 1973–4, has become a non-threatening paragon of liberal accommodation to an unchanging elite agenda of pharaonic redevelopment projects. The former rebel from east of the River is now the jaded booster of a 'Downtown renaissance' that promotes super-cathedrals, billionaire sports franchises, mega-museums, Yuppie lofts, and drunken Frank Gehry skyscrapers at the expense of social justice and affordable housing. He endorses an evil plan to expel the majority of the homeless from Downtown in order to satisfy the greed of its landowners and gentrifiers.

Villaraigosa, to be sure, owed his victory to the renascent power of the Los Angeles County Federation of Labor and, like his immediate predecessors, Richard Riordan and James Hahn, he is an earnest advocate of negotiation and incremental social progress: always within the parameters, of course, of what billionaire patrons like Eli Broad and Ron Burkle will allow. Westsiders, struggling to reconcile their obscene real-estate equities with their residual social consciences, may find reassurance in the fact that Los Angeles continues to be governed by a smug coalition of corporate philanthropy and emasculated liberalism – with Villaraigosa as a Latin Bradley – but the blunted thrust of regime change has different, less-happy implications for the rest of the city.

If there was ever a time for fire in the belly and a radical politics of hope, it is now. Despite the mountain of gold that has been built downtown, Los Angeles remains vulnerable to the same explosive convergence of street anger, poverty, environmental crisis, and capital flight that made the early 1990s its worst crisis period since the early Depression. Los Angeles, of course, will not fall into the ocean, but it could resume the arc of decline that began in the early 1990s: slowly bleeding high-wage jobs, skilled workers, and fiscal resources. No great American city – the recent case of New Orleans aside – is so susceptible to downward mobility over the next generation.

Why do I continue to be so pessimistic? Taking 1990 as a baseline, consider some of the most important structural trends and social changes of the generation that has followed the original 'conjuncture' of *City of Quartz*.

PREFACE

1. REGIONAL (IM)MOBILITY

In 1990 the Los Angeles County Transportation Commission's ambitious program of subway and light-rail construction held the promise of increased mobility and reduced pollution. But in 2006, the imminent future is massive immobility and staggering congestion. Right now locals pay a 'congestion tax' – ninety-three hours per commuter per year lost in traffic delays – that is the highest in the United States, and twice as high as it was in 1982. In the worst scenario, it could double again in another decade.

In the late Bradley years – it should now be clear – Los Angeles wrote the textbook on bad transport planning and even worse project management. The big-ticket projects of this era turned out to be costly fiascos: a Wilshire subway that didn't actually go down Wilshire Boulevard, or to the Eastside, for that matter; a light rail to the airport that didn't actually go to LAX; and a Alameda corridor that was designed to take truck-hauled containers off the Long Beach Freeway, but has failed to do so. Everyone loves to ride the subway, but few appreciate that it is underwritten by huge operating subsidies – almost $27 per passenger – that have been financed out of the pockets of bus riders. Between 1991 and 1997, as fares increased, the bus system lost 17 per cent of its passenger volume or 71 million trips: hardly a victory for mass transit. Overall, mass transit accounts for only one out of every fifty trips within the region.

Likewise, both city and county have allowed politically powerful developers – like Maguire Thomas at Playa Vista or Newhall Ranch in the Santa Clara River Valley – to dump huge new volumes of traffic into the most congested nodes without any real mitigation. The projected 70,000-resident Tejon Ranch near Gorman (property formerly owned by the Chandler dynasty of the *Los Angeles Times*) will be even worse: the beginning of gridlock that someday may extend to Bakersfield in the San Joaquin Valley. Regionally, we are no closer to real planning or coordination of housing, jobs and transportation than we were fifty years ago. There is much talk about 'smart growth' and 'new urbanism,' but, with few exceptions, the regional norms are still dumb sprawl and senile suburbanism. Some politicians still invoke magic bullets and sci-fi fixes, like 200 mph maglev trains, but Sacramento – which has recently siphoned off $2.5 billion in transportation funds to cover the budget deficit – is unable even to fill the potholes in our aging freeways. Southern California, as a result, is quickly turning into one huge angry parking lot. Congestion will inevitably drive away more jobs and business, while also fueling an ugly neo-Malthusian politics – already audible on the AM dial – of blaming immigrants (whose environmental footprint is actually the smallest) for declining physical and social mobility.

2. BRANCHVILLE

In the late 1980s, boosters of the now forgotten 'L.A. 2000' scheme were claiming that L.A. would soon become the new command center of the California and Pacific Rim economies, the 'headquarters of the 21st century'. The more incautious – perhaps they had smoked too much jimson weed – even foresaw Downtown as a second Manhattan, thanks to the Archimedean lever of Japanese investment. What a delirious vision.

In fact, Japanese capital – suffering huge losses – couldn't bail out of Downtown fast enough during the recession of the early 1990s. Financial consolidations, in the wake of the savings and loan meltdown and bank deregulation, left Los Angeles for the first time in its history without a single major locally headquartered bank. Indeed, apart from the odd oil company and some of the entertainment giants, Los Angeles is hardly a headquarters city at all. The final insult, of course, was Otis Chandler's decision – forced by the scandals and bloodbaths on Spring Street – to put a silver stake through his grandfather's heart and sell the *Times*, the flagship of local capitalism, to the Chicago *Tribune* empire.

Thus Los Angeles has entered the twenty-first century, as it did the twentieth, largely as an economic colony of corporations and investors headquartered elsewhere: San Francisco, Charlotte, New York, Chicago and Tokyo. A dozen or so billionaires, including Sumner Redstone, Kirk Kerkorian, Marvin Davis and David Geffen, still receive mail at L.A. zip codes but, with the exception of Eli Broad (the new uber-patron of Downtown culture), their commitment to the region is unclear, even inscrutable. Rupert Murdoch is currently the biggest fish in the pond, but is he a local player? Hardly anyone knows. An 'elite' – in the aggressive, almost militarized sense of Harry Chandler and his friends in the 1920s – hardly exists in Los Angeles anymore. Power and wealth, of course, remain massively concentrated, but there is a real sense of transience. Too many of the *nouveaux riches* keep their bags packed, ready to bolt the city if it again catches fire or erupts in mayhem.

3. MANUFACTURING DECLINE

By 1990, the Los Angeles region had lost most of the 'Fordist' industries that once made it the nation's second-largest center of auto and tire manufacture. Of its fourteen largest non-defense plants, twelve, including Kaiser in Fontana and GM in Southgate, had been shut down and their machinery exported to China. Yet, unlike anywhere else, the region actually gained manufacturing jobs in the 1980s through expanding aerospace payrolls and a light manufacturing boom – apparel, toys, furniture – centered around Downtown. For a decade, Los Angeles surpassed Chicago, with the largest manufacturing workforce in the country.

But in the 1990s, Los Angeles County lost one-third of that compensatory industrial job base, as defense jobs were transferred to other regions, and light manufacturing was exported to border *maquiladoras* or to China. In an era of national Republican hegemony, the heavily Democratic Los Angeles region has lost its former competitive advantage in Washington: witness the blatant partisan politics in the early 1990s behind the transfer of thousands of Lockheed jobs from Burbank to Newt Gingrich's congressional district in Marrietta, Georgia. The recent announcement that Boeing will be terminating the assembly of 717s in the former McDonnell Douglas plant in Long Beach marks the end of a historical era.

For fifty years, Southern California's military–industrial economy was irrigated by an aqueduct of tax dollars from Washington: in some years, the net gain – via the inter-regional transfer of tax resources – was as much as $6 to $8 billion. Now the fiscal differential flows the other way: Los Angeles County – like Michigan or Ohio in the 1950s – now pays more in federal taxes than it receives in federal expenditures. Between 1983 and 1996 real per capita federal spending in Southern California fell by a whopping 14 per cent.

The decline of manufacturing jobs in the regional core (Los Angeles and Orange counties), moreover, has not been compensated for by small increases in the Inland Empire and San Diego counties. In addition, over the next few years Los Angeles may lose half of its apparel employment to China. The burden of deindustrialization, of course, is most heavily felt in

Los Angeles' new-immigrant neighborhoods, where the garment industry has been a major employer. As manufacturing employment shrinks, an already precarious low-wage workforce is further compressed into a limited spectrum of service-sector jobs in restaurants, hotels, offices, theme parks, and private homes.

This service-heavy economy, based upon a myriad of poorly-capitalized small businesses, is especially vulnerable to fluctuations in economic weather. Indeed both the rate of business formation, and the rate of business failure, remain higher than in most other metropolitan regions. This generates plenty of heartwarming stories about successful ethnic enterprise, but it also ensures an equally high rate of broken dreams and bankruptcy. Too many ethnic donut stores, nail parlors, *tiendas*, taco wagons, landscaping services, auto repair shops, and hairdressing studios survive only by dint of heroic feats of family self-exploitation. The employees of the micro-enterprise sector, moreover, tend to eke out survival at the barest minimum: caught in a gigantic low-wage, largely off-the-books, economic ghetto.

4. THE NEW INEQUALITY

In 1988, as I was writing *City of Quartz*, the Los Angeles County Board of Supervisors threatened to shutdown the ER at the California Medical Center. This was the beginning of what has become Los Angeles' permanent health care crisis as County government has struggled unsuccessfully to maintain enough hospital beds to deal with the needs of 2.5 million uninsured residents. The County has been caught in a scissors between declining fiscal capacity (the legacy of Proposition 13 in 1978) and the refusal of so many local employers to provide health benefits to their workers. In Southcentral L.A. one in two adults lacks any form of health insurance. Less than one-third of private employers in California as a whole, and even less in Los Angeles County, pay the full cost of their workers' health insurance premiums.

As a result, in 1995, 1999, and again in 2002, the supervisors almost closed USC-County General Hospital itself: a 'Chernobyl-like' meltdown of health care only narrowly avoided by desperate measures at the last minute, including an emergency parcel tax and a grudging federal bailout. Although USC-County is still open, sixteen vital community health clinics have been closed, as has the ER at scandal-plagued Martin Luther King

General in Willowbrook. The working poor in Los Angeles, in conse-quence, have only marginally better access to health care than they might possess in Mexico City or Rio de Janeiro.

The County health crisis – still just a step away from system breakdown and catastrophe – is emblematic of the larger deficit of investment in a humane social safety net. Los Angeles, as it did in 1990, continues to house the poor in the street (an estimated 90,000 homeless in the County), and the mentally ill in jails. The so-called civic 'recovery' of the mid-1990s and the ensuing dotcom boom years did disappointingly little to reduce the mass of poverty in the city; indeed, according to the L.A. Coalition to End Hunger and Homelessness, the number of people living in 'high poverty' in Los Angeles doubled during the 1990s. Los Angeles, according to United Way, remains 'the nation's poverty capital' with the largest number of poor of any metropolitan area. The City's family poverty rate is double the national average, and an amazing 59 per cent of students in public schools qualify for free or reduced-price lunch programs. (More broadly, the L.A.–Riverside–Orange County area has the highest percentage of families in poverty and the lowest percentage of high school graduates of the nation's fourteen largest metropolitan areas.)

Most of the poor, or at least poor parents, are in the labor force, and the persistence of such high levels of poverty through the last decade is evidence of labor markets that provide few footholds for occupational or income mobility. In part, this is the result of the educational shortfall in the labor force: an extraordinary 78 per cent of adults in Los Angeles County are *not* college graduates, and 1.8 million are illiterate. Adult education, in other words, is an enormous, largely unmet public need (as well as the vital precondition to reskilling and economic mobility).

Meanwhile, Los Angeles Unified School District continues its slow decline: two-fifths of current high school students do not graduate with their class. The Latino graduation rate is the worst: only 53 per cent. But wages in California over the last generation have increased only for workers with a college degree: those with high school or less have lost ground in the last decade. This may partially explain why Latino poverty in L.A. County soared from 22 to 35 per cent during the early 1990s recession, then fell back to an uncomfortable plateau of 30 per cent, where it has remained stuck ever since.

The other side of poverty and vulnerability, of course, is inequality, and the Los Angeles metropolitan area has almost Latin-American extremes of wealth and poverty. During the 1990s, real household incomes fell throughout much of Southern California, but the worst drop in the median income was in the City of Los Angeles, where it fell by 9.1 per cent. At the same time, the percentage of households in poverty increased from 18 to 22 per cent, while the percentage with an annual income of more than $100,000 increased from 9.7 to 15.7 per cent. Almost 700,000 working adults in L.A. County have incomes below the poverty line, and seven of the ten fastest-growing occupations in the city, including cashier and security guard, pay less than $25,000 per year. The *Times* editorialized in 2000 that L.A. and California had entered a 'new Gilded Age' where 'the income gap between rich and poor is wider than at almost any time in history and magnified by the sudden wealth and lavish living of a growing elite'.

Meanwhile, the heirs of Howard Jarvis – almost thirty years on – continue to repel all assaults on the perverse edifice of Proposition 13. Land inflation remains the most destabilizing force in Southern California life, but Prop. 13, as Peter Shrag has so powerfully shown, ensures that the greater part of the real-estate windfall annually passes through the economy, on its way to buy Hummers, Laker tickets, and vacation homes, without paying a tithe to schools and the creation of the human capital on which the future of California will rest. Luxury lifestyles are subsidized, as it were, on both ends: by a seemingly infinite supply of cheap service labor, and by the tax advantages that accrue to real-estate and sumptuary consumption.

5. TERMINAL SUBURBS

Real-estate inflation is the tax that one portion of society – older, more affluent homeowners and corporate landowners in coastal areas – levies on the rest of society: especially younger, less affluent families. It is also the economic passport that allowed hundreds of thousands of largely white, affluent Southern Californians to vote with their feet and leave the region in the 1990s. The City of Los Angeles alone lost 200,000 white, non-Latino residents in the 1990s; the County, almost one-fifth of its total white population. This Anglo exodus – to a much smaller extent, also a Black

PREFACE

out-migration – explains the ironic fate of the 'slow-growth' movement that in the 1980s so dominated the suburban landscape.

Fifteen years ago it was apparent that residential development had reached the last frontier of available land within an hour of the coast. Today, this final build-out is in progress from Santa Barbara to San Diego. The dirt is almost gone. In Orange County, the *Los Angeles Times* reported two years ago, there was room left for maybe 40,000 additional homes in Irvine and Rancho Mission Viejo east of San Juan Capistrano. Currently, Orange County has more than 3,600 residents per square mile; Los Angeles County around 2,200. Believe it or not, the Los Angeles–Anaheim–Riverside metropolitan area now has a higher density (8.31 people per acre) than the New York regional plan area (7.99) or San Francisco–Oakland (7.96).

Homeowners associations, of course, still remain potent forces in local politics, and suburban coalitions still wrangle with developers over the scale and pace of land conversion. Likewise, the secession movement in the San Fernando Valley – which so shrewdly seized the center of attention in L.A. city politics for five years – can be construed as the virtual apotheosis of earlier slow-growth and NIMBYite protests. Yet it was also, I believe, a last hurrah.

Fifteen years on, slow-growth forces have won many small battles but lost the war. It is clear that thousands of households have resolved the contradictions of growth and residential quality of life by using their Southern California equity to purchase shares in dream retirements or new lives in amenity-rich areas throughout the West. The white flight from Southern California in the 1990s is unique in California history and was instigated by a number of different factors, ranging from recession, fear of crime and natural disaster, to the irresistible attractions of golf-centered utopias in the Arizona and Nevada deserts.

Local planners in exurban boomtowns like St. George, Utah and Casa Grande, Arizona estimate that about 40 per cent of their new residents are émigré Southern Californians. Similar numbers have been quoted by Hal Rothman and other experts on the supernova-like growth of southern Nevada. These 'off-worlds,' to use the terminology of *Blade Runner*, seem to be part of a larger sorting-out process by which white, religiously-conservative 'red America' is taking its distance from heavily immigrant and liberal 'blue America'. Within Southern California itself, meanwhile, neighborhood diversity is too often an artifact of one group moving in, another moving out. Although there are some convincing examples of apparently stable suburban diversity – Cerritos, Quartz Hill or Moreno Valley – the larger tendency is still toward regional re-segregation represented by largely monochromatic Simi Valley, Laguna Hills, and Temecula Valley.

6. SPURNING THE PEACEMAKERS

Homicide is still the largest single cause of death for children under eighteen in Los Angeles County. Years ago, I used the Sheriff Department's 'gang-related homicide' data to estimate that some 10,000 young people had been killed in the L.A. area's street wars, from the formation of the first Crips sets in 1973–4 until 1992. This, of course, is a fantastic, horrifying figure, almost three times the death toll of the so-called 'Troubles' in Northern Ireland over a roughly similar time span. It is even more harrowing when we consider that most of the homicides have been concentrated in a handful of police divisions. Add to the number of dead the injured and permanently disabled, as well as those incarcerated or on parole for gang-related violations, and you have a measure of how completely Los Angeles – its adult leaderships and elites – has betrayed several generations of its children.

Soon after I published *City of Quartz*, I wrote and narrated an hour-long film for Channel 4 in the UK. In the documentary, I interviewed dozens of gang members, as well as community activists, on both the South and Eastside; none expressed even a grain of optimism about reducing gang violence. All the more extraordinary, then, when on the eve of the Rodney King riot, the leaderships of the major Black gangs in Watts announced a truce: a truce that endured for more than a decade and was replicated by local truces in other war-torn parts of the city. The initial response of the LAPD and Sheriff's – especially the corrupt and tainted anti-gang unit, CRASH – was to do everything possible to sabotage and undermine the truce. To the credit of Chief Willie Williams, he pulled the dogs off; to the discredit of Mayor Riordan and his business backers, they refused any dialogue with the truce organizers.

It had been obvious for most of a generation that the only people who can end the street wars are the warriors themselves. Mindless punishment and super-incarceration have been societal disasters: locking away tens of thousands of young people in hyper-violent prisons, dominated by in-stitutionalized race wars, without any semblance of education, rehabilita-tion or hope. The real function of the prison system, indeed, is not to safeguard communities, but to warehouse hatred for the day when it returns to the street. In contrast, the organizers of the gang truce movement offered an unprecedented framework for dialogue with the youth of the city: a chance to turn street warriors into community organizers and peacemakers. But with the heroic exceptions of Congress-woman Maxine Waters and State Senator Tom Hayden, no elected politician even bothered to listen. Funds from Rebuild L.A. went to the usual suspects – politically connected developers and ministers – while almost nothing trickled down to the housing projects or mean streets. Unlike 1965, there was no social postmortem on the causes of the riot, nor any serious new investment in youth employment and recreation, despite the proven track record of programs like the California Conservation Corps.

The failure to acknowledge the gang truce or build on its early successes was a first-rate tragedy, whose price we are now paying in an inexorable, deadly resumption of gang warfare. The gravest danger, as always, is inter-ethnic violence, spreading from the chronic warfare between Blacks and Latinos that is tolerated in the county jails and state prisons. Our over-crowded penal institutions, governed by a cynical calculus of social incapacitation, are expressive of the mean Victorian ethos that currently commands California politics.

7. CITY OF ORGANIZERS?

Finally, a cautious note of optimism. The local labor movement is largely missing from *City of Quartz*, yet – as I argued later in a little book called *Magical Urbanism* – Los Angeles over the last fifteen years became the principal R&D center for the future of the American labor movement. The militant, creative organizing campaigns of the janitors, hotel workers and drywall workers kept hope alive in L.A. during the tough years of the 1990s and helped train a new generation of activists. As elite power become more politically diffuse and uncertain, the renovated L.A. County

Federation of Labor emerged as the single most important electoral and social force in the city. The successful Living Wage campaign demonstrated that local government could play a proactive role in restructuring labor markets and preventing the race to the bottom in wages and benefits. The long, bitter but ultimately successful campaign to defend the rights of catering and cleaning workers at USC – culminating in hunger strikes and mass arrests – took the battle into an inner sanctum of elite privilege and self-righteousness. Los Angeles in the 1990s became a city of organizers.

But Los Angeles' new progressive politics, buoyed by the dynamism of the new unionism, has arrived at a watershed. Clearly, the labor movement needs to stay on the political offensive, expanding its clout into additional areas of vital interest to local working people, especially the politics of land-use, transportation, healthcare and housing. It requires an expansive vision and comprehensive program, yet the labor movement has mortgaged its future to a Democratic Party, large elements of which are in full retreat from traditional New Deal commitments. In striving to remake it, labor runs the risks of having its own new unity and militancy unmade instead. Indeed, some would argue that the Democratic Party is the inevitable graveyard of political principle.

Labor's forward march in Los Angeles, and with it the future of the urban region, depends, in my opinion, upon further consolidation of a programmatic vision, built around a human needs agenda, that is not hostage to any individual campaign or political personality. Los Angeles needs, in short, a more, not less, ideological politics. I find nothing praiseworthy in current calls for more 'centrism' or 'pragmatism': euphemisms for the continual process of incremental adjustment to the rightward drift of the Democratic Party. In contrast, conservative Christian groups have built impressive political bases in local suburban politics largely through unyielding, programmatic tenacity. Odd to say, but many con-servatives seem to have a better grasp of Gramsci than many on the Left. Above all, they understand the principle that a hegemonic politics must represent a consistent continuum of values: it must embody a morally coherent way of life.

Upton Sinclair – the most famous Socialist in Southern California in the 1920s and 1930s – understood this instinctively and completely. His EPIC movement of 1934 brilliantly used the ethic of the New Testament to argue the compelling case for production for use and full employment. He campaigned on the straightforward principle that the right to earn a living for one's family transcends the right to own idle property. His campaign was a crusade that lit fires in the hearts of millions of ordinary Californians, most of whom had never previously paid any attention to ideas from the Left.

But what is the equivalent crusade today? What moral imperative should organize and give passion to a progressive politics for Los Angeles and California? The answer, I think, has been provided by the extraordinary, if underpublicised hearings that Los Angeles state senators Gloria Romero and Richard Alarcon conducted several years ago, which focused on the scandal of poverty, particularly child poverty in California. They argued with real eloquence that California – one of the richest societies in world history – needs to declare war on the poverty and youth violence in its inner cities and farm communities. This is the great issue – not tax relief for corporations and SUV owners, or persecution of undocumented immigrants – that should be the moral center of local and state politics.

The gigantic demonstrations of Latino immigrants and their allies in the spring of 2006, which reclaimed downtown Los Angeles in the name of El Pueblo, revealed the social power of the city's blue-collar neighborhoods and suburbs. The challenge to labor activists and community organizers is to harness this emergent power to a consistent progressive program, and the centerpiece of that program, in my opinion, should be a social and economic bill of rights for the city's children. At the end of the day, the best measure of the humanity of any society is the life and happiness of its children. We live in a rich society with poor children, and that should be intolerable.

San Diego, April 2006

PROLOGUE

THE VIEW FROM
FUTURES PAST

The best place to view Los Angeles of the next millennium is from the ruins of its alternative future. Standing on the sturdy cobblestone foundations of the General Assembly Hall of the Socialist city of Llano del Rio – Open Shop Los Angeles's utopian antipode – you can sometimes watch the Space Shuttle in its elegant final descent towards Rogers Dry Lake. Dimly on the horizon are the giant sheds of Air Force Plant 42 where Stealth Bombers (each costing the equivalent of 10,000 public housing units) and other, still top secret, hot rods of the apocalypse are assembled. Closer at hand, across a few miles of creosote and burro bush, and the occasional grove of that astonishing yucca, the Joshua tree, is the advance guard of approaching suburbia, tract homes on point.

The desert around Llano has been prepared like a virgin bride for its eventual union with the Metropolis: hundreds of square miles of vacant space engridded to accept the future millions, with strange, prophetic street signs marking phantom intersections like '250th Street and Avenue K'. Even the eerie trough of the San Andreas Fault, just south of Llano over a foreboding escarpment, is being gingerly surveyed for designer home sites. Nuptial music is provided by the daily commotion of ten thousand vehicles hurtling past Llano on 'Pearblossom Highway' – the deadliest stretch of two-lane blacktop in California.

When Llano's original colonists, eight youngsters from the Young Peoples' Socialist League (YPSL), first arrived at the 'Plymouth Rock of the Cooperative Commonwealth' in 1914, this part of the high Mojave Desert, misnamed the Antelope Valley,[1] had a population of a few thousand ranchers, borax miners and railroad workers as well as some armed guards to protect the newly-built aqueduct from sabotage. Los Angeles was then a city of 300,000 (the population of the Antelope Valley today), and its urban edge, now visible from Llano, was in the new suburb of Hollywood, where D. W. Griffith and his cast of thousands were just finishing an epic romance of the Ku Klux Klan, *Birth of a Nation*. In their day-long drive from the Labor Temple in Downtown Los Angeles to Llano over ninety miles of rutted wagon road, the YPSLs in their red Model-T trucks passed by scores of billboards, planted amid beet fields and walnut orchards, advertising the impending subdivision of the San Fernando Valley (owned by the city's richest men and annexed the following year as the culmination of the famous 'water conspiracy' fictionally celebrated in Polanski's *Chinatown*).

Three-quarters of a century later, forty thousand Antelope Valley commuters slither bumper-to-bumper each morning through Soledad Pass on their way to long-distance jobs in the smog-shrouded and overdeveloped San Fernando Valley. Briefly a Red Desert in the heyday of Llano (1914–18), the high Mojave for the last fifty years has been preeminently the Pentagon's playground. Patton's army trained here to meet Rommel (the ancient tank tracks are still visible), while Chuck Yeager first broke the sound barrier over the Antelope Valley in his Bell X-1 rocket plane. Under the 18,000 square-mile, ineffable blue dome of R-2508 – 'the most important military airspace in the world' – ninety thousand military training sorties are still flown every year.

But as developable land has disappeared throughout the coastal plains and inland basins, and soaring land inflation has reduced access to new housing to less than 15 per cent of the population, the militarized desert has suddenly become the last frontier of the Southern California Dream. With home prices $100,000 cheaper that in the San Fernando Valley, the archetypical suburban fringe of the 1950s, the Antelope Valley has nearly doubled in population over the last decade, with another quarter million new arrivals expected by 2010. Eleven thousand new homes were started in 1988 alone. But since the Valley's economic base, not counting real-estate agents, consists almost entirely of embattled Cold War complexes – Edwards Air Force Base and Plant 42 (altogether about eighteen thousand civilian jobs) – most of the new homebuyers will simply swell the morning commute on the Antelope Valley Freeway.

The pattern of urbanization here is what design critic Peter Plagens once called the 'ecology of evil'.[2] Developers don't grow homes in the desert – this isn't Marrakesh or even Tucson – they just clear, grade and pave, hook up some pipes to the local artificial river (the federally subsidized California Aqueduct), build a security wall and plug in the 'product'. With generations of experience in uprooting the citrus gardens of Orange County and the San Fernando Valley, the developers – ten or twelve major firms, headquartered in places like Newport Beach and Beverly Hills – regard the desert as simply another abstraction of dirt and dollar signs. The region's major natural wonder, a Joshua tree forest containing individual specimens often thirty feet high and older than the Domesday Book, is being bulldozed into oblivion. Developers regard the magnificent Joshuas, unique to this

THE FUTURE PAST
General Assembly Hall / Hotel, Llano del Rio

desert, as large noxious weeds unsuited to the illusion of verdant home-steads. As the head of Harris Homes explained: 'It is a very bizarre tree. It is not a beautiful tree like the pine or something. Most people don't care about the Joshuas.'[3]

With such malice toward the landscape, it is not surprising that developers also refuse any nomenclatural concession to the desert. In promotional literature intended for homebuyers or Asian investors, they have started referring to the region euphemistically as 'North Los Angeles County'. Meanwhile they christen their little pastel pods of Chardonnay lifestyle, air-conditioned and over-watered, with scented brand-names like Fox Run, Mardi Gras, Bravo, Cambridge, Sunburst, New Horizons, and so on. The most hallucinatory are the gated communities manufactured by Kaufman and Broad, the homebuilders who were famous in the 1970s for exporting Hollywood ramblers to the suburbs of Paris. Now they have brought back France (or, rather, California homes in French drag) to the desert in fortified mini-*banlieus*, with lush lawns, Old World shrubs, fake mansard roofs and *nouveaux riches* titles like 'Chateau'.

But Kaufman and Broad only expose the underlying method in the apparent madness of L.A.'s urban desert. The discarded Joshua trees, the profligate wastage of water, the claustrophobic walls, and the ridiculous names are as much a polemic against incipient urbanism as they are an assault on an endangered wilderness. The *eutopic* (literally no-place) logic of their subdivisions, in sterilized sites stripped bare of nature and history, masterplanned only for privatized family consumption, evokes much of the past evolution of tract-home Southern California. But the developers are not just repackaging myth (the good life in the suburbs) for the next generation; they are also pandering to a new, burgeoning fear of the city.

Social anxiety, as traditional urban sociology likes to remind us, is just maladjustment to change. But who has anticipated, or adjusted to, the scale of change in Southern California over the last fifteen years? Stretching now from the country-club homes of Santa Barbara to the shanty *colonias* of Ensenada, to the edge of Llano in the high desert and of the Coachella Valley in the low, with a built-up surface area nearly the size of Ireland and a GNP bigger than India's – the urban galaxy dominated by Los Angeles is the fastest growing metropolis in the advanced industrial world. Its current population of fifteen million, encompassing six counties and a corner of

Baja California, and clustered around two super-cores (Los Angeles and San Diego–Tijuana) and a dozen major, expanding metro-centers, is predicted to increase by another seven or eight million over the next generation. The overwhelming majority of these new inhabitants will be non-Anglos, further tipping the ethnic balance away from WASP hegemony toward the poly-ethnic diversity of the next century. (Anglos became a minority in the city and county of Los Angeles during the 1980s, as they will become in the state before 2010.[4])

Social polarization has increased almost as rapidly as population. A recent survey of Los Angeles household income trends in the 1980s suggests that affluence (incomes of $50,000 plus) has almost tripled (from 9 per cent to 26 per cent) while poverty ($15,000 and under) has increased by a third (from 30 per cent to 40 per cent); the middle range, as widely predicted, has collapsed by half (from 61 per cent to 32 per cent).[5] At the same time the worst popular fears of a generation ago about the conse-quences of market-driven overdevelopment have punctually come true. Decades of systematic under-investment in housing and urban infra-structure, combined with grotesque subsidies for speculators, permissive zoning for commercial development, the absence of effective regional planning, and ludicrously low property taxes for the wealthy have ensured an erosion of the quality of life for the middle classes in older suburbs as well as for the inner-city poor.

Ironically the Antelope Valley is both a sanctuary from this maelstrom of growth and crisis, and one of its fastest growing epicenters. In the desperate reassurance of their gated subdivisions, the new commuter population attempts to recover the lost Eden of 1950s-style suburbia. Older Valley residents, on the other hand, are frantically trying to raise the gangplanks against this ex-urban exodus sponsored by their own pro-growth business and political elites. In their increasingly angry view, the landrush since 1984 has only brought traffic jams, smog, rising crime, job com-petition, noise, soil erosion, a water shortage and the attrition of a distinctively countrified lifestyle.

For the first time since the Socialists left the desert (in 1918 for their New Llano colony in Louisiana) there is wild talk of a 'total rural revolu-tion'. The announcement of several new mega-projects – instant cities ranging from 8,500 to 35,000 units, designed to be plugged into the

Valley's waiting grid – have aroused unprecedented populist ire. On one recent occasion, the representative of the Ritter Ranch project in rustic Leone Valley was 'ambushed by an angry mob . . . screaming and bitching and threatening to kill [him]'. In the Valley's two incorporated municipalities of Lancaster (the international headquarters of the Flat Earth Society) and Palmdale (the fastest growing city in California for most of the 1980s), more than sixty different homeowners' associations have joined together to slow down urbanization, as well as to contest the state's plan for a new 2,200-bed prison for Los Angeles drug and gang offenders in the Mira Loma area.[6]

Meanwhile the myth of a desert sanctuary was shattered shortly after New Year's Eve 1990 when a stray bullet from a gang member's gun killed a popular high-school athlete. Shortly afterwards, the trendy Quartz Hill area, advertised as the emergent 'Beverly Hills' of the desert, was wracked by a gun-battle between the local 5 Deuce Posse and some out-of-town Crips. The *grand peur* of L.A. street gangs suddenly swept the high desert. While sheriffs hunted fugitive teenagers with dogs – like escapees from a Georgia chain-gang – local businessmen formed the semi-vigilante Gangs Out Now (GON). Intimidated by official warnings that there were six hundred and fifty 'identified gang members' in the Valley, the local high school attempted to impose a draconian dress code banning 'gang colors' (blue and red). Outraged students, in turn, protested in the streets.[7]

While the kids were 'doin' the right thing', the local NAACP was demanding an investigation of three suspicious killings of non-whites by sheriffs' deputies. In one case the deputies gunned down an unarmed Asian college student while in another a Black man accused of wielding a three-pronged garden tool was shot eight times. The most egregious incident, however, was the slaying of Betty Jean Aborn, a homeless middle-aged Black woman with a history of mental illness. Confronted by seven burly sheriffs after stealing an ice-cream from a convenience store, she supposedly brandished a butcher's knife. The response was an incredible volley of twenty-eight rounds, eighteen of which perforated her body.[8]

As the desert thus announced the arrival of the *fin de siècle* with a staggering overture of bulldozers and gunfire, some old-timers – contemplating the rapidly diminishing distance between the solitude of the Mojave and the gridlock of suburban life – began to wonder out loud whether there was any alternative to Los Angeles after all.

THE MAY POLE

Class war and repression are said to have driven the Los Angeles Socialists into the desert. But they also came eagerly, wanting to taste the sweet fruit of cooperative labor in their own lifetimes. As Job Harriman, who came within a hair's-breadth of being Los Angeles's first Socialist mayor in 1911, explained: 'It became apparent to me that a people would never abandon their means of livelihood, good or bad, capitalistic or otherwise, until other methods were developed which would promise advantages at least as good as those by which they were living.' What Llano promised was a guaranteed $4 per day wage and a chance to 'show the world a trick they do not know, which is how to live without war or interest on money or rent on land or profiteering in any manner'.[9]

With the sponsorship not only of Harriman and the Socialist Party, but also of Chairman W.A. Engle of the Central Labor Council and Frank McMahon of the Bricklayers' Union, hundreds of landless farmers, unemployed laborers, blacklisted machinists, adventurous clerks, persecuted IWW soapbox orators, restless shopkeepers, and bright-eyed bohemians followed the YPSLs to where the snow-fed Rio del Llano (now Big Rock Creek) met the edge of the desert. Although they were 'democracy with the lid off . . . democracy rampant, belligerent, unrestricted', their enthusiastic labor transformed several thousand acres of the Mojave into a small Socialist civilization.[10] By 1916 their alfalfa fields and modern dairy, their pear orchards and vegetable gardens – all watered by a complex and efficient irrigation system – supplied the colony with 90 per cent of its own food (and fresh flowers as well). Meanwhile, dozens of small workshops cobbled shoes, canned fruit, laundered clothes, cut hair, repaired autos, and published the *Western Comrade*. There was even a Llano motion picture company and an ill-fated experiment in aviation (the homemade plane crashed).

In the spirit of Chautauqua as much as Marx, Llano was also one big Red School House. While babies (including Bella Lewitzky, the future modern dancer) played in the nursery, children (among them Gregory Ain, the future modern architect) attended Southern California's first Montessori school. The teenagers, meanwhile, had their own Kid Kolony (a model industrial school), and adults attended night classes or enjoyed the Mojave's largest library. One of the favorite evening pastimes, apart from dancing to the colony's notorious ragtime orchestra, was debating Alice Constance Austin's design for the Socialist City that Llano was to become.

Although influenced by contemporary City Beautiful and Garden City ideologies, Austin's drawings and models, as architectural historian Dolores Hayden has emphasized, were 'distinctively feminist and California'. Like Llano kid Gregory Ain's more modest 1940s plans for cooperative housing, Austin attempted to translate the specific cultural values and popular enthusiasms of Southern California into a planned and egalitarian social landscape. In the model that she presented to colonists on May Day 1916, Llano was depicted as a garden city of ten thousand people housed in graceful Craftsman apartments with private gardens but communal kitchens and laundries to liberate women from drudgery. The civic center, as befitted a 'city of light', was composed of 'eight rectangular halls, like factories, with sides almost wholly of glass, leading to a glass-domed assembly hall'. She crowned this aesthetic of individual choice within a fabric of social solidarity with a quintessentially Southern California gesture: giving every household an automobile and constructing a ring road around the city that would double 'as a drag strip with stands for spectators on both sides'.[11]

If Austin's vision of thousands of patio apartments radiating from the Bonaventure Hotel-style Assembly Hall, surrounded by socially owned orchards, factories and a monumental dragstrip sounds a bit far-fetched today, imagine what Llanoites would have made of a future composed of Kaufman and Broad *chateaux* ringed by mini-malls, prisons and Stealth Bomber plants. In any event, the nine hundred pioneers of the Socialist City would enjoy only one more triumphant May Day in the Mojave.

The May Day festivities of 1917 commenced at nine o'clock in the morning with intra-community athletic events, including a Fat Women's Race. The entire group of colonists then formed a Grand Parade and marched to the hotel where the Literary Program followed. The band played from a bunting-draped grandstand, the choral society sang appropriate revolutionary anthems like the 'Marseillaise', then moved into the Almond Grove for a barbecue dinner. After supper a group of young girls injected the English into the radical tradition by dancing about the May Pole. At 7:30 the dramatic club presented 'Mishaps of Minerva' with newly decorated scenery in the assembly hall. Dancing consumed the remainder of the evening.[12]

Despite an evident sense of humor, Llano began to fall apart in the later half of 1917. Plagued by internal feuding between the General Assembly and the so-called 'brush gang', the colony was assailed from the outside by creditors, draft boards, jealous neighbors, and the Los Angeles *Times*. After the loss of Llano's water rights in a lawsuit – a devastating blow to its irrigation infrastructure – Harriman and a minority of colonists relocated in 1918 to Louisiana, where a hard-scrabble New Llano (a pale shadow of the original) hung on until 1939. Within twenty-four hours of the colonists' departure, local ranchers ('who precariously represented capitalism in the wilderness') began to demolish its dormitories and workshops, evidently with the intention of erasing any trace of the red menace. But Llano's towering silo, cow byre, and the cobblestone foundation and twin fireplaces of its Assembly Hall, proved indestructible: as local patriotic fury subsided, they became romantic landmarks ascribed to increasingly mythic circumstances.

Now and then, a philosophical temperament, struggling with the huge paradox of Southern California, rediscovers Llano as the talisman of a future lost. Thus Aldous Huxley, who lived for a few years in the early 1940s in a former Llano ranch house overlooking the colony's cemetery, liked to meditate 'in the almost supernatural silence' on the fate of utopia. He ultimately came to the conclusion that the Socialist City was a 'pathetic little Ozymandias', doomed from the start by Harriman's 'Gladstone collar' and his 'Pickwickian' misunderstanding of human nature – whose history 'except in a purely negative way . . . is sadly uninstructive'.[13]

Llano's other occasional visitors, lacking Huxley's vedic cynicism, have generally been more charitable. After the debacle of 1960s–70s communitarianism (especially the deadly trail that led into the Guyanese jungle), the pear trees planted by this ragtime utopia seem a more impressive accomplishment. Moreover, as its most recent historians point out, Huxley grossly underestimated the negative impact of wartime xenophobia and the spleen of the Los Angeles *Times* upon Llano's viability. There but for fortune (and Harry Chandler), perhaps, would stand a brave red *kibbutz* in the Mojave today, canvassing votes for Jesse Jackson and protecting Joshuas from bulldozers.[14]

THE DEVELOPERS' MILLENNIUM?

But, then again, we do not stand at the gates of Socialism's New Jerusalem, but at the hard edge of the developers' millennium. Llano itself is owned by an absentee speculator in Chicago who awaits an offer he cannot refuse from Kaufman and Broad. Setting aside an apocalyptic awakening of the neighboring San Andreas Fault, it is all too easy to envision Los Angeles reproducing itself endlessly across the desert with the assistance of pilfered water, cheap immigrant labor, Asian capital and desperate homebuyers willing to trade lifetimes on the freeway in exchange for $500,000 'dream homes' in the middle of Death Valley.

Is this the world-historic victory of Capitalism that everyone is talking about?

On May Day 1990 (the same day Gorbachev was booed by thousands of alienated Moscovites) I returned to the ruins of Llano del Rio to see if the walls would talk to me. Instead I found the Socialist City reinhabited by two twenty-year-old building laborers from El Salvador, camped out in the ruins of the old dairy and eager to talk with me in our mutually broken tongues. Like hobo heroes out of a Jack London novel, they had already tramped up and down California, but following a frontier of housing starts, not silver strikes or wheat harvests. Although they had yet to find work in Palmdale, they praised the clear desert sky, the easy hitchhiking and the relative scarcity of La Migra. When I observed that they were settled in the ruins of a *ciudad socialista*, one of them asked whether the 'rich people had come with planes and bombed them out'. No, I explained, the colony's credit had failed. They looked baffled and changed the subject.

We talked about the weather for a while, then I asked them what they thought about Los Angeles, a city without boundaries, which ate the desert, cut down the Joshua and the May Pole, and dreamt of becoming infinite. One of my new Llano *compañeros* said that L.A. already was everywhere. They had watched it every night in San Salvador, in endless dubbed reruns of *I Love Lucy* and *Starsky and Hutch*, a city where everyone was young and rich and drove new cars and saw themselves on television. After ten thousand daydreams like this, he had deserted the Salvadorean Army and hitchhiked two thousand five hundred miles to Tijuana. A year later he was standing at the corner of Alvarado and Seventh Streets in the MacArthur Park district near Downtown Los Angeles, along with all the rest of yearning, hardworking Central America. No one like him was rich or drove a new car – except for the coke dealers – and the police were as mean as back home. More importantly no one like him was on television; they were all invisible.

THE DEVELOPERS' MILLENNIUM
Tract homes, Mojave Desert

His friend laughed. 'If you were on TV you would just get deported anyway and have to pay some *coyote* in Tijuana $500 to sneak you back to L.A.' He argued that it was better to stay out in the open whenever possible, preferably here in the desert, away from the center. He compared L.A. and Mexico City (which he knew well) to volcanoes, spilling wreckage and desire in ever-widening circles over a denuded countryside. It is never wise, he averred, to live too near a volcano. 'The old gringo *socialistas* had the right idea.'

I agreed, even though I knew it was too late to move, or to refound Llano. Then, it was their turn to interrogate me. Why was I out here alone, amongst the ghosts of May Day? What did *I* think of Los Angeles? I tried to explain that I had just written a book. . . .

NOTES

1. Despite the incautious claims of Lynne Foster in her recent Sierra Club guide (*Adventuring in the California Desert*, San Francisco 1987), there is absolutely no evidence that 'many thousands of pronghorn antelope roamed the area' in the nineteenth century. On the contrary, small numbers of pronghorn were introduced in the Space Age, partially to allow the Valley to live up to its name!

2. 'Los Angeles: The Ecology of Evil', *Artforum*, December 1972.

3. Los Angeles *Times*, 3 January 1988; Antelope Valley *Press* 29 October 1989.

4. For demographic projections, see Southern California Association of Governments (SCAG), *Growth Management Plan*, Los Angeles, February 1989. To the rather arbitrary five-county SCAG area I have added projections for San Diego and Tijuana.

5. County research quoted on KCET-TV's, 'A Class by Itself', May 1990.

6. Los Angeles *Business Journal*, 25 December 1989; *Press* 14 and 19 January 1990.

7. Ibid., 17 and 19 January.

8. *Daily News*, 4 June 1989. (It was months before the Los Angeles *Times* reported the Aborn murder in its main edition.)

9. Harriman quoted in Robert Hine, *California's Utopian Colonies*, San Marino, Calif. 1953, p. 117; and Dolores Hayden, *Seven American Utopias*, Cambridge, Mass. 1976, pp. 289–90.

10. Llano chronicler Ernest Wooster quoted in Nigey Lenon, Lionel Rolfe, and Paul Greenstein, *Bread and Hyacinths: Job Harriman and His Political Legacy*, unpublished manuscript, Los Angeles 1988, p. 21.

11. Cf. Hayden, pp. 300–1 (on Austin's design); and Sam Hall Kaplan, *L.A. Lost and Found*, New York 1987, p. 137 (on Ain's attempts to design for cooperative living).

12. Hines, p. 127.

13. 'Ozymandias, The Utopia that Failed', in *Tomorrow and Tomorrow and Tomorrow . . .* , New York, 1956, pp. 84–102.

14. Of course I deliberately beg the question of the Joshuas ploughed away to build Llano (ominously they have never grown back), not to mention what would have come of Austin's car in every red garage or where the water for 10,000 singing tomorrows would have been 'borrowed' from.

CHAPTER ONE

SUNSHINE OR *NOIR*?

LOS ANGELES INTELLECTUALS: AN INTRODUCTION

> Los Angeles, it should be understood, is not a mere city. On the
> contrary, it is, and has been since 1888, a *commodity*; something to be
> advertised and sold to the people of the United States like automobiles,
> cigarettes and mouth wash. *Morrow Mayo*[1]

In the summer of 1989, a well-known fashion magazine constantly on the
prowl for lifestyle trends reported from Los Angeles that 'intellectualism'
had arrived there as the latest fad. From celebrities buying armloads of
'smart-looking eyeglasses' to the 'people of L.A. who . . . have elevated
intellectualism to a life style', the city was supposedly booming with bookish
behavior for its own sake: 'There's a real feeling here about becoming
intellectual, removing superficiality, getting culture.'[2] The magazine's
West Coast editor noted approvingly that the 'new intellectualism' was
sweeping Los Angeles on the same wave of messianic hype that had brought
its local predecessors, 'the perfect body' and 'New Age spirituality'.
Angelenos, moreover, had already recognized that the crucial point of the
new pastime was that 'books are for sale' and that a surge of commodity
fetishism and feverish entrepreneurship would accompany the laying on of
Culture.[3]

As this anecdote implies, to evoke 'Los Angeles intellectuals' is to invite
immediate incredulity, if not mirth. Better then, at the outset, to refer to a
mythology – the destruction of intellectual sensibility in the sun-baked
plains of Los Angeles – that conforms more to received impressions, and
that is at least partially true. First of all, Los Angeles is usually seen as
peculiarly infertile cultural soil, unable to produce, to this day, any
homegrown intelligentsia. Unlike San Francisco, which has generated a
distinctive cultural history from the Argonauts to the Beats, Los Angeles's
truly indigenous intellectual history seems a barren shelf. Yet – for even
more peculiar reasons – this essentially deracinated city has become the
world capital of an immense Culture Industry, which since the 1920s has
imported myriads of the most talented writers, filmmakers, artists and
visionaries. Similarly, since the 1940s, the Southern California aerospace
industry and its satellite think-tanks have assembled the earth's largest single

concentration of PhD scientists and engineers. In Los Angeles immigrant mental labor is collectivized in huge apparatuses and directly consumed by big capital. Almost everyone is either on a corporate payroll or waiting hopefully at the studio gate.

Such relations of 'pure capitalism', of course, are seen as invariably destructive of the identity of 'true' intellectuals, still self-defined as artisans or rentiers of their own unique mental productions. Snared in the nets of Hollywood, or entrapped by the Strangelovian logic of the missile industry, 'seduced' talents are 'wasted', 'prostituted', 'trivialized', or 'destroyed'. To move to Lotusland is to sever connection with national reality, to lose historical and experiential footing, to surrender critical distance, and to submerge oneself in spectacle and fraud. Fused into a single montage image are Fitzgerald reduced to a drunken hack, West rushing to his own apocalypse (thinking it a dinner party), Faulkner rewriting second-rate scripts, Brecht raging against the mutilation of his work, the Hollywood Ten on their way to prison, Didion on the verge of a nervous breakdown, and so on. Los Angeles (and its alter-ego, Hollywood) becomes the literalized Mahagonny: city of seduction and defeat, the antipode to critical intelligence.

Yet this very rhetoric (which infuses a long tradition of writing about Los Angeles, since at least the 1920s) indicates powerful critical energies at work. For if Los Angeles has become the archetypal site of massive and unprotesting subordination of industrialized intelligentsias to the programs of capital, it has also been fertile soil for some of the most acute critiques of the culture of late capitalism, and, particularly, of the tendential de-generation of its middle strata (a persistent theme from Nathanael West to Robert Towne). The most outstanding example is the complex corpus of what we call *noir* (literary and cinematic): a fantastic convergence of American 'tough-guy' realism, Weimar expressionism, and existentialized Marxism – all focused on unmasking a 'bright, guilty place' (Welles) called Los Angeles.

Los Angeles in this instance is, of course, a stand-in for capitalism in general. The ultimate world-historical significance – and oddity – of Los Angeles is that it has come to play the double role of utopia *and* dystopia for advanced capitalism. The same place, as Brecht noted, symbolized both heaven and hell. Correspondingly, it is the essential destination on the

ORANGES ON SIDEWALK
Temple-Beaudry district

itinerary of any late twentieth-century intellectual, who must eventually come to take a peep and render some opinion on whether 'Los Angeles Brings It All Together' (official slogan), or is, rather, the nightmare at the terminus of American history (as depicted in *noir*). Los Angeles – far more than New York, Paris or Tokyo – polarizes debate: it is the terrain and subject of fierce ideological struggle.

With apologies for the schematic compression inevitable in so cursory a survey, I explore, first, the role played by successive migrations of intellectuals (whether as tourists, exiles or hired hands), in relation to the dominating cultural institutions of their time (the Los Angeles *Times*, Hollywood, and, most recently, an emergent university-museum mega-complex), in constructing or deconstructing the mythography of Los Angeles. I am interested, in other words, not so much in the history of culture produced *in* Los Angeles, as the history of culture produced *about* Los Angeles – especially where that has become a material force in the city's actual evolution. As Michael Sorkin has emphasized, 'L.A. is probably the most mediated town in America, nearly unviewable save through the fictive scrim of its mythologizers'.[4]

I begin with the so-called 'Arroyo Set': writers, antiquarians, and publicists under the influence of Charles Fletcher Lummis (himself in the pay of the *Times* and the Chamber of Commerce), who at the turn of the century created a comprehensive fiction of Southern California as the promised land of a millenarian Anglo-Saxon racial odyssey. They inserted a Mediterraneanized idyll of New England life into the perfumed ruins of an innocent but inferior 'Spanish' culture. In doing so, they wrote the script for the giant real-estate speculations of the early twentieth century that transformed Los Angeles from small town to metropolis. Their imagery, motifs, values and legends were in turn endlessly reproduced by Hollywood, while continuing to be incorporated into the ersatz landscapes of suburban Southern California.

As the Depression shattered broad strata of the dream-addicted Los Angeles middle classes, it also gathered together in Hollywood an extraordinary colony of hardboiled American novelists and anti-fascist European exiles. Together they radically reworked the metaphorical figure of the city, using the crisis of the middle class (rarely the workers or the poor) to expose how the dream had become nightmare. Although only a few works directly attacked the studio system,[5] *noir* everywhere insinuated contempt for a depraved business culture while it simultaneously searched for a critical mode of writing or filmmaking within it. Although some principal *noir* auteurs, like Chandler, went little further than generalized petty-bourgeois resentment against the collapse of the Southern California dream, most claimed Popular Front sympathies, and some, like Welles and Dmytryk, alluded to the repressed reality of class struggle. Despite the postwar witch hunt that decimated Hollywood progressives, *noir* survived through the 1950s to re-emerge in a new wave in the 1960s and 1970s. The huge popularity of Didion, Dunne, Wambaugh, *Chinatown*, *Blade Runner*, the Chandler and Cain remakes, and, finally, the arrival of the 'post-*noir*' of James Ellroy's *Los Angeles Quartet*, stand as proof of the genre's durability. Although recuperated as an ambience shorn of its 1940s radical affinities, *noir* has nonetheless remained the popular and, despite its intended elitism, 'populist' anti-myth of Los Angeles.

While the cinematic translation of the *noir* vision of Los Angeles engaged some of the finest European writers and directors resident in Hollywood in the 1940s (giving them an invaluable medium for political and aesthetic resistance), the relationship between the city and the community of anti-fascist exiles deserves separate consideration. It was a potent common moment in the cultural histories of Southern California and Europe, generating its own mythology that helped shape critical reaction to the postwar Americanization of Europe. Without necessarily subscribing to the 'nightmare' anti-myth of *noir*, the exile sense of Los Angeles was unremittingly pessimistic. Here was the ultimate city of capital, lustrous and superficial, negating every classical value of European urbanity. Driven by one epochal defeat of the Enlightenment to the shores of Santa Monica Bay, the most unhappy of the exiles thought they discerned a second defeat in Los Angeles as the 'shape of the things to come', a mirror of capitalism's future.

It is hard to exaggerate the damage which *noir*'s dystopianization of Los Angeles, together with the exiles' denunciation of its counterfeit urbanity, inflicted upon the accumulated ideological capital of the region's boosters. *Noir*, often in illicit alliance with San Francisco or New York elitism, made Los Angeles the city that American intellectuals love to hate (although, paradoxically, this seems only to increase its fascination for postwar

European, especially British and French, intellectuals). As Richard Lehan has emphasized, 'probably no city in the Western world has a more negative image'.[6] To repair this image, especially among the cultural elites, local corporate patrons have sponsored a third major immigration of intellectuals, comparable to the Hollywood-bound diaspora of the 1930s, but now dominated by architects, designers, artists and culture theorists.

As Los Angeles – propelled by financial, real-estate and military booms – has rushed forward to Manhattanize its skylines (increasingly with offshore capital), it has attempted to Manhattanize its cultural super-structure as well. The largest land developers and bankers have coordinated a major cultural offensive, whose impact has been redoubled, after decades of mere talk, by a sudden torrent of arts capital, including the incredible $3 billion Getty endowment, the largest in history. As a result, a wealthy institutional matrix has coalesced – integrating elite university faculties, museums, the arts press and foundations – single-mindedly directed toward the creation of a cultural monumentality to support the sale of the city to overseas investors and affluent immigrants. In this sense, the cultural history of the 1980s recapitulated the real-estate/arts nexus of early twentieth-century boosterism, although this time around with a pro-motional budget so large that it could afford to buy the international celebrity architects, painters and designers – Meier, Graves, Hockney, and so on – capable of giving cultural prestige and a happy 'Pop' veneer to the emergence of the 'world city'.

These, then, are the three major collectivized interventions by intel-lectuals in the culture formation of Los Angeles: what I somewhat awkwardly abbreviate as the *Boosters*, the *Noirs*, and the *Mercenaries*. The *Exiles*, as a fourth, more parenthetical, intervention, have linked the indigenous process of city-myth production and its *noir*-ish antipode to European sensibilities about America and its West Coast. They have integrated the spectre of 'Los Angeles' into fundamental debates about the fate of Modernism and the future of a postwar Europe dominated by American Fordism.

It may be objected that this historical typology is one-sidedly slanted towards literateurs, filmmakers, musicians and artists – that is, toward fabricators of the *spectacle* – and neglects the role of practical intellectuals – planners, engineers, and politicians – who actually build cities. And where are the scientists, Southern California's most precious crop, who have shaped its rocket-propelled postwar economy? In fact, the fate of science in Los Angeles exemplifies the role reversal between practical reason and what Disneyites call 'imagineering'. Where one might have expected the presence of the world's largest scientific and engineering community to cultivate a regional enlightenment, science has consorted instead with pulp fiction, vulgar psychology, and even satanism to create yet another layer of California cultdom. This ironic double transfiguration of science into science fiction, and science fiction into religion, is considered in a brief account of the *Sorcerers*.

It is hard to avoid the conclusion that the paramount axis of cultural conflict in Los Angeles has always been about the construction/interpretation of the *city myth*, which enters the material landscape as a design for speculation and domination (as Allan Seager suggests, 'not [as] fantasy imagined but [as] fantasy seen').[7] Even though Los Angeles's emergence from the desert has been an artifact of giant public works, city-building has otherwise been left to the anarchy of market forces, with only rare interventions by the state, social movements or public leaders. The city's most Promethean figure – water engineer William Mulholland – was enigmatic and taciturn to an extreme (his collected works: the Los Angeles Aqueduct and the injunction 'Take it'). Although, as we briefly note, residential architecture has episodically served as a rallying point for cultural regionalism (for example, the Craftsman bungalow of the 1910s, the 'case-study' home of the 1940s, the Gehry house of the 1970s), celluloid or the electronic screen have remained the dominant media of the region's self-expression. Compared to other great cities, Los Angeles may be *planned* or *designed* in a very fragmentary sense (primarily at the level of its infrastructure) but it is infinitely *envisioned*.

Yet we must avoid the idea that Los Angeles is ultimately just the mirror of Narcissus, or a huge disturbance in the Maxwellian ether. Beyond its myriad rhetorics and mirages, it can be presumed that the city actually exists.[8] I thus treat, within the master dialectic of sunshine and *noir*, three attempts, in successive generations, to establish authentic epistemologies for Los Angeles.

First, and at some length in the section called *Debunkers*, I examine immigrant writer Louis Adamic's anti-romantic insistence upon the centrality of *class violence* in the constitution of the social and cultural landscapes of Los Angeles, an interpretation that was carried further in detail and scope by his close friend, Carey McWilliams. McWilliams's *Southern California Country (An Island on the Land)* is analyzed as the climax – and terminus – of Popular Front attempts to unmask Booster mythology and to recover the historical roles of labor and oppressed minority groups.

Secondly, I survey the careers of several very different avant gardes (the Black Arts Movement, the Ferus Gallery group, the alternative Hollywood of Kenneth Anger, the solo flight of Thomas Pynchon) which formed a Los Angeles cultural underground during part or all of the 1960s. These collaborations (*Communards*) – broken up or expatriated by the early 1970s – represented the coming-of-age of the first L.A.-bred bohemia (indeed, in some cases, tracing their roots back to local high-school cliques of the 1940s), unified by their autobiographical search for representative phenomenologies of daily life in Southern California in experiences as different as those of Black jazz musicians, white hotrodders and gay bikers.

Thirdly, in a concluding section I sketch, in broad and very tentative outline, the fledging attempts (after an intellectual/cultural hiatus in the 1970s) to contest the current corporate celebration of 'postmodern' Los Angeles. I argue that neither the neo-Marxist academics of the 'Los Angeles School' nor the community intellectuals of 'Gangster Rap' have yet fully disengaged themselves from the official dream machinery. On the other hand, the cultural definition of the poly-ethnic Los Angeles of the year 2000 has barely begun.

THE BOOSTERS

The missions are, next to our climate and its consequences, the best capital Southern California has. *Charles Fletcher Lummis*[9]

In 1884 a malarial journalist from Chillicothe, Ohio decided to change his fortune and improve his health by going to Southern California. Unlike the thousands of other health-seekers beginning to discover the curative powers of sunshine, Charles Fletcher Lummis did not take the train. He walked. On his arrival in Los Angeles 143 days later, the owner of the *Times*, Colonel (later General) Harrison Gray Otis, was so impressed that he appointed Lummis city editor.

When Otis greeted the footsore Lummis, Los Angeles was just a back-country town (the 187th largest in the 1880 Census) tributary to imperial San Francisco, with little water or capital, and no coal or port. When Otis died thirty-five years later, Los Angeles was the biggest city in the West, approaching a million inhabitants, with an artificial river tapped from the Sierras, a federally subsidized harbor, an oil bonanza, and block after block of skyscrapers under construction. Unlike other American cities that maximized their comparative advantages as crossroads, capitals, seaports, or manufacturing centers, Los Angeles was first and above all the creature of real-estate capitalism: the culminating speculation, in fact, of the generations of boosters and promoters who had subdivided and sold the West from the Cumberland Gap to the Pacific.

The first boom occurred a few years after Lummis's arrival and brought one hundred thousand fortune- and health-seekers to Los Angeles County. After the collapse of this railroad-engineered land rush, Colonel Otis – representing the toughest of the new settlers – took command of the city's business organizations on behalf of panic-stricken speculators. To revive the boom, and to launch a reckless competition with San Francisco (the most unionized city in the world), he militarized industrial relations in Los Angeles. Existing unions were locked out, picketing was virtually outlawed, and dissidents were terrorized. With sunshine and the open shop as their main assets, and allied with the great transcontinental railroads (the region's largest landowners), a syndicate of developers, bankers and transport magnates led by Otis and his son-in-law, Harry Chandler, set out to sell Los Angeles – as no city had ever been sold – to the restless but affluent babbitry of the Middle West. For more than a quarter century, an unprecedented mass migration of retired farmers, small-town dentists, wealthy spinsters, tubercular schoolteachers, petty stock speculators, Iowa lawyers, and devotees of the Chautauqua circuit transferred their savings and small fortunes into Southern California real estate. This massive flow of wealth between regions produced population, income and consumption structures seemingly out of all proportion to Los Angeles's actual production base: the paradox of the first 'postindustrial' city in its preindustrial guise.

As Kevin Starr emphasizes in his widely acclaimed account of the cultural history of Southern California in the Booster Era (1885–1925), *Inventing the Dream*, this transformation required the continuous inter-action of myth-making and literary invention with the crude promotion of land values and health cures. In his view, the partnership of Lummis and Otis was the prototype for the conscription of a whole generation of Eastern (usually Brahmin) intellectuals as the cultural agents of the Boom. The original cadre consisted of the journalists and errant *littérateurs*, led by Lummis, whom Otis brought to the *Times* during the Gilded Age: Robert Burdette, John Steven McGroaty ('the Poet of the Verdugo Hills'), Harry Carr, and others.

Through the talents of such men, Otis promoted an image of Southern California that dominated the popular imagination at the turn of the century and is alive to this day: a melange of mission myth (originating in Helen Hunt Jackson's *Ramona*), obssession with climate, political conservatism (symbolized in open shop), and a thinly veiled racialism, all put to the service of boosterism and oligarchy.[10]

The mission literature depicted the history of race relations as a pastoral ritual of obedience and paternalism: 'graceful Indians, happy as peasants in an Italian opera, knelt dutifully before the Franciscans to receive the baptism of a superior culture, while in the background the angelus tolled from a swallow-guarded campanile, and a choir of friars intoned the *Te Deum*'.[11] Any intimation of the brutality inherent in the forced labor system of the missions and haciendas, not to speak of the racial terrorism and lynchings that made early Anglo-ruled Los Angeles the most violent town in the West during the 1860s and 1870s, was suppressed.

If Jackson's *Ramona* transformed selected elements of local history into romantic myth (still popular to this day), Lummis was the impresario who promoted the myth as the motif of an entire artifical landscape. In 1894, as federal troops occupied Los Angeles and Otis fretted that the local Pullman strikers might draw out other workers in a general strike, Lummis organized the first Los Angeles Fiesta as a public distraction. The next year, with the class war temporarily abated, he orchestrated the Fiesta around a comprehensive 'mission' theme, influenced by *Ramona*. Its electric regional impact can only be compared to the national *frisson* of the contemporary

Columbian Exposition in Chicago: as the latter inaugurated the neo-Classical revival, the former launched an equally frenzied local 'Mission revival'.

The romanticized and idyllic theme was quickly picked up and exploited by a gallery of entrepreneurs who knew a good thing when they saw it. Everything from furniture suites and candied fruit to commercial and residential architecture stressed the mission motif.[12]

Some of the missions themselves were restored as pioneer theme-parks, especially San Gabriel Arcangel where a specially constructed theater next to the old church housed McGroarty's *Mission Play* – 'the American Ober-ammergau' – which was eventually seen by tens of thousands. At a New York advertising convention in the early 1930s, the mission aura of 'history and romance' was rated as an even more important attraction in selling Southern California than weather or movie-industry glamor.[13] Of course, as Starr notes, this capitalization of Los Angeles's fictional 'Spanish' past not only sublimated contemporary class struggle, but also censored, and repressed from view, the actual plight of Alta California's descendants. Pio Pico, the last governor of Mexican California and once the richest man in the city, was buried in a pauper's grave virtually as Lummis's floral floats were passing down Broadway.[14]

From the middle nineties, Lummis edited the influential magazine *Out West (Land of Sunshine),* 'whose masthead . . . reads like a Who's Who . . . of California letters',[15] and oversaw a full-fledged *salon* that gathered around his famous bungalow, El Alisal, along the rocky Arroyo Seco, between Los Angeles and Pasadena (the famed winter retreat of Eastern millionaires). Lummis's 'Arroyo Set' regrouped Henry James's Yankee intelligentsia in an altogether more libidinal setting: indeed one of the Set's major credos, best expressed in Grace Ellery Channings's evocations of an Italianized Southern California, was the power of sunshine to reinvigorate the racial energies of the Anglo-Saxons (Los Angeles as the 'new Rome' and so on).

Lummis's passions for Southwest archeology (he founded the famed Southwest Museum a few blocks from El Alisal), mission preservation, physical culture (emulating the imagined knightly lifestyle of the dons), and racial metaphysics were recapitulated by other Arroyans. Thus the retired

tobacco manufacturer and essayist Abbot Kinney crusaded simultaneously
for the Mission Indians, the mass planting of eucalpytus, citrus culture, the
conservation of Yosemite Valley, and Anglo-Saxon racial purity through
eugenics. As a speculator and developer, he also realized the supreme
incarnation of the Mediterranean metaphor: Venice, California, with its
canals and imported gondoliers. In a similarly polymathic vein, Joseph
Widney was an early president of the University of Southern California, a
fervent booster (*California of the South*, 1888), and author of the epic *Race Life
of the Aryan Peoples* (1907), which argued that Los Angeles was destined to
become the world capital of Aryan supremacy. Meanwhile, with the avid
support of Otis, the doctrines of Nietzsche were being Southern-Californized
by the *Times*'s literary editor and Arroyan child prodigy, Willard Huntington
Wright. (Wright would later, as editor of the *Smart Set*, metamorphose from
booster to debunker, repudiating Los Angeles's 'provincialism' at every
opportunity, while celebrating the invigorations of sexual promiscuity.)

   The Arroyo Set also defined the visual arts and architecture of turn-of-
the-century Los Angeles. George Wharton James, a desert health faddist like
Lummis, organized the Arroyo Guild, a shortlived but seminal point of
intersection between the mission-myth romantics and the Pasadena
franchise of the Arts-and-Crafts movement dominated by the celebrated
Greene brothers. A synthesis of the two currents, of course, was the typical
Craftsman bungalow with its Navajo and 'Mission Oak' interior
decoration.[16] If the ultimate bungalow was really a 'cathedral in wood'
(like the Greene Brothers' incredible Gamble House) affordable only by the
very rich, the masses could buy small but still stylish imitations in 'do-it-
yourself' kits that could be thrown up on any vacant lot. For an entire
generation these 'democratic bungalows', with their domestic miniaturiza-
tion of the Arroyo aesthetic, were praised not only for making Los Angeles
a city of single-family homes (a staggering 94 per cent of all dwellings by
1930) but also for assuring 'industrial freedom'. Thus when the United
States Commission on Industrial Relations visited Los Angeles in 1914 it
heard F.J. Zeehandelaar of the Merchants and Manufacturers Association
brag that working-class home ownership was the keystone of the Open Shop
and a 'contented' labor-force. Bitter union leaders, on the other hand,
denounced the mortgage payments on the little bungalows as a 'new
serfdom' that made Los Angeles workers timid in face of their bosses.[17]

AN ARROYO CATHEDRAL
Gamble House (1908), Pasadena

The preeminence of the Arroyo Set in defining the cultural parameters of Los Angeles's development, and in investing real-estate speculation and class warfare with an aura of romantic myth, began to come to an end after World War One. Lummis's special relationship with Otis was not part of the inheritance that Harry Chandler took over in 1917. The *Times*'s subsidy to Lummis was cut, the movies arrived as more effective promoters of immigration than *The Land of Sunshine*, and, in any case, the Mission Romantics became older and more disenchanted in rapidly urbanizing and auto-congested Southern California. Taos and Carmel began to usurp the Arroyo's role as elite culture center of the Southwest. By the early 1920s, bungalows and rugged outdoor living were passing out of vogue; the upper middle classes, enriched by oil speculations or Hollywood, were preferring servants and massive 'Spanish Colonial Revival' homes. Yet the upscale popularity of the Spanish Colonial style testified to one of the two most durable legacies of the Arroyans: the creation of an ersatz history which, through its comprehensive incorporation into landscape and consumption, became an actual historical stratum in the culture of Los Angeles.[18] (Contemporary mini-malls and fastfood franchises, with their Franciscan arches and red-tiled roofs, are still quoting chapter and verse from the Mission Myth – not to mention the Mission-style design of the new Ronald Reagan Presidential Library in Simi Valley.) The other major legacy, of course, was the ideology of Los Angeles as the utopia of Aryan supremacism – the sunny refuge of White Protestant America in an age of labor upheaval and the mass immigration of the Catholic and Jewish poor from Eastern and Southern Europe.

THE DEBUNKERS

It seems somehow absurd, but it is nevertheless a fact, that for forty years, the smiling, booming, sunshine City of the Angels has been the bloodiest arena in the Western world for Capital and Labor.
Morrow Mayo[19]

'The weather is beautiful . . .'
The only words spoken by a Wobblie before his arrest in the
1921 San Pedro free speech fight

One of these immigrants, and the first (at least among the non-Jews) to become a major American writer, was Louis Adamic. His personal odyssey carried him from Carniola in the Austro-Hungarian Empire to the milltowns of Pennsylvania, then with the American Expeditionary Force to the trenches of the Somme. Like so many other demobilized veterans, he decided to try his luck in Los Angeles, ending up broke and homeless in Pershing Square (as old Central Park had just been renamed). What the *Times* would later call the 'Forty Year War' of capital and labor was drawing to its bitter close. The city's once powerful Socialist movement (they came within a hair's-breadth of the mayoralty in 1911) had retreated to Llano in the Mojave, while one AFL union after another had been broken in a succession of violent metal trades strikes and street transport lockouts. Only IWW seamen and longshoremen defied the Merchants and Manu-facturers Association crusade to make the open shop complete. Adamic was swept up in this final battle of the local class war, befriending the IWW organizers, relishing their gallows humor and indiscipline, and ultimately recording their suicidal bravery in his *Laughing in the Jungle* (1932) – an 'autobiography of an immigrant in America' that was also an extraordinary documentary of Los Angeles in the 1920s from the standpoint of its radical outcasts and defeated idealists.

Adamic's 'epistemological position' was curious. Although in his guts he sided with the IWW's doomed struggle, he remained intellectually aloof from their 'naive belief' in revolution and One Big Union. As he put it, 'I was not a regular Socialist, but a "Menckenite".' He soon became part of a like-minded *salon* of Los Angeles bohemians, gravitating around bookdealer Jack Zeitlin's home in Echo Park, that included architect Lloyd Wright, photographer Edward Weston, critic-librarian Lawrence Clark Powell, artist Rockwell Kent and a dozen others.[20] Yet Adamic was also uncomfortable with these genteel rebels; as Carey McWilliams (a young member of the circle) would later observe, he had an 'instinctive hostility to typically middle-class concepts'. Eventually he withdrew to a Slavic neighborhood in San Pedro, Los Angeles's bustling port ('It was a normal seaport town . . . there were no tourists and sick old people from Iowa and Missouri').[21]

From this base in the harbor – with one foot in the literati camp (Mencken had begun to publish Adamic in the *American Mercury*) and the other in the proletariat – Adamic chronicled Los Angeles of the oil-and-God-crazy 1920s. To him it was an incredible burlesque mirror of the philistinism and larceny of Coolidge America ('additional proof of the accuracy of Marx's generalization that history repeats itself, first as tragedy and then as farce').[22] As McWilliams recalled:

He thrived on Los Angeles. He reveled in its freaks, fakirs, and frauds. He became the magazine biographer of such eccentrics as Otoman Bar-Azusht Ra'nish and Aimée Semple McPherson. Lost in the files of the strange assortment of magazines published by R. Haldeman-Julius will be found a long list of Adamic's contributions to Los Angeles. He was its prophet, sociologist and historian.[23]

Adamic's most original contribution to the debunking of the Booster myth was his emphasis on the centrality of class violence to the construction of the city. Others had already attacked Los Angeles's philistinism and skewered its apologists with Mencken-like sarcasm. (Indeed as early as 1913, Willard Huntington Wright was complaining in *The Smart Set* about the 'hypocrisy, like a vast fungus, [that] has spread over the city's surface'.)[24] In his historically interesting but vapidly written 1927 novel, *Oil!*, Upton Sinclair (who had been a leading participant in the IWW free speech fight at the Harbor) debunked the oil boom and evoked the oppression of labor in Los Angeles. But Adamic was the first to carefully chart the sordid, bloody history of the Forty Year War and attempt a muckraking reconstruction of its central events: the bombing of the *Times* in 1910 and the subsequent trial of the labor conspiracy led by the McNamara brothers. *Dynamite: The Story of Class Violence in America* (1931), although scarcely flattering to the California labor bureaucracy, painted a demonic portrait of General Otis and the ruling-class brutality that had driven labor to desperation. Equally it warned readers in the early Depression years that until employers bargained with unions in good faith, outbreaks of violent class warfare were inevitable.

Shortly after publishing the first version of *Dynamite*, Adamic synthesized his various Haldeman-Julius ephemera and pages from his diary in a famous essay, 'Los Angeles! There She Blows!' (*The Outlook*, 13 August 1930), later quoted in 'The Enormous Village' chapter of *Laughing in the Jungle*. This essay was widely noticed by the critical literati, exerting a seminal influence on McWilliams, as well as upon Nathanael West, who in *The Day of the Locust* (1939), would further develop Adamic's image of Los Angeles's 'spiritually and mentally starving' little people, the 'Folks'. Also impressed was writer and satirist Morrow Mayo, who 'paraphrased' and amalgamated Adamic's *Outlook* and McNamara pieces in his own *Los Angeles* (1933). Although *Laughing in the Jungle* was the incomparably more powerful work, Mayo's lurid, vignette-style history (for example, from 'Hell-Hole of the West' to 'The Hickman Horror') scored its own points against the Los Angeles Chamber of Commerce. Mayo was particularly effective in reworking Adamic's 'enormous village' theme:

Here is an artificial city which has been pumped up under forced draught, inflated like a balloon, stuffed with rural humanity like a goose with corn . . . endeavoring to eat up this too rapid avalanche of anthropoids, the sunshine metropolis heaves and strains, sweats and becomes pop-eyed, like a young boa constrictor trying to swallow a goat. It has never imparted an urban character to its incoming population for the simple reason that it has never had any urban character to impart. On the other hand, the place has retained the manners, culture, and general outlook of a huge country village.[25]

Not all debunking of the 'enormous village' was merely literary. The Group of Independent Artists of Los Angeles, who held their first exhibition in 1923, represented an analogous, even earlier, critical current in local art. A united front for the 'New Form', including Cubism, Dynamism, and Expressionism, they attacked the landscape romantics – the Eucalyptus painters, Laguna seascape painters, Mission painters, and so on – who perpetuated Helen Hunt Jackson in watercolor. Dominated by the 'Synchromist' painter Stanton Macdonald-Wright, who had caroused with the Cubists in Paris before World War One, and the radical Lithuanian exile Boris Deutsch, the Group of Independents were transformed by their encounter with revolutionary Mexican muralism in the late 1920s.[26] David Siquieros, who passed through Los Angeles in the early Depression, contributed a famous 'lost work' that was roughly the equivalent of Adamic's *Dynamite* in its Marxist view of Los Angeles history. Commissioned in 1930 to decorate Olvera Street – the contrived 'Mexican' tourist precinct next to the old Plaza – with a 'gay mural', Siquieros instead painted *Tropical America*: a crucified *peon* under a snarling eagle evokes the imperial savagery at the origin of the Anglo occupation. Although quickly white-washed by his shocked patroness, Siquieros's great mural survived long enough to impress the young Jackson Pollock; reportedly 'echoes of its imagery enter[ed] his later work'.[27]

Adamic's and Mayo's indictment of Los Angeles's 'fake urbanity', as well as the attack of the Group of Independents on landscape romanticism, simultaneously unearthed a truism and gave birth to a lasting stereotype. The anti-urban, Garden City ethos celebrated by the Arroyans was turned over to expose its malignant aspect. Intellectual emigrés, beginning to arrive in numbers from Europe in the early 1930s, were particularly disturbed by the absence of urban culture in a city-region of two million inhabitants. Alfred Döblin – the famed literary portraitist of Berlin – would actually denounce Hollywood as a 'murderous desert of houses ... a horrible garden city'. (When asked to comment on the suburban lifestyle, he added: 'Indeed, one is much and extensively in the open here – yet, am I a cow?')[28]

Unfortunately Adamic was not around to add his voice to the dis-enchantment of the exiles, or, alternatively, to guide them to the 'saner' working-class areas of the city which he knew so intimately. Awarded a Guggenheim fellowship to pursue his writing on the new immigrants, he moved to New York at the beginning of the Depression. After his departure, the mantle of Los Angeles Debunker passed to his friend, the lawyer, writer and journalist Carey McWilliams. Adamic's profound influence upon McWilliams's view of Los Angeles was acknowledged in a small volume of essays, *Louis Adamic and Shadow-America*, which the latter circulated in 1935. McWilliams reflected at length on Adamic's Menckenesque critique of Los Angeles as America, as well as upon the margin of class consciousness and 'peasant sense' that distinguished Adamic from other L.A. bohemians of the 1920s. (McWilliams also registered some of his own, surprisingly left-wing opinions, including a reference to 'the daintily eclectic fascism of Mr Roosevelt'.)[29] A few years later, coincident with the sensation of Steinbeck's *Grapes of Wrath* (1939), McWilliams published his brilliant exposé of California agribusiness, *Factories in the Field*, that led to his appointment as Commissioner of Immigration and Housing by California's newly-elected Democratic governor, Culbert Olson. Through the war years McWilliams also kept up his leading role in the progressive politics of Los Angeles, organizing the defense for the Eastside Chicanos framed in the infamous 'Sleepy Lagoon' case of 1943, and reporting in the *Nation* and *New Republic* on the successful struggle to end the Open Shop.

In 1946, as the culmination of nearly twenty years of literary and political engagement in the region, McWilliams published his magisterial *Southern California Country: Island on the Land*, as a volume in the 'American Folkway Series' edited by Erskine Caldwell. A self-described 'labor of love', *Southern California Country* completed the debunking project initiated by Adamic in his 'Los Angeles! There She Blows!' piece almost a generation before.[30] It was a devastating deconstruction of the Mission Myth and its makers, beginning with a recovery of the *Mexican* roots of Southern California and the seldom-told story of genocide and native resistance during the 1850s and 1860s. But McWilliams went far beyond L.A.-bashing polemic or Menckenesque condescension. Picking up where Adamic had left off in his narratives of Los Angeles labor, McWilliams sought to integrate historical narrative with economic and cultural analysis. *Southern California Country* adumbrates a full-fledged theory of the singular historical conditions – ranging from militarized class organization to 'super-boosterism' – that made possible the breakneck urbanization of Los Angeles without the concomitant development of a large manufacturing base or commercial hinterland. McWilliams carefully explained how this 'sociology of the boom' was responsible for the city's anti-urban bias and sprawling form ('it reflects a spectacle of a large metropolitan city without an industrial base').

Three years later, *California: The Great Exception* placed the rise of Southern California within the larger framework of California's unique evolution as a civilization and social system. The year 1949 also saw the publication of his groundbreaking history of Mexican immigration, *North from Mexico*, which restated, now on epic scale, the fundamental contribution of Mexican labor and craft to the emergence of the modern Southwest. This magnificent quartet of books, together with earlier studies of California writers (Ambrose Bierce and Adamic), constitutes one of the major achievements within the American regional tradition, making McWilliams the Walter Prescott Webb of California, if not its Fernand Braudel. In his *oeuvre*, in other words, debunkery transcended itself to establish a commanding regional interpretation.

But no 'McWilliams School' followed. *Southern California Country* was falsely assimilated into the 'guidebook' genre, and, despite continuing popularity, produced little commentary and few progeny. The implicit political groundwork of McWilliams's writing – the labor-reformist popular front in California – was demolished by Cold War hysteria. Called to New York to oversee an emergency 'civil liberties' issue of the *Nation*, McWilliams stayed there for the next quarter of a century as the magazine's editor.[31] Meanwhile, research on Southern California devolved once again into trivial genealogy or boosterism; until the late 1970s, with the appearance of Gottlieb and Wolt's massive history of the *Times*,[32] fewer serious monographs, let alone synoptic studies, were annually produced about the region than of any other major metropolitan area.[33] Virtually alone among big American cities, Los Angeles still lacks a scholarly municipal history – a void of research that has become the accomplice of cliché and illusion. The chapters that would update and complete *Southern California Country* are absent; Los Angeles understands its past, instead, through a robust fiction called *noir*.

THE NOIRS

From Mount Hollywood, Los Angeles looks rather nice, enveloped in a haze of changing colors. Actually, and in spite of all the healthful sunshine and ocean breezes, it is a *bad* place – full of old, dying people, who were born old of tired pioneer parents, victims of America – full of curious wild and poisonous growths, decadent religious cults and fake science, and wildcat enterprises, which, with their aim for quick profit, are doomed to collapse and drag down multitudes of people . . . a jungle. *Louis Adamic*[34]

You can rot here without feeling it. *John Rechy*[35]

In 1935 the famous radical author Lewis Corey (née Louis Fraina) announced in his *Crisis of the Middle Class* that the Jeffersonian Dream was moribund: 'That middle-class ideal is gone beyond recall. The United States today is a nation of employees and of propertyless dependents.' As jobless accountants and ruined stockbrokers stood in the same breadlines as truckdrivers and steelworkers, much of the babbitry of the 1920s was left with little to eat except for obsolete class pride. Corey warned that the downwardly mobile middle stratum, 'at war with itself', was approaching a radical crossroads, and would turn either toward socialism or fascism.[36]

This invocation of the dual immiseration and radicalization of the middle classes applied more literally, and appositely, to Los Angeles during the early 1930s than anywhere else in the country. The very structure of the long Southern California boom – fueled by middle-class savings and channeled into real-estate and oil speculations – ensured a vicious circle of crisis and bankruptcy for the mass of retired farmers, small businessmen and petty developers. Indeed, the absence of heavy industry (together with the deportation of tens of thousands of unemployed manual workers back to Mexico) meant that the Depression in Los Angeles was foregrounded and amplified in the middle classes, producing a political fermentation that was at times bizarre.

Political observers inured to the bedrock conservatism of Southern California's Midwest immigrants were incredulous in 1934 when Upton Sinclair, the region's most notorious socialist, captured more than a hundred thousand cross-over Republican votes for his 'End Poverty in California' (EPIC) program with its quasi-revolutionary advocacy of 'production for use'. (In an interview thirty years later, Los Angeles EPIC organizer Reuben Boroughs confirmed that the movement primarily 'spoke to the broken down middle class' with little attention to labor or to the unemployed.)[37] Four years later, journalists were warning of the potential for local fascism as the voting tide switched toward the shadowy 'Ham and Eggs' movement with its weird combination of pension reform and brown-shirt demagoguery.[38] Agitated middle-class voters also embraced the temporary sensations of Technocracy, Inc., the Utopian Society, and the Townsend Plan. Symptomatically, the epicenters of this turbulence were the suburban growth-poles of the roaring twenties: Glendale (a hotbed of EPIC) and Long Beach (with 40,000 elderly Iowans, the birthplace of the Townsend Plan and stronghold of Ham and Eggs).

These Depression-crazed middle classes of Southern California became, in one mode or another, the original protagonists of that great anti-myth usually known as *noir*. Beginning in 1934, with James M. Cain's *The Postman Always Rings Twice*, a succession of through-the-glass-darkly novels – all produced by writers under contract to the studio system – repainted the image of Los Angeles as a deracinated urban hell. 'Writing against the myth of El Dorado, they transformed it into its antithesis; that of the dream running out along the California shore . . . [they created] a regional fiction obsessively concerned with puncturing the bloated image of Southern California as the golden land of opportunity and the fresh start.'[39]

Noir was like a transformational grammar turning each charming ingredient of the boosters' arcadia into a sinister equivalent. Thus, in Horace McCoy's They Shoot Horses Don't They? (1935) the marathon dance hall on Ocean Pier became virtually a death camp for the Depression's lost souls. The 'changeless monotonous beautiful days without end . . . unmarred by rain or weather' of William Faulkner's noir short story, Golden Land (1935) were a Sisyphean imprisonment for the matriarch of a Midwestern family corrupted by L.A. success. Similarly, Cain, in Double Indemnity (1936) and Mildred Pierce (1941), evoked poisoned bungalows, whose white-walled, red-tiled normality ('as good as the next, and perhaps a little better') barely hid the murderous marriages within. In Nathanael West's The Day of the Locust (1939), Hollywood became the 'Dream Dump', a hallucinatory landscape tottering on apocalypse, while in successive Chandler novels the climate ('earthquake weather' and mayhem-inspiring Santa Ana winds) was increasingly eerie; there were even 'ladies in the lakes'.

Collectively, the déclassé middle strata of these novels are without ideological coherence or capacity to act except as McCoy's sleepwalkers or West's stampeding 'flea people'. Individually, however, their petty-bourgeois anti-heroes typically expressed autobiographical sentiments, as the noir of the 1930s and 1940s (and again in the 1960s) became a conduit for the resentments of writers in the velvet trap of the studio system. Thus the very first hardboiled Hollywood detective, Ben Jardinn, the hero of a 1930 serial in The Black Mask, echoed the studio-weary cynicism of his creator, Raoul Whitfield, bit actor turned hack screenwriter.[40] Likewise, Tod Hackett in The Day of the Locust is portrayed in a situation similar to West's own: brought to the Coast by a talent scout for the studios and forced to live 'the dilemma of reconciling his creative work with his commercial labors'.[41] Chandler's Marlowe, by the same token, symbolized the small businessman locked in struggle with gangsters, corrupt police and the parasitic rich (who were usually his employers as well) – a romanticized simulacrum of the writer's relationship to studio hacks and moguls.[42]

NOIR UNDER CONTRACT
Paramount Gates, Hollywood

Budd Schulberg, on the other hand, examined the exploitative relation-ship between writer and mogul from the top down. A studio brat (son of Paramount's production chief) turned Communist writer, he portrayed Hollywood capitalism with almost documentary realism in *What Makes Sammy Run?* (1940). Sammy Glick, the rising young mogul, battens off the creativity of the friends and employees whom he, in turn, betrays and crushes. As one of Schulberg's characters observes, 'he is the *id* of our society'.[43]

Schulberg's psychoanalytic perspective, however, was exceptional. One of the distinguishing traits of first-generation 'Los Angeles fiction' was its emphasis on economic self-interest rather than depth psychology. Thus something like the labor theory of value supplied a consistent moralizing edge in the novels of Chandler and Cain. There is a constant tension between the 'productive' middle class (Marlowe, Mildred Pierce, Nick Papdakis, and so on), and the 'unproductive' *déclassés* or idle rich (the Sternwoods, Bert Pierce, Monty Beragon, and so on). Unable to accumulate any longer through speculation or gambling, or having lost their inheritance (or merely desiring to speed it up), the *noirs déclassés* invariably choose murder over toil. Invariably, too, the fictional opposition between these different middle strata suggests the contrast between the 'lazy', speculative Southern California economy (real-estate promotions and Hollywood) and America's hard-working heartlands.

These motifs of the 1930s 'Los Angeles Novel' – the moral phen-omenology of the depraved or ruined middle classes; the insinuation of the crisis of the semi-proletarianized writer; and the parasitical nature of Southern California – underwent interesting permutations in the *film noir* of the 1940s. Sometimes *film noir* is described in shorthand as the result of the encounter between the American hardboiled novel and exiled German expressionist cinema – a simplistic definition that leaves out other seminal influences, including psychoanalysis and Orson Welles. For our purposes, however, what was significant was the way in which the image of Los Angeles was reworked from novel to screenplay (sometimes incestuously as in Chandler rewriting Cain or Faulkner rewriting Chandler), then translated to the screen by such leftish *auteurs noirs* (some of them emigrés) as Edward Dmytryk, Ring Lardner Jr., Ben Maddow, Carl Foreman, John Berry, Jules Dassin, Abraham Polonsky, Albert Maltz, Dalton Trumbo and Joseph Losey.

In their hands, *film noir* sometimes approached a kind of Marxist *cinema manqué*, a shrewdly oblique strategy for an otherwise subversive realism.[44]

After the first adaptations of Cain and Chandler, *film noir* began to exploit Los Angeles settings in new ways. Geographically, it shifted increasingly from the Cainian bungalows and suburbs to the epic dereliction of Downtown's Bunker Hill, which symbolized the rot in the heart of the expanding metropolis.[45] Sociologically, 1940s *noir* was more typically concerned with gangster underclasses and official corruption than with the pathology of the middle class; politically, the implicit obsession with the fate of the petty producer was supplanted by representations of political re-action and social polarization. Of course, *film noir* remained an ideologically ambiguous aesthetic that could be manipulated in dramatically different ways. Thus Howard Hawks chose to flatten the deep shadows of *The Big Sleep* (Chandler's most anti-rich novel) into an erotic ambience for Bogart and Bacall, while the more toughminded Edward Dmytryk and Adrian Scott (both future members of the Hollywood Ten) evoked premonitions of fascism and brainwashing in their version of *Farewell, My Lovely* (*Murder, My Sweet*).

The experiments of *film noir* were mirrored by new directions in hardboiled Los Angeles writing during the 1940s. John Fante, who together with Adamic and Cain had been discovered by Mencken's *American Mercury* in the early Depression, founded a one-man school of 'wino writing' that autobiographically chronicled life in Bunker Hill's single-room-occupancy hotels and Main Street taxi dancehalls during the Depression and war years.[46] Charles Bukowsky would later acquire a hyped-up celebrity (including two 'autobiographical' films) for his derivative, Fantesque descriptions of a Hollywood demimonde of fallen 'stars in bars' – a world better evoked in the phantasmagorical autobiography of jazzman and junkie Art Pepper.[47]

Aldous Huxley's two Los Angeles novels (*After Many a Summer Dies the Swan* [1939] and *Ape and Essence* [1948]), on the other hand, prefigured the postwar fantastic novel (on a spectrum that includes Thomas Pynchon's *Crying of Lot 49* [1966] as well as Kim Stanley Robinson's *The Gold Coast* [1988]) that exploited Southern California's unsure boundary between reality and science fiction. As David Dunaway has pointed out, Huxley's important contributions to Los Angeles's anti-mythography are seldom acknowledged these days. If *Swan*, with its grotesque and scarcely veiled portraits of William Randolph Hearst and Marion Davis, inspired Welles's *Citizen Kane* (1940), then *Ape and Essence*, with its savage vision of the post-apocalypse, was the 'predecessor of science fiction films on the environmental destruction of Los Angeles and human devolution' – a list that includes *Planet of the Apes*, *Omega Man*, and *Blade Runner*.[48]

The early science fiction of Ray Bradbury, meanwhile, showed a strong *noir* influence derived from his sci-fi mentor, Leigh Brackett, who styled herself after Chandler and Hammett. Bradbury's uniqueness was that he was a son of the Folks turned 'poet of the pulps'. A Depression emigré from Wisconsin, he attended L.A. High (but never learned to drive) and became an enthusiastic member of West's dreaded fanocracy:

I was one of Them: the Strange Ones. The Funny People. The Odd Tribes of autograph-collectors and photographers. The Ones who waited through long days and nights, who used other people's dreams for their lives.[49]

Bradbury's *Martian Chronicles* (1950) revolves around contradictions between the Turnerian, 'westering' quest for new frontiers and poignant nostalgia for small-town America. In a sense, Bradbury took the angst of the dislocated Midwesterner in Los Angeles and projected it as extra-terrestrial destiny. As David Mogen has pointed out, Bradbury's Mars is really Los Angeles's metaphysical double: 'a product of fantasies imposed upon it . . . magical promises and disorienting malevolence'.[50]

But the most interesting transit across Los Angeles's literary scene in the 1940s was probably the brief appearance of Black *noir*. Los Angeles was a particularly cruel mirage for Black writers. At first sight to the young Langston Hughes, visiting the city in the Olympic year of 1932, 'Los Angeles seemed more a miracle than a city, a place where oranges sold for one cent a dozen, ordinary Black folks lived in huge houses with "miles of yards", and prosperity seemed to reign in spite of the Depression.'[51] Later, in 1939, when Hughes attempted to work within the studio system, he discovered that the only available role for a Black writer was furnishing demeaning dialogue for cotton-field parodies of Black life. After a humiliating experience with the film *Way Down South*, he declared that 'so far as Negroes are concerned, [Hollywood] might just as well be controlled by Hitler'.[52]

Hughes's disillusionment in Los Angeles was recapitulated, more harrowingly, by the experience of Chester Himes. At the beginning of the war, Himes (who had spent the early Depression in the Ohio State Penitentiary on a robbery charge) headed West with his wife Jean for a fresh start as a screenwriter for Warner Brothers. Despite a formidable reputation as a short story writer for *Esquire* (the first 'convict writer' of renown), Himes encountered an implacable wall of racism in Hollywood. As his biographer describes the incident, 'he was promptly fired from . . . Warner Brothers when Jack Warner heard about him and said, "I don't want no niggers on this lot" '.[53] Racebaited from the studios, Himes spent the rest of the war years as an unskilled laborer in internally segregated defense plants wracked by outbursts of white violence. As he recalled later in his autobiography, it was a searing experience:

Up to the age of thirty-one I had been hurt emotionally, spiritually, and physically as much as thirty-one years can bear: I had lived in the South, I had fallen down an elevator shaft, I had been kicked out of college, I had served seven and one half years in prison, I had survived the humiliating last five years of the Depression in Cleveland; and still I was entire, complete, functional; my mind was sharp, my reflexes were good, and I was not bitter. But under the mental corrosion of race prejudice in Los Angeles I had become bitter and saturated with hate.[54]

Himes's Dostoyevskian portrait of Los Angeles as a racial hell, *If He Hollers Let Him Go* (1945), is *noir* as well-crafted as anything by Cain or Chandler. Set in the long hot summer of 1944, it narrates how white racism, acting in utterly capricious circumstances, launches the self-destruction of Bob Jones, a skilled 'leaderman' in the shipyards. As a critic has noted, 'fear is the novel's major theme . . . the progressive deterioration of a personality under the deadly pressure of a huge and inescapable fear'.[55] Himes's next novel, *Lonely Crusade* (1947), is also given a nightmare setting in the racially tense Los Angeles war economy. This time fear eats the soul of Lee Gordon, a Black UCLA graduate and union organizer under the influence of the Communist Party. Together, Himes's two Los Angeles novels, ignored in most critical treatments of the *noir* canon,[56] constitute a brilliant and disturbing analysis of the psychotic dynamics of racism in the land of sunshine.

However inadvertently, Himes's caricature of the local 'red conspiracy' in *Lonely Crusade* also prefigured the emergence of an 'anticommunist *noir*' in the Korean War years. While the Hollywood Inquisition was cutting down the careers of a majority of the writers, directors and producers of hardcore *film noir*, a redbaiting, bastard offspring – frequently set in Los Angeles – appeared on the B-movie circuit (for example, *Stakeout on 101*) and the drugstore paperback-rack (Mickey Spillane's sado-McCarthyite thrillers). Meanwhile through the 1950s, Ross Macdonald (Kenneth Millar) continued to churn out reasonably well-written detective *noir* in a Chandleresque mode, usually with some pointed contrast between the primitive beauty of the Southern California seacoast and the primitive greed of its entrepreneurs.[57]

A major revival of *noir* occurred in the 1960s and 1970s as a new generation of emigré writers and directors revitalized the anti-myth and elaborated it fictionally into a comprehensive counter-history. Thus Robert Towne (influenced by Chandler and West) brilliantly synthesized the big landgrabs and speculations of the first half of the twentieth century in his screenplays for *Chinatown* and *The Two Jakes*. Where *Chinatown* established a 1920s genealogy for 1930s and 1940s *noir*, *The Two Jakes* and John Gregory Dunne's *True Confessions* extrapolated it into the postwar suburban boom; while Ridley Scott's *Blade Runner* (cleverly reworking the plot of Philip K. Dick's *Do Androids Dream of Electric Sheep?*) depicted a stunningly Chandleresque Los Angeles of the third millennium. More recently, Ray Bradbury, returning to the genre for the first time in forty years, has 'softboiled' *noir* in an unabashedly nostalgic mode to recall Venice Beach of the 1950s – before urban renewal and gentrification – in his *Death is a Lonely Business* (1985).

Parallel to this project of a *noir* history of Los Angeles's past and future (which actually has come to function as a surrogate public history), other writers in the 1960s re-experienced the moral chill that shivered down the spines of Cain's and West's anti-heroes. John Rechy's *City of the Night* (1963) captured, from the standpoint of its gay 'Lost Angels', the image of the city as a fugitive midnight hustle – 'the world of Lonely America squeezed into Pershing Square' between anonymous sex acts and gratuitous police brutality. But where Rechy could ultimately find a certain nihilistic exhilaration along the shore where 'the sun gives up and sinks into the black, black sea',[58] Joan Didion found only nausea. More haunted than anyone by Nathanael West's dystopia, she described the moral apocalypse of 1960s Los Angeles in her novel *Play It As It Lays* (1970) and her volume of essays, *Slouching Toward Bethlehem* (1968). For Didion – on the edge of a nervous breakdown – the city of the Manson murders was already a helter-skelter of demeaned ambition and random violence. Her visceral revulsion was recalled years later by Bret Easton Ellis, L.A.'s 'bratpack' writer of the 1980s. His *Less Than Zero* (1985), a Cainian novel of gilded Westside youth, offered the darkest Los Angeles yet: 'Images of parents who were so hungry and unfulfilled that they ate their own children. . . . Images so violent and malicious that they seemed to be my only point of reference for a long time afterwards. After I left.'[59]

Finally, sixty years after the first short stories in *The Black Mask* and *The American Mercury* announced the genre, Los Angeles *noir* passes into delirious parody in the over-the-top writing of James Ellroy, the self-proclaimed 'Demon Dog of American Literature'. Although other contemporary tough-guy novelists, including Arthur Lyons, Robert Campbell, Roger Simon, T. Jefferson Parker and Joseph Wambaugh, keep pace with the Chandler/Macdonald tradition on its native turf, Ellroy's sheer frenzy transports his work to a different plane.[60] His *Los Angeles Quartet*,[61] depending on one's viewpoint, is either the culmination of the genre, or its *reductio ad absurdum*. At times an almost unendurable wordstorm of perversity and gore, *Quartet* attempts to map the history of modern Los Angeles as a secret continuum of sex crimes, satanic conspiracies, and political scandals. For Ellroy, as for Dunne in *True Confessions*, the grisly, unsolved 'Black Dahlia' case of 1946 is the crucial symbolic commencement of the postwar era – a local 'name of the rose' concealing a larger, metaphysical mystery. Yet in building such an all-encompassing *noir* mythology (including Stephen King-like descents into the occult), Ellroy risks extinguishing the genre's tensions, and, inevitably, its power. In his pitch blackness there is no light left to cast shadows and evil becomes a forensic banality. The result feels very much like the actual moral texture of the Reagan–Bush era: a supersaturation of corruption that fails any longer to outrage or even interest.

Indeed the postmodern role of L.A. *noir* may be precisely to endorse the emergence of *homo reaganus.* In an afterword to the fiftieth anniversary edition of *What Makes Sammy Run?*, Budd Schulberg confesses consternation that his savage portrayal of avarice and ambition has been recuperated as a 'handbook for yuppies':

The book I had written as an angry exposé of Sammy Glick was becoming a character reference. . . . That's how they're reading it in 1989. And if that's the way they go on reading it, marching behind the flag of Sammy Glick, with the big dollar sign in the square where the stars used to be, the twentieth-century version of Sammy is going to look like an Eagle Scout compared to the twenty-first.[62]

Pynchon forsees even worse 'repressive desublimations' (a Marcusean expression peculiarly apt to the context) of *noir*. In *Vineland* (1990) – his wily, California-centered novel about 'the restoration of fascism in America' – he envisions the Disneyfication of *noir* to sell deodorants and mineral water to Schulberg's coming hyper-yuppies. In a memorable scene, his 'mall-rat' teeny-boppers, Praire and Che, rendezvous at Hollywood's 'new Noir Center':

This was yuppification run to some pitch so desperate that Praire at least had to hope the whole process was reaching the end of its cycle. . . . Noir Center here had an upscale mineral-water boutique called Bubble Indemnity, plus The Lounge Good Buy patio furniture outlet, The Mall Tease Flacon, which sold perfume and cosmetics, and a New York style deli, The Lady 'n' Lox . . .[63]

THE EXILES

Shirley Temple lived across the street. Schoenberg was incensed when guides on the frequently-passing tour buses would point out her home and not his. *Dika Newlin*[64]

Between the Nazis' seizure of power and the Hollywood witch hunts, Los Angeles was the address in exile of some of Central Europe's most celebrated intellectuals.[65] Desperate and 'very modest' (Eisler), having just escaped the camps and the Gestapo, they arrived with few initial demands upon their sanctuary. They were stunned by the opulence of the movie colony. Even the most shirtless among them usually received so-called 'life-saving' contracts from the studios that guaranteed work visas and $100 weekly stipends. The more famous joined the exclusive salons established in Santa Monica and the Palisades by the pre-Hitler immigration of European film stars and directors.[66] Yet, despite their acknowledgement that Los Angeles did indeed appear like 'paradise', many of the anti-fascist exiles grasped at the first opportunity to leave for New York or, later, to return to the ruins of war-ravaged Europe. However, their recoil from 'paradise' is only seemingly paradoxical.

In part they were tormented by their own incestuous choice. Adorno in *Minima Moralia: Reflections from Damaged Life* (a journal he kept in Los Angeles during the war) recalled the 'isolation [which] becomes worse through the formation of exclusive, politically controlled groups, suspicious of their members, hostile towards those branded as different. . . . Relations among outcasts are even more poisonous than among the residents.'[67] (Adorno certainly knew what he was talking about; Brecht thought that the Los Angeles *soirées* of the Institute for Social Research (the 'Frankfurt School') resembled 'graduate seminars in a wartime bunker'.)[68] Segregated from native Angelenos, the exiles composed a miniature society in a self-imposed ghetto, clinging to their old-world prejudices like cultural life-preservers.

But their collective melancholia was also a reaction to the landscape. With few exceptions they complained bitterly about the absence of a European (or even Manhattan) *civitas* of public places, sophisticated crowds, historical auras and critical intellectuals. Amid so much open land there seemed to be no space that met their criteria of 'civilized urbanity'. Los Angeles, for all its fleshpots and enchantments, was experienced as a cultural antithesis to nostalgic memories of pre-fascist Berlin or Vienna. Indeed, as the September song of exile wore on, Los Angeles became increasingly symbolized as an 'anti-city', a Gobi of suburbs.

The formation of a critical consensus about Los Angeles/Hollywood (the two hopelessly conflated in the minds of most exiles) was, moreover, a seminal moment in the European reconceptualization of the United States. What had been largely romance – European fantasies of cowboys, Lindbergh and skyscrapers – was now mediated through actual experience in a city that stood in the same quasi-utopian relationship to the rest of the United States as America as a whole had stood to the Weimar imagination of the

1920s. Put another way, exile in Southern California ultimately trans-formed the terms for understanding the impact of Modernism, at least in the minds of the intellectuals influenced by the Institute for Social Research, which had moved to Santa Monica at the beginning of the war.[69]

Adorno, who wrote the *Dialectic of Enlightenment* with Max Horkheimer in Los Angeles during the war, said after his return to Frankfurt years later, 'It is scarcely an exaggeration to say that any con-temporary consciousness that has not appropriated the American experi-ence, even if in opposition, has something reactionary about it.'[70] In Los Angeles where Adorno and Horkheimer accumulated their 'data', the exiles thought they were encountering America in its purest, most prefigurative moment. Largely ignorant of, or indifferent to, the peculiar historical dialectic that had shaped Southern California, they allowed their image of first sight to become its own myth: Los Angeles as the crystal ball of capitalism's future. And, confronted with this future, they experienced all the more painfully the death agony of Enlightenment Europe.[71]

The Frankfurt critique of the 'Culture Industry' became the primary theoretical representation of this encounter. The focus of their time in Los Angeles being Hollywood, and its specular double 'Hollywood!', the Germans were soon adding a Hegelian polish to homegrown *noir* sensibility. They described the Culture Industry not merely as political economy, but as a specific spatiality that vitiated the classical proportions of European urbanity, expelling from the stage both the 'masses' (in their heroic, history-changing incarnation) and the critical intelligentsia. Exhibiting no apparent interest in the wartime turmoil in the local aircraft plants nor inclined to appreciate the vigorous nightlife of Los Angeles's Central Avenue ghetto, Horkheimer and Adorno focused instead on the little single-family boxes that seemed to absorb the world-historic mission of the proletariat into family-centered consumerism under the direction of radio jingles and *Life* magazine ads. The sun rises over Mount Hollywood in Adorno and Horkheimer's famous opening section of 'The Culture Industry':

Even now, the older houses just outside the concrete city center look like slums, and the new bungalows on the outskirts are at one with the flimsy structures of world fairs in their praise of technical progress and their built-in demand to be discarded after a short while like empty food cans. Yet the city housing projects designed to perpetuate the individual as a supposedly independent unit in a small hygienic dwelling make him all the more subservient to his adversary – the absolute power of capitalism.[72]

Despite their heady discovery, however, Horkheimer and Adorno were scarcely the Columbus and Magellan of this brave new world. The Los Angeles landscape of movie studios and single-family homes was already being chronicled by curious European observers long before the Weimar diaspora arrived in force. In the late twenties, for example, the foremost muckraker of German-language journalism, Egon Erwin Kisch, had set his acerbic wit against Open Shop Los Angeles. Famous for his exposé of the Colonel Redl affair which shook the Hapsburg Empire on the eve of World War One, Kisch was a prominent member of the Austrian Communist Party by the time he arrived in Los Angeles. His ironic travelogue, *Paradies Amerika*, echoed Adamic in its savage satirization of make-believe landscapes and speculative manias. Unimpressed with a city seemingly built only on sunshine, Kisch asked, 'Will this immense real-estate business end as a boom, as a speculative maneuver followed by a crash?'[73]

A few years later, after the 'crash' — and as the 1932 Olympics riveted world attention on Los Angeles, the 'mystery' of its growth, and its excess of cults – the German geographer Anton Wagner, who had relatives in the old German colony at Anaheim, meticulously mapped, photographed and described the Los Angeles Basin. His *Los Angeles . . . Zweimillionenstadt in Sudkalifornien* (1935) was a monument to old-fashioned Teutonic scholarship; Reyner Banham praised it forty years later as 'the only comprehensive view of Los Angeles as a built environment'.[74] Although awash with garbled pseudo-scientisms and racial allusions, *Los Angeles* offered an extraordinarily detailed panorama of the city's districts and environs in the early Depression. Wagner was particularly fascinated by the penetration of the principle of the movie set into the design of 'façade landscapes', particularly Hollywood's elaborate, but doomed, attempt to generate a Europeanized 'real urban milieu':

Here, one wants to create the Paris of the Far West. Evening traffic on Hollywood Boulevard attempts to mimic Parisian boulevard life. However, life on the Boulevard is extinct before midnight, and the seats in front of the cafes, where in

Paris one can watch street life in a leisurely manner, are missing. . . . At night the illuminated portraits of movie stars stare down from lampposts upon crowds dressed in fake European elegance – a declaration that America yearns to be something other than American here. . . . Yet, in spite of the artists, writers and aspiring film stars, the sensibility of a real Montmartre, Soho, or even Greenwich Village, cannot be felt here. The automobile mitigates against such a feeling, and so do the new houses. Hollywood lacks the patina of age.[75]

This notion of 'counterfeit urbanity', which, as we have seen, was already a cliché in the Menckenite critique of Los Angeles, would be further elaborated in the writing of the exiles (some of whom, presumably, were disembarking at San Pedro as Professor Wagner, maps in hand, was returning to his academic sinecure in the Third Reich). The contemporary 'adventures in hyperreality' of Eco and Baudrillard in Southern California, which have caused such a stir, strictly follow in these earlier footsteps. For example, in the German version of his Hollywood book, *Shadows in Paradise*, Erich Maria Remarque perfectly anticipated Eco and Baudrillard's idea of the city as 'simulacrum':

Real and false were fused here so perfectly that they became a new substance, just as copper and zinc become brass that looks like gold. It meant nothing that Hollywood was filled with great musicians, poets and philosophers. It was also filled with spiritualists, religious nuts and swindlers. It devoured everyone, and whoever was unable to save himself in time, would lose his identity, whether he thought so himself or not.[76]

But for most exiles the perceived lifelessness of the city grew to even more unbearable proportions once one left the Parisian stage-set of Hollywood Boulevard. Remarque reportedly fled from Los Angeles because he could not enjoy himself during his customary morning walk. 'Empty sidewalks, streets and houses' were too redolent of the 'desert' from which Los Angeles originally had been conjured.[77] For his part, Hanns Eisler denounced the 'dreadful idyll of this landscape, that actually has sprung from the mind of real-estate speculation because the landscape does not offer much by itself. If one stopped the flow of water here for three days, the jackals would reappear and the sand of the desert'.[78]

Yet not all Europeans were estranged by either the façade or the desert behind it. Aldous Huxley – part of a 'Bloomsbury' set of expatriate British pacifists that included Christopher Isherwood, Gerald Heard, and, briefly, Lord Russell (at UCLA) – relished precisely those qualities of the local landscape that the Germans most despised. In a headlong escape from both war and Hollywood, Huxley moved his family to a ranch in the desert near the ruins of the original 'anti-Los Angeles' of Llano del Rio.[79] Here, while he searched for the 'godhead' in the silence of the Mojave, his wife Maria devoured the astrology columns in the *Times* that Adorno made fun of. Huxley and Heard, embracing mysticism, health-food and hallucinogens, would later in the 1950s become the godfathers of Southern California's 'New Age' subculture.[80]

It would be amusing to know if Huxley and Brecht ever discussed the weather. None of the anti-fascist exiles seemed more spiritually desolated by Los Angeles than the Berlin playwright and Marxist aesthetician. As he put it in a famous poem:

> On thinking about Hell, I gather
> My brother Shelley found it was a place
> Much like the city of London. I
> Who live in Los Angeles and not in London
> Find, on thinking about Hell, that it must be
> Still more like Los Angeles.[81]

Yet Brecht's desperate ennui was compounded out of strange contradictions. One moment he was complaining that his Santa Monica bungalow was 'too pleasant to work in', the next he was promoting Los Angeles as a 'hell' of Shelleyan proportions. It borders on the absurd, as Lyon and Fuegi point out, 'to imagine an original European like Brecht shopping in an American supermarket, or passing the California driver's test, or in a drugstore picking up canned beer and running into Arnold Schoenberg'.[82] (Huxley, by contrast, first opened the 'doors of perception' with mescaline in the 'world's biggest drugstore' on La Cienega.)[83] By the same token, however, it is odd that the creator of *Mahagonny*, who in Berlin favoured lumpen demimondaines and working-class conversation, should have shown so little apparent interest in exploring Los Angeles's alternative side: Boyle Heights dancehalls, Central Avenue nightclubs, Wilmington honky-tonks, and so on. Real-life Mahagonny was always to hand, as was a thriving local labor movement, largely led from the left. But if the 'stench of oil' occasionally penetrated his garden in Santa Monica, Brecht fabricated the myth of the convergence of heaven and hell without really knowing what the 'hellish' parts of Los Angeles looked like.[84]

Not all the Germans, of course, spent their time in Los Angeles in existential despair. Thomas Mann (according to Brecht) pictured himself in the Pacific Palisades as a 'latter-day Goethe in search of the land where the lemons grow'.[85] Schoenberg may have resented Shirley Temple, but he loved playing tennis with his other Brentwood neighbor, George Gershwin, as well as the sunlight that flooded his study each morning while he composed.[86] Max Reinhart, for his part, boasted that Southern California would become 'a new center of culture. . . . there is no more hospitable landscape'.[87] Indeed for a while the more famous of the exiles could fancy themselves Hollywood sahibs: happy white people under the palm trees, feeding themselves on an economy run by invisible servants. But even the most suntanned of the exiles, including Mann and Reinhardt, woke up to the fact that behind the Mediterraneanized affluence lurked exploitation and militarism.

In the first place, virtually all the Europeans railed against Hollywood's proletarianization of the intelligentsia. Here the complaints of the Weimar and Bloomsbury groups echoed the already alienated writers' colony (the Screen Writers Guild had been formed in 1933), and retraced a theme, as I have argued, that was central to Los Angeles fiction. Thrown into a 'totally alien, opaque environment, where creative ideas, artistry and originality did not count, where everything was tuned to the ways one finds in workshops and offices',[88] the exiles experienced artistic degradation amid affluence. Despite his initial euphoria about the cultural prospects of Southern California, Max Reinhardt found himself expected to punch a studio timeclock like any factory worker – 'in 1942 he left dejectedly for New York City'. Brilliant, anti-fascist actors of the Weimar theater like Fritz Kortner, Alexander Grenach, and Peter Lorre were restricted by studio bosses to ridiculous impersonations of the Nazi leadership.[89] Stravinsky's big break was rearranging the *Rite of Spring* as a soundtrack for dancing brooms in Disney's *Fantasia*, while Schoenberg, otherwise invisible, tutored studio composers who made musical suspense for *noir* thrillers and monster movies.[90] Marxists, who earlier in Germany had praised the advent of collectivized intellectual production and the disappearance of the author, now bitterly denounced Taylorized 'breadwork', as Brecht called it, and the futility of 'writing for nobody'.[91] For Adorno, Hollywood was nothing less than the mechanized cataclysm that was abolishing Culture in the classical sense. ('In America, one will . . . not be able to dodge the question, whether the term culture, in which one grew up, has become obsolete. . . .')[92]

Secondly, whatever their material situation, secluded (Adorno) or integrated (Billy Wilder), forgotten (Heinrich Mann and Man Ray) or celebrated (Thomas Mann), dependent on charity (Döblin) or housed in the Palisades (Feuchtwanger), the exiles were all vulnerable to changes in the political climate. Concentrated in the movie colony under an increasingly hostile public eye, they played out their final role in Los Angeles as scapegoats of the Hollywood Inquisition. With the entire industry increasingly held hostage by cold war brainwashing, and ten of their American colleagues on the road to prison (with hundreds more blacklisted for a generation), many of the exiles chose to take the first boat back to the Old World. Others hung on, as best they could, writing or directing the occasional *noir* film that intimated the cancer of political and cultural repression.

Later, back in *Modell Deutschland* (which he had chosen over Brecht's DDR), Horkheimer reorganized the Frankfurt School and began to publish the rest of his and Adorno's notes from the mid twentieth century's 'most advanced point of observation'. The Frankfurters briefed the new European intelligentsia about the coming order for which the Marshall Plan was laying the foundation. Bittersweet memories of 'exile in paradise' (New York and Los Angeles) were sublimated into a preemptive critique of cultural Americanization and the consumer society. Southern California, meanwhile, might have forgotten that it had ever housed the Institute for Social Research, except for the unexpected arrival of Frankfurt's most famous prodigal son, Herbert Marcuse, in the early 1960s – the last of the exile generation to arrive on the West Coast.

Recruited from Brandeis to anchor the philosophy program at the spectacular new sea-cliff campus of the University of California at San Diego, Marcuse willingly walked back into the same storm of rabid anti-radicalism and anti-intellectualism from which Brecht, Eisler and scores of others had fled in the late 1940s. During what Barry Katz has called his 'years of cheerful pessimism', Marcuse took Adorno's 'collapse of culture' thesis a step further, positing a 'democratic totalitarianism' undermining the very possibility of critical subjectivity. Undoubtedly he found plentiful confirmation for this claim in surrounding San Diego County, with its eerie landscape conjugation of seaside resorts and Marine Corps bases.

But even in this 'one-dimensional society', Marcuse welcomed emergent 'forces of liberation': praising soul music and jazz (which Adorno excoriated), supporting Angela Davis and the Panthers, and urging his students to spread the gospel of classical Marxism across California.[93] He was able to make the organic connection to indigenous radicalism that had eluded a majority of his exile comrades in the 1940s. Unfortunately the Last Dialectician in Lotusland fell afoul not only of rising Nixonian hysteria (every day brought fresh death threats from San Diego's fascist fringe), but, fatally, of the fickle attention of the Culture Industry. Unwonted media celebrity first 'gurufied' Marcuse (*Time* magazine's 'Pied Piper of Insurgent Youth'), then stamped his thoughts with the killing censorship of a fad whose time has passed.

Yet the spectre of Frankfurt Marxism (Horkheimer, Adorno and Marcuse) still haunts Southern California, even if their once ironic observations have been reduced to guidepost clichés for the benefit of Postmodernism's Club Med. If the Weimar exiles appeared in Los Angeles as tragedy, then today's Fifth Republic tourists come strictly as farce. What was once anguish seems to have become fun. As a local critic has observed with regard to a recent visit of the current Parisian philosopher king:

Baudrillard seems to enjoy himself. He loves to observe the liquidation of culture, to experience the delivery from depth. . . . He goes home to France and finds it a quaint, nineteenth-century country. He returns to Los Angeles and feels perverse exhilaration. 'There is nothing to match flying over Los Angeles by night. Only Hieronymous Bosch's Hell can match the inferno effect.'[94]

THE SORCERERS

If Southern California is to continue to meet the challenge of her environment . . . her supreme need . . . is for *able, creative, highly endowed, highly trained men in science and its appplications.*
Robert Millikan[95]

> In the South of California has gathered the largest and most miscellaneous
> assortment of Messiahs, Sorcerers, Saints and Seers known to the history
> of aberrations. *Farnsworth Crowder*[96]

Not every Los Angeles intellectual of renown ended up behind a studio gate
in the 1940s. Even adjusting for the relative exchange values of literary and
scientific prestiges, the famed writers' stable at MGM was small cheese
compared to the extraordinary concentration of Nobel laureates gathered
around the recently founded California Institute of Technology in Pasadena
from the mid 1920s onward. With a permanent or visiting faculty that
included Einstein, Millikan, Michelson, von Karman, Oppenheimer,
Dobzhansky, Pauling and Noyes, Cal Tech was the first institution in the
West to claim national preeminence in a major science, physics.[97] More
importantly, Cal Tech was no mere ivory tower, but the dynamic nucleus
of an emergent technostructure that held one of the keys to Southern
California's future. While its aeronautics engineers tested airframe designs
for Donald Douglas's DC-3 in their wind tunnel and its geologists solved
technical problems for the California oil industry, other Cal Tech scientists
were in Pasadena's Arroyo Seco, above Devil's Gate Dam (where NASA's Jet
Propulsion Laboratory stands today), helping launch the space age with
their pathbreaking rocket experiments. Cal Tech, together with the Department of Defense, substantially invented Southern California's postwar,
science-based economy.

But Cal Tech itself was largely the invention of George Ellery Hale,
pioneering astrophysicist and founder of the Mount Wilson Observatory.
Smitten with Pasadena and its extraordinary concentration of retired,
'surplus' wealth, Hale envisioned a vast scientific-cultural triangle around
the *Observatory* ('already the greatest asset possessed by Southern California,
not excluding the Los Angeles Chamber of Commerce'), the *Institute*, and
the *Huntington Library* (whose creation he also influenced).[98] The indefatigable Hale (closely associated with the Carnegie interests) was also the
chief catalyst in organizing the National Research Council in 1917 to
support Woodrow Wilson's war mobilization. The NRC was the scientific-
military-industrial complex in embryo, bringing together the nation's
leading physical scientists, the military's chief engineers, and the heads of
science-based corporations like AT&T and GE. Moreover it was the model

for the triangular regional collaboration that Hale wanted to establish around Cal Tech, and whose ultimate offshoot was the Los Angeles aerospace industry.[99]

In order to realize this dream, Hale convinced one of his NRC colleagues, and America's leading physicist, Robert A. Millikan, to forsake his beloved University of Chicago for the presidency of Cal Tech. A key factor in Millikan's recruitment was apparently a promise by Southern California Edison to provide him with a high-voltage laboratory for experiments in atomic physics. Hale and Millikan shared an almost fanatical belief in the partnership of science and big business. It was their policy that Cal Tech be allied to 'aristocracy and patronage' and shielded 'from meddling congressmen and other representatives of the people'.[100]

Their chief apostle in mobilizing the local aristocracy was Edison director Henry M. Robinson, also president of the First National Bank and intimate of Herbert Hoover ('his Colonel House'). Robinson had personally advanced science in Southern California by applying Einstein's theories to capitalism in a little book entitled *Relativity in Business Morals*. (Critics suggested that Robinson had acquired experimental evidence for his treatise while participating in the great Julian Petroleum swindle of the 1920s.)[101] With unbounded enthusiasm for alloying physics and plutocracy, Robinson helped Millikan and Hale recruit more than sixty local millionaires (Mudd, Kerckhoff, O'Melveny, Patton, Chandler, and so on) into the California Institute Associates, the most comprehensive elite group of the era in Southern California.

In his role as Cal Tech's chief booster, Millikan increasingly became an ideologue for a specific vision of science in Southern California. Speaking typically to luncheon meetings at the elite California Club in Downtown Los Angeles, or to banquets for the Associates at the Huntington mansion, Millikan adumbrated two fundamental points. First, Southern California was a unique scientific frontier where industry and academic research were joining hands to solve such fundamental challenges as the long-distance transmission of power and the generation of energy from sunlight. Secondly, and even more importantly, Southern California 'is today, as was England two hundred years ago, the westernmost outpost of Nordic civilization', with the 'exceptional opportunity' of having 'a population which is twice as Anglo-Saxon as that existing in New York, Chicago or any of the great cities of this country'.[102]

Millikan's image of science and business reproducing Aryan supremacy on the shores of the Pacific undoubtedly warmed the hearts of his listeners, who like himself were conservative Taft–Hoover Republicans. An orthodox Social Darwinist, Millikan frequently invoked Herbert Spencer (the 'great thinker') in his fulminations against socialism ('the coming slavery'), the New Deal ('political royalists'), Franklin Roosevelt ('Tammanyizing the United States'), and 'statism' in general. In the face of breadlines, he boasted 'the common man . . . is vastly better off here today in depressed America than he has ever been at any other epoch in society'. Yet, as private support for scientific research collapsed during the Depression years, Millikan reconciled his anti-statism with Cal Tech's financial needs by advocating military research as the one permissible arena where science and industry could accept federal partnership – an $80 million windfall to Cal Tech in the war years.[103]

In an important sense, this utter reactionary, who was totally out of step with younger, more progressive scientific leaderships in places like Berkeley and Chicago, defined the parameters – illiberal, militarized and profit-driven – for the incorporation of science into the economy and culture of Southern California. Nowhere else in the country did there develop such a seamless continuum between the corporation, laboratory and classroom as in Los Angeles, where Cal Tech via continuous cloning and spinoff became the hub of a vast wheel of public-private research and development that eventually included the Jet Propulsion Laboratory, Hughes Aircraft (the world center of airborne electronics), the Air Force's Space Technology Laboratory, Aerojet General (a spinoff of the latter), TRW, the Rand Institute, and so on.

But the rise of science in Southern California had stranger resonances as well. Just like Hollywood, that other exotic enclave, Cal Tech struck sparks as it scraped against the local bedrock of Midwestern fundamentalism. It was not unusual for Albert Einstein to be lecturing at Cal Tech on his photoelectric equation, while a few blocks away Aimée Semple McPherson was casting out the devil before her Pasadena congregation. At the height of the Scopes Trial controversy, and amid the efforts of the Bryan Bible League of California to make the King James Bible a required textbook in schools, Millikan – 'to a great many people in Southern California (Babbitts and quacks included) the greatest man in the world' – intervened to reconcile God and Science. Millikan went on the stump as a 'Christian scientist' proclaiming, via radio, a national lecture tour and a book, that there was 'no contradiction between *real* science and *real* religion'. The 'debunker' Morrow Mayo, disgusted by the capitulation of America's leading scientist to the fundamentalist backlash of the 1920s, described his performance as follows:

When he got through with science and religion, they were so wrapped up in each other that a Philadelphia lawyer could never untangle them. The closest this great scientist ever came to a definite stand was a full gallop on a supernatural race-track running from Fundamentalism to theism, but his powers of occult observation would have done credit to any crystal-gazer in Los Angeles. . . . The whole thing was a conglomeration of metaphysical aphorisms and theological sophistry, suffused in a weird and ghostly atmosphere of obscurantism, with occasional and literal references to Santa Claus.[104]

At the same time that Millikan was trying to soothe evangelical ire with reassurances about Jesus, the electron and Santa Claus, Los Angeles's powerful 'New Thought' movement was avidly assimilating Einstein and Millikan to Nostradamus and Annie Besant as 'Masters of the Ages'. Contemporary 'science', in the guise of astounding powers and arcane revelations, became the progenitor of an entire Southern California cult stratum. As Farnsworth Crowder explains the origin of 'good vibrations' in his 'Little Blue Book' classic, 'Los Angeles – The Heaven of Bunk-Shooters':

Science is the first-assistant Messiah inspiring many a sect. . . . What psychology will not suppply can be lifted from the physical sciences. Einstein, Michaelson, Millikan and company are unwitting contributors. . . . Whatever waves, oscillates, vibrates, pulses or surges contributes, by analogy, to the explanations of harmony, absent treatment, telepathy, magnetic healing, vibratory equilibrum, spiritualism or any other cloudy wonder. Surpassing are the powers of these scientific sects. One awed citizen referring to a busy group of vibrators cloistered in the hills, whispered, 'My lord, man! – they wouldn't *dare* release their secrets. The race isn't ready – not advanced enough. The world would go to pieces. It would be like giving everybody a handful of radium. Ignorant people would have too much power.'[105]

In Southern California physics and metaphysics continued to rub shoulders in a variety of weird circumstances. Crowder specifically had in mind those 'superscientists', the Rosicrucians and Theosophists, as well as more ephemeral sects (the Church of Psychic Science, the Metaphysical Science Association, and so on), who exploited the public's simultaneous awe and mystification in the face of strange new disciplines like quantum mechanics and psychoanalysis. Before the emergence of a full-fledged, alternative 'science fiction' milieu in the 1940s, and in the absence of any truly popular culture of science, they filled in the cracks between ignorance and invention, and mediated between science and theology. A more bizarre liaison, however, directly connected the oldest metaphysic, the Luciferian Magick or Black Art, to Cal Tech and the founders of the American Rocket State, and then, through an extraordinary *ménage à trois*, to the first world religion created by a science-fiction writer.

Cal Tech's connection with the emergence of Scientology can be briefly retold here (relying heavily on Russell Miller's account). Sometime during the 1930s one Wilfred Smith founded a Pasadena branch ('the Agape Lodge') of the *Ordo Templi Orientis* (OTO) – a German-origin brotherhood of magicians (and spies) that had come under the spell of Aleister Crowley, the notorious Edwardian sorcerer and 'most hated man in England'.[106] For several years the Agape Lodge quietly succored Satan and his 'Great Beast' (Crowley) with contributions, while secretly diverting Pasadenans with the amusements of sexual necromancy. Then, sometime in 1939, the Lodge fell under the patronage and leadership of John Parsons, a young L.A. aristocrat and pioneer of Cal Tech rocketry (later a founder of the Jet Propulsion Laboratory). During the day, Parsons worked at the Cal Tech labs or the Devil's Gate test range with the great Theodore von Karman, perfecting propellant systems for liquid-fuel rockets; at night, he returned to his mansion on Pasadena's 'millionaires row' (South Orange Grove Avenue) to perform blasphemous rituals (with, for example, naked pregnant women leaping through fire circles) in his secret OTO 'temple' under the long-distance direction of Crowley.[107]

Aside from being a world-famous rocket pioneer and a secret wizard, Parsons was also a devoted science fiction fan who attended meetings of the Los Angeles Fantasy and Science Fiction Society to hear writers talk about their books. One day in August 1945, to Parsons's delight, a LAFSFS acquaintance showed up at the Orange Grove mansion with a young naval officer, Lt. Commander L. Ron Hubbard, who had already established a reputation as a master of sci-fi pulp. Captivated by Hubbard's 'charm' and expressed desire to become a practitioner of Magick, Parsons welcomed him as house guest and sorcerer's apprentice. Hubbard reciprocated by sleeping with Parsons's mistress. Perturbed by this development, but not wishing to show open jealousy, Parsons instead embarked on a vast diabolical experiment, under Crowley's reluctant supervision, to call up a true 'whore of Babylon' so that she and Parsons might procreate a literal Antichrist in Pasadena.

'With Prokofiev's *Violin Concerto* playing in the background', Hubbard joined Parsons in the 'unspeakable' rites necessary to summon the 'scarlet woman', who, after many mysterious happenings (inexplicable power failures, occult lights, and so on), was found walking down South Orange Grove Avenue in broad daylight. After Parsons seduced the young woman in question, Hubbard and Parsons's previous mistress ran off with the rocket scientist's money to Florida. There is no need to relate the ensuing complex chain of events, except to say that Parsons – the renowned explosives expert – managed to blow himself and his Orange Grove mansion skyhigh in June 1952. Debate still rages as to whether it was an accident, suicide or murder.[108]

Hubbard, meanwhile, was ready to employ the occult dramaturgy and incantatory skills that he had imbibed in Parsons's OTO temple to more lucrative uses. Frustrated with the small-change earnings of a pulp sci-fi writer, he founded a pseudo-science, Dianetics, which he eventually transformed into a full-fledged religion, Scientology, with a cosmology derived from the pages of *Astounding Science Fiction*. Russell Miller, in his fascinating biographical debunking of the Hubbard myth, described the notorious Shrine Auditorium rally, at the height of the original Dianetics craze in 1950, when Hubbard introduced the world to his own equivalent of Parsons's 'scarlet woman':

As the highlight of the evening approached, there was a palpable sense of excitement and anticipation in the packed hall. A hush descended on the audience when at last Hubbard stepped up to the microphone to introduce the 'world's first clear'. She was, he said, a young woman by the name of Sonya Bianca, a physics major and pianist from Boston. Among her many newly acquired attributes, he claimed she had 'full and perfect recall of every moment of her life', which she would be happy to demonstrate.

SCI-FI RELIGION
Hollywood

'What did you have for breakfast on 3 October 1942?' somebody yelled. . . . 'What's on page 122 of *Dianetics?*' . . . someone else asked. Miss Bianca opened her mouth but no words came out. . . . As people began getting up and walking out of the auditorium, one man noticed that Hubbard had momentarily turned his back on the girl and shouted, 'OK, what colour necktie is Mr Hubbard wearing?' The world's first 'clear' screwed up her face in a frantic effort to remember, stared into the hostile blackness of the auditorium, then hung her head in misery. It was an awful moment.[109]

Despite this temporary setback, Hubbard went on to become filthy rich (and increasingly paranoid) from peddling his amalgam of black magic, psychotherapy and science fiction to gullible hippies in the 1960s. Five years after his death was announced to two thousand of his followers gathered in the Hollywood Palladium, Hubbard's original *Dianetics* was enjoying a resurrection on bestseller lists – a discouraging reminder of science's fate in local culture.

THE COMMUNARDS

L.A. needs the cleansing of a great disaster or founding of a barricaded commune . . . *Peter Plagens, 1972*

Los Angeles has almost no cultural tradition – particularly no modernist tradition – to overthrow. *Peter Plagens, 1974*[110]

Living in Skid Row hotels, jamming in friends' garages, and studying music theory between floors during his stint as a elevator operator at Bullocks Wilshire, Ornette Coleman was a cultural guerrilla in the Los Angeles of the 1950s. Apotheosized a generation later as 'the most influential single figure to emerge in African-American music since Charlie Parker', he spent the Eisenhower years as a lonely, messianic rebel: bearded, dressed in eccentric clothes, 'the complete antithesis of the clean-cut, Hollywood High School undershirt and tidy crew-cut image of the cool jazz musician'.[111] The revolution that Coleman, a Texan, and a small circle of Los Angeles-bred musicians (Eric Dolphy, Don Cherry, Red Mitchell, Billy Higgins and Charlie Haden) were trying to foment was 'free jazz'[112] – an almost 'cataclysmic'

widening of the improvisational freedom that Charlie Parker and Dizzy
Gillespie had pioneered in the 1940s. At the time of Coleman's revolutionary
1958 album, *Something Else!*, they were a veritable 'underground within the
underground', on the margin of a 'hard bebop' community that was itself
locked out of Los Angeles's white-dominated 'cool jazz' scene.[113]
Coleman's underground situation was indicative, not only of the color
bar in Los Angeles cultural institutions (just beginning to break down in
music with the integration of the Musicians' Union, initiated by Charlie
Mingus and Buddy Collette), but of the predicament of L.A.'s young
Modernists in general. Abstractionism in either jazz or painting faced
similar repression. If the so-called 'bebop invasion' of Los Angeles in 1946
had been repelled and Bird incarcerated in Camarillo, abstract expressionism fared little better in face of cold war hysteria married to cultural
philistinism. Ancillary to the great Hollywood witch-hunt, a satellite
inquisition in 1951 was mounted against 'subversive modern art' at the (old)
County Museum in Exposition Park.

A group called Sanity in Art swore they detected maps of secret defense
fortifications sequestered in abstract paintings, and one painter, Rex Brandt, was
accused by an investigating committee for the City Council of incorporating
propaganda in the form of a thinly disguised hammer-and-sickle within a seascape.
Finally, the City Council resolved that the artists were 'unconscious tools of
Kremlin propaganda' and didn't rescind that opinion for eight years.[114]

If Los Angeles's architectural modernists of the Exile generation (Richard
Neutra and Rudolph Schindler) and their younger contemporaries (Raphael
Soriano, Gregory Ain, and Harwell Harris) fared better in the early cold war
than jazz musicians or modern artists, it was partly because of the circum-
scription of their project. Their Hollywood Hills pleasure domes and 'case-
study' homes corresponded better to evolving middle-class sensibility on
Los Angeles's *nouveau riche* Westside.[115] Yet increasing acceptance of the
International Style in domestic architecture was accompanied by a new
intolerance for public housing – virtually outlawed by a 1952 ordinance
directed against 'socialistic projects'.

On the whole, however, the younger generation interested in new
forms and practices was driven towards bohemia. For partisans of hard(er)

jazz and its canvass counterpart (New York's abstract expressionists had already acknowledged bebop's seminal influence on their work), as well as what might be labelled 'late surrealism' in both art and film – that is to say, for the Los Angeles 'hipster' generation that came of age in the late 1940s and 1950s – there was little alternative but to form temporary 'communes' within the cultural underground that burgeoned for almost a decade.

One of the qualities shared by these diverse groups was their concern for critically reworking and re-presenting subcultural experience – a quality that made them the first truly 'autobiographical' intelligentsia in Los Angeles history. For Coleman, Dolphy, and other local jazz guerrillas, that shared existential ground was Black Los Angeles's distinctive Southwestern blues tradition. Coleman had started his musical career honking out heavy, if slightly unorthodox, blues riffs in Texas and Louisiana juke joints, later playing the emergent 'R&B' sound that synthesized blues and swing. Los Angeles in the late 1940s, with the greatest number of independent studios, was the capital of R&B recording, while Central Avenue's dazzling 'Main Stem' offered an extraordinary spectrum of jazz, blues and R&B, dominated by musicians from the Southwest circuit of Texas, Oklahoma, Kansas and Lousiana (the region that had sent the most Black migrants to work in the West Coast's war plants).

However, with the slow decline of the Central Avenue scene, partly as a result of police antipathy to 'race mixing' in the clubs, and with Black musicians excluded from lucrative studio jobs, the music of the younger ghetto jazzmen became leaner and harder, seeking through introspection and experiment to fashion a hegemonic alternative to the deracination of the 'cool jazz' played in beach nightclubs.[116] In 1961, after Coleman, following Dolphy, had left for New York, the pianist and composer Horace Tapscott founded the Union of God's Musicians and Artists Ascension (UGMAA) and the Pan Afrikan Peoples' Arkestra. Like the similar jazz collectives organized by Sun Ra and Roscoe Mitchell in Chicago, UGMAA communalized and utopianized the struggle for free music – striving simultaneously to become a performance laboratory, people's school, and local cultural arm of the Black Revolution.[117]

The art counterpart to the jazz underground (although never with such radical aspirations) was the informal cooperative organized by a score of younger artists during the late 1950s around Edward Kienholz's and Walter

Hopps's Ferus Gallery on La Cienga Boulevard. 'A motley batch of beatniks, eccentrics, and "art types" ', they became the 'seminal source for the blossoming of modernist art in Los Angeles during the sixties'.[118] The Ferus core, including Billy Al Bengstrom, Ed Moses, Craig Kauffman, Robert Irwin, Larry Bell and Ed Ruscha (along with Kienholz himself) were far too individualistic to form an identifiable 'L.A. school', but they were temporarily unified by common passions. One was their desire to break the academicist stranglehold over Los Angeles's backwater art world, although they differed on the means towards that end (abstract expressionism versus hard-edge abstractionism, for example). Another was a biographical and aesthetic camaraderie based on enthusiasm for the hotrod and motorcycle subcultures that had developed in Southern California from the 1940s.

In his talks with Lawrence Weschler, Robert Irwin (who had attended L.A.'s Dorsey High School with Eric Dolphy) repeatedly emphasized the importance of custom-car 'folk art' to the emergence of the Ferus group and the 'L.A. Look' which they eventually created. Earlier, critic Nancy Marmer, in contrasting the Northern and Southern California avant gardes, had made the same point:

Aside from the backdrop influence of Hollywood and the hypertrophied 'neon-fruit supermarket', there has also existed in California an idiosyncratic welding of sub-cultures and a body of small but curiously prophetic art, whose influence, if not always direct, is at least in an askew relation to contemporary Pop Art. For example, the Los Angeles hot-rod world, with its teenage rites, baroque car designs, kandy-kolors, its notion of a high-polish craftsmanship, and, perhaps most influential, its established conventions of decorative paint techniques, has flourished in the southern part of the state since the 1940s. If the imagery ('Mad Magazine Bosch', one writer has called it) has fortunately not been especially important, the custom-coach techniques of air-brush manipulation, 'candy apple-ing', and 'striping' have been variously suggestive.[119]

In the evolving work of motorcycle racer Billy Al Bengston's heraldic auto surfaces, Ed Ruscha's gas station and parking lot books, Craig Kaufmann's Plexiglas paintings, and Larry Bell's Minimalist cubes, folk car culture was transformed into the 'cool , semitechnological, industrially pretty art' that became the patented 'L.A. Look' of the 1960s.[120] It was the avant-garde counterpart to the 'Endless Summer' depicted in Roger Corman movies, the

Gidget novels (based on a Hollywood writer's actual surfer-girl daughter), and the falsetto lyrics of Beach Boys' songs. It was the mesmerizing vision of a white kids' car-and-surf-based Utopia.

Kienholz was the major exception. As Anne Bartlett Ayres has pointed out, his 'assemblages developed as a shadow side to the famous "L.A. Look" ',[121] a kind of hotrod *noir* juxtaposed to the Pop luster of his colleagues. His *Back Seat Dodge – 38* of 1964 – a work that so infuriated a right-wing County supervisor that he tried to have the new County Museum of Art shut down because of it – summarized the Southern California Dream in a single *noir tableau*. Literally hotrodding, Kienholz 'chopped' a '38 coupé and set it in a 'Lovers' Lane' complete with discarded beer bottles on the grass and 'mushy' music. Dead lovers, locked in a grim missionary embrace on the front seat, seemed to symbolize an adolescence gone to seed in eternity – Frankie Avalon and Annette Funicello petting after the Holocaust. Kienholz's imagery – set in a fateful year – anticipated the worst.

This car–sex–death–fascism continuum also emerged as a dominant vision in L.A. underground film. In the notes to his 'lost' classic, *Kustom Kar Kommandos* (1964–65), Kenneth Anger – comparing L.A. eroticized custom cars to 'an American cult-object of an earlier era, Mae West' – emphasized that for the Southern California teenager, 'the power-potentialized customized car represents a poetic extension of personality'.[122] Anger – leader of the Hollywood film underground at various times in the 1950s and early 1960s – knew all about Southern California adolescence. This Hollywood brat reputedly 'played the role of the child prince in Max Reinhardt's movie of *A Midsummer Night's Dream* and had Shirley Temple for a dancing partner at cotillions of the Maurice Kossloff Dancing School', before launching his filmmaking career at age eleven. Another avid follower of Aleister Crowley, Anger was obsessed with the diabolics of Hollywood, homosexuality and speed machines of all kinds. His book, *Hollywood Babylon* has been described as 'a slander catalogue amounting to a phenomenology of the myth of the scandal in Hollywood', while two of his films, *Scorpio Rising* (1962) (which contains the seed of the 1980s film *Blue Velvet* in one of its segments) and *Kommandos*, explored the Nietzschean porno-mythology of motorcycle gangs and hotrodders.[123]

Adding to the L.A. car-culture phenomenologies of the Ferus artists and Anger, as well as inaugurating an improvisational voice that has been compared to Joyce but sounds more like Dolphy or Coleman, Thomas Pynchon's *The Crying of Lot 49* (1966) provided the ultimate freeway-map ontology of Southern California. A former technical writer in the West Coast aerospace industry (forced to produce eroticized descriptions of Bomark missiles and the like), Pynchon understood (better than some of the Ferus Gallery's Pop artists) that in Southern California custom cars and their makers grew up into ICBMs and *their* makers. As radically 'decentered' as any contemporary Althusserian could have wished, *Lot 49* wastes no time grappling with the alienation of its subject (as in Joan Didion's 'L.A. car book', *Play It As It Lays*) but moves immediately into a postmodern lane. It maps a baroquely layered but ultimately one-dimensional reality (Marcuse à la Klein bottle?) 'in which the city is at once an endless text always promising meaning but ultimately only offering hints and *signs* of a possible and final reality . . . like a "printed circuit" ' – or a freeway.[124]

But the Endless Summer of the avant garde (expressed in the new painting as a 'bright ethereality') came to an abrupt end in August 1965. Southcentral Los Angeles exploded in rage against police abuse and institutional racism, creating for a few days the 'barricaded commune' (Plagens) and 'burning city' (West) that Los Angeles intellectuals had frequently dreamt about as a kind of liberation from the Culture Industry. In fact, the Watts Rebellion, as well as the police attack on peaceful anti-war demonstrators at Century City in July 1967, politically galvanized artists and writers on the first broad scale since the Hollywood witch-hunt. Pynchon wrote a stirringly sympathetic and unpatronizing piece called 'A Journey into the Mind of Watts' (really a meditation on urban segregation), Ruscha painted *The Los Angeles County Museum on Fire* (1965–8), Schulberg organized a Watts Writers' Workshop, anti-war artists contributed scores of pieces to the 'Artists' Peace Tower' on the Sunset Strip, the underground *Los Angeles Free Press* flourished, and Kienholz's tableaux denounced war (see his *Portable War Memorial* [1968]).[125]

Most importantly, the Rebellion inspired unity and élan in Southcentral Los Angeles, giving birth to a local version of the Black Arts Movement across a full spectrum of practices from Tapscott's Arkestra to the rap poetry of the Watts Prophets. Bernard Jackson and J. Alfred Cannon founded the Inter-City Cultural Center in 1966 which grew into a flourishing theater center with its own press and school. Wanda Coleman,

Kamau Daaood, Quincy Troupe, K. Curtis Lyle, Emory Evans, and Ojenke established a distinctive Watts idiom in fiction and poetry, while Melvin Van Peebles pioneered an alternative Black cinema with his outlaw odyssey, *Sweet Sweetback's Badasssss Song*. The Watts Festival, meanwhile, brought cultural cadres together with the community in annual celebrations of unity and rebellion.

But the heroic moment of Underground Los Angeles Culture quickly passed. As a local art historian pointed out, 'the high -flying spirit of the '60s . . . crashed and burned.'[126] The local dearth of jazz clubs and modernist galleries/collectors irresistibly drove part of the late 1950s and early 1960s avant garde (including L.A.'s *Artforum* magazine) to Manhattan (or, sometimes, in the case of experimental film and poetry, to San Francisco). After a student rebellion in 1966, Disney endowers moved Chouinard Art Institute, reborn as the California Institute of the Arts, to an isolated suburban fringe where their conservative proprietary interests would be maximized. Inner-city cultural institutions, meanwhile, were starved of financial support and media attention. Then, amidst the recession of avant-garde hopes, there were suddenly the seductions of Los Angeles's own emergent corporate arts nexus.

Maurice Tuchman, the curator of the County Museum of Art, 'conceived [in the late 1960s] the somewhat dubious notion of placing artists with corporate sponsors in a vast Art and Technology program'.[127] With the patronage of 'Missy' Chandler of the *Times* dynasty, Tuchman 'married' seventy-six artists to forty major local corporations.[128] As Peter Plagens notes, the resulting exhibition in 1971 was the 'swan song of sixties art' — a programmatic turning-point towards the mercenary, corporate-dominated arts dispensation of the late 1970s and 1980s.

The exhibition's catalogue is not so much the narrative of a completed project, but an interim report on a hoped-for ongoing metamorphosis of modern art, centered in Los Angeles. Its candid and lengthy description/documentation of every attempted collaboration between the museum-matched artists and corporation admits to every artist's arrogance . . . as well as the easy alignment of artists with hard-core capitalism and war-related industries (while the war in Vietnam was at its height).[129]

The 'L.A. Look', which in the early 1960s suggested the possibility of a critical-artistic strategy that interpreted the city from an indigenous sensibility, progressively collapsed into mere self-affirming veneer, 'mock worship of California's earthly paradise'.[130] Christopher Knight, writing about the 1970s, has described the implosion of the Los Angeles arts scene as a febrile, Popish 'regionalism' – based on pastel sentimentality and 'a distrust of intellectualism' – which attempted to fill the cultural vacuum left from the defeat of the 1960s. But out of this 'morass of determined provincialism' no 'broadly convincing local aesthetic' emerged, only a 'gruesome' celebration of trivialized made-in-Los-Angeles productions.[131]

The itinerary of Edward Ruscha probably best typifies the post-1960s gentrification of the Ferus generation. Although he still describes himself as an 'underground artist', he has become in fact a reigning art god whose own Brobdingnagian portrait looms over Downtown in a five-story-high mural by Kent Twitchell. As critics have pointed out, Ruscha's progression has been from advertising art, via some brief subversions in the 1960s, to 'advertising art advertising itself as art that hates advertising'.[132] If Ruscha-like images now emblematize L.A.'s good life on the walls of myriad corporate waiting rooms and beachfront condos, it is perhaps because (as Edward Lucie-Smith suggests) 'willed neutrality is [his] essence'.[133] His slogans and trademarks shimmering on the warm, dayglo Los Angeles landscape, which once seemed ironic, now are reassuring advertisements for the postmodern condition:

Ruscha wants to mirror the dream-like state which many people find typical of California living, to give the feeling that there is no longer any hierarchy – of ideas, emotions or events. He is the essence of California cool.[134]

While Pop was cooling down into neo-boosterism, the survivors of the original L.A. underground totted up the body count: Eric Dolphy dead of a heart attack in a Berlin nightclub in 1964;[135] Kenneth Anger lost in a Rimbaud-like flight into obscurity after the theft of his personal film archive in 1967. Pynchon, of course, went successively deeper into his personal underground, becoming the B. Traven of West Coast writing (*Vineland* [1990], however, celebrates the inter-generational continuity of a counter-culture of resistance). Kienholz – disgruntled by the superficial 1970s art scene – simply moved back to his hometown in Idaho.

What survived best was what was most deeply rooted in local soil: the 'Watts Renaissance' and the other ethnic community arts movements (including Chicano muralism) which were inspired by its example. Although, as we shall see, the corporate culture bonanza of the 1980s has actually impoverished the arts infrastructure in inner-city communities, new vigor has come from rap as well as from the arrival of an exile contingent of younger Latin American artists, poets and writers. A remarkable local example of the perdurance of communitarian cultural values is the magisterial five-suite history of Black America (*Roots and Folklore*) recently composed by John Carter, another Texas blues-rooted L.A. jazz veteran. In this work, as well as in the dogged persistence of Horace Tapscott, Bernard Jackson and numerous other inner-city cultural workers, a fragile continuity is preserved between the progressive avant gardes of the past and future.

THE MERCENARIES

With galleries and museums springing up like weeds, with the Getty Trust and its money glittering like the spires of Oz, with the hot-shot L.A. Festival grabbing important performance premieres even before the Brooklyn Academy of Music . . . well, what other choice is there? L.A., the Jewel in the Pacific Rim, has got to be the arts mecca of the coming century. Even *New York* magazine says so. . . .
Linda Frye Burnham[136]

I think of the best efforts of the '60s, of all the pain we went through. Now we find we're sinking to the bottom.
C. Bernard Jackson (director, Inner-City Cultural Center)[137]

Like the anti-hero of *Less Than Zero*, Didion and Dunne – publicly critical of almost every aspect of Los Angeles in the 1980s – voted with their feet. Yet, even the defection to New York of the city's most celebrated writers was hardly noticed amidst the tide of prominent new arrivals. The stretch limousines from LAX continued to disgorge Houston architects, London painters, New York critics, Tokyo designers, Boston composers, Oxford historians, and Parisian fakirs.[138] Indeed the current continental and international shift of the intelligentsia to the West Coast invites comparison to the great Hollywood immigration of the 1930s. The 'push' factors of this migration are predictably diverse: ranging from the impact of Thatcherite cuts upon the British university system to the relative decline of architectural commissions in the rest of the Sunbelt. More important, however, is the major 'pull' factor: a boom in cultural investment at the level of the design professions, fine arts institutions, and elite university departments – as well as a new siren song from the studios. The broad trend of this immigration, moreover, is thoroughly mercenary, as the new wave of designers, artists and professors have come to praise Caesar – in this case, international real-estate capital.

The large-scale developers and their financial allies, together with a few oil magnates and entertainment moguls, have been the driving force behind the public-private coalition to build a cultural superstructure for Los Angeles's emergence as a 'world city'. They patronize the art market, endow the museums, subsidize the regional institutes and planning schools, award the architectural competitions, dominate the arts and urban design taskforces, and influence the flow of public arts monies. They have become so integrally involved in the organization of high culture, not because of old-fashioned philanthropy, but because 'culture' has become an important component of the land development process, as well as a crucial moment in the competition between different elites and regional centers. Old-fashioned material interest, in other words, drives the mega-developers to support the general cultural revalorization of Los Angeles, and, more specifically, to endorse the concentration of cultural assets in nodes of maximum development.

This culture strategy has a long history behind it. Since the 1920s, the 'Downtown elite' (composed of old guard families, led by the Chandler dynasty of the *Times*, who had sunk their patrimonies in Downtown real estate), faced with the centrifugal movement of investment westward along Wilshire Boulevard, have struggled to 'recenter' the region around a revitalized central business district. At various times, they have tried to repell, or assimilate, the autonomous 'Westside' power structure that arose out of Jewish interests in the entertainment, savings-and-loan, and suburban real-estate sectors. Contrastingly, the Jewish elites have pursued their own spatial strategy of centering academic and cultural institution-building on the Westside. More recently, as offshore capital has partially supplanted this old ruling-class antinomy, central-place rivalries have been subsumed into a more ambitious neo-regionalism geared up to compete with San Francisco and New York.

Public cultural investment has been an integral variable in these 'place wars' since at least the mid 1940s, when twenty-five of the most powerful Downtown leaders formed the Greater Los Angeles Plans Incorporated (GLAPI) to plot a strategy to 'recenter' the rapidly suburbanizing region. In their original conception an opera house on Bunker Hill was visualized both as a beachhead for the renewal of that neighborhood, and as a counterweight to the westward drift of cultural life. Direct public financing of the proposed opera house, however, was defeated in the 1951 municipal election, and again in 1953, despite the appendage of a sports arena for the masses. This led GLAPI to switch to a public-private financing strategy and to replace the opera proposal with the idea of an omnibus 'music center'. The leadership of the fundraising drive (coordinated with simultaneous initiatives to clear Bunker Hill and build Dodger Stadium) passed in the 1950s to Dorothy ('Buffy') Chandler, wife of the *Times* publisher, mother-in-law of 'Missy', and empress of the paper's society page.

In a fascinating reconstruction of the *Times*'s role in the politics of culture in postwar Los Angeles, Robert Gottlieb and Irene Wolt explain how Buffy, to the consternation of the anti-semitic old guard, 'crossed over' to the Westside to find allies for the music center amongst the Jewish Hillcrest Country Club elite.[139] Her masterstroke was to manipulate the bitter rivalry between the savings-and-loan *nouveaux riches*, Mark Taper and Howard Ahmanson, so as to extract the decisive donations that allowed the Music Center – with its Dorothy Chandler Pavillion, Mark Taper Forum and Ahmanson Theater – to finally open in 1964, alongside of the final evictions from Bunker Hill. For a brief moment, it seemed as if the renaissance of Downtown property values and the arrival of high culture in Los Angeles were meant to go hand in hand.[140]

But, as if to precisely counterbalance the Music Center's pretensions to anchor Culture securely in Downtown, the Los Angeles County Museum of Art, heavily endowed by the Ahmansons and other Westside patrons, opened a few months later in the Jewish Hancock Park area. Since the late 1940s the Westside had been staking claims for a distinctive cultural identity beyond mere affinity with Hollywood. *Arts and Architecture* magazine, which organized the postwar case-study homes project, crusaded for the International Style amongst affluent Westsiders with the same zeal that *Land of Sunshine* had once advocated the Mission Revival. Indeed, John Entenza, *Arts and Architecture*'s editor/publisher (1940–62), was transfixed with a Miesian vision of Wilshire Boulevard and the Hollywood Hills every bit as compelling as Lummis's Craftsman ideal of the Arroyo and Pasadena. From his case-study home in Santa Monica Canyon (the Westside's El Alisal), Entenza presided over a latter-day *salon* that included such important local design pundits as Peter Krasnow, Charles Eames and Alvin Lustig. Any perusal of *Arts and Architecture*'s 1950s files reveals the extent to which architectural and design Modernism became emblematic of a Westside cultural divide separating new money from old, Jew from Gentile, transplanted New Yorker from hereditary Pasadenan.

In this period of crosstown *Kulturkampf*, while Joan Didion was distilling her most dyspeptic imagery, a visiting British design historian, Reyner Banham, was penning the first serious celebration of the city since the booster days of the 1920s. Chief ideologue of the 1950s British 'Independent Group' – the midwife to the Pop Art explosion of the 1960s – Banham had once defined Pop as a 'firing squad without mercy or reprieve' against hieratic art traditions.[141] From this perspective, Southern California, with its aggressive Present-mindedness, was a land purified by an exemplary design terror.[142] *Los Angeles: The Architecture of the Four Ecologies* (1971) found virtue in almost everything disdained by traditional critics, including the automobile,[143] surfboards, hillside homes, and something called 'Los Angeles architecture'. Rejecting the Exiles' criterion of comparability with 'classical' urban space, Banham claimed that Los Angeles's polymorphous landscapes and architectures were given a 'comprehensible unity' by the freeway grid in a metropolis that spoke the 'language of movement, not monument'. He found the city's 'essential dream' – 'the dream of the urban homestead . . . the great bourgeois vision of the good life in a tamed countryside' – a 'sympathetic ecology for architecture' and excoriated the elitism of critics who failed to consult the actual desires of the masses. Lest anyone mistake the punchline of his book, Banham also made a companion BBC television documentary, *Reyner Banham Loves Los Angeles* (1972).

The effect of Banham's intervention was quite extraordinary. Supported by his own brilliant prose, as well as by a new aesthetic climate prepared to reverse historic judgements in favor of 'pop' sensibilities of all kinds, *Los Angeles ... the Four Ecologies* became a turning-point in the valuation of the city by the international intelligentsia. Adopted universally as *the* textbook on Los Angeles, it established standards – vernacular, decentralist and promiscuous – that continue to frame art-world views of what is happening in California south of the Tehachapis. In face of this resurgent neo-boosterism, it was left to a local art critic, Peter Plagens, to register a principled dissent against the enshrining of Banham's book:

When the frail last defenses of the progressive architect are bartered on the counter of hipness, when an ostensibly perceptive specialist takes a look at this obvious dung-heap and pronounces it a groove, then the capitalist quick-buck juggernaut will all the more quickly kill off the green that's left.[144]

Although Plagens's bitter warning about the ideological appropriation of Banham was ignored, the latter's admirers were forced to admit that he had been in error on at least one important point. In a note on Downtown – 'because that is all downtown Los Angeles deserves' – Banham had dismissed the 'recentering' strategy and depreciated the city's need for a conventional center.[145] Given the Downtown doldrums of the early 1970s, it was impossible for him to have foreseen the landrush in the 1980s of Japanese and Canadian capital, in the context of epochal geopolitical shifts, that has made Downtown 1990 second only to Tokyo as a financial pole of the Pacific Rim. Nor would it have been easy in 1971 to envision how the traditional Downtown–Westside rivalry – which Buffy Chandler had tried to reconcile in the late 1950s – would be increasingly pacified by a functional sorting-out of central-place roles (i.e., Downtown as international financial center, Century City as the capital of entertainment law, LAX as aerospace headquarters, and so on), and by the gradual inter-elite acceptance of an ecumenical regionalism vis-à-vis the world market.

This new geography of power has concentrated cultural affluence in two overweening arts acropolises. On Bunker Hill, along a Grand Avenue axis, the 1964 Music Center has been joined by Arata Isozaki's Museum of Contemporary Art [1986] (which 'fills the box labeled "Culture" ') soon to be followed by the Bella Lewitzky Dance Gallery and Frank Gehry's monumental Disney Concert Hall.[146] Other world-celebrity architects and

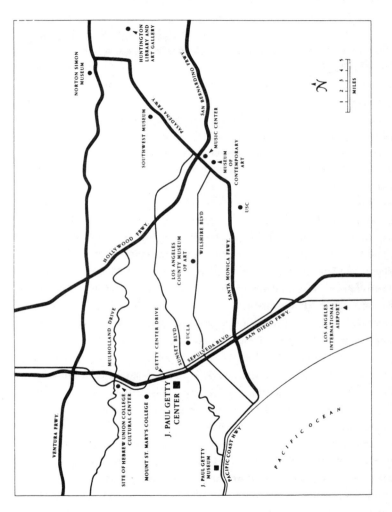

THE MUSEUM ARCHIPELAGO

artists, including Michael Graves and David Hockney, are involved in private developments focused around the Los Angeles Public Library, at the southern foot of Bunker Hill. Meanwhile, sixteen miles west, in the Sepulveda Pass near Westwood, Richard Meier ('perhaps the world's leading architect')[147] is designing the $300 million J. Paul Getty Center: a museum, library and research center for the largest arts endowment in history ($3 billion plus). On the other side of the San Diego Freeway, in Westwood proper, octogenarian Armand Hammer is preparing his own megalomaniacal art mausoleum, while the over-endowed, over-built campus of UCLA bulges with the expatriate cream of European postmodernism (including in a recent year Baudrillard, Derrida and Jencks).

As previously mentioned, large developers dominate every level of this new cultural superstructure. The chairman, for example, of the mayor's recent blue-ribbon taskforce on the arts was Thomas Maguire III, the region's biggest commercial developer, who sponsors the feature 'Art and Culture' on local public television and whose Library Tower Downtown incorporates artwork from David Hockney. Southern California's largest homebuilder, Eli Broad, is the dominating presence on the board of the Museum of Contemporary Art, which raises land values in $1.2 billion California Plaza. Donald Bren, meanwhile, the state's leading *latifundista* as owner of the Irvine Company, is reported to 'live only for his art collection'. And, lately, the new rentier elite of Japanese corporations Downtown has also discovered that culture fertilizes real estate. Shuwa Investments, which owns more than $1 billion of prime local property, has offered Mayor Bradley the initial contribution towards a 'Statue of Liberty' for Los Angeles (the favored proposal is actually a deconstructivist 'steel cloud' designed to be laid over the Hollywood Freeway next to the Civic Center).

The political clout of developers like Maguire, Broad and Shuwa (all major campaign donors to the mayor and the city council) ensures that municipal cultural policy maximally favors big Downtown or Westside projects, where on-site public art or adjacent museums inflate property values. The Community Development Agency's vaunted 'culture tax' of one per cent on new development – intended to promote 'the integration of the arts into all aspects of the built environment'[148] – has largely functioned as a sleight-of-hand subsidy to Downtown developers, whose expenditures on monumental kinetic forms, sullen pastel plinths, and fascist steel cubes, are

CATCHING UP WITH MANHATTAN
Century City

partially recompensed by reduced landleases or advantageous density transfers.

Moreover, the boom in public art and cultural monumentality has gone hand-in-hand with a culture depression in most of the inner city. As Linda Frye Burnham points out, the gleaming new museums and trendy Downtown loft district are a 'Potemkin Village, so many façades hiding the fact that L.A. artists are in a desperate state, fighting over scraps, without career opportunities, funds or housing'.[149] Since the late 1970s, school board financing for music and arts instruction has plummeted, key community arts workshops have closed, local jazz venues have folded one after another, Black dance has been shut out in the cold, community theater has withered, Black and Chicano filmmakers have lost much of their foundation support, and the world-famous East L.A. mural movement has almost disappeared. Such vital generators of community self-definition as the Watts Towers Arts Center, the Inner City Cultural Center, and the Bilingual Foundation of the Arts have had to make drastic cutbacks to survive the 'age of arts affluence'.[150] The inner city, in other words, has been culturally hollowed out in lockstep with the pyramiding of public and private arts capital in Westwood and Bunker Hill. As a result Black and Chicano cultural avant gardes have either been decimated or forced to retreat from their community constituencies to the cooptative shelter of the universities and corporate arts establishment.[151]

The current Culture boom, and its attendant celebrity-intellectual influx, therefore, must be seen as an epiphenomenon of the larger social polarization that has revitalized Downtown and enriched the Westside at the expense of vast debilitated tracts of the inner city. Although Los Angeles now boasts of competing with New York's culture worlds, it has none of the latter's vast arts and literary patrimony, derived from successive radical bohemias and avant gardes. Even the expected 'trickle-down' from corporate culture largely fails to reach, or nurture, street culture in Los Angeles. As a result of a deliberate 'deregionalization' of cultural investment – symbolized by the 1979 decision to change the name of the future Los Angeles Museum of Modern Art to the Museum of Contemporary Art ('signifying that it would present art from an international rather than regional perspective')[152] – the arts fund is either spent on imported culture (especially from New York) or used to entice

CULTURE SUPPORTING REAL ESTATE
Museum of Contemporary Art, Downtown

celebrity immigrants. The $35.2 million which the Getty family recently paid for a sixteenth-century work by the little-known painter Pontormo was many times the city's annual budget for culture in Southcentral and East Los Angeles.

Given this conjuncture of arts bonanza and scorched earth, it is not surprising that imported intellectuals feel like missionaries in a cultural *tabula rasa*. Peter Sellars, the director of the corporate-endowed Los Angeles Festival (which has replaced the more populist Los Angeles Street Scene), is a modal example of the new mandarins who are 'redefining' the city. His curriculum vitae modestly relates that 'in addition to the festival, he's visiting professor in the World Arts and Cultures Department at UCLA, an artist in residence at Northwestern University, writing a book of essays on contemporary performance and preparing to launch into cinema as director of his first feature film'. Although 'huge parts of the city are unformed and confusing', Sellars loves Los Angeles because it is 'the ground floor', 'a gawky adolescent . . . [full of] nascent energy'. 'There is certainly that sense of genuine immaturity, but . . . I don't think that's entirely to be deplored – I think it's interesting.'[153]

Such condescending enthusiasm has become the hallmark of the *colon* intelligentsia (Sellars has been in L.A. two years). Yet, at the same time, the arts elites, without any concession to the have-not cultural world, have begun to recognize the evident contradictions in their *nouveau riche* strategy (followed by all Sunbelt cities) of buying Culture straight off the rack of the world market. Over the last few years strenuous efforts have been made to discover seductive motifs that can act as brand labels for 'culture made in L.A.'. As in the early 1900s when the Mission Revival helped dissimulate local class struggle, there is a many-sided effort to fashion a new, emollient ideology for 'postmodern' Los Angeles that emphasizes the glamorous upside of the current social polarization and stakes a claim for the city's cultural leadership. In the absence of a single controlling metaphor like the 'Mission', however, the present mythmaking proceeds on several different tracks.

One track, represented by Sellars's Los Angeles Festival and funded by Pacific Rim capital, aims to display Los Angeles as a bazaar of ethnic (although not necessarily indigenous) cultures. Since Los Angeles is the only city in the world whose ethnic diversity approaches or exceeds New York's, (eighty-six different languages were recently counted amongst its school-children), multiculturalism seems an obvious emblem for its new globe-trotting pretensions. Yet (so far) this is still largely an import strategy, focused on an emerging network of transactions between elite cultural institutions, and designed to pluralize the tastes of Los Angeles's upscale arts consumers. As previously explained, it signifies no necessary commit-ment to the city's own community arts centers or diverse street cultures, who generally lack the corporate support that endorses Japanese theater or European ballet. At its worst, 'corporate multiculturalism' is an attitude that patronizes imported diversity while ignoring its own backyard. Thus, when Black performers protested that their community was 'virtually shut out' of the 1987 Festival, they received the haughty reply 'that the black community was represented in the multicultural program through foreign black artists, classical jazz performers and others'.[154]

Another major arts logo for 1990s Los Angeles is the deconstructed Pop architecture of Frank Gehry – heralded as the first major indigenous style since the bungalow. Gehry's work has the peculiar quality of trans-muting *noir* into Pop through a recycling of the elements of a decayed and polarized urban landscape (for example, rude concrete, chain-link, empty back walls, and so on) into light and airy expressions of a happy lifestyle (law schools, aquariums, movie libraries, etc.). It is a kind of architectural alchemy that makes the best of 'bad urban spaces', like downtown Hollywood or the Pico-Union barrio, by (as we shall see in chapter four) combining delightful geometries with complex physical security systems. Not surprisingly Gehry, who has characterized some of his own proposals as 'stage sets', has struck up a lucrative relationship with Disney CEO Michael Eisner to design 'entertainment architecture' for the Disney World expansion in Florida as well as the Disney Concert Center on Bunker Hill.[155] As the 'human face' of the corporate architecture that is trans-forming Los Angeles – uprooting neighborhoods and privatizing public space – Gehry has acquired a popular authority over regional taste that at times recalls the historic functions of Lummis, or even Disney.

The Los Angeles Festival's sponsorship of 'Pacific Rim consciousness', along with Gehry's gestures toward an architectural synthesis of 'Los Angelesness', have been mirrored by the combined efforts of planners, developers and business leaders to coin a 'new urban archetype' to emblematize the city's official future. Under siege from angry homeowner and environmental groups protesting out-of-control development, and anxious to bolster his image for the 1986 gubernatorial race, Mayor Bradley established a corporate-dominated blue-ribbon committee to prepare a 'strategic plan for Los Angeles'. Coming on the heels of the Los Angeles Olympics (a landmark in the current booster cycle), the committee was able to mobilize an unusual degree of attention from Los Angeles's usually divided elites (including, for the first time, representatives of Asian capital). The resulting report, *L.A. 2000: A City for the Future* (1988), has become the manifesto of a 'new regionalism', aiming to forge a unity of vision between mega-developers and the haute intelligentsia.[156]

Interestingly, the report's epilogue (by historian Kevin Starr) reminds readers that the last 'coherent' Los Angeles, that of the 1920s, found 'community on a civic level' because it 'had a dominant establishment and a dominant population'.[157] The report clearly implies that because of the decline of the Anglo *herrenvolk* – i.e., the absence of a dominant culture group in an increasingly poly-ethnic, poly-centered metropolis – a 'dominant establishment' is more essential than ever. While explicitly warning of the '*Blade Runner* scenario' – 'the fusion of individual cultures into a demotic polyglottism ominous with unresolved hostilities' – the report opts for the utopia of the 'Crossroads City': 'an extraordinary city of cities, a congregation of liveable communities'.[158] Although it repeatedly points out the total failure to create a social infrastructure to integrate new immigrants or old poor, the social justice dimension of the report consists basically of low-cost, cosmetic programs with an occasional, half-hearted allusion to the daunting scale of effort required. The central thrust of the report is an emphasis on 'growth management' to be implemented through rationalized regional government agencies supported by state environmental planning and a regional 'goals consensus'. Symptomatically, the Southern California economy is depicted as a happy black box generating endless growth. There is no consideration whatsoever of possible contradictions within this perpetual motion machine.

This optimistic, technocratic vision of Los Angeles entering the new millennium received unusual intellectual reinforcement eighteen months later with the publication of Kevin Starr's whiggish history of the city's Promethean past: *Material Dreams: Southern California Through the 1920s*

(1990). Elaborating the themes of his epilogue to *L.A. 2000*, Starr claims that Los Angeles was conjured out of the desert as a willed act of imagination by a visionary pantheon of artists, architects, engineers, and entrepreneurs. Although particular settings (for instance, Santa Barbara in the 1920s, the utopian beginnings of Los Angeles architecture, and so on) are brilliantly evoked, Los Angeles in the Open Shop era is depicted without a *noir* cloud on the horizon. There is no hint of class or racial violence, nor, for that matter, of any historical causality other than seminal individuals attempting to materialize their dreams. It is an account that begs comparison to the hagiographic 'brag books' – so common in the early twentieth century – that depicted local history as the heroic activity of the 'leading men of business and industry'. But Starr's evident concern is less to praise the forefathers than to encourage his contemporaries in the conceit that they too are fountainheads of the 'Southern California dream'. *Material Dreams*, by convincing us that its heroes 'designed' the city's past, offers a hubristic coda for today's mercenary intellectuals to claim that they are designing its future.[159]

EPILOGUE: GRAMSCI VS *BLADE RUNNER*

> Los Angeles seems endlessly held between these extremes: of light and
> dark – of surface and depth. Of the promise, in brief, of a meaning
> always *hovering* on the edge of significance. *Grahame Clarke*[160]

If one were to attempt to distinguish the new Boosterism from the old, it might be said that while the Mission Revivalism of Lummis's generation relied upon a fictional past, the World City hoopla of today thrives upon a fictional future. If the imaginary idyll of padres and their happy neophytes erased a history of expropriation and racial violence, then the singing tomorrows of *L.A. 2000* and the Central City Association are a preemptive repression of the *Blade Runner* scenario that too many Angelenos fear is already inevitable. As Adamic and McWilliams in the 1930s and 1940s debunked the white supremacist pseudo-history of the Boosters, so today's oppositional intellectuals must contest the mythology of managed and eternal growth. As always, that contestation will be primarily a guerrilla war across a diversity of terrains, from UCLA to the streets of Compton.

One brave beginning has been made at UCLA – an institution otherwise more attuned these days to Paris than to Pasadena or Pacoima. The self-proclaimed 'L.A. School' is an emerging current of neo-Marxist researchers (mostly planners and geographers) sharing a common interest in the contradictory ramifications of urban 'restructuring' and the possible emergence of a new 'regime of flexible accumulation'. Their image of Los Angeles as prism of different spatialities is brilliantly encapsulated by Edward Soja in an essay – 'It All Comes Together in Los Angeles', that has become the latter-day counterpart of Adamic's famous 'Los Angeles! There She Blows!'

One can find in Los Angeles not only the high technology industrial complexes of the Silicon Valley and the erratic sunbelt economy of Houston, but also the far-reaching industrial decline and bankrupt urban neighborhoods of rustbelt Detroit or Cleveland. There is a Boston in Los Angeles, a Lower Manhattan and a South Bronx, a São Paulo and a Singapore. There may be no other comparable urban region which presents so vividly such a composite assemblage and articulation of urban restructuring processes. Los Angeles seems to be conjugating the recent history of capitalist urbanization in virtually all its inflectional forms.[161]

During the 1980s the 'L.A. School' (based in the UCLA planning and geography faculties, but including contributors from other campuses) developed an ambitious matrix of criss-crossing approaches and case-studies. Monographs focused on the dialectics of de- and re-industrialization, the peripheralization of labor and the internationalization of capital, housing and homelessness, the environmental consequences of untrammeled development, and the discourse of growth. Although its members remain undecided whether they should model themselves after the 'Chicago School' (named principally after its *object* of research), or the 'Frankfurt School' (a philosophical current named after its *base*), the 'L.A. School' is, in fact, a little bit of both. While surveying Los Angeles in a systematic way, the UCLA researchers are most interested in exploiting the metropolis, à la Adorno and Horkheimer, as a 'laboratory of the future'. They have made clear that they see themselves excavating the outlines of a paradigmatic postfordism, an emergent twenty-first century urbanism.[162] Their belief in the region as a crystal ball is redoubled by Fredric Jameson's famous evocation (in his 'Cultural Logic of Late Capitalism') of Bunker Hill as a 'concrete totalization' of postmodernity.[163]

POLYETHNIC L.A.
Corner, Vermont and Olympic

By exposing the darkest facets of the 'world city' (Los Angeles's 'new Dickensian hell' of underclass poverty in the words of UCLA geographer Alan Scott) the 'L.A. School' ridicules the utopias of *L.A. 2000*. Yet, by hyping Los Angeles as the paradigm of the future (even in a dystopian vein), they tend to collapse history into teleology and glamorize the very reality they would deconstruct. Soja and Jameson, particularly, in the very eloquence of their different 'postmodern mappings' of Los Angeles, become celebrants of the myth. The city is a place where everything is possible, nothing is safe and durable enough to believe in, where constant synchronicity prevails, and the automatic ingenuity of capital ceaselessly throws up new forms and spectacles – a rhetoric, in other words, that recalls the hyperbole of Marcuse's *One-Dimensional Man*.

The difficulties of breaking completely free of Los Angeles's ideological conceits are equally illustrated across town in the ghettoes of Watts and Compton, with the emergence of 'gangster rap'. George Lipsitz, in his engaging 'Cruising Around the Hegemonic Bloc' (1986),[164] has argued that Los Angeles's spectrum of ethnic rock musicians, muralists, breakdancers, and rappers constitute a kind of 'organic intelligentsia' fomenting a cultural strategy for a 'historical bloc of oppositional groups'. Seemingly confirming this thesis, NWA (Niggers With Attitude) and their lead rapper Eazy-E have sowed consternation in law-and-order circles with the phenomenal popularity of their 1989 albums, 'Straight Outta Compton' (500,000 copies) and 'Eazy-Duz-It' (650,000). Disdaining recent attempts to whitewash a musical style that was meant to be the authenic sound of the ghetto ('we make these records for our people first'), NWA are 'pushing the imagery much further than anyone before them'; '[they] feature sirens and gunshots as backdrops to their brutal and ugly X-rated tales of drug-dealing, gangbanging and police confrontations'.[165] As Eazy-E explains it, gangster rap has become Los Angeles's alternative press:

We're telling the real story of what it's like living in places like Compton. We're giving [the fans] reality. We're like reporters. We give them the truth. People where we come from hear so many lies that the truth stands out like a sore thumb.

But one of the most persistent 'truths' that NWA report is their own avarice: 'We're not making records for the fun of it, we're in it to make money.' In contrast to their New York Rap counterparts, Public Enemy (now defunct), who were tribunes of Black nationalism, Los Angeles gangster rappers disclaim all ideology except the primitive accumulation of wealth by any means necessary. In supposedly stripping bare the reality of the streets, 'telling it like it is', they also offer an uncritical mirror to fantasy power-trips of violence, sexism and greed. And no more than Charles Bukowski or Frank Gehry (other purveyors of L.A. 'social realism') have the gangster rappers managed to avoid retranslation by becoming celebrities. Surrounded by benignly smiling white record company execs and PR men, NWA brandish customized assault rifles and talk darkly about recent 'drive-bys' and funerals of friends – a 'polished' image like any other in the business.[166]

This apparent synergy between gangster culture and Hollywood (an old motif) raises some doubts about Lipsitz's thesis of a counter-hegemonic convergence. Writing about another of Los Angeles's outlaw subcultures, the punk scene of the late 1970s and early 1980s, David James expresses pessimism that any contemporary culture practice, however transitory or marginal, can escape 'virtually overnight' assimilation and repackaging by the 'hegemonic media'. The experience of NWA, and less subtly of the entire burgeoning *Colors* genre, suggests that Hollywood is eager to mine Los Angeles's barrios and ghettoes for every last lurid image of self-destruction and community holocaust. If the dream factories are equally as happy to manufacture nightmare as idyll, what happens to the oppositional power of documentary realism (a question, of course, that transcends the class struggle over the ideological figuration of Los Angeles)? James's own bleak answer, informed by Los Angeles case-studies, is that 'exemplary moments' of negation can now only be visualized as transient skirmishes at the very margin of culture; resistance becomes permanently 'conjectural'.[167]

Somewhere between Lipsitz's Gramscian optimism and James's Frankfurtian pessimism lies the real possibility of oppositional culture in Los Angeles. As Gramsci almost certainly would have pointed out, a radical structural analysis of the city (as represented by the 'L.A. School') can only acquire social force if it is embodied in an alternative experiential vision – in this case, of the huge Los Angeles Third World whose children will be the Los Angeles of the next millennium. In this emerging, poly-ethnic and *poly-lingual* society – with Anglos a declining minority – the structural conditions of intervention in popular culture are constantly in flux. Who can predict how the long years of struggle which lie ahead, before new Latino immigrants can hope to attain social and political equality, will affect the culture of the Spanish-speaking inner city? Will the city-within-the-city become colonized by a neo-Taiwanese work ethic of thrift and submission, disintegrate into a clockwork-orange of warring gangs, produce an oppositional subculture (like the Yiddish radicalism of ragtime New York) – or, perhaps, all three? Equally, will the boundaries between different groups become faultlines of conflict or high-voltage generators of an alternative urban culture led by poly-ethnic vanguards?

Certainly 'interculturalism' is an ambiguous slogan these days: defining the agenda of both 'hegemonic' culture institutions (touting the idea of a Pacific Rim nexus of corporate-sponsored art and performance) and their guerrilla opposition (dreaming of an unprecedented coalition of have-not street artists from different communities). While heeding the traditional warning – from Louis Adamic to David James – that intellectual and cultural oppositions in the capital of the Culture Industry are always conjunctural (if not conjectural), it remains to give something back to George Lipsitz's observation that when Los Angeles's street cultures rub together in the right way, they emit light of unusual warmth and clarity.

NOTES

1. *Los Angeles*, New York 1933, p. 319.
2. See *Glamor*, August 1989.
3. Ibid.
4. Michael Sorkin, 'Explaining Los Angeles', *California Counterpoint: New West Coast Architecture 1982*, San Francisco Art Institute 1982, p. 8.
5. Notably Fitzgerald's *The Last Tycoon*, West's *The Day of the Locust*, and Schulberg's *What Makes Sammy Run*.
6. 'The Los Angeles Novel and the Idea of the West', in David Fine, ed., *Los Angeles in Fiction*, Albuquerque 1981, p. 30.
7. Quoted in Mark Winchell, *Joan Didion*, Boston 1980, p. 122.
8. No one has explained better than Michael Sorkin (see above) how a 'Los Angeles discourse' – mystification presenting itself as understanding – has come to be organized into a series of interchangeable tropes and 'mist-shrouded essences', ranging from 'the weather' and 'the apocalypse', to 'Disney', 'cars' and 'the future'.
9. Quoted in Kevin Starr, *Inventing the Dream: California Through the Progressive Era*, Oxford 1985, p. 85.

KILL MICKEY!
Downtown

10. Ibid., p. 76.

11. Ibid., p. 58. Starr exhaustively mines Franklin Walker's pioneering survey of the local cultural landscape, *A Literary History of Southern California*, Berkeley 1950.

12. Joseph O'Flaherty, *Those Powerful Years: The South Coast and Los Angeles, 1887–1917*, Hicksville, New York 1978, p. 67.

13. John Ogden Pohlmann, *California's Mission Myth*, PhD thesis, Department of History, UCLA, Los Angeles 1974, p. 385.

14. Starr, ibid., p. 86.

15. Ibid., p. 113.

16. A manic revival of the 'Mission Revival' has swept over Southern California during the 1980s as gentrifiers and collectors have rediscovered the heirlooms of the Lummis era. *Business Week*, 31 July 1989, reports that an ordinary Mission Oak couch, factory-made by the Stickley Brothers at the turn of the century, and only worth $100 five years ago, now sells for $20,000. At a recent Christie's auction, Barbra Streisand – apparently a neo-Arroyan by taste – paid $363,000 for a single Mission Oak sideboard. The craze is so formidable that only drastic action by the Pasadena City Council has prevented some of the Greene Brothers' most famous homes from being dismantled for the sale of their parts.

17. United States Commission on Industrial Relations, 'Open and Closed Shop Controversy in Los Angeles', United States Congress, *Senate Documents*, 64 Congress, 1 Session, number 415, pp. 5, 493–5, 518.

18. According to Dudley Gordon, who for many decades was the curator of a small, continuing Lummis cult, the latter's writings remained extremely popular in Spain long after they were out of print in California – the Spanish, uncritically relishing as fact the entire 'Mission Myth'. (See the interview in Lionel Rolfe's unpublished manuscript, *Notes of a California Bohemian*, n.d.)

19. Mayo, p. 137.

20. This essentially harmless Echo Park bohemia is described in Kevin Starr's, *Material Dreams: Southern California Through the 1920s*, Oxford 1990; and in Lionel Rolfe's unpublished *Notes of a California Bohemian*, which includes a wonderful interview with Jake Zeitlin, in which the aged bookdealer recounts the role of Miriam Lerner, private secretary to oil millionaire Edward Doheny (as well as an ardent member of the Young People's Socialist League and Edward Weston's model/lover), in getting jobs for young L.A. bohemians at Doheny gas stations or, in Zeitlin's case, even mowing the tycoon's lawn.

21. See *Laughing in the Jungle*, New York 1932, p. 211; and Carey McWilliams, *Louis Adamic and Shadow-America*, Los Angeles 1935, pp. 23–4, 32.

22. McWilliams, p. 26.

23. Ibid.

24. Quoted in Carey McWilliams, *Southern California Country: An Island on the Land*, New York 1946, p. 157.

25. *Los Angeles*, New York 1933, p. 327.

26. San Francisco Museum of Modern Art, *Painting and Sculpture in California: The Modern Era*, San Francisco 1977, pp. 27–9, 93. There is virtually no historical literature on Southern California's prewar art avant gardes, or their relationship to contemporary social struggles.

27. See Ellen Landau, *Jackson Pollock: An American Saga*, New York 1989, p. 46. Pollock's brother Sande was a member of the small workshop of young artists who studied with Siqueiros and helped install his mural. However, Pollock's other recent biographers, Steven Naifeh and Gregory White Smith, dispute Landau's account of the mural's impact on Jackson. According to them he was 'strangely untouched' by his first encounter with Siqueiros in Los Angeles, coming under his spell only later in New York as they worked together on banners and posters for the 1936 Union Square May Day demonstration. (See Landau, p. 284 passim.)

28. Quoted in Erna Moore, 'Exil in Hollywood: Leben und Haltung deutscher Exilautoren nach ihren autobiographischen Berichten', in Spalek and Strelka, eds, *Deutsche Exilliterature seit 1933. Teil 1: Kalifornien*, Bern and Munich 1976, p. 28 (our translation).

29. *Louis Adamic*, p. 77.

30. See Carey McWilliams, *The Education of Carey McWilliams*, New York 1978, pp. 119–20.

31. Ibid, p. 119 passim.

32. Robert Gottlieb and Irene Wolt, *Thinking Big: The Story of the Los Angeles Times*, New York 1977. This book is the new foundation for serious writing and analysis about Southern California.

33. The major exception, between McWilliams and Gottlieb and Wolt, was Robert Fogelson's *The Fragmented Metropolis: Los Angeles, 1850–1930* Cambridge, Mass. 1967 – an important historical study of demography, planning and power, shamefully out of print.

34. Quoted in McWilliams, *Louis Adamic*, pp. 80–81.

35. *City of Night*, New York 1963, p. 87.

36. *Decline of the Middle Class*, New York 1935, pp. 15, 21–23, 34, 342–3, 361.

37. 'Reuben W. Borough and the California Reform Movements', transcript, Oral History Program, UCLA, Los Angeles 1968.

38. Carey McWilliams described pensionites shouting 'Ham and Eggs!' with 'the frenzy of storm-troopers yelling "Sieg Heil!" All meetings of the Payroll Guarantee Association are opened with the shouted salutation "Ham and Eggs!" and each speaker who appears on the platform must preface his remarks with the salutation. If he neglects to do so, the crowd will shout "Ham and Eggs!" until he does.' (*Southern California Country*, pp. 305–6.).

39. David Fine, 'Introduction' in Fine, ed., *Los Angeles in Fiction*, Albuquerque 1984, p.7. H.L. Mencken was again decisive in preparing the way for the emergence of the genre. His sentimental-cynical journalistic style, his disdain for euphemism, and his patronage of underground writers – all made him *noir*'s godfather. He premiered the short stories of Cain and Fante in his *American Mercury*, as well as founding *The Black Mask* (subsequently sold to Eltinge Warner) which printed early Hammett, Gardner and Chandler. Mencken, ironically, disliked detective fiction. (For a recognition of his influence, see Kinsley Widmer, 'The Way Out: Some Life-Style Sources of the Literary Tough Guy and the Proletarian Hero', in David Madden, *Tough Guy Writers of the Thirties*, Carbondale, Ill. 1968, p. 6.)

40. Ron Goulart, *The Dime Detectives*, New York 1988, pp. 100–105. Other jaded Hollywood literary proletarians who wrote *noir*-ish detective stories in this vein included John Butler, W.T. Ballard, Frank Gruber, Roger Torrey and Norbert Davis. (Ibid., 'The New Wild West', chapter six.)

41. Gerald Locklin, 'The Day of the Painter; the Death of the Cock: Nathanael West's Hollywood Novel' in Fine, p. 68.

42. Marlowe, the avenging burgher, totters precariously on the precipice of fascist paranoia. Each successive Chandler novel focuses on a new target of Marlowe's dislike: Blacks, Asians, gays, 'greasers', and, always, women. In this regard it is useful to recall the genealogy of the hardboiled detective hero: the special 1923 issue of *The Black Mask* on the Ku Klux Klan that introduced Carroll John Daly's nativist detective 'Race Williams' as the prototype of tough guy crusaders against (foreign-born) corruption. (Cf. Goulart, pp. 27–32; and Philip Durham, 'The *Black Mask* School', in Madden, pp. 51–79.).

43. *What Makes Sammy Run?*, New York 1940, p. 119. The first edition sold few copies, but sparked a vehement debate amongst left-wing writers, some of whom considered the Glick character 'anti-semitic'. See Neal Gabler, *An Empire of Their Own: How the Jews Invented Hollywood*, New York 1988, pp. 335–8.

44. 'Many left-oriented screenwriters and directors were logically drawn to the *film noir* . . . [which] positively reeked of the facts of life. It was easier to instill a feeling that all was not perfect in American society by way of the ambiguities of *film noir* than to take on the system and risk the cooptation of any subversive message.' (Carlos Clarens, *Crime Movies*, New York 1980, pp. 195–6.)

What a 'real' Marxist Hollywood film would have looked like remains a matter for arcane conjecture. Perhaps the best potential candidate was the remarkable screenplay of *An American Tragedy* which Sergei Eisenstein and Ivor Montagu wrote in 1930 during the Soviet director's brief and troubled stay in Hollywood. Dreiser supposedly loved the script, but Paramount – alarmed by its 'monstrous challenge to American society' – killed the project. See W.A. Swanberg, *Dreiser*, New York 1965, pp. 369–77.

45. An interesting convention of *film noir*, overlapping with the avant garde of documentary film-making, was the emergence of the metropolis itself (typically as 'naked city', 'divided city', etc.) as protagonist and star. Thus, the 1950 *film noir*, *Once a Thief*, actually lists 'Los Angeles' in the credits as one of the 'characters'. (See Dana Polan, *Power and Paranoia*, New York 1986, p. 235.)

46. See *Wait Until Spring Bandini* (1938), *Ask the Dust* (1939), *Dago Red* (1940), and the posthumously published 1930s novel, *1933 Was a Bad Year* (1985).

47. See Art and Laurie Pepper, *Straight Life: The Story of Art Pepper*, New York 1979. Son of one of the San Pedro Wobblies admired by Adamic, Pepper grew up in Watts, studied bebop on Central Avenue, did graduate work on heroin in Boyle Heights, and became emeritus at San Quentin. His tormented autobiography eclipses that of any character in the Bukowskian hell.

48. David King Dunaway, *Huxley in Hollywood*, New York 1989, pp. 222–3.

49. From 'W.C. Fields and the S.O.B. on Rollerskates', quoted in David Mogen, *Ray Bradbury*, Boston 1986, p. 5.

50. Ibid., p. 93.

51. Quoted in Arnold Rampersad, *The Life of Langston Hughes*, vol. I, New York 1986, p. 236.

52. Ibid., p. 371.

53. Stephen F. Milliken, *Chester Himes: A Critical Appraisal*, Columbia, Mo. 1976, p. 56.

54. *The Quality of Hurt*, New York 1972, p. 75.

55. Milliken, p. 75.

56. Himes, for example, is never mentioned in any of the twelve essays on Los Angeles fiction in the Fine anthology.

57. See Jerry Speir, 'The Ultimate Seacoast: Ross Macdonald's California', chapter six in Fine, ed.

58. *City of Night*, New York 1963, pp. 93, 87.

59. *Less Than Zero*, New York 1985, pp. 207–8.

60. A different tangent, of course, from the original *noir* generation is the reworking of West's image of the little people stranded in the hollowness of the L.A./Hollywood/California Dream. Probably the best contemporary representative of this genre (also covered by Sam Sheppard) is Burbank-born playwright John Steppling, who charts broken lives along Los Angeles's 'low-rent periphery'. For a discussion of his work, see Jan Breslauer, 'Chronicles of the Dream Coast', *LA Weekly*, 26 January–1 February 1990.

61. The *Los Angeles Quartet* includes *The Black Dahlia* (1987), *The Big Nowhere* (1988), *L.A. Confidential* (1990), and *White Jazz* (forthcoming). Ellroy produces his 'post-Noir' potboilers in a basement office in Eastchester, New York – 3,000 miles from the scene of the crime.

62. Quoted in the Los Angeles *Times*, 13 February 1990.

63. *Vineland*, New York 1990, p. 326.

64. Dika Newlin, *Schoenberg Remembered*, Pendragon, New York 1980, p. 42. This is the diary of a thirteen-year-old whizz kid who studied with Schoenberg in the 1930s.

65. The emigré French composer Milhaud marveled that Los Angeles could contain 'a whole *world* of artists, writers and musicians'. Altogether some ten to fifteen thousand European refugees – mostly professionals – were allowed to settle on the West Coast. Perhaps half that number lived for some period in Southern California. (See Gerald Nash, *The American West Transformed: The Impact of the Second World War*, Bloomington, Ind. 1985, pp. 194–5.)

66. There were also some 'precocious' refugees from reaction, like the radical Jewish painter Boris Deutsch who arrived from Lithuania in 1920.

67. Quoted in Gross, 'Adorno in Los Angeles: The Intellectual in Emigration', *Humanities in Society*, Fall 1979, p. 342. Old differences were magnified, not forgotten in exile. Despite repeated efforts of friends to get them together, Shoenberg and Stravinsky lived in Los Angeles for thirteen years (sitting 'on opposite sides of the Wilshire Ebell Theater at the premiere of the *Genesis Suite*') before finally agreeing to speak to each other. (See Igor Stravinsky and Robert Craft, *Dialogues*, Berkeley 1982, p. 106.)

68. See Anthony Heilbut, *Exiled in Paradise: German Refugee Artists and Intellectuals in America*, Boston 1983, p. 161.

69. *Noir* had its own, separate sphere of influence upon postwar European (especially French and Italian) culture. Cain – more than anyone – helped precipitate a new kind of fiction and cinema: *The Postman Always Rings Twice* was the model for Camus's *The Outsider* as well as being 'stolen' by Visconti as *Ossessione*, which Godard later remade. (Cf. David Madden, 'Introduction', *Tough Guy Writers of the Thirties*, Carbondale, Ill. 1968, p. xvii; and Otto Friedrich, *City of Nets: Hollywood in the 1940s*, New York 1986, p. 235.)

70. See Martin Jay, *The Dialectical Imagination*, Berkeley 1985, p. 123.

71. See Gross, p. 344.

72. Max Horkheimer and Theodor Adorno, *Dialektik der Aufklerung*, Frankfurt 1972: pp. 120–21 (our translation).

73. *Paradies Amerika*, Berlin 1948, p. 134.

74. *Los Angeles: The Architecture of Four Ecologies*, London 1971, pp. 236, 247. Wagner has never been translated and *Los Angeles . . . Zweimillionenstadt in Sudkalfornien* is now a rare item in library special collections.

75. Ibid., p. 156ff (our translation).

76. Quoted in Hans Wagener, 'Erich Maria Remarque', Spalek and Strelka, eds, p. 595.

77. Ibid.

78. Hanns Eisler, *Fragen Sie mehr ueber Brecht: Gespraeche mit Hans Bunge*, Darmstadt 1986, p. 44 (our translation).

79. See his famous essay 'Ozymandias, the Utopia That Failed', a cautionary tale of communal living, in *Tomorrow and Tomorrow and Tomorrow*, New York 1956.

80. See David King Dunaway's fascinating *Huxley in Hollywood*, New York 1990. Most devotees, as well as critics, of California's 'New Age' seem to believe that it emerged fully-formed out of the 1960s 'age of Aquarius'. In fact it has a complex subcultural genealogy, being related, via Huxley and Heard, to Bloomsbury and an earlier Pre-Raphaelite bohemia, as well as deriving, more locally, from a concatenation of Arroyo-ite Aryanism (especially the emphasis on racial physical perfectionism) and Hollywood cult tradition (including a Satanic chromosome or two from the influential Crowleyites).

81. Brecht, 'On Thinking About Hell', *Poems: 1913–1956*, Part Three, London 1976, p. 367.

82. Ibid., 1976, p. 280.

83. Dunaway, pp. 285–303.

84. See discussion in Patty Lee Parmalee, *Brecht's America*, Miami 1981.

85. Quoted in Bruce Cook, *Brecht in Exile*, New York 1982, p. 58. Mann, of course, wrote *Doctor Faustus* in Los Angeles.

86. Cf. Malcolm MacDonald, *Schoenberg*, London 1978, p. 46; Julian Brand, *The Berg–Schoenberg Correspondence*, New York 1987, p. 458. MacDonald points out that Schoenberg was a popular figure at UCLA, and that 'he also taught John Cage privately, asking no fee "as long as he would devote his life to music" '. (p. 45)

87. Quoted Nash, p. 197. Indeed having the Gods of European Culture in Los Angeles during the 1930s and 1940s did stimulate many young writers and musicians. For the impact of meeting Thomas Mann in 1947 on one North Hollywood teenager, see Susan Sontag's memoir, 'Pilgrimage', *New Yorker*, 21 December 1987.

88. Erna Moore, 'Exil in Hollywood: Leben und Haltung deutscher Exilautoren nach ihren autobiographischen Berichten', in Spalek and Strelka, p. 25ff.

89. Nash, ibid.

90. Kevin MacMahon, private communication.

91. Of course, the studio writing departments *were* real factories. ' "You had to punch the Clock", Milton Sperling recalled. "They would walk around and see if everybody was typing. There'd be a lookout in the writers' building. When Warner or Cohn would be seen coming toward the building, somebody would say 'He's coming' and all the typewriters would start. . . . He [Jack Warner] couldn't understand why people weren't always typing." ' (In Neal Gabler, *An Empire of Their Own: How the Jews Invented Hollywood*, New York 1988, p. 324.)

92. 'Wissenschaftliche Erfahrungen in Amerika', in *Stichworte. Kritische Modelle II*, Frankfurt 1969, p. 147 (our translation).

93. See Barry Katz, *Herbert Marcuse*, London 1985.

94. Leddy, *L.A. Weekly*, 1989, p. 11.

95. *The Autobiography of Robert A. Millikan*, New York 1950, p. 242.

96. Farnsworth Crowder, 'Los Angeles: The Heaven of Bunk-Shooters', in *How 'Wicked' Is Hollywood?*, 'Little Blue Book No. 1591' (Haldeman-Julius), Girard (Kansas) n.d., p. 18.

97. By the mid 1920s, just a few years after its refounding, Cal Tech was surpassing all other American universities in the both the number of major physics publications by its faculty, and the number of national and international research fellows attracted to its laboratories. See Robert Kargon, *The Rise of Robert Millikan*, Ithaca 1982, p. 117.

98. On the attraction of Orange Grove Avenue's 'millionaires' row', see Carey McWilliams, *California: The Great Exception*, New York 1949, pp. 260–62. On the Observatory as region-builder, see Millikan, pp. 230–31.

99. Ibid., pp. 92–101.

100. Ibid., p. 104.

101. See Guy Finney, *The Great Los Angeles Bubble (A Present-Day Story of Colossal Financial Jugglery and of Penalties Paid)*, Los Angeles 1929.

102. 'Some Exceptional Opportunities in Southern California', Robert A. Millikan Archives, Cal Tech, Pasadena, box 27.9 (two drafts), n.d.

103. Kargon, pp. 162–3.

104. Morrow Mayo, *Los Angeles*, New York 1933, pp. 313–15.

105. Crowder, pp. 45–7.

106. One cannot be entirely unsympathetic towards Crowley, however. During the Russian Revolution he did write to Trotsky expressing his agreement with the elimination of capitalism and proposing to be put in charge of the 'extirpation of Christianity on earth'. Trotsky did not reply. See Wilson, p. 137.

107. Cf. Colin Wilson, *Aleister Crowley: The Nature of the Beast*, Wellingborough 1987, p. 147; Russell Miller, *Bare-Faced Messiah: The True Story of L. Ron Hubbard*, New York 1987, p. 113 passim; Frank Malina, 'The Jet Propulsion Laboratory', in Arthur Clarke, ed., *The Coming of the Space Age*, London 1967, p. 67 passim.

108. Miller, pp. 116–30.

109. Miller, p. 165.

110. 'Los Angeles: The Ecology of Evil', *Artforum*, Vol 11, December 1972, pp. 67–76; and *Sunshine Muse*, New York 1974, p. 139.

111. Valerie Wilmer, *As Serious As Your Life: The Story of the New Jazz*, London 1977, p. 70; and Barry McRae, *Ornette Coleman*, London 1988, p. 16.

112. The Big Apple-biased perspective of jazz criticism often overlooks the seminal role of this Los Angeles underground in launching the New Wave dominated by Coleman, Coltrane, Taylor and Dolphy. A similar argument could be made about the neglect of the Los Angeles origins (from Martha Graham to Alvin Ailey) of much of modern 'New York' dance.

113. See Robert Gordon, *Jazz West Coast*, London 1986, p. 183 passim.

114. Peter Plagens, *Sunshine Muse*, p. 23.

115. The Case-Study House program sponsored by John Entenza's *California Arts and Architecture* magazine between 1945 and 1960 allowed the younger modernists to conduct exhaustive experimentation on Los Angeles's social and cultural ideal-type: the detached, single-family home. The exhibition of the first six homes (by Soriano, Ain, and others), which attracted nearly 370,000 viewers, has been sometimes compared to New York's Armoury Show (1913) as a local premiere of Modernism. The Case Study experience was the subject of a major, uncritical retrospective by the 'Temporary Contemporary' (the satellite facility of the Museum of Contemporary Art) in 1989 which once again attracted tens of thousands of viewers.

116. Ironically, many of the white 'cool' jazzmen had first apprenticed themselves in the 1940s to Central Avenue's integrated music culture and continued, through the 1950s, to personally prefer the 'harder' and 'freer' sound in the ghetto.

117. See John Litweiler, *The Freedom Principle: Jazz After 1958*, New York 1984, pp. 296–7.

118. Lawrence Weschler, *Seeing is Forgetting: The Name of the Thing One Sees*, Berkeley 1982, p. 42.

119. 'Pop Art in California', in Lucy Lippard, ed., *Pop Art*, New York 1966, p. 140.

120. Plagens, *Sunshine Muse*, p. 120.

121. 'Berman and Kienholz: Progenitors of L.A. Assemblage', in Maurice Tuchman, ed., *Art in Los Angeles: Seventeen Artists in the 1960s*, Los Angeles 1982, p. 12.

122. Quoted in P. Adams Sitney, *Visionary Film: The American Avant-Garde, 1943–1978*, Oxford 1974, p. 125.

123. Ibid., p. 93 passim.

124. Clarke, p. 142.

125. Cf. Thomas Pynchon, 'A Journey Into the Mind of Watts', *New York Times Magazine*, 12 June 1966; and Budd Schulberg, ed., *From the Ashes: Voices of Watts*, New York 1967.

126. See Christopher Knight, 'The Resurrection of John Baldessari', *Times*, 18 March 1990.

127. Weschler, p. 123.

128. Maurice Tuchman, *A Report on the Art and Technology Program of the Los Angeles County Museum of Art, 1967–1971*, LACMA, Los Angeles 1971, pp. 9–10 (on 'Missy' Chandler's role). In 1975 the *Los Angeles Free Press* exposed an unethical cash nexus between Tuchman and a gallery which sold work to the County Museum. See William Hackman, 'Seven Artists in Search of a Place to Hang', *California Magazine*, November 1986, p. 95, 108.

129. Plagens, p. 165.

130. Ibid., p. 145. On the art front, Plagens has evaluated the potential of the 1960s avant garde as follows: 'In the heyday of Los Angeles art, in 1966–9, there was a myth operative in the land, even in certain renegade minds east of the Hudson, that Los Angeles was the art center of the twenty-first century. . . . Not so, for a couple of reasons. . . . If art stayed with hard, opaque, permanent, hand-wrought painting and sculpture, Los Angeles would never have the density, the cultural surplus, to pull it off; the honor would probably go to Houston, the South Bronx of 2001. If there were to be a Warhol *doppelgänger*, he wouldn't live in the bowels of lower Hollywood; if he kept a modest studio for fifteen years in the Thai-restaurant-adult-movie stretch of North Western Avenue, he wouldn't be another Warhol.' (See 'Ed Ruscha, Serious' in *The Works of Ed Ruscha*, San Francisco Museum of Modern Art 1982, p. 39.)

131. See Knight, who praises the Santa Monica-based Baldessari, a major figure in the rise of Conceptual Art in the 1980s, precisely for his 'cosmopolitan worldliness' and rejection of L.A.'s 'provincial regionalism'.

132. Harold Rosenberg, quoted in Peter Plagens, *Ruscha*, p. 40. Plagens struggles heroically in this essay to defend Ruscha as a wry moralist who 'aspires to innocence . . . to cleanse the view from the beach' (p. 39). But is sixties' innocence, twenty-five years later, still 'innocent'?

133. *American Art Now*, New York 1985, p. 52.

134. Ibid.

135. See Vladimir Simosko and Barry Tepperman, *Eric Dolphy: A Musical Biography and Discography*, Washington, D.C. 1974.

136. 'Art in Limbo', *L.A. Weekly*, 18–24 March 1988.

137. Jackson was speaking to a 1988 conference on the state of the Black theater at Stanford University. See Lawrence Christon, 'Black Theater: Its Decline Since 1960', Los Angeles *Times Calendar*, 31 January 1988.

138. An almost random list of new arrivals would include the editor and publisher of the Los Angeles *Times*, the president of the California Institute of the Arts, the director of the Los Angeles Festival, and the dean of UCLA's architecture and planning school.

139. *Thinking Big: The Story of the Los Angeles Times*, New York 1977, pp. 306–20.

140. Los Angeles was never meant to forget Buffy's crowning moment. As Kevin McMahon notes: 'The white silk Yves Saint-Laurent gown Dorothy wore to the gala opening of her music center is still in a display next to the men's room in the downstairs lounge. The historic object is draped over a dark velvet mannequin and dramatically spot-lit. It has yellowed and looks pretty awful.' (private communication).

141. Quoted in Dick Hebdige, 'In Poor Taste: Notes on Pop', in The Institute for Contemporary Art, ed., *Modern Dreams: The Rise and Fall of Pop*, New York 1988, p. 77.

142. As Plagens once put it, 'the question, at least for Southern California, is not so much whether the area was/is ripe for Pop, but whether the whole ambience – from showbusiness to aircraft industry to the Gobi of suburbia – is not preemptively Pop in itself.' (*Sunshine Muse*, p. 139.)

143. Banham's early essay on the libidinalized automobile, 'Vehicles of Desire' (*Art*, September 1955), signaled that he was proleptically, or telepathically, on the same wavelength as the Ferus artists and Kenneth Anger.

144. 'Los Angeles: The Ecology of Evil', *Artforum*, vol. II, December 1972, pp. 67–76.

145. *Los Angeles: The Architecture of Four Ecologies*, London 1972, p. 201 passim.

146. For a provocative discussion of Downtown culture politics, see Jo-Anne Berelowitz, 'The Jewel in the Crown: Bunker Hill, MOCA, and the Ideology of Urban Redevelopment', discussion paper, Dept. of Art History, UCLA 1988.

147. Los Angeles *Times*, 19 May 1989. Meier reportedly 'has brooded about whether the Getty Center should have been located in a less affluent area and has concluded that "by being where it is, the way you see Los Angeles . . . it belongs to the whole city" '. (Ibid.)

148. CRA brochure. Photographer and design critic Alan Sekula describes this 'Pop reification of real-estate' as the master cultural trend of Los Angeles in the 1980s (interview, December 1989).

149. Frye, ibid. She also reveals that Los Angeles spends $1.53 per capita on the arts in contrast to New York's $8.87 or even Miami's $5.20.

150. A parallel problem is the lack of effective Black or Chicano/Mexican controlled television, comparable to the outlets operated by the Asian or evangelical communities. The major Spanish-language station is controlled by Cuban exiles, while the only Black-owned station – long inactive – is being purchased by evangelicals. The net result is a brutally twin-tiered metropolitan 'information order'.

151. For example, Chicano artists in Southern California have become increasingly reliant upon corporate sponsors, especially beverage companies and breweries, to show their work around the country. As journalist Reuben Martinez discovered, this usually entails a large dose of censorship. ' "One thing we want to stay away from is upsetting people", says Michele Bernhardt, a Canadian Club representative [sponsor of the 'Mira!' show]. "There are strong right-wing sentiments in this country now, and we don't want to put out anything controversial." ' (See 'Toward a Rainbow Culture', *L.A. Weekly*, 18–24 March 1988.)

152. Berelowitz.

153. Interviewed by Lizanne Fleming ('New Kid in Town'), *Pasadena Weekly*, 2 February 1990. Consider also this description of Sellars's Frank Lloyd Wright living room: 'At least half of the room's walls are covered with volumes ranging in subject matter from Russian and Soviet theater and Islamic art to shamanism and Jungian psychology. One shelf mixes theatrical classics with an eclectic stack of worn paperbacks by Jackie Gleason, Sid Caesar and Rudy Vallee.' (Ibid.)

154. Los Angeles *Times*, 24 February 1990. Festival Director Sellars, to be fair, has since promised to address community concerns. 'This is the most segregated city I've ever lived in. But as you set foot on this stage, you are created equal.' (Ibid.) He has not explained, however, where the Black community is expected to find financial support that would give its arts activities equal footing with wealthier ethnic segments of the corporate-dependent Festival.

155. Interviewed by Ross Miller, 'The Master of Mudpies'. Referring to Gehry, Isozaki, Graves and other current Disney 'starchitects', critic Suzanne Stephens observes, 'Yesterday, every architect in America dreamed of building office towers for enlightened developers. Today, they want to work for Michael Eisner.' (Quoted in Leon Whiteson, 'Disney Design', Los Angeles *Times*, 25 January 1990.)

156. Formulated under the leadership of a vice-president of Bankamerica, *L.A. 2000* is now being implemented by the '2000 Partnership' – a public-private organization headed by the former CEO of Lockheed.

157. *L.A. 2000*, p. 86.

158. Ibid.

159. Kevin Starr, *Material Dreams*, Oxford 1990. This is the third volume in Starr's ambitious *Americans and the California Dream*. A latter-day Bancroft who enjoys celebrity in elite circles in both San Francisco (where he was City Librarian) and Los Angeles (where, as we have seen, he 'contextualized' *L.A. 2000*), Starr may be the only official 'California intellectual' in the culturally polarized state.

160. 'The Great Wrong Place?: L.A. as Urban Milieu', in Clarke, ed., *The American City*, London 1988, p. 142.

161. Edward Soja, *Postmodern Geographies: The Reassertion of Space in Critical Social Theory*, London 1989, p. 193.

162. Los Angeles's monopoly on 'future vision', however, is now being challenged by other 'advanced points of observation', especially the city's largest suburb. A parallel 'Orange County School' of researchers, based at the University of California at Irvine, and patronized by a large Rockefeller Foundation grant, are exploring that area's claim to be the ideal-typical postindustrial society.

163. The original version of this essay appeared in *New Left Review* 146 (July–August 1984) as 'Postmodernism, or the Cultural Logic of Late Capitalism'. For a critique of Jameson's specific Los Angeles coordinates, see Mike Davis, 'Urban Renaissance and the Spirit of Postmodernism', in E. Ann Kaplan, ed., *Postmodernism and its Discontents*, London 1988, pp. 79–87.

164. In *Cultural Critique*, Winter 1986/7, pp. 157–77.

165. Robert Hilburn, 'Rap', Los Angeles *Times Calendar*, 2 April 1989.

166. Berelowitz op. cit.

167. Cf. description of NWA interview in Hunt.

168. See his 'Poetry/Punk/Production: Some Recent Writing in L.A.', in Kaplan, pp. 163–86.

CHAPTER TWO

POWER LINES

WHO RULES LOS ANGELES?

There is no power structure here – only people who think they are it.
Otis Chandler[1]

Popular images of power in Los Angeles are curiously contradictory. On the one hand is the common belief, almost folk legend, that L.A. is ruled by an omnipotent Downtown establishment, headed by the *Times* and some big banks, oil companies and department stores. On the other hand is Chandler's lofty avowal, echoed by journalists of the 'there is no "there" there' school, that power in Southern California is fragmented and dispersed, without a hegemonic center.

Both images exploit partial truths. For the half century between the Spanish-American and Korean wars, the Otis–Chandler dynasty of the *Times* did preside over one of the most centralized – indeed, militarized – municipal power-structures in the United States. They erected the open shop on the bones of labor, expelled pioneer Jews from the social register, and looted the region through one great real-estate syndication after another. Important residues of their power – and looting – remain inscribed in Downtown, influencing the present Bradley regime, even if the Old Guard is being supplanted by more powerful players from Tokyo, Toronto and New York.

At the same time, the great-grandson of General Harrison Gray Otis is correct to emphasize the current uncertainty of 'who rules L.A.'. Beginning with the rise of enclaved entertainment and aircraft industries in the 1920s and 1930s, and the decentralization of business along the Wilshire corridor during the same period, the Chandlerian power structure – which gave much of the darkness to L.A. *noir* – rapidly lost its regional monopoly. A separatist, predominantly Jewish and Democratic Westside wove its distinctive social and political networks into a competing hierarchy of power. More recently, the globalization of the regional economy has introduced new actors and power centers, destabilizing old-fashioned patrician cultures.

Obviously the poly-centered complexity of the contemporary system of elites is no longer susceptible to the diktat of any single dynasty or Mr Big. But if Los Angeles has long ceased being a hick town with a single 'executive committee of the ruling class', it is still far from being a mere gridwork of diffused wealth and power. Political power in Southern California remains organized by great constellations of private capital, which, as elsewhere, act as the permanent government in local affairs. What is exceptional about Los Angeles is the extreme development of what remains merely tendential in the evolution of other American cities.

First of all, elite formation in Los Angeles has tended to obey the rules laid down by the region's unpredictable geology as sudden shifts in the economic base produce fundamental recompositions at the level of power blocs. Despite the interlude of Chandlerian business discipline, Los Angeles has always had a far more *porous* elite culture than New York, Chicago, Philadelphia or San Francisco. As Frederic Jaher emphasizes, each new wave of wealth has 'imposed its ways on the community, rather than defer to older elites'.[2] This intrusive imperialism now operates in favor of the Japanese *zaibatsu* and Manhattan-based banks, as it did briefly, but spectacularly, for the recently deposed junk-bond kings of Beverly Hills.

Secondly, elite genealogy in Los Angeles has reversed the typical American sequence of WASP dominance followed by Catholic and Jewish bids at power. Here the early preeminence of non-Protestant elites was superseded by a long era of WASP exclusionism as once cosmopolitan Los Angeles became, culturally and demographically, the most nativist and fundamentalist of big cities. The social and political purge of elite Jews in particular precipitated a bifurcated ruling class, perhaps unique in the United States.

Thirdly, the sprawling character of the city's modern development, which already by 1925 anticipated the general tendency of American urbanism in the 1960s, weakened the crucial spatial integuments of a centralized municipal Establishment. Since World War One, an increasingly self-identified Downtown elite has been trying to prevent power leaks outward and to reinforce the regional centrality of the old Central Business District. This has only led to an escalation of Darwinian place wars as new centers and their elites, from Century City to Orange County's Golden Triangle, have challenged the squirearchy of Downtown L.A. Moreover, the extreme political fragmentation of the metropolis, surpassing even Balkanized greater Chicago or Boston, has allowed powerful private interests to capture local governments for selfish use as tax-proof

THE TIMES'S MARTYRS CRYPT
Hollywood Cemetery

enclaves. This 'competitive marketplace of muncipalities' – celebrated by ultra-laissez-faire Public Choice theorists – has reduced the incentive for comprehensive elite organization on a regional scale.

Fourthly, the *internationalization of class formation* has recently made a quantum leap in Los Angeles beyond any other North American city. The most WASPish of big cities in 1960, Los Angeles now contains more poly-ethnic diversity than New York, with a huge manual working class of Latinos and a growing rentier stratum of Asian investors. On an elite level, Japanese capital, arriving like a *tsunami* in the early 1980s, has already become a discreet but major player in city politics. Meanwhile great waves of Chinese, Korean and Armenian middle-class immigrants, augmented by Israelis, Iranians, and others, have made Los Angeles the most dynamic center of ethnic family capitalism on the planet.

Finally, because mass politics are so extraordinarily stunted in Los Angeles, elite interest brokerage is transacted invisibly with minimum patronage costs or 'trickle-down' to inner-city or labor constituencies. Except for the periods immediately following the defeat of the open shop in the late 1930s and the Watts Rebellion of 1965, modern Los Angeles power structures have not had to respond to significant reformist pressures from the left. This is partly the perverse legacy of local, early-twentieth-century progressivism, which by eliminating partisan competition in city and county governments depreciated citizen participation. It is also the result of extreme racial gerrymandering, especially of the Chicano Eastside, which has historically diluted the political clout of the non-Anglo working class. More recently, the tide of undocumented immigration from Mexico and Central America has magnified the discrepancy between who labors and who votes. Despite the epochal demographic transition that has made Anglos a minority group in Los Angeles, the most significant constraint on elite decision-making comes from affluent Anglo homeowners (see chapter three) whose electoral weight is greater than ever.

Although other American cities betray some of these tendencies – that is, Faustian economic restructuring, social porosity, elite anti-semitism, central place competitions, internationalization of class formation, extreme political fragmentation, and disfranchisement of the inner city – none (to borrow the city's official slogan) 'brings it all together like Los Angeles'. The most permanent boomtown in American history, Los Angeles has always been 'the Great Gatsby of American cities'.[3] Through the ebb and flow of individual fortunes, the real city-making will of Los Angeles has been incarnated in a succession of power structures made coherent by common *accumulation strategies*, and distinguished by specific modes of insertion into the larger power structures of the Californian and national (today, international) economies. In almost every case, moreover, the new strategies and elites have been generated by restructurings of the political economy of land development. As a general rule, changing modes of land speculation have tended to determine the nature of Los Angeles's power structures.

In the genealogy that follows, I sketch a generational narrative of power elites framed within a tripartite periodization according to historically dominant modes of land development. First, in the century from the declaration of the Bear Flag Republic to the surrender of Japan – that is, across the long arc of Manifest Destiny – Los Angeles grew from an insignificant Mexican pueblo of fewer than three thousand souls to a metropolis of over three million. In this first century of Anglo rule, development remained fundamentally latifundian and ruling strata were organized as speculative land monopolies whose ultimate incarnation was the militarized power structure, established by General Otis, which controlled the city for almost three generations after 1889.

By the end of World War Two, however, it became impossible to speak of a single, hegemonic power structure, as Los Angeles was increasingly polarized between Downtown and Westside 'growth coalitions' with competing economic, political and cultural pretensions. In an era of 'Keynesian suburbanization', merchant building and home mortgage industries generated much of the Westside's rising power, while the Chandlerian Old Guard remained fixated on the redevelopment of their Downtown patrimonies. Although militant uprisings of the inner city encouraged a certain rapprochement between Jewish and gentile business leaderships (ironically represented in the 'liberal' Bradley regime), Los Angeles remained effectively a 'city with two heads' until the 1980s.

During the last decade increasing land scarcity has interacted with the arrival of Asian investment to initiate a far-reaching recomposition of traditional elites. As the second city of a vast Pacific Rim 'co-prosperity sphere' dominated by Tokyo, Los Angeles has become both imperium and colony. Parochial power struggles between Downtown and the Westside have been overshadowed by new geopolitics and land economics, leaving the problem of who will rule Los Angeles in the year 2000 a surprisingly open question.

SUNSHINE AND THE OPEN SHOP

SCHEMING SONS-IN-LAW (1840s–1850s)

If in Northern California the armies of goldseekers brutally overran the native *Californio* society, in the South the preferred weapon of conquest was marriage. The old *haciendados* of the Los Angeles region – the *gente de razón* whom we recall today principally by picturesque street names (Pico, Figueroa, Sepulveda, and so on) – were nonviolently dispossessed by their own scheming Yankee sons-in-law.

In the late 1820s, Mexican Alta California, particularly the rich rangelands around Missions San Gabriel and San Fernando which were the object of a protracted struggle between the Church and secularizing land-grantees, became a maritime colony of Boston. Hides from the great ranchos provided the leather for the shoe factories of New England's Industrial Revolution while Yankee traders furnished the rudiments of Victorian civilization to the remote Southern California coast. As clipper ships became a regular sight in the Catalina Channel, however, more than one sailor was enchanted by the possibilities of life ashore – especially by the lucrative opportunities to grasp the commercial intermediary roles disdained by the indigenous ranchers.

One of the earliest, and eventually the most successful, of these Yankee shipjumpers was 'Don' Abel Stearns, who arrived in the late 1820s and, after a politic conversion to Catholicism, became the son-in-law of Juan Bandini, a leading landowner. His Massachusetts compatriot, 'Juan' Temple, opened Los Angeles's first store and scored an even bigger coup by marrying the daughter of Manuel Nieto, the greatest cattle baron in the province, whose ranges extended from the San Gabriel to the Santa Ana rivers. A score of other Yankees, as well as a handful of vagabond Europeans, followed the matrimonial trail to fortune blazed by Stearns and Temple. By the eve of the Conquest, and before the arrival of any of Polk's dragoons, the economy of Southern California had already been decisively Americanized by intermarriage, with Stearns – looking in his daguerrotypes every inch the Old Testament patriarch – the wealthiest man in Alta California and the master of Los Angeles's foreign commerce.[4]

Although the decline of the hide trade and the War of Conquest temporarily depressed the rancho economy, the Gold Rush stimulated an almost insatiable demand for beef to feed one hundred thousand placer miners. As the price of range cattle increased from $2 to $50 per head, Stearns and the Anglo-Californians waxed in power and wealth. Then, during the Civil War, catastrophe struck: first, a devastating drought that left the bones of a million cattle bleaching the hillsides of Los Angeles County; secondly, the introduction of stockraising, using improved breeds, in the southern San Joaquin Valley by the famous cattle baron and land pirate, Henry Miller. Visionaries dreamt of vast irrigation works to revive the Southern California economy, but there was no local capital. Heavily in debt, with their stock destroyed, and trapped in decades-long litigation of their land titles, the *haciendados* began to lose control of their patrimonies.

NORTHERN CARPETBAGGERS (1860s–1870s)

The destruction of Southern California's cattle-based economy contrasted with the soaring wealth of San Francisco resulting from the silver bonanza in the Comstock and the building of the Central Pacific Railroad. While the Gold Rush itself failed to leave behind a well-defined California ruling class, the corporate exploitation of the Comstock and the federal railroad subsidies/landgrants created an independent pole of capital in San Francisco ruling over a Pacific Slope empire from the Aleutians to Baja. It was this fabled Medicean San Francisco – of 'Ralston's ring', the 'Big Four', and the 'Comstock Kings' – which, after the end of the Civil War, invaded the Los Angeles region and reshaped its economy.

San Francisco capital arrived in two separate contingents. Early in the Gold Rush days, German-Jewish merchants from Silesia and Alsace began to wrest control of Los Angeles's commerce from Stearns and the Anglo-Californians. By the late 1860s, when Isaias W. Hellman – destined to be Los Angeles's greatest Gilded Age financier – opened the doors of his first bank, these merchant families had integrated Southern California into a vast financial-commercial network spread across most of the West, controlled from San Francisco (usually via a division of labor between older and younger brothers), and linked internationally to capital centers in New York, Paris and Frankfurt.[5]

Exploiting the drought-induced collapse of land values to ten cents per acre (the entire assessed valuation of all of Los Angeles County was only $1,600,000 in 1863), a second stream of *nouveaux riches* Comstock millionaires and wealthy retainers of the Central Pacific Railroad began to buy up the bankrupt ranchos of the South.[6] The transition between eras and ruling groups was dramatically marked by the liquidation in 1868 of the ruined estate of Abel Stearns. A syndicate of San Francisco investors led by Alfred Robinson and Sam Brannan (the famous Mormon vigilante of the 1850s) subdivided the great domain stretching from San Pedro to San Bernardino. William Clary, historian of the O'Melveny legal dynasty which battened off the sale of the ranchos, points out that the Stearns sale 'set the pattern for all future California real-estate promotions. It was the first time that a systematic attempt was made to promote nationally the climatic and other attractions of Southern California.'[7]

Within a decade of the breakup of the Stearns empire, virtually every major landgrant (with the signal exception of the Dominquez rancho in the South Bay) had been alienated to Northern California interests: the Long Beach area to Bixby and Flint (who bought out Juan Temple), southern Orange County to Irvine and Flood (later, O'Neil), Catalina Island to Lick, a brace of ranches in the San Gabriel Valley to 'Lucky' Baldwin, the Santa Clara Valley of the South to Newhall, the southern San Fernando to Lankershim and Van Nuys, the northern San Fernando to the Porter brothers and McClay, while Senator Jones of Nevada became the 'father' of Santa Monica. Still lacking an irrigation infrastructure, there was little market for the sub-division of these vast holdings into farms. Forced to preserve their *latifundia* intact for another generation, the Northerners experimented with sheep raising, then, after wool prices slumped, with bonanza wheat and barley farming. This generated a novel maritime commerce for Los Angeles as flour from the San Fernando Valley was shipped around the Horn to Liverpool.

The chief profiteers from the sale of the ranchos were Isaias Hellman and his partner, ex-Governor John Downey, who through shrewd usury

THEY RULED THE VALLEY
Lankershim/Van Nuys needle, Evergreen Cemetery

during the drought years came to hold liens on the choicest properties. In 1871 they founded the Farmers and Merchants Bank which for thirty years was the city's leading financial center. The collaboration of Hellman and Downey, which survived even the former's capture of control of the bank in 1875, symbolized a broader ethnic coexistence. Many of the carpet-baggers were Irish (Downey, O'Neill, O'Melveny, Baldwin, and so on) and, interestingly, as in San Francisco they tended to form easy alliances with the German-Jewish merchant community. The two groups entrenched them-selves in the all-powerful local Democratic Party, and the Jews, in stark contrast to their exclusion in the next century, regularly participated in all the insignia of municipal power, from the city council to the vigilance committee's frequent 'necktie parties'. (Today, in the little Masonic Museum in El Pueblo Historical Park, a visitor can still find abundant evidence, in membership lists, period portraits and testimonials, of the ecumenical commingling of elites during the 1870s.)[8]

As Remi Nadeau has documented, the first coordinated initiative of this new ruling class – the centerpiece of their common accumulation strategy – was lobbying to make Los Angeles the primary rail center of the Southwest. After the collapse of the rancho economy, the city had been saved by its commerce with the silver camps of Cerro Gordo and the Panamint Mountains (near Death Valley). As the Southern Pacific built its way down the San Joaquin Valley in the early 1870s, Los Angeles leaders feared that one of the new Valley railheads might siphon off this essential bullion trade. Looking further ahead, the local backers of the Southern Pacific (SP), led by banker Hellman and lawyer O'Melveny, hoped to pre-empt San Diego's bid to become Southern California's transcontinental railroad terminus. Although the SP extorted extravagant land and cash subsidies to build a spur to the Los Angeles River, Hellman and O'Melveny overrode railroad critics with glittering visions of the prosperity imminently in the wake of the iron horse.[9]

OTIS AND THE BOOMERS (1880s–1910s)

The railroad was at first a cruel disappointment, demanding much in tribute and delivering little in new trade. While Los Angeles (population 11,183 in

1880) waited seven long years for the SP to complete its southern branch through New Orleans, local produce had to be routed through Ogden where fruit shipments perished in the cold of the high passes. As late as 1883, local seers envisioned a purely parochial future. Ostrich raising was still described as a 'prominent industry' and naturalist John Muir saw the region's best hope in beekeeping.[10]

The completion of the SP's Sunset Route in 1883, followed by the arrival of the competing Santa Fe in 1886, transformed the geographic and economic setting of Southern California. With immense investments tied up in their new transcontinental lines, and as the region's largest landowners, the railroads acquired a huge stake in the rapid development of Los Angeles and adjoining counties.[11] (Eager to show off the charms of its new fiefdom, the SP once offered Oscar Wilde a special train and private car if he would visit Los Angeles.) On a scale hitherto not dreamt possible, they created a growth blueprint based on the conversion of latifundian dry agriculture into subdivided irrigated horticulture. As Richard Orsi has emphasized, by the early 1880s the railroads were the 'leading patron[s] of scientific farming in California'. Citrus culture, especially, seemed an ideal development strategy: attracting thousands of affluent investors, raising land values, reinforcing the region's 'Mediterranean' image, promoting tourism, stimulating town-building, and, above all, dramatically raising the unit value of railroad shipments.[12]

To realize this vision the railroads allied their immigration and advertising departments, their land agents and tourist bureaux, to local promotional forces. As the SP and Santa Fe began a rate-cutting war in 1886, Los Angeles – a mystery-place to most Americans – suddenly became the urgent destination of around a hundred thousand land speculators and curious tourists. As the San José *Times-Mercury* complained: 'The average Eastern mind [now] conceives of California as a small tract of country situated in and about Los Angeles.'[13]

As we saw in the previous chapter, the boom of 1886–9 was a human frenzy not unlike the Gold Rush of 1849. A contemporary observer said 'it looked as if the whole human family were coming here to live "on climate and swapping corner lots"'.[14] In 1887 alone, two thousand real-estate agents transacted over $100 million in land sales (several times the region's previous net value), and sixty new towns were laid out, mostly along competing railroad routes.[15] Although the boom abruptly collapsed in 1889, turning many 'millionaires of a day' into paupers, it left behind an impressive infrastructure of irrigation districts and suburban traction companies (heavily financed by San Francisco and Chicago capital), as well as fifty thousand new residents.

The British vice-consul surveying the wreckage of the boom in early 1890 noted that the chief obstacle to Los Angeles's renewed growth was the pitiable state of its 'harbor', the wholly unimproved and unprotected anchorage at San Pedro. Conditions there were so bad, particularly during the season when the southeastern gales blew, that Los Angeles was forced to use New Orleans (via the Sunset Route) as an alternative port.[16] As historian William Issel has pointed out, it was the 'Free Harbor fight' during the 1890s – simultaneously waged for federal subsidies to improve San Pedro and against Southern Pacific's scheme for a captive port at Santa Monica – that 'stimulated the emergence of a group of leaders who rapidly came to regard themselves as the city's natural leadership class'.[17]

The chief organizer of the Free Harbor League, of course, was General Otis, who welded together the 'natural' ruling class of the 1890s, while simultaneously making the *Times* (the only one of four dailies to unequivocally support the municipal harbor) the leading paper in the region.[18] Many of the 'carpetbaggers' of the previous generation, like Lankershim, Cole and Slauson, who had sided with the SP, never recovered the power they lost as a result of the Free Harbor victory. Their successors included two very distinctive strata of newcomers. On the one hand were the professional developers working with the railroads – Hobart Whitley, Moses Sherman, Eli Clarke, H.L. Wilcox and so on – who had followed the Western land boom to its final frontier on the Pacific.[19] On the other hand was an odd coterie of refugee Easterners, mostly from Brahmin backgrounds, who whether from illness (Dwight Willard and Harry Chandler were consumptives), or from business failure (Otis, as we have seen, was a disappointed federal office-seeker), had come out to Los Angeles seeking their 'last chance'.

Although this composite elite was scarcely more than a defeated band of land speculators, under Otis's slogan of a 'New Beginning', they launched the most ambitious city-building program in American history. With the immodest ambition of surpassing San Francisco in a generation, they kept Los Angeles on a war footing – fully mobilized for self-promotion and improvement. Their chief allies, of course, remained the railroads, and it is indicative of transcendent common interests that, even while the Free Harbor League was battling the SP, the Chamber of Commerce (dominated by the same personages) was cooperating with the 'Octopus' to promote Los Angeles in the East. All sides agreed that the realization of the ultimate speculators' dream – the subdivision of the great Southern California *latifundia* – required the construction of an immense artificial infrastructure.

Critics (especially San Franciscans) mocked the hubris that declared Los Angeles 'one of the world's great cities in the making', yet within twenty years a Bismarckian municipal will – manifest in both public works and private monopoly – had created the world's biggest manmade port, aqueduct and inter-urban electric railroad system. The same iron will, as we have seen, also smashed the labor movement in Los Angeles with the aim of giving the Otis-organized Merchants and Manufacturers Association a competitive advantage over their regional rivals in union citadel San Francisco. Permanent class warfare also reinforced bourgeois political discipline. When middle-class Progressives (the Good Government League or 'Goos Goos') attempted to break away from the strictly 'Otistown' vision of Los Angeles's future, they were driven back into line by the dramatic 1909–12 electoral gains of the Socialist Party (which captured both working-class resentment against the open shop and anti-Progressive support from the Southern Pacific machine).[20]

In its inner logic this third-generation power structure resembled a McKinleyite version of the *Cosa Nostra*. At the pinnacle of regional power were two 'families' of speculators headed by rival 'godfathers'. On one side was the *Times* dynasty of Otis and his son-in-law Harry Chandler. On the other side, was the 'Pacific Electric mob': the alliance of Isaias Hellman and Henry Huntington, which also included San Francisco millionaires Christian de Guisne and Antoine Borel.[21] Hellman, the principal carry-over from the *ancien régime* of the 1870s, had moved to San Francisco in 1890 to run the Wells Fargo Bank, but continued, even at a distance, to dominate Los Angeles finance until his death in 1920. In particular he helped SP heir Huntington finance the consolidation of the region's suburban railroads into the fabled Pacific Electric system. Hellman and Huntington, two of the richest men in the West, loathed General Otis, and it is interesting to speculate what might have been the consequence of an all-out war between their rival factions.

Instead, the godfathers kept the peace by sharing with each other the super-profits of Los Angeles's next boom. Manipulating water politics and captive city officials, Otis, Chandler, Hellman and Huntington – along with a score of other leading capitalists (including even Christian Socialist John Randolph Haynes) – joined in syndicates to monopolize the subdivision of Hollywood, the San Fernando Valley and much of northeastern Los Angeles. As Towne and Polanski's *Chinatown* suggests (in a history more syncretic than fictional), the windfall profits of these operations welded the ruling class together and capitalized lineages of power (notably, the *Times-Mirror* empire) that remain in place today.

HARRY CHANDLER'S TOWN (1920s–1940s)

After the death of Otis in 1917, Harry Chandler – sitting on more than fifty corporation boards – emerged as the unquestioned leader of L.A.'s fourth-generation Anglo power structure, 'the generalissimo of the forces that engineered the great postwar boom'.[22] Indeed Los Angeles in the 1920s was in many respects a de facto dictatorship of the *Times* and the Merchants and Manufacturers Association, as the LAPD's infamous 'red squad' kept dissent off the streets and radicals in jail.[23] The social base of this authoritarian regime was the great influx of Middle Western babbitry between 1900 and 1925 – one of the great internal migrations of American history. In an era when transatlantic immigration was making most big US cities more foreign-born, Catholic and Jewish, Los Angeles's non-Protestant white population was in relative decline. Moreover the new WASP ascendency found its essential economic support in the arrival of Mexican labor in massive numbers after the fall of the Porfiriato in 1910. Evoking Los Angeles in 1920, Robert Fogelson describes an ethnic polarization which, except for the dramatic reversal between majority and minority populations, prefigured the city of the 1990s:

WATER IS POWER
Los Angeles Aqueduct (1913), San Francisquito Canyon

Unlike most eastern and midwestern metropolises, which were divided between native Americans and European immigrants, Los Angeles was divided between an overwhelming native white majority and a sizable colored minority. Nowhere on the Pacific coast, not even in cosmopolitan San Francisco, was there so diverse a mixture of racial groups, so visible a contrast and so pronounced a separation among people, in the 1920s.[24]

One of the first casualties of this recomposition of demography and power was the integrated social status of Los Angeles Jews. By the early 1900s elite Jews, including the pioneer dynasties of the 1840s and 1850s, were being excluded from the corporate directorships, law firms, philanthropies and clubs that in many cases they had helped to establish.[25] At the same time Jewish financial preeminence, represented by Hellman's Farmers and Merchants Bank (which also regrouped remnants of the 1870s gentile elite), declined in face of the steady rise of the regional branch banking empires led by Joseph Sartori (Security Bank) and Henry Robinson (First National). The Jewish old guard, faced with growing anti-semitism on all sides, began a defensive withdrawal into its own segregated elite culture (represented first by the Concordia Club, followed by the Hillcrest Country Club).

Catholic capitalists, interdependent with the local Democratic machine, also retreated in the face of the economic hegemony of the Chandler clique and the political supremacy of militant Protestantism. The once mighty Southern California Democratic party – led in its 1890s heyday by Senator Stephen White, the hero of the 'free harbor' fight – was reduced to quarrelsome, ineffectual cabals in the era of one-party, Republican government. Its fractious disarray exposed the competition of several sub-elites, divided by religion and petroleum. Thus on one side was the Catholic rump of the old party machine, led by Isidore Dockweiler, railroad lawyer and holdover from the days of the SP 'Octopus'. On the other side was a gaggle of Wilsonian carpetbaggers who had moved to Los Angeles during the early 1920s real-estate and oil booms in the hope of repairing their fallen fortunes. They were led by the late president's son-in-law, William Gibbs McAdoo who, driven from New York by the popularity of Al Smith, mobilized a constituency of Southern Democrats, ex-Bryanites, and the Ku Klux Klan (then waxing in power throughout Southern California). Although oil man Edward Doheny (of Teapot Dome infamy) was the most prominent Catholic in Los Angeles, he heavily financed McAdoo, presumably because the latter was even more passionately 'pro-oil' than anti-Catholic. (At the 1924 Democratic convention, 'Smith supporters in the balcony constantly jeered "Oil, Oil, Oil" at every mention of McAdoo'.)[26]

Indeed Southern California in the oil-crazed 1920s was a land of blue-eyed sheiks, some of whom formed a new stratum of the Chandlerian ruling class, while others ended up filling cells in San Quentin.[27] But even oil speculation, in the fiercely anti-semitic climate of the period, was organized via the financial equivalents of restrictive covenants or segregated drinking fountains. During the Julian Petroleum frenzy, the biggest and phoniest of the promotions, separate stock pools were set aside for Jewish and gentile capital. Unsurprisingly when the bubble burst, and the underlying swindle was exposed, wiping out thousands of investors and plunging Southern California into a recession, the prosecution focused on a few Jewish scape-goats, refusing to follow obvious leads pointing (as we saw in the last chapter) to banker Henry Robinson and other members of the WASP establishment.[28]

As a school for scandal, only the Downtown construction boom rivaled the oil rush. When the Otis–Chandler–Hellman–Huntington syndicates bought out the *latifundistas* of the San Fernando Valley, the latter plowed their capital gains into Downtown real estate. Their eponymous skyscrapers (the Van Nuys, Lankershim, San Fernando, and so on.) dominated the skyline until the early 1920s when, in turn, the fourth generation began to shift the spoils of their suburban speculations into a new expansion of Downtown. Chandler led the syndicates that financed the Biltmore Hotel (with Letts and the Chaffeys) and the Subway Terminal Building (with Sartori), as well as promoting improvements (Coliseum, Union Station, Civic Center, and so on) that reinforced Downtown property values in general.[29]

But neither the oil nor Downtown booms – nor, for that matter, oranges and movies – provided an adequate economic foundation for Los Angeles's dramatic ascent during the 1920s to become the nation's fourth largest metropolitan district. Homegrown wealth and commerce were insufficient to support the region's lavish superstructures of consumption, tertiary employment and geriatrics. As Upton Sinclair noted, Los Angeles was fundamentally 'parasitic' on prosperity produced in other regions – a kind of 'cloud society', like Swift's Laputa, levitated by the influx of wealthy migrants and retirees from the Heartland.[30]

Chandler and other fourth-generation leaders, like Sartori and Robinson, were acutely aware that the real-estate growth machine created by the previous generation required continuous transfers of savings from the rest of the country. Although the All Year Club under Chandler's directorship launched a massive campaign in the 1920s to keep affluent immigrants and tourists coming westward, there was universal elite agreement that what Los Angeles needed most was industry. As the *Times* itself polemicized:

Los Angeles has existed for too long with an economic base of local real estate and building interests. We need more factories, new industries, and more interstate commerce and the development of foreign trade.[31]

With the *Times*'s proprietor again in the saddle, the Open Shop forces crusaded to attract Eastern corporations to Los Angeles's 'sunny land of industrial freedom'. By 1930 they had wooed scores of corporate branch plants and nearly 50,000 new manufacturing jobs to the county.[32]

Yet the Chandlerian power structure was ultimately defeated by its own successes. Each of its major accumulation strategies – that is, the recapitalization of Downtown and the promotion of branch-plant industry – brought unexpected consequences that weakened or diffused its hegemony. For example, the conversion of so much of the elite's patrimony into Downtown real estate failed to anticipate the centrifugal influence of Southern California's precocious automobilization, which already by 1925 had attained a density (one car per 1.6 persons) which the rest of the nation would not reach until the late 1950s. By entangling Downtown streetcar lines in a gridlocked conflict over right of way, while simultaneously offering harassed commuters the option of virtually unlimited personal mobility outside the central business district, the automobile subverted Downtown's central-place monopoly and created wind fall-profit opportunities for the developers of the first suburban, auto-centered shopping complexes.[33]

Indeed by the late 1920s Downtown forces were embroiled in a losing battle to prevent A.W. Ross from establishing his 'Miracle Mile' on Wilshire

Boulevard's Westside. While middle-class suburbanization in the direction of the ocean began to disperse traditional Central Business District (CBD) functions along a Wilshire axis (Downtown's share of retail trade plummeting from 90 per cent in 1920 to 17 per cent in 1950), the inclusive real-estate syndicate system – so essential to elite cohesion in the previous generation – collapsed. Just as the city became more decentralized, so too did control over its major profit-making activity, the subdivision of the suburban frontier. The fourth-generation elite – now self-consciously defined as a 'Downtown Establishment' – would struggle in vain for the next forty years to 'recenter' growth around their enormous fixed investments in the CBD.[34]

Industrialization undermined their power in more subtle ways. The branch plants were the *maquiladoras* of the 1920s: usually located in manufacturing zones outside the city limits and assembling parts shipped in from the East. Save for Chandler's ties to Donald Douglas and Warner Brothers, Frederic Jaher has found little evidence of the integration of local and outside capital:

In fact, the major financing and the direction of these ventures emanated usually from banks and corporations based mostly on the Atlantic coast. [Likewise] half the oil industry production was controlled by huge national corporations and the leading independents were run largely by recent arrivals.[35]

'Hollywood' (encompassing also the movie enclaves in Burbank, Universal City and Culver City) exemplified this growing disjuncture between regional economic power and the Downtown-oriented elite. The most important fact about the movie colony was not so much its financial domination by Wall Street and the Bank of Italy, but simply that it was headed by Eastern European Jews who, despite their legendary wealth and conservative politics, could not play golf or send their kids to the same schools with the Chandlerian elite. Even Louis B. Mayer, during the 1930s the chairman of the California Republican Party and the highest paid executive in the United States, was excluded from social inner sanctums enjoyed by middle-level WASP realtors and used-car dealers.[36]

The *hochdeutsche* Jewish clans like the Hellmans and Newmarks were initially disdainful of Hollywood's vulgar *nouveaux riches*, but they were gradually reconciled by the common pressures of anti-semitism and the reinvigorating wealth of the movie moguls. The Hillcrest Country Club, founded in 1920 on the edge of Beverly Hills and the Fox studios, was the melting pot of new and old Jewish elites, where the ingredients for a future 'Westside' power structure were first combined. As Neal Gabler explains:

The Hollywood Jews at Hillcrest were also rearranging the power configurations within the Jewish community. Hillcrest not only signified the grudging acceptance of the Hollywood Jews by the German Jews, whose power was, in any case, declining by the time the Depression hit; Hillcrest forged an alliance between these groups.[37]

A CITY WITH TWO HEADS

The enclave manufacturing economy proved to be the Trojan Horse of Otistown: as early as 1927, Hollywood opened a breach in employer ranks by accepting the Studio Master Agreement with unions; later, auto and tire branch plants would impose national contracts and labor standards. The Open Shop, in any case, was being closed down by a strange municipal reform movement that united latterday 'Goos Goos' with the CIO to sweep away civic corruption *and* anti-picketing laws. Despite dire warnings from the 'Better America Federation' and other fronts for the Merchants and Manufacturers Association that unionization would turn Los Angeles back into a desert, the war in the Pacific arrived in time to bring the region its real industrial revolution.

Although it is doubtful if Harry Chandler or any of his wealthy friends recognized much in the name 'Keynes' beyond the dimly perceived bugaboo of 'British Socialism', the Los Angeles economy in the 1940s was being 'Keynesianized' in its own peculiar fashion. First, the inter-regional capital flows that had been the source of Southern California's prosperity were now institutionalized in national defense appropriations that shifted tax resources from the rest of the country to irrigate the Los Angeles area's air-craft plants and military bases: a huge regional subsidy that in later years was estimated to average $17–20 billion per annum.[38]

Secondly, the land-conversion process, already raised to an economy of scale by prewar syndicates and developers, was now transformed into a true mass production industry. Federally guaranteed mortgages, veterans benefits, and a protected savings-and-loan sector – along with the higher wages of the aircraft plants – provided a stable mass demand for the products of local 'merchant builders' who industrialized land-assembly and construction in the infant suburbs of the San Fernando Valley and the southeastern coastal plain.

These new structures of accumulation transformed conditions for the reproduction of elite power. The militarization of the Los Angeles economy conferred the largest single quotient of economic power upon enclaved aircraft corporations, financed from Wall Street and historically indifferent to the fate of Downtown. At the same time, the strategic position of the savings-and-loan industry within the postwar housing revolution opened up new power roles for ethnic and political outsiders. Fortunately, Harry Chandler, who died in 1944 at age eighty, wasn't around to witness the slow unravelling of his *ancien régime*.

THE WESTSIDE EMERGES (1950s)

In the reconversion period (1944–7) the Chandlerian generation of Downtown leaders began to be replaced by their sons and protégés. The most prominent circle had been chums of Norman Chandler since college days in the 1920s: Bud Haldeman (whose father was an open-shop leader and whose son would star in Watergate), Preston Hotchkis (the Bixby Ranch heir), John McCone (future CIA chief) and Reese Taylor (eventually president of Union Oil). But these grandsons of the nineteenth-century boosters would not themselves be the architects of the great suburban boom of the 1950s. Their structural position in the Southern California economy was increasingly that of a classical rentier stratum, preoccupied with the cultivation of patrimonies, especially their common stake in Downtown. Moreover, the 'tired blood' or 'spoiled rich boy' syndrome, which seemingly afflicts all dynasties after the second generation, made them dependent upon their fathers' henchmen or their wives.

Indeed the actual direction of the affairs of the Downtown elite during the 1950s was a hybrid of matriarchy and regency. Norman Chandler, although nominally the heir to the throne, left the generalship of protracted struggles to his father's chief proxy, Kyle Palmer (whom David Halberstam judged 'the political boss of California' between 1930 and 1960), or, alternately, to his ambitious wife Buffy. (According to Halberstam, Buffy learned about power dealing literally through listening at the keyhole as her father-in-law did business with Herbert Hoover.)[39] Another one of Harry Chandler's old associates, insurance executive Asa Call, also played 'Mr Big' roles opposite Palmer and Mrs Chandler. He was usually assisted by O'Melveny and Myers's partner James Lin Beebe and furniture merchant Neil Petree. Later, when the Republican elite began to split up between 'Old Right' and 'New Right' wings, oilman Henry Salvatori emerged as the *éminence grise* of the most conservative camp.

This sclerotic power bloc, increasingly reliant upon a Ptolemaic system of lobbyists and retainers, made three major moves in the late 1940s and 1950s to repair its declining hegemony. First, Beebe and Petree, as heads of the Chamber of Commerce's powerful Traffic and Transit Committee, launched a plan in 1948 to integrate rail rapid transit into a radial, Downtown-centered freeway grid. The Chamber's aim was to protect CBD property values by reinforcing Downtown's transit centrality – in this case, to capture the retail trade of the burgeoning San Fernando Valley before another entrepreneur repeated A.W. Ross's 1920s feat of creating an alternative suburban shopping complex.

Although 'Rail Rapid Transit – Now!' was endorsed by hundreds of Downtown businessmen as well as by larger San Fernando Valley developers, it was condemned as 'socialistic' by a counter-coalition composed of Westside developers, outlying commercial interests (including the proprietors of the new Crenshaw Shopping Center), the Wilshire and Miracle Mile Chambers of Commerce, the Los Angeles Realty Board, and independent cities like Long Beach and Santa Monica. In the end, this suburban united front turned a narrow majority of the City Council against the Chamber's plan – 'an astonishing defeat' of Downtown leadership in the opinion of the episode's historian.[40]

Aided by local McCarthyism, the Old Guard was more successful in 1953 in restoring a pliant, *Times*-dominated regime in City Hall. The pretext of their municipal counter-revolution was the 'creeping socialism' (their turn to make the accusation) of Mayor Fletcher Bowron's low-rent public housing program, especially where it cut across elite plans for

Downtown – as in Chavez Ravine, or, potentially, Bunker Hill. What Bowron would latter denounce as 'a small, immensely wealthy, incredibly powerful group' – i.e., Chandler, Call, Petree and Beebe – drafted right-wing Congressman Norris Poulson as the torch-bearer of their crusade against 'socialism'. According to Gottlieb and Wolt, Poulson accepted the nomination only after being assured by Chandler that the mayor was 'entitled to strut around in a Cadillac and chauffeur supplied by the city'. With Norman Chandler's editorial pages pounding away at Bolshevism and public housing, Poulson got his ride in the Cadillac. Within a few years, the *Times*-made mayor, in return, gave the Downtown interests what they really wanted: the removal of 12,000 low-income residents to pave the way for Bunker Hill redevelopment and Dodger Stadium in Chavez Ravine.[41]

Exhilarated by their easy recapture of City Hall, Chandler, Palmer, Call and company combined forces with their traditional ally, the Knowland dynasty of Oakland, to carry the counter-revolution statewide in 1958. The traditional *bête noir* of Old Guard Republicanism in California was less the Democratic Party than the hugely popular, labor-supported and welfarist regime of liberal Republican Governor Earl Warren (1942–54). Partially to block Warren's presidential ambitions, the Old Guard, led by Kyle Palmer and Norman Chandler, engineered the rise of Richard Nixon from Congress to vice-presidency.[42]

After Warren's elevation to the Supreme Court, Chandler–Knowland forces focused on trimming the wings of his moderate Republican successor, Goodwyn Knight. Their strategy was to force Knight to trade positions with Senator William Knowland, who would then use the sup- posedly stronger base of the governor's mansion for a presidential bid in 1960. In tandem with the Knowland campaign, moreover, was a right-to- work initiative which featured hysterical denunciations of 'Walter Reuther's threat to California'. This blatant, overweening attempt to restore the Open Shop backfired in a historic Democratic landslide led by Pat Brown that buried Old Guard Republicanism forever.

Most shockingly for Los Angeles's Downtown elite, the 1958 Republican debacle also signalled the emergence of Westside power centers willing and able to contest their historical monopoly on statewide political influence. One of the Old Guard's chief grievances with Governor Knight, together with his 'coddling of labor', was his reliance upon the support of

Westside savings-and-loan king Howard Ahmanson. Reputedly the richest man in California, Ahmanson was despised for, apart from his Jewishness, being a 'pink Republican – too rich to be a Democrat and too liberal to be a true Republican'. Knight's attempt to depose state Republican finance chief Asa Call (L.A.'s Mr Big) and replace him with Ahmanson had provoked a final break between the two wings of the party.[43]

Yet, while Ahmanson was Knight's financial right hand, he was also quietly bankrolling Jesse Unruh, a liberal Democratic assemblyman from Southcentral Los Angeles who had intimate connections with younger Jewish Democrats on the Westside. When Knight was humiliatingly forced to cede the gubernatorial candidacy to Knowland, Ahmanson paid Unruh's salary to run Pat Brown's highly successful Southern California campaign. This was the beginning of the celebrated 'Ahmanson–Unruh system', wherby Westside money (Bart Lytton of Beverly Hills was another major contributor) provided Unruh with the 'juice' to capture the Speakership and eventual control of the Legislature. With 'Big Daddy' Unruh strategically dispursing savings-and-loan money to younger Democratic candidates, much of the party's ostensible 'liberal wing' became a satellite of Los Angeles's *nouveaux riches*.[44]

Where did the money to buy such power come from? Although some of the new wealth on the Westside arose from the military aerospace boom of the later 1950s, the locus of power, as in previous generations, remained real-estate speculation. But, as we have stressed, the game was now played within the new rules of Keynesian suburbanization set by the FHA and Fannie Mae. Two rising groups of entrepreneurs dominated the 1950s building boom from their Westside headquarters outside the radius of Downtown power. First were the merchant builders, mostly 1940s newcomers, like Nate Shapell, Larry Weinberg, Louis Boyar, Ray Watt, Bill Lyon, and (later) Eli Broad. Secondly were the savings-and-loan empires that funneled mortgage capital from all over the country to Southern California homebuilders. In the 1950s this was an extraordinarily dynamic industry with a deposit base growing 21 per cent per annum. The preeminent local firms were Ahmanson's Home Federal Savings (number one in the USA) and Mark Taper's First Charter Corporation (number three). Moreover the building and savings-and-loan sectors were complexly integrated by strategic combinations (for instance, Taper's alliance with Boyar and

Weinberg to mass-produce the suburb of Lakewood) as well as by the massive reinvestment of builders' profits in the thrift industry.[45]

The rise of this boom-fueled, federally subsidized building-and-thrift complex on the Westside shifted the ethnic and geographic axes of regional power. Before World War Two only a handful of large developers (most notably Joseph Toplitzky) had been Jewish; after the war, abetted by Jewish immigration to the Westside and Valley, suburb development became virtually a Jewish-dominated industry at both the construction and financial ends. As Vorspan and Gartner note, 'The Jewish builder replaced the Jewish film magnate as the entrepreneur par excellence.'[46] But the builders were less rivals than communal reinforcements to the second-generation studio heirs and movie producers gathered around the Hillcrest Country Club. With the building-and-thrift and entertainment sectors as two pillars, a growing sportswear industry (financed and integrated by the Jewish-owned Union Bank) completed the tripod of *landsman* economic power. Moreover, as we saw in the last chapter, in a decade when Downtown construction had virtually ceased, the Westside building boom – whether represented by hillside homes or new savings-and-loan headquarters – generalized architectural Modernism as a distinctive emblem of the Westside society dominated by the Jewish elites. Although other American cities may have had plural elites or competing cliques, none could claim a situation so dichotomous, on so many levels, as the separate upper-class universes of Downtown and the Westside.

RESPONDING TO URBAN CRISIS (1960s–1970s)

A city with two power structures, however, is like a beast with two heads. As the 1960s dawned, Los Angeles was divided in direction and torn in loyalty. Increasingly, Downtown redevelopment and Westside expansion appeared as zero-sum games, with the possibility that the real leadership of the city would be wrested away by the younger and more dynamic West-siders. Moreover the Old Guard restoration in City Hall under Poulson was first hollowed out by increasing suburban representation on the City Council, and then overthrown entirely by the unexpected victory of Sam Yorty in the 1961 mayoral election.

Yorty – the most notorious perennial candidate in California politics – beat Poulson by appealing histrionically to a variety of suburban discontents ranging from trash separation ('the oppression of the housewife') to over-taxation. Although inveighing against the *Times* and the 'Downtown establishment', Yorty – a renegade Democrat rapidly moving toward the right – had no evident connection to the Westside power structure. Rather, he won as a filibuster exploiting an accumulation of anti-elite resentments in the electorate.

One of his main campaign pledges, directed to win votes in South-central L.A., had been to fire Chief Parker of the Los Angeles Police Department (LAPD), an avowed white supremacist held responsible by Los Angeles Blacks for a police reign of terror. Instead, Yorty threw his weight behind the police and the growing white resistance to civil rights demands (exemplified by a 1964 initiative repealing California's new open housing law). A major consequence of this combination of white repression and intransigence was the Watts Rebellion of 1965. As arson fires crept perilously close to the southern edge of the CBD, and National Guard troops occupied the social-register USC campus, Downtown business leaders contemplated the possible ruin of their redevelopment strategy.

If on one hand, they confronted the McCone Commission's prediction 'that by 1990 the core of the Central City of Los Angeles will be inhabited almost exclusively by more than 1,200,000 Negroes',[47] on the other, they faced the competition of the Westside's new 'downtown' – the Century City complex near Beverly Hills. Nervous mortgage bankers and leasing agents started talking about a wholesale corporate defection westward, even the 'death of Downtown'. Such apocalyptic talk, in the wake of the uprising of the inner city, galvanized the Old Guard into action (as Régis Debray once put it, 'revolutions revolutionize counter-revolutions').

According to Wolt and Gottlieb, Daniel Bryant of Bekins convinced Asa Call to convene a discreet steering committee of Downtown's biggest corporations, known as the Committee of 25, and including Norman Chandler, Neil Petree, Henry Salvatori, Wiliam French Smith (later Reagan's attorney general), Norman Topping (of the University of Southern California), and John McCone (who chaired the commission on the riots which whitewashed the LAPD's role and raised alarmist images of Black power). The Committee of 25 was intended to function as a shadow government of the chief burghers, bringing their consensual opinion to bear upon the mayor and the council. (We shall consider in a later chapter how the elite 'militarized' Downtown redevelopment in response to Watts.)[48]

But this secretive group was rent by divisions over fundamental strategy. First, should they endorse the politics of racial polarization by supporting Yorty? Secondly, should the Committee of 25 be broadened to include representatives from the Westside Jewish power structure? On both scores, the Chandler dynasty, now officially led by Norman's son Otis, broke ranks with the majority of the Old Guard. As we saw in the last chapter, Otis's mother Buffy had long encouraged *rapprochement* with Westside society – a stance, incidentally, that mirrored the *Times*'s increasing orientation to affluent groups within the entire region. Now the Chandlers, to the horror of California Club types and John-Birchite members of their own family clan, joined with once-despised 'Westside liberals' to support the unsuccessful 1969 mayoral challenge of Black councilman Thomas Bradley, while the rest of the Committee of 25 backed Yorty's vicious, race-baiting campaign.[49]

The schism in the Downtown power structure wrought by the *Times*'s creeping liberalization opened the way for complex realignments. As the city languished through its first aerospace recession and third Yorty term, a group of prominent Westside Jewish liberals, led by the so-called 'Malibu Mafia' (Max Palevsky, Harold Willens and Stanley Sheinbaum), undertook to create a broader and more affluent support base for Bradley's rematch with Yorty. With multi-millionaire Palevsky as chair of the campaign, political consultant David Garth was imported from New York to co-ordinate a media blitz using Hollywood stars, priests and rabbis. Meanwhile, Westside Democratic chieftains like Paul Ziffren, Grey Davis and Nelson Rising tapped money sources usually reserved for crucial national or state campaigns, while a comprehensive grassroots effort was organized by liberals and Black ministers. The *Times* hammered the final nails in Yorty's coffin with a series of denunciatory editorials.

Bitter anti-Bradley forces blamed Yorty's defeat on this unholy convergence of Westside money and the editorial power of the Chandlers. In the eyes of many Central City Association types, Bradley, if not quite the 'Black Panther' or 'Communist' decried by Yorty, was, at the very least, a 'militant' and stooge for Jewish Westside Democracy. A particular sore point was the new mayor's chief deputy, Maury Weiner, a talented left-liberal rumoured to be a 'fellow-traveler'. Relations between City Hall and the Committee of 25 considerably improved, however, after Weiner was destroyed by a vice arrest politically engineered by the LAPD. His replacement was a Pasadena Republican, Ray Remy (later head of the Los Angeles Chamber of Commerce) who smoothed communications between the mayor – rapidly showing himself to be a cautious moderate – and the Downtown establishment.[50]

What eventually emerged, transcending the mass politics of Bradley's coalition between Southcentral and West Los Angeles, was an intricate citywide accommodation of elites. Bradley won over a hostile Committee of 25 with his promotion of Downtown redevelopment, rather than community development in Watts and East L.A., as the showpiece program of his administration. Bradley supporters who had expected dramatic initiatives to address inner-city poverty and unemployment were shocked as mayoral taskforces headed by Asa Call, Philip Hawley (Broadway stores) and Red Schnell (Prudential Insurance) set corporate-oriented economic development and transportation goals. By year three of the Bradley era even Henry Salvatore (godfather to Goldwater and Reagan) was forking out contributions to the mayor while the Chamber of Commerce sang the praises of an administration that it had originally denounced.[51]

The Westside power structure, which in the 1980s would take its distance from Bradley and his CBD-oriented policies, initially welcomed the new dispensation that forced Downtown leaders to negotiate the city's future with them. Although the influence of the liberal 'Malibu Mafia' rapidly faded in City Hall, their place was taken by Lew Wasserman of MCA – Ronald Reagan's agent and Hollywood's last tycoon. Bradley's role as a bridge between Los Angeles's two elite cultures was symbolized by an extraordinary 1975 fundraiser on his behalf that was jointly hosted by Wasserman and Asa Call – the Mr Bigs of their respective halves of the city.[52] If not a reconciliation, it was at least a consummation.

THE NEW SPRAWL OF POWER

The black-tie, elite 'Woodstock' of the Wasserman–Call dinner was also a last hurrah. From the late 1970s the narrative of power in Los Angeles gradually ceased to be a Harold Robbins potboiler about Downtown versus the Westside. Certainly such antagonisms remain, but the older social establishments have dramatically shrunk in importance as new power configurations have emerged, shaped by the extraordinary economic forces of the 1980s. The scale of the power dispersal that has occurred over the last fifteen years can be illustrated by the muckraking research of Robert Gottlieb (now an eminent authority on California water) in the mid 1970s. In various pamphlets as well as in his massive history of the *Times* (with Irene Wolt), Gottlieb was able to draw a detailed map of how power in Los Angeles was distributed between the Downtown and Westside establishments which I have discussed in previous pages.[53]

To draw a similar power map of Los Angeles in 1990, with the same confident coordinates as a guide to the stars' homes, is virtually impossible. We are living through a comparatively rare event (although, as we have seen, more common in Los Angeles than elsewhere), a genuine 'revolution from above', as elites are reshuffled and new power centers consolidated. Amongst the great US cities perhaps only Los Angeles – with its social porosity, spatial poly-centricity and adjacency to the Pacific Rim – is currently susceptible to such an upheaval in its higher circles.

For example there has been a dramatic increase in the number of major individual players and their mobilized wealth. Donald Bren, Marvin Davis, the Kobayashi Family, Donald Trump – not to mention the fallen Michael Milken – are billionaire dealmakers who in a day's work routinely break up or assemble aggregations of capital equivalent to the entire patrimonies of Old Guard families. And 'offshore' capital, not just the Japanese but the Chinese, Koreans, Canadians and Manhattanites as well, now have the capacity, in the context of Los Angeles's wide-open economy, to suddenly transform any scenario by huge buy-outs or injections of new investments (witness Shuwa's billion-dollar landing in Downtown in 1976 or Trump's sudden arrival in 1990).

This current volatility of power is best understood in light of what might be characterized as the 'post-Keynesian' transformation of the Los Angeles economy.[54] A Dickensian social polarization between rich and poor (discussed at length in latter chapters) has been the single most dramatic cause/effect expression of this transition, but three other large-scale processes are equally notable. First has been the conversion of the tract lot – the basic input of Los Angeles's major 'mass production' industry – into a luxury good affordable only by a shrinking minority of local residents. Second has been the rise of a new economic geometry that is turning Los Angeles's old suburban belts into 'outer cities' in their own right. Third has been the internationalization of the regional economy, which makes Los Angeles elites tributary to the great financial centers in Shinjuku and Lower Manhattan.

How have the traditional Southern California power blocs responded to these epochal changes? We still remain too much within the maelstrom of restructuring to offer a summary judgment. Instead, four brief case studies suggest some tentative theses about the relationship between old elites and new realities: first, the re-monopolization of land development; second, the Japanese colonization of Downtown; third, the *Times*'s attempt to 'regionalize' its circulation and influence; and fourth, the complex combination of generational succession and foreign takeover in Hollywood.

THE NEW OCTOPUS

For two generations between 1870 and 1910, a period that Progressives regarded as California's 'dark ages', the almighty Southern Pacific Railroad (Frank Norris's 'Octopus') acted behind the scenes of both major parties to dictate state politics from the governor's mansion to City Hall. As Californians used to learn in school, Hiram Johnson's Progressive 'revolution' of 1910 – which smashed the SP machine in Sacramento – was designed to prevent any private economic combination from ever again controlling the state. Yet in the 1980s an invisible third party emerged that recapitulates, perhaps even exceeds, the influence of the SP machine in its heyday, and which, like the Octopus, operates across partisan boundaries at every level of government.

This ascendent power is a re-monopolized land development industry. It is 're-monopolized' in the sense that urban development has been re-integrated around speculative land ownership in a mode that differs strikingly from what was described earlier as the 'Keynesian suburban-ization' of the 1950s and early 1960s. In those days the crucial liaison was between the merchant builder and the thrift financier; land was relatively cheap and easily assembled from thousands of small orchard and farm owners. The supply of money not land was the crucial variable in determining the power structure of development.

As we shall see in more detail in the next chapter, all this started changing during the Vietnam boom as developable coastal land – the raw material of the Southern California dream – began to disappear. Resulting land inflation, which went ballistic in the late 1970s and again in the late 1980s, profoundly reshaped the distribution of wealth and opportunity. Relative land scarcity also led to a rapid decline of 'mom and pop' builders, soon followed by the middle strata of developers. Control over land conversion has been increasingly centralized in huge companies capable of banking scarce remaining blocs of coastal plain, or financing whole new residential or industrial cities in distant interior basins.

In the Los Angeles region this 'new Octopus' – monopolizing the development of the metropolitan edge and the infill of 'holes' in the core – consists of three distinct, although interlocking, types of enterprise.

First, a handful of great land bankers, some the direct heirs of nineteenth-century *latifundistas*, monopolize community and industrial development in southern Orange, southwestern and northern Los Angeles counties: the Mission Viejo/Santa Margarita Ranch group (the Flood–O'Neill patrimony alienated to Philip Morris in the 1970s); the Irvine Ranch (now Donald Bren); C.J. Segerstrom & Sons (whose bean field has become the 'postmodern downtown' around South Coast Plaza in Costa Mesa); Watson Land Company (the Dominguez legacy in the Carson 'zaibatsu alley' area); and the Newhall Land and Farming Company (developers of Santa Clarita and Canyon County).

Second, about fifteen or twenty 'community builders', based primarily in Orange County or on the Westside of Los Angeles, and including many of the key Jewish firms of the 1950s, dominate the remaining frontiers of 'starter homes' in the Inland Empire (western Riverside and San Bernardino counties) and the Antelope Valley: Lewis Homes, Kaufman and Broad, the Lusk Company, Goldrich and Krest, Shapell Industries, Watt Industries, and so on. To this category should also be added the principal developers of outlying commercial and industrial centers: Koll Company, the Haagen Company, Ahmanson Commercial Company, and others.

Third, many members of the California Business Roundtable have discovered, in an era of skyrocketing land values and corporate raiding, that their landholdings are now amongst their most valuable, and liquidifiable, assets. Thus land-intensive industries have led the way to become major developers in their own right: aerospace (Hughes/Summa at Westchester and Playa del Rey, Douglas at Santa Monica and Long Beach), entertainment (MCA and Disney in the Valley), energy (Chevron at Ontario), and transportation (Union Pacific at Fox Hills, and Southern Pacific in western San Bernardino County) – to give a very partial list.

Not surprisingly, land development is still Southern California's most lucrative large industry with annual profit margins as high as 50 per cent (contrasted to the 12–18 per cent profits of the oil industry at the height of the last boom).[55] The giant Irvine Ranch in Orange County – 'nearly five times larger than the island of Manhattan . . . [and] the largest private real estate holding in a major US metropolitan area' – is perhaps the best example of the wages of land monopoly. Although the ranch is an unfolding fifty-year plan of private urbanization (including the 'utopian' city of Irvine, an adjacent University of California campus, and the world's largest office-and-science park), it earns fabulous profits simply by leaving its rare land to age on site like fine wine. Thus as land values in Irvine soared an unbelievable 233 per cent in 1988, the Irvine Company mined $630,000 in new equity from each undeveloped acre. The Company's total land inflation jackpot is currently the subject of legal controversy. In 1983 the Company officially declared its worth as $1 billion; now some real-estate experts put its value in excess of $10 billion – making its owner, Donald Bren, possibly the richest person in North America and leaving Henry George (California's nineteenth-century foe of land monopoly) squirming in his grave.[56]

By raising the stakes to such immense proportions, land scarcity has driven the baronial and fiercely competitive personalities comprise the upper strata of the real-estate industry to unite as an interest bloc to perpetuate the political conditions of growth. On the one hand, the long-range, multi-phase nature of most contemporary projects imposes the need to stabilize land-use zoning and ensure state support for infrastructure. On the other hand, rising resistance to new development from homeowner-based 'slow growth' movements (the subject of the next chapter) has necessitated expensive investments in organizing political counter-responses. This combination of exigencies has resulted in the creation of a vast lobbying and campaign finance network whose supply of 'juice' exceeds anything ever offered politicians in the days of the SP or Ahmanson and Unruh.

Although political journalists have frequently compared the developers' role in corrupting the current state legislature to the pre-1910 'Associated Villainies',[57] the favorite habitat of the new Octopus is the county. This least democratic unit of government has control over land use in unincorporated growth fringes and generally offers developers the biggest bang for their campaign buck. It is not surprising, therefore, that conservative, pro-developer majorities control the boards of supervisors in every Southern California county except Santa Barbara.

Los Angeles County is the most important case if only because it is such a vast bureaucracy, traditionally overshadowing in size the City of Los Angeles, and, for that matter, every other local government in the country except for New York's (now defunct) Board of Estimate. As the *Times* has frequently complained, the County is also an 'Ice Age' throwback lacking 'basic checks and balances' as well as 'cohesion, direction, efficiency and accountability'. Its 'five little kings' – all white men, with a three-to-two conservative majority – fuse administrative, legislative and juridical authority over personal fiefdoms with populations larger than Detroit. In a typical local version of the Sacramento 'juice' system, the political warchest of Supervisor Pete Schabarum (now retiring) was heavily endowed by fifteen large developers, enabling him to transfer hundreds of thousands of dollars in the early 1980s to elect two clones, Deane Dana and Mike Antonovich, whose seats were then made impregnable with massive contributions from thirty other corporate developers. As we shall see in the next chapter, Schabarum's majority handsomely repaid developers by opening up hundreds of thousands of acres of land to subdivision that planners and citizens' groups desperately wanted preserved as open space.[58]

If the land development industry is conceived as a regional, or even statewide, power structure superimposed on older and more parochial elites,[59] what is particularly fascinating is the unscrupulous way in which developers' largesse nourishes conservatives and liberals alike. One of the dirty little secrets of Los Angeles politics is that Mayor Bradley – originally the standard-bearer of the most liberal wing of Southern California Democracy – shares to an astonishing extent the same developer financial base as leading local Republicans. Thus Irvine Company's Bren, financial godfather to Senator Pete Wilson and the largest Republican contributor in the state, has also been a major backer of Bradley, as has Richard Riordan, Downtown lawyer–developer–banker, who engineered the overthrow of California's liberal Supreme Court majority in 1986.

But perhaps the most revealing example of the mutual advantages of two-way political swinging is Alexander Haagen, Southern California's leading retail developer, who simultaneously shares beds with Bradley and the Republican supervisors. Through his intimate connections with City Hall, he has achieved a lucrative monopoly over the retail recolonization of South-central Los Angeles; his city-subsidized, fortified shopping centers (described in chapter five) earn handsome returns. Meanwhile, following a friendly $29,000 campaign contribution to Supervisor Mike Antonovich, he made a cool $9 million in a few days buying and promptly reselling a former Sears center in Antonovich's district to the County Department of Public Works.[60]

Unfortunately these kind of examples could be multiplied *ad nauseam*. They exemplify a new elite politics which operates on a 'bipartisan' plane not so much because corporate developers have ceased to be ardent Republicans, but because urban Democrats like Bradley have ceased to represent the distinctive interests of popular constituencies. In California, of course, where the 'juice' has always flowed, this is an old story. More interesting, perhaps, is the new mobility of power – whether welded associationally or individually. From a certain historical perspective it may be as significant that Haagen is deeply involved in the microcosm of Fontana politics, deep in the Inland Empire, as that he contributes to both sides of Los Angeles's political macrocosm. Contrasted to older, place-fixed power-structures, whatever the 'new Octopus' lacks in social cohesion, it more than makes up for in regional ubiquity. Today's big developers navigate the fragmented political geography of Southern California with an ease and familiarity that would have astonished even Harry Chandler.

THE PERILS OF CO-PROSPERITY

As we saw in the last chapter Reyner Banham was not the only one to mistake the future of Downtown Los Angeles. The grand design (an actual

1972 masterplan known as the 'Silverbook') of the Committee of 25 and the Central City Association has been realized, under the aegis of the Bradley regime, to an extent few believed possible. If there were just five new highrises above the old height limitation of thirteen stories in 1975, there are now nearly fifty, crowned by Maguire Thomas's overweening 73-story Library Tower (although Donald Trump is threatening to build a 125-'hyper-skyscraper' along Wilshire Boulevard). Yet, as Downtown has soared, the rising ante of speculation has forced many of the original corporate members of the Committee of 25, including large regional banks and oil companies with troubled cashflows, to sell equity and withdraw to the sidelines.[61]

Downtown in a word simply became too big for local interests to continue to dominate, and recentering came effectively to mean inter-nationalization. Thus in 1979 the *Times* reported that a quarter of Downtown's major properties were foreign-owned; six years later the figure was revised to 75 per cent (one authority has claimed 90 per cent).[62] The first wave of foreign investment in the late 1970s, as in Manhattan, was led by Canadian real-estate capital, epitomized by Toronto-based Olympia and York. The Reichmann clan who own Olympia and York collect skyscrapers in the way that the merely rich collect rare stamps or Louis XIV furniture. Yet since 1984 they, along with the New York insurance companies and British banks, have been swamped by a *tsunami* of Japanese capital.

Of all the complex factors involved in the contemporary 'Nippon-ization' of the Southern California economy, two are particularly out-standing. First is the bizarre fact that the region's leading foreign export by volume is simply empty space; more than half the containers which arrive in San Pedro filled with computers, cars and televisions return with nothing in them.[63] Although it is impossible to know the regional balance of trade with any accuracy, in the mid 1980s the state as a whole averaged $20 billion deficits in a commerce of nearly $30 billion with Japan.[64] This one-way trade generates both the need for huge onshore infrastructures of import services, finance and sales administration, as well as mechanisms for recycling the Japanese surplus.

The second factor, helping define the mode of recycling, has been the differential in land prices across the Pacific. If land inflation in Los Angeles has radically transformed the economics of local urbanization, it remains yet minuscule compared to the neutron-star densities of property values in Tokyo. In face of the refusal of the ruling Liberal-Democrats to plow Japan's trade windfalls into higher wages and a Keynesian housing reflation (as demanded by the Socialist opposition), trade-generated surplus capital has instead flooded into stock and real-estate speculations reminiscent of Coolidge's America. What the Japanese call *zaitech*, the strategy of using diverse financial technologies to shift cashflow from production to speculation, began to be internationalized in the mid 1980s with a special orientation toward Southern California. In particular, the 'super-yen' put the skyscrapers along Downtown's new Gold Coast at rummage-sale discounts vis-à-vis their most dowdy Tokyo equivalents.

From the standpoint of the Japanese establishment, however, a noxious side-effect of *zaitech* has been the fostering of a stratum of swashbuckling billionaires – the equivalent of our corporate raiders – known as *nottori-ya* or 'hijackers'. It was the most notorious of the Tokyo *nottori-ya*, Shuwa Company Ltd, who stunned L.A.'s Old Guard by purchasing nearly $1 billion of Downtown's new skyline, including the twin-towered ARCO Plaza, in a single two-and-a-half month buying spree. This was the preface to what by 1990 was a bulging portfolio of twenty-five major Los Angeles area properties. In contrast to the polite, grey-flannel anonymity of other Japanese investors, Shuwa's boss, Shigeru Kobayashi, and his son Takaji, have brazenly emulated the example of Ahmanson and earlier generations of Los Angeles *nouveaux riches*. In what *Business Week* euphemistically described as 'following the Japanese tradition of bringing gifts to new neighbors', the Kobayashis donated $1 million to the Ronald Reagan Presidential Library in Simi Valley, contributed generously to Mayor Bradley's ill-fated 1988 gubernatorial campaign, and gave the city of Los Angeles a $100,000 downpayment on the 'steel cloud' mentioned in the previous chapter.[65]

For his part, Mayor Bradley has extended a warm welcome to the *nottori-ya* as well as their more respectable corporate compatriots. To a greater extent than any other muncipal leader, including even Atlanta's globe-trotting Andrew Young, Bradley has integrated foreign capital into the top rungs of his coalition.[66] Although no one can recall the mayor making strenuous efforts to defend the 50,000 local high-wage manufacturing jobs wiped out by imports since 1975, he has been unflagging in his promotion of the movement of free capital across the Pacific while denouncing critics of Japanese power as 'racists'.[67] His administration has kept landing fees at LAX amongst the lowest in the world, vastly expanded port facilities, given special zoning exemptions and development-right subsidies to foreign investors Downtown (especially Shuwa), and made expatriate Chinese bankers the recipients of 'affirmative action' (embroiling Bradley, in one case, in a scandal involving illegal city deposits with Henry Hwang's Far East National Bank).[68]

Surprisingly, there has been little outcry from the remnants of the Old Guard over Japanese ownership of a third of Downtown or City Hall's tropism toward the East. With a fifth of all Japanese North American real-estate investment flowing into Los Angeles ($3.05 billion in 1988 alone), major pillars of the WASP power structure have decided to join, rather than fight, this 'co-prosperity sphere'. Following an initial phase of skyscraper trophy-taking, capped by the Shuwa purchases, the *zaibatsu* are now in a second phase of joint-venture projects with leading local developers, ranging from Mitsubishi's collaboration with Prudential to build the huge Citicorp complex Downtown, to Nippon Credit Bank's partnership with Trammel Crow in City of Industry. Meanwhile the sale of Southern California real estate is being promoted in Asia with the same fervor that it was once sold in the Midwest. Major Southland realtors, like Beverly Hills-based Fred Sands, are specially packaging Los Angeles property to entice the mass market of Japanese yuppies – today's Iowans. 'We're looking at middle-class Japanese buyers, because the middle class there often has $1 million to $2 million worth of equity in their homes.'[69]

The consequence of these myriad trade flows and real-estate deals (Southern California, so far, has only a small fraction of Japan's US manufacturing investment) is the city's growing financial dependence upon Tokyo. (In a few years it may be more accurate to speak of a financial triangle of Los Angeles, New York and Tokyo, but Manhattan money-center banks have had to bide time setting up shop in Los Angeles, awaiting full inter-state financial deregulation in 1991, while Japanese banks have enjoyed a spectacular headstart.) Fifty billion dollars in direct Japanese bank assets, led by Union Bank, are complemented by financial joint ventures like Security Pacific's wide-ranging alliance with Mitsui. Meanwhile nearly $1 billion in County pension funds have been invested in mixed Japanese stocks, while the City issues yen-denominated bonds and parcels of Downtown exchange hands entirely in yen.[70]

An obvious result of growing financial integration is that control over the Los Angeles economy is being alienated, with incalculable consequences, to power centers six thousand miles away. The Downtown 'renaissance', after all, is only a perverse monument to US losses in the global trade war. When the Japanese economy seemed invincible and its supply of exportable capital infinite, this deficitary dialectic did not trouble local elites. But 1980s blind faith in the 'Pacific Century' began to buckle at the knees following the *kamikaze* dive of the Tokyo stock market in early 1990. Los Angeles's leaders were rudely awoken for the first time to the real nature of colonial subservience upon the inscrutable workings of a Japanese economy bloated with fictional capital. For example, when the Bank of Japan recently decided to raise its discount rate, it drove Tokyo investors to desert Disney Corporation stocks *en masse* for domestic bonds. The result was unexpected distress and confusion in Burbank. This was an infinitesimal foretaste of what a general real-estate slump in Tokyo or a Japan-centered recession might do to those sectors of the Los Angeles economy – like Downtown or Hollywood – hopelessly addicted to ever-increasing fixes of recycled debt.

THE PARADOXICAL *TIMES*

If part of the Downtown Old Guard has been put out to pasture while another fraction has been reduced to a satellite by offshore capital, the *Times* remains both the major link to past glory and the traditional institution that has tried hardest to adapt itself to the new sprawl of power. As we indicated earlier, the publishing empire's liberal turn in the late 1960s was co-resonant with its marketing shift toward the college-educated middle classes. Since the mid 1970s the *Times* – self-defined as the 'nation's first daily news magazine' – has tracked Yuppie demographics across the entire girth of the Southland, from San Diego to Ventura, with specially tailored regional editions.[71] When the rival Hearst-owned *Herald-Examiner* finally died in November 1989 from circulation wounds inflicted years earlier in a bitter strike, the *Times* appeared to have triumphantly fulfilled General Otis's manifest destiny.[72]

But the 'gray lady' is, in fact, plagued with problems. For one thing, Chandler blood has continued to tire. Early in the decade the family *consigliere* and former UCLA chancellor, Franklin Murphy, retired, soon followed by his boss, Otis Chandler (who is rumored to enjoy surfing more than high finance). Even 'Missy' Chandler, daughter-in-law and successor to Buffy on the arts and charity scene, has recently pulled back. This leaves fewer Chandlers at large in the city than at any time since the Spanish-American War. At the same time the Goliath *Times* has been getting shellacked by newspaper Davids in critical suburban markets. The *Times*'s original strategy in the early 1960s of simply buying out all of its regional competitors was vetoed by federal anti-trust action. Now, despite enormous capital and careful planning, it finds itself on the losing end of four different regional circulation wars. In affluent, fast-growing San Diego County it has failed to gain ground against an entrenched Copley dynasty, while in its formerly captive market of the San Fernando Valley it barely holds its own against the upstart *Daily News*, owned by Jack Kent Cook, which has already crossed the Santa Monicas to compete with the *Times* for the blue-collar readership of the defunct *Herald-Examiner*. Meanwhile a regional newspaper-in-the-making for the suburbs of the San Gabriel Valley, the Los Angeles Newspaper Network (an alliance of Pasadena, Whitter and West Covina papers owned by the Thompson and Singleton chains), claims to have drawn even with *Times*'s circulation and advertising revenue.[73]

But the *Times*'s real Vietnam has been in Orange County – the land of the nation's highest median house prices – where the conservative Orange County (ex-Santa Ana) *Register* has buried a whole generation of the Chandlers' best and brightest. Tom Johnson, ironically an L.B.J. protégé, was brought in from a Texas farm team in 1980 to become *Times* publisher with the specific mission of penetrating the Orange curtain. In late 1989, after pouring tens of millions of dollars into futile marketing campaigns south of the border, he was 'demoted upwards'. Joan Didion has revealed that the newly installed 'leaner, meaner' regime of the 1990s – publisher David Laventhol and editor Shelby Coffey III – are widely resented within the *Times* as authoritarian 'Eastern' snobs (that is, they exemplify the 'mercenary' migration analyzed in the last chapter).[74]

But the underlying issue of these circulation wars transcends the competencies of the *Times* management or the competitive packaging of news entertainment. As one of the senior *Times* editors interviewed by Didion recognized, the paper has lost ground because of the 'aggressive disidentification with Los Angeles of the more recent and more uniformly affluent communities in Ventura and San Diego and Orange Counties'. Ironically, the once monolithically reactionary and middlebrow *Times* – flagship of Downtown power – is now at the receiving end of a regional backlash against the cultural and political liberalism of Los Angeles's Westside. At the same time there is also growing suburban estrangement from Los Angeles's inverse image of being an alien, third-world city. Yet the overly cautious and bourgeois *Times* has also had little impact upon the Latino metropolis of three million people within Los Angeles County. Its desultory experiments with monthly bilingual inserts have only highlighted its lack of vision and audacity.[75]

But we should not overstate the problems facing the fifth (now largely absentee) generation of the Chandler dynasty. The position of the *Times* as a regional power-center is more paradoxical than anything else. Its increasing liberalism and catering to the highbrow have ensured its dominance over metropolitan Yuppie publics – making it now as essential to breakfast with cappuccino on the West Coast as the (less liberal) New York *Times* on the East. Over the last decade its editorial page, which for generations thundered against 'red menaces' and 'socialistic' public expenditures, has assumed statewide leadership in calling for a return to Keynesian budgets and social investment – precipitating thereby an acrimonious public exchange with Governor Deukmejian (an Old Guard throwback whom earlier Chandlers would have adored). Yet the paper is losing crucial battles to shape a truly regional, 'supercity' news market, while simultaneously remaining irrelevant to the city's most rapidly growing ethnic groups. The *Times*'s dilemma, in other words, almost precisely outlines the problem of ruling-class hegemony in a postmodern city of secessionist suburbs and burgeoning barrios.

MONEY-MACHINE IN TRANSITION

In contrast to fading or colonized Downtown institutions, Tinseltown's influence in local and national politics has immeasurably increased over the last generation. In an age where Republicans have reaped the major benefits of the PAC revolution in campaign finance, and where Labor and other traditional constituencies are in steep decline, the national Democratic Party has been driven to rely more than ever upon liberal Hollywood's combination of finance and fantasy. The money-grubbing pilgrimages of Democratic hopefuls to Malibu and Brentwood have become as important rites of presidential campaigning as the Iowa primary or even the Convention itself. The Hollywood Primary, as it were, has become the first, sometimes decisive, test of the sales potential of presidential timber in the face of the party's most important constituency of fundraisers and media managers.

Locally, a veritable aqueduct of Westside entertainment and savings-and-loan money has irrigated the 'postmodern political machine' run by Congressmen Berman, Waxman, and Levine. Recognized by the *New Republic* as the most powerful regional Democratic grouping in the country, and operating with equal facility in local, state and national arenas, Berman–Waxman–Levine, Inc. are the most potent expression to date of the Westside's political ascendency. Unlike old-fashioned machines they do not depend on patronage resources or grassroots cadre. Instead they rely upon a behind-the-scenes cold fusion of Hillcrest Country Club money, direct-mail technology, and Congressional seniority to promote the careers of protégés and allies. With the decline of the legendary Burton machine in the Bay area (of which Assembly Speaker Brown is a veteran), B-W-L Inc. have become the potential kingmakers of California Democracy. Current major subsidiaries include minority Congressmen Julian Dixon and Marty Martinez, state Senators Herschel Rosenthal and Gary Hart, as well as Assemblyman Burt Margolin and City Controller Rick Tuttle.[76]

Formerly chief allies of the Bradley regime, B-W-L Inc. have increasingly taken their distance from City Hall, identifying with the 'slow-growth' and anti-Downtown discontent of the suburbs. Indeed they were actively engaged in trying to overthrow Bradley until the *Times* blew the whistle on the Koch-like strategy behind the campaign of Westside Council-member Zev Yaroslavsky. The disclosure of a racist campaign memorandum written by Congressman Berman's (legendarily uncouth) brother Michael forced Yaroslavsky to fold his tents. Having gone to the brink of a split with Black Democrats, B-W-L Inc., responding to the anxiety of the entire Westside Jewish establishment, retreated instead.

Also working the fast lanes of Westside power, often in tandem with B-W-L Inc., but sometimes in apparent opposition, are Manatt, Phelps, Rothenberg and Phillips – a major power center vaguely disguised as a law partnership. Charles Manatt was the 1980s successor to two previous Westside corporate lawyers, Eugene Wyman and Paul Ziffren, as Los Angeles's emissary in national Democratic affairs. Serving from 1981 to 1985 as chairman of the Democratic National Committee, he created the Democratic Business Council to align the national party more closely with the Business Roundtable's agenda: a strategy which, through the priority it attached to fiscal conservatism, helped to demolish Mondale's chances in 1984.

Manatt's firm continues to specialize in marriage counseling between Democrats and big business (especially the entertainment and real-estate industries), while its partners interlock comprehensively, and without scruple, with virtually every Democratic notable or coterie in the city. Thus in 1984, Manatt associate Mickey Kantor (formerly Jerry Brown's chief L.A. operative) chaired Mondale's California campaign, while another Manatt attorney, John Emerson (now chief deputy city attorney), ran Gary Hart's. This 'heads Manatt wins, tails Manatt wins' strategy was repeated in 1988 during the controversy over Occidental Petroleum's attempt to legalize oil drilling on the shores of Santa Monica Bay. While Kantor extolled Armand Hammer's oil rigs as a revolt against Westside 'elitism', his colleague, Lisa Specht, represented angry homeowner and environmental groups with equal self-righteousness. Currently Manatt, Phelps is supplying the major legal muscle to defend Mayor Bradley against sundry corruption and conflict-of-interest allegations, although it may be fairly surmised that the firm is also working to help groom his successor.[77]

The neo-liberalism of B-W-L Inc. and the post-liberalism of Manatt, Phelps define the institutional parameters, as it were, of Westside Democratic power. But competitive fundraising still depends principally upon individual entrepreneurs or wealthy cliques. An important generational succession is taking place in Hollywood that echoes the larger recomposition of elites in the city. Fading from the scene, first of all, are the famous 'Malibu Mafia' that engineered the election of Bradley in 1973, and then helped finance a stream of liberal victories in the aftermath of Watergate. Although Norman Lear is still kicking around, his energies have been long concentrated on 'People for the American Way', his antidote to moral majorities. Into the vacuum left by Palevsky and Lear, meanwhile, have rushed baby-boom glitzocrats – potentially powerful but colorlessly centrist young studio management from Fox, Disney and New World who were early backers of Dukakis in 1988. On their left flank is the Hollywood Women's Political Committee, which has molded part of the 1980s 'bratpack' into an aggressive liberal feminist cadre.[78]

On the other end of Hollywood's political spectrum, Ron and Nancy survive in mummified splendor in Bel-Air Estates, jointly financed by Japanese *zaibatsu* and federal taxpayers. The famous 'kitchen cabinet' led by Justin Dart and Holmes Tuttle, however, has been whittled down by death and decrepitude. Even at its height in the late 1970s it was strictly a venture capital operation around Reagan, with little impact as a local power structure. Ironically the Reagan associate who remains politically most virile is his old agent, Lew Wasserman of MCA, now the Supreme Being of Democratic fundraising in Hollywood.

Wasserman organizes the largest, nominally Democratic but anti-ideological camp of entertainment industry leaders. Generally speaking the only cause for which they are willing to bleed is that of their studio's balance-sheet. When Wasserman nods in any candidate's direction they can trust that the rigorous bottom-line calculation has already been made. Although he and his grand vizier, Sidney Sheinberg, are mostly concerned with the impact of national politics on the entertainment industry, MCA, via ownership of Universal City, is the biggest real-estate developer in the entire San Fernando Valley and an active tentacle of the 'new Octopus' when it needs to be.

But this entire constellation of power, old and new, revolves around historic Jewish and Democratic predominance in Hollywood – a fact that can no longer be taken for granted. Like Downtown, Hollywood has been put on a global auction bloc. It is the 'software' center of a madly evolving, $150 billion world entertainment complex (growing 15 per cent annually). The *Economist* estimates that nearly $100 billion has been invested in raiding and restructuring the industry since 1988. Locally this has meant the offshore purchase of four out of five major recording companies, and four out of nine movie studios, as well as a flood of foreign capital into independent production and so-called 'mini-studios'. If media raiders like

Rupert Murdoch's Australian-based News Group (which bought Fox in 1985) are primarily looking for undervalued assets, the electronic hardware giants like Sony (which now owns CBS records, Columbia and Tri-Star) are creating vertically integrated entertainment monopolies for the millennium.[79]

The acquisition of Hollywood's dream machinery is a fitting capstone to Japanese capitalism's humbling of the United States in the age of Reagan and Bush. Although the ex-president, speaking in Tokyo, can praise the *zaibatsu* for bringing a new rectitude to Babylon, no one can predict the implications of foreign ownership for the future of political fundraising in the studios, or, for that matter, the industry's central role in national Jewish affairs. Like Downtown, Hollywood is becoming a colony of the world economy.[80]

DARE GA L.A. WO UGOKASHITE IRUKA

This is polite Japanese for 'who rules L.A.?' It is a question that will be increasingly asked by curious and confused newcomers, especially from societies where power remains organized in great dynastic hierarchies. Although Episcopalian bankers and San Marino debutantes on one side of town, and Hillcrest Country Club habitués on the other, will continue to dominate the local Social Register for another generation (biological echoes of the ruling classes of the 1880s, 1920s and 1950s) – real power is gravitating elsewhere. The stellar success of Los Angeles as a real-estate, media and technology mecca is overwhelming its traditional upper classes, diminishing their autonomy and clout. This is not to suggest that they are somehow being pauperized – indeed they are becoming wealthier – but, rather, that they are surrendering power, which is different from mere money, to others more strategically established in the new circuits of land monopoly and global finance. L.A. 2000, despite official hype about being 'THE city of the 21st century', will largely be an entrepot for megabanks and technology monopolies headquartered elsewhere. It will also, undoubtedly, continue to be the urban equivalent of the Spanish Main for corporate buccaneers and *nottori-ya* from all over the world. Its old WASPish elites, especially, recumbent in their luxury, may linger primarily as consumers, *compradores* or just breeding stock.

NOTES

1. Quoted in Sophia Spalding, 'Power Shift in L.A.', unpublished manuscript, 1989.
2. Frederic Jaher, *The Urban Establishment: Upper Strata in Boston, New York, Charleston, Chicago and Los Angeles*, Urbana 1978, p. 577.
3. Kevin Starr, 'An Epilogue: Making Dreams Come True', *L.A. 2000 – A City for the Future*, Los Angeles 1988, p. 84.
4. These opportunistic 'Yankee Hidalgos', however, drew the wrath of other sons of the Puritans like Richard Henry Dana, Jr., author of *Two Years Before the Mast* (1852), who despised the 'hated coast' of Southern California and the Anglo-Californians who 'left their consciences behind at Cape Horn'. See the discussion in Franklin Walker, *A Literary History of Southern California*, Berkeley 1950, pp. 22–32.
5. See Robert Cleland and Frank Putnam, *Isaias W. Hellman and the Farmers and Merchants Bank*, San Marino 1965.
6. Statistics from Robert Cleland, *The Cattle on a Thousand Hills*, Los Angeles 1951, p. 159. Los Angeles County, in other words, comprised barely 1 per cent of the state's wealth in 1863.
7. William Clary, *O'Melveny and Myers: 1885–1965*, privately printed, Los Angeles 1966, p. 211.
8. This is not to deny the existence of elite anti-semitism, most notably amongst the first generation Anglo-Californians who blamed the Jews, especially Isaias Hellman, for foreclosing on their ranchos during the 1860s. This grievance resurfaced in an ugly mode following the collapse of the Temple and Workman Bank, last redoubt of the Sons-in-Law, in the 1875 Panic which was again blamed on Hellman's machinations. See Max Vorspan and Lloyd Gartner, *History of the Jews of Los Angeles*, Philadelphia 1970, p. 42.
9. See chapter six, Remi Nadeau, *City-Makers*, New York 1948. The Southern Pacific had little domestic capital available in the long depression years of the 1870s, so the Big Four sent Michael Pease, a San Francisco capitalist who also owned the Alamitos Ranch in Los Angeles, to Germany to sell bonds. The 'invisible hand' that made possible the rail integration of Los Angeles into the national economy was actually the savings of middling German investors. (See Jackson Graves, *Seventy Years in California*, Los Angeles 1927, p. 100.)
10. Cf. *A Southern California Paradise*, Pasadena 1883, p. 53; and John Muir, *Mountains of California*, vol. 2, Boston 1894 , p. 120. During the 'golden age of beekeeping' in the early 1880s, there were more than 50,000 hives in Southern California, largely tended by consumptives seeking the fresh air. (See John Baur, 'The Health Seekers and Early Southern California Agriculture', *Pacific Historical Review* 20, 1951.)
11. In 1918 the Southern Pacific alone owned 2,598,775 acres of five Southern California counties (including 137,463 acres in Los Angeles County). See California Commission on Immigration and Housing, *A Report on Large Landholdings in Southern California*, Sacramento 1919, p. 10.
12. Cf. Richard Orsi, 'The Octopus Reconsidered: The Southern Pacific and Agricultural Modernization in California, 1865–1915', *California Historical Quarterly*, LIV-3 Fall 1975; Edna Parker, 'The Southern Pacific Railroad and Settlement in Southern California', *Pacific Historical Review* 6, 1937.
13. Quoted in Glenn Quiett, *They Built the West*, New York 1934, p. 275.
14. George Burton Ward, *Men of Achievement in the Great Southwest*, Los Angeles 1904, p. 24.
15. Cf. Glenn Dumke, *The Boom of the Eighties in Southern California*, San Marino 1944, p. 4; and *Industries of Los Angeles*, Los Angeles 1888, pp. 11, 23.
16. Great Britain, Foreign Office, Vice-Consul Mortimer, *The Trade and Commerce of Los Angeles*, London 1890, p. 4.

17. William Issel, ' "Citizens Outside the Government": Business and Urban Policy in San Francisco and Los Angeles, 1890–1932', manuscript copy (courtesy of author), 1988.

18. According to Charles Willard, the circulation of the *Times* before the harbor battle was little more than any of its three competitors; by the end of the fight, its circulation exceeded all rival papers combined. (*The Free Harbor Contest at Los Angeles*, Los Angeles 1899, pp. 102–3.)

19. Whitley had developed towns all along the Rock Island line in Oklahoma, Wilcox had made a fortune in Topeka real estate, Sherman had been the first major developer in Phoenix, and so on.

20. When the Socialist candidate came within a hair's-breadth of winning the mayoralty in the 1909 (Harper recall) election, the local radical press – referring to the unholy alliance of the saloon owners and railroad machine with labor – lamented that there was 'not much honor in an election of our comrade by such a combination'. The 'real socialist vote' was estimated at 3,000 (see *Common Sense*, 3 April 1909).

21. *Men of Achievement in the Great Southwest* (p. 33) characterized them as 'L.A.'s Big Four', though only Huntington actually lived in Southern California. Huntington, in a famous trade with E.H. Harriman of the SP, exchanged his inter-urban red car system for the municipal streetcar system.

22. See Robert Gottlieb and Irene Wolt, *Thinking Big: the Story of the Los Angeles Times*, New York 1977, pp. 121–6.

23. Indeed, after the generalization of the Open Shop throughout California in 1919–23, the entire state tottered on the brink of becoming a one-party regime dominated by a trio of right-wing publishers: Chandler, Hearst (L.A. and San Francisco) and Knowland (Oakland). The major political opposition came within the Republican Party from remnant Progressives and religious fundamentalists. For an extraordinary group photograph of the California ruling class of the 1920s, see *California Journal of Development* 16:5, State Chamber of Commerce's Development Association, May 1926.

24. Robert Fogelson, *The Fragmented Metropolis: Los Angeles 1850–1930*, Cambridge, Mass. 1967, p. 83.

25. One case in point was the law firm founded by I.W. Hellman's old associate, Henry O'Melveny, which between 1909 and 1956 refused to hire Jewish associates. The same anti-semitic principle was *de rigueur* throughout major Downtown law firms. See the *Times*'s 'L.A. Law' series, 28 September 1987.

26. Royce Delmatier, Clarence McIntosh and Earl Waters, *The Rumble of California Politics*, New York 1970, p. 207.

27. In 1988 the top three corporations headquartered in Los Angeles were Arco, Occidental and Unocal.

28. See Guy Finney, *The Great Los Angeles Bubble*, Los Angeles 1929.

29. Civic Center redevelopment also specifically rescued Chandler investments in the declining northside of Downtown. Thus the old *Times* building, assessed at only $250,000, was peddled to the city in the 1920s for more than six times that figure. See *Reuben Borough and California Reform Movements*, transcript, Oral History Program, UCLA 1968, p. 170.

30. Gottlieb and Wolt, p. 146.

31. *Times*, 9 June 1927.

32. Cf. Edgar Hampton, *How the Open Shop Promotes General Prosperity in Los Angeles*, Los Angeles 1929; Industrial Department, Los Angeles Chamber of Commerce, *General Industrial Report of Los Angeles County, California*, Los Angeles 1930. John Steven McCroarty attributed the national discovery of Los Angeles's manufacturing potential to the survey conducted by the War Industries Board in 1917. (See his *History of Los Angeles County*, Chicago 1923, p. 355.)

33. Cf. Scott Bottles, *Los Angeles and the Automobile*, Berkeley 1987; Martin Wachs, 'Autos, Transit, and the Sprawl of Los Angeles: the 1920s', *APA Journal*, Summer 1984.

34. For the 'Battle of the Miracle Mile', compare 'The Miracle of the Miracle Mile', in Ralph Hancock, *Fabulous Boulevard*, New York 1949, pp. 149–64; and Marc Weiss, *The Rise of the Community Builders*, New York 1987, pp. 86–101.

35. Jaher, p. 667.

36. Through the 1970s Jews were excluded from the California and University Clubs Downtown, the Los Angeles Country Club, and Pasadena's Valley Hunt Club. See Jon Bradshaw, 'The Strange Land of Clubs', *West Magazine*, 6 August 1972.

37. Neal Gabler, *An Empire of Their Own: How the Jews Invented Hollywood*, New York 1988, p.276.

38. Cf. California, Assembly Committee on Economic Development and New Technologies, *Hearing*, 4 December 1984, pp. 1, 3, 7 ; Committee on State Finance, *The Impact of Federal Expenditures on California*, Sacramento, August 1986, pp. 2, 4.

39. David Halberstam, *The Powers That Be*, New York 1979, pp. 97,118; Robert Meyers, 'The Big New Tilt in the L.A. Power Game', *Los Angeles*, p. 50.

40. See Sy Adler, 'Why BART But no LART?', *Planning Perspectives* 2, 1987, pp. 149–74.

41. Cf. Wolt and Gottlieb, pp. 257–70; Thomas Hines, 'Housing, Baseball and Creeping Socialism', *Journal of Urban History* 8:2, February 1982.

42. Halberstam gives Palmer and Chandler extraordinary credit for manufacturing Nixon. He also claims that Palmer was personally closer to Nixon, because they both shared 'fewer scruples' than Chandler. See Halberstam, pp. 256–63.

43. Lou Cannon, *Ronnie and Jessie: A Political Odyssey*, Garden City 1969, pp. 97–100.

44. As Cannon (ibid.) points out: 'Ahmanson's diversified approach to money-making and politics and Unruh's encompassing attitude toward power transformed the California political system and overfilled the vacuum that Samish [notorious king of the lobbyists during the 1940s] left and which he in turn had inherited from the Progressives' destruction of the Southern Pacific machine.'

45. A still fundamental analysis of the financing of the 1950s boom is Hyman Minsky, 'Commercial Banking and Rapid Economic Growth in California', in Minsky, ed., *California Banking in a Growing Economy: 1946–1975*, Berkeley 1965, pp. 79–134.

46. Vorspan and Gartner, p. 235. They estimate from 'private information from Jewish businessmen' that in the late 1950s Jewish builders were responsible for half of Southern California's new homes and shopping centers. They also note the 'significant trend . . . as Jewish builders began to invest their substantial capital in new banks and in savings and loan associations'. (Ibid.)

47. *Times*, 4 November 1965.

48. Gottlieb and Wolt, pp. 457–8. The public face of elite activism in Downtown was represented by the Committee for Central City Planning, whose membership more or less recapitulated the twenty-five, and whose avowed goal was to accelerate the redevelopment process.

49. On how 'older Establishment types' regarded the *Times* 'traitors', see Meyers, p. 50. For Otis Chandler's reciprocal disdain of 'the California Club crowd', see Jaher, p. 684.

50. For Bradley's courtship of the Downtown business community, see J. Gregory Payne and Scott Ratzan, *Tom Bradley: The Impossible Dream*, Santa Monica 1986, pp. 137–51.

51. Ibid.

52. In a controversial series on 'Jewish Los Angeles', Robert Scheer detailed the political fundraising rivalries of Wasserman and the Malibu group (*Times*, 30 January 1978).

53. See Gottlieb and Wolt, 'Who Rules Los Angeles?', chapter 34.

54. My *Prisoners of an American Dream*, London 1986, is largely devoted to a analysis of the post-liberal landscape of global capital mobility and domestic social polarization after Reaganomics.

55. According to A. Donald Anderson, 'How Real Estate Leaders Plan to Subdivide the Land of Opportunity', *Management*, UCLA, Fall 1985, p. 20.

56. Diane Wagner, 'Lord of the Land', *California Business*, February 1987; Orange County *Register*, 30 June 1989; and *Times*, 21 January 1990.

57. See, for instance, Mark Dowie's account of how Speaker Willie Brown's constituency has shifted from an original base of unions and community groups to mega-developers like Olympia and York and Southern Pacific Development Corporation ('The King of Juice', *California Magazine*, February 1986).

58. See *Times*, 30 March 1986 and 27 April 1987.

59. I do not mean to suggest, however, that elite memberships necessarily exclude one another. Certainly many old-line Jewish homebuilders, for example, continue to function as leaders of a distinctive Westside power structure, while simultaneously acting in concert with other developers. What is historically novel is the tendential unity of the development community.

60. *Times*, 7 October 1987 and 7 November 1987.

61. Los Angeles *Business Journal*, 11 January 1988.

62. Cf. Dick Turpin in *Times*, 21 September 1986; confirmed by the *National Real Estate Investor*, December 1986, p. 102; the higher estimate is from Howard Sadlowski, *Times*, 17 June 1984.

63. *Times*, 6 July 1988. Symtomatically, the next leading volume exports are waste paper, scrap iron and a variety of raw materials.

64. Cf. *California Magazine*, September 1986, p. 49 and January 1987, p. 25.

65. Cf. *Business Week*, 11 July 1988 and *Times*, 20 August 1989. The latter source reports Japanese opinion that Kobayashi is 'buying social status in the United States and trying to bring it home'. In fact the Kobayashis seem only to be purchasing more notoriety as two 1989 lawsuits allege that son Takaji beat up one of his Los Angeles employees, while his cousin sexually harassed another. (Ibid.)

66. Aside from Shuwa, other major Japanese contributors to Bradley include Sumitomo, Mitsui Fudosan, Bank of Tokyo and Nissan Motors (see *Business Week*, ibid.)

67. Contrasted to the vast scale of new Asian, Canadian and European investment in Los Angeles County, it should be pointed out that the largest local 'minority-owned business' (i.e., owned by any Black, Latino, Native American or Asian-American) is an automobile dealership in the city of Glendora, followed by a fish cannery, tamale company and Berry Gordy's refugee Motown Records. See Los Angeles *Business Journal*, 26 March 1988.

68. The City Council's ethics committee probe of Bradley's relations with Hwang was led by Hollywood's Michael Woo. Scion of the acknowledged leader of the local Chinese financial community, his father's generous campaign contributions to Hollywood's political boss, state Senator David Roberti, supposedly paved the way to his Council seat. With eyes on the prize of the mayoralty, Council member Woo is rapidly becoming the most powerful Asian-American politician in the state.

69. *Southern California Real Estate Journal*, 24 April–7 May 1989; *Times*, 8 March and 16 April 1989. The only Japanese investment that actually raised ruling-class hackles was the purchase of a half share in the elite Riviera Country Club. The Japanese and other Asians are valued as economic allies, but despised as social equals.

70. Los Angeles *Business Journal*, 12 October 1987; *Times*, 21 December 1987.

71. More plebeian papers (like the departed *Herald-Examiner*) tend to be 'headline-driven' and thus more vulnerable to competition from television. The *Times* strategy was to emphasize news content (of which it has more than any other paper in the nation) like *Time* or *Newsweek* magazines.

72. With nearly a million expatriate Canadians estimated to be living in Southern California (the largest immigrant ethnicity after Mexicans), the Toronto Sun Publishing Company carefully considered but ultimately rejected the purchase of the *Herald-Examiner*.

73. Los Angeles *Business Journal*, 12 February 1990; and Dan Cook, 'Extra! Extra!', *California Business*, April 1989.

74. Joan Didion, 'Letter From Los Angeles', *The New Yorker*, 26 February 1990, pp. 91–3, 97.

75. Ibid. The *Times*, which publishes eight regional editions, has never shown any interest in addressing the local media needs of the Black community. As suggested in the last chapter, Southcentral L.A. is excluded from all regional 'informational orders', corporate or bohemian, in every medium.

76. *New Republic*, 7 July 1986, pp. 18–19; *Herald-Examiner*, 28 April 1985 and 25 March 1986; Michele Willens, 'Dance of the Democrats: the West Side Shuffle', *California Journal*, April 1982.

77. *Times*, 3 August 1988.
78. *Times* 9 March 1987; Bill Bradley, 'Look Out, Tom and Jane', *L.A. Business*, April 1988.
79. See profile of his holdings in *Times*, 6 May 1990.
80. Wild charges by Giancarlo Paretti, the new Catholic owner of the Cannon Group (which was formerly Israeli), that he has been victimized by a 'Jewish media cartel' have certainly provoked a measure of disquiet in the Hillcrest Country Club. (Symptomatically, another formerly key Los Angeles Jewish business institution, Union Bank, recently passed into a second generation of foreign ownership, from British to Japanese.)

CHAPTER THREE

HOMEGROWN REVOLUTION

Some would say that it could only have happened in the Valley. Joy Picus, the L.A. city councilmember from the west San Fernando Valley, was under siege day and night from a group called the 'West Hills Open Zone Victims'. They harangued her with petitions and phone calls, haunted her on the stump, and ambushed her outside her field office. They said she was cold-hearted and haughty, unmoved by their extremity. From their agitated tone the innocent observer would have guessed that they had been the victims of some great, uncompensated communal tragedy: a plane crash or gas explosion next to an elementary school, a suddenly revealed Love Canal in their backyards, or, perhaps (as the Rod Sterling or Thomas Pynchon concept of 'open zone' suggests), something stranger, even occult.

In fact no one in the neighborhood had died, the school was intact, the pollution problem was no worse than in any other part of the smog-choked Valley, and there had been no encounters of a third kind. What *had* happened to raise the victims' spleen was that the coldhearted Picus had let them remain, as they had always been, residents of Canoga Park. To fathom the depth of their anger, it is necessary to rehearse a few simple facts of life about Los Angeles's single-family suburbs:

fact one: Los Angeles homeowners, like the Sicilians in *Prizzi's Honor*, love their children, but they love their property values more.

fact two: 'Community' in Los Angeles means homogeneity of race, class and, especially, home values. Community designations – i.e. the street signs across the city identifying areas as 'Canoga Park', 'Holmby Hills', 'Silverlake', and so on – have no legal status. In the last analysis, they are merely favors granted by city councilmembers to well-organized neighborhoods or businessmen's groups seeking to have their areas identified.

fact three: The most powerful 'social movement' in contemporary Southern California is that of affluent homeowners, organized by notional community designations or tract names, engaged in the defense of home values and neighborhood exclusivity.

Thus it was that more than three thousand homeowners in the foothills of western Canoga Park petitioned Picus in early 1987 to redesignate their area as 'West Hills'. The members of the West Hills Property Owners

Association complained that they were forced to look down from the patios of their hilltop $400,000 homes on mere $200,000 hovels in the flatlands east of Platt Avenue. Implicitly referring to the pigmentation as well as home values on the other side of the tracks, the secessionists whined that Canoga Park was 'bad ... very slummish' and that 'our area is more expensive ... because we paid a heck of a lot more in the first place'.[1] To further fuel West Hills' search for 'community', local realtors spread the rumor that redesignation would raise home values by an instant $20,000.

Picus, a very moderate Democrat, was in no mood to become a suburban Lincoln saving West Hills for Canoga Park. The power in her district is divided between influential developers (Voit's Warner Center) and anti-development (or 'slow growth') homeowners' associations. Under investigation by the City Attorney for receiving improper campaign contributions from developers, she was particularly eager to mollify homeowners. With a phone call from Picus to the city Department of Transportation, West Hills was born.

For disconsolate homeowners just east of the new non-entity, however, the redesignation was a calamity that cheated them out of a $20,000 windfall. 'They took out the cream of the crop of the homes and we were not even told. [We] thought everybody had a right to be asked if they wanted to be included.' Months later, after relentlessly dogging Picus, the homeowners from the orphan fringe between Shoup and Platt avenues finally won admittance into the exclusive West Hills club. But Picus might as well have been trying to pass a peace-pipe between Armenians and Azerbaijanis. As a local, unsympathetic observer explained:

This raised the ire of the original West Hills petitioners, who obviously were loath to see their gains diluted; their 'sense of community' carries a 'small is beautiful' qualifier. Not to be confused with Solomon, Picus tried to divide the baby by declaring the newly admitted neighborhoods 'open zones', to be referred to as Canoga Park or as West Hills as each inhabitant might deem appropriate. ... Unsurprisingly, this satisfied no one – least of all the once-scorned, once-embraced, scorned-again inhabitants of the open zones.[2]

Sucked waist-deep into the nomenclatural quicksand of West Hills by her revision of the 'community's' imaginary boundaries, Picus only sank further

THE $20,000 SIGN

with each attempt at extrication. Caught between those who wanted to pull up the gangplanks around the narrowest construction of the area, and those who wanted to roll back the secession entirely ('thus returning all property owners to their original positions'), Picus floundered hopelessly. Her attempt at a complicated League-of-Nations plebiscite in the three contentious areas (that is, the original West Hills, the 'Open Zone', and much maligned Canoga Park) came off poorly and brought new charges of 'her abhorrence of leadership'. At the end of the day, all sides derided her, political analysts calculated major, perhaps fatal damage to her political career, and the mere mention of 'West Hills' at press conferences was enough to drive the unfortunate councilmember to apoplexy.[3]

SUNBELT BOLSHEVISM

The slow-growth movement is not a fad, it is a major revolution.
L.A. Councilmember Marvin Braude[4]

The Frankenstein of West Hills is a familiar kind of terror to suburban politicians in the Los Angeles area. Many of them live in fear of being ground to bits – as Joy Picus nearly was – by the incessant conflict of microscopically parochial interests. It is, I suppose, another example of how Southern California stands simplistic social theory on its head. Elsewhere affluent homeowners are imagined to be the contented bulwark of the status quo. But south of the Tehachapis they act like *sans culottes*, wielding the parish pump as a guillotine. Indeed it was precisely Valley homeowners like the West Hills group who were the shock troops of Howard Jarvis's tax revolt in 1978: an epochal event that helped end the New Deal era and pave the way for Reaganomics.

Now, more than a decade later, angry homeowners are engaged in a more diffuse, but no less significant struggle over the politics of growth. With roots in literally hundreds of homeowners' associations, a so-called 'slow-growth movement' has emerged out of the Brownian motion of local landuse grievances (like the Canoga Park redesignation) to challenge the most powerful economic interest in California today: the land development industry. Like Proposition 13 earlier, the new revolt seemed to erupt out of the crabgrass with little prior warning.

The first rumble was in January 1985 when a coalition of homeowners won a court order stopping the City of Los Angeles from allowing highrise development flagrantly in excess of its own General Plan. Their precedent planted the seed for the success of Proposition U in November of 1986. Heralded by the *Times* as the 'first major challenge to Los Angeles's growth ethic in a hundred years', Proposition U reduced developable commercial density in the city by half and imposed a ten-point growth management plan.[5] A year later, Councilmember Pat Russell, the key strategist of Mayor Bradley's 'pro-growth' majority on the Council, was dramatically upset by a darkhorse slow-growth advocate.

In the meantime homeowner-backed slow-growth insurgencies dominated the 1987–8 local elections in scores of Los Angeles suburbs and outlying cities.[6] In spite of the absence of a county-wide growth control initiative, these local skirmishes yielded an impressive balance-sheet of new building restrictions and development moratoria. Already superheated real-estate markets reacted with hysteria. Anticipating that the slow-growth movement would further constrict the limited supply of developable land, hordes of house-hungry buyers rushed into the market: a self-fulfilling prophecy that led to Tokyo-type escalations in median home values in Los Angeles and Orange counties during 1987.

Land inflation only fanned the flames of growth protest throughout the suburbanizing, 'pro-growth' frontiers of Southern California. In the Reaganite fastnesses of southern Orange County (where only semi-liberal Irvine breaks the mold) the traditional conservative consensus was splintered by a bitter struggle between latifundian developers and wealthy homeowners. The initially commanding lead of the 'Sensible Growth Initiative', with its stringent 'quality of life' standards for new development, was barely surmounted in the June 1988 election by the unprecedented scare campaign (stressing higher taxes and job flight) mounted by Donald Bren and his fellow *haciendados*. Chastened by the close-call in Orange County, developers in neighboring Riverside County, home of two of the fastest growing suburban fringes in the country (Moreno Valley and Elsinore–Temecula), spared no expense in vilifying their own fledgling slow-growth movement. Measure B (November 1988) which would have restricted future development in the county's unincorporated areas was beaten three to two after pro-growth forces outspent slow-growth fifty-five to one. A similar developer-financed, pro-growth *blitzkrieg* edged out popular growth-control initiatives in San Diego County.

Having portrayed the slow-growth movement as virtually invincible in 1986, the press now claimed that the 1988 developers' counter-offensive had left the movement in shambles.[7] In fact, the struggle, which had begun as largely unreported guerrilla skirmishes, was changing from a war of maneuver – with dramatic results at the polls – to an increasingly complex war of position, involving the courts, the state legislature, and various regulatory bodies, as well as local government. And, whatever the immediate balance of forces, there is no question that growth controversies continue to polarize and reshape the Southern California political land-scape. But what interpretation do we give to that vague cipher known as 'slow growth'? And where on a traditional spectrum of political and social forces can we locate a 'movement' composed of strange molecules like the West Hills homeowners?

To some analysts the Southern California slow-growth rebellion of the late 1980s merely seemed a recapitulation of the experience of affluent Bay Area counties in the previous decade. Beginning with Petaluma's famous 1973 experiment in growth management, more than two dozen cities, along with the designer counties of Marin and Napa, had imposed some kind of moratorium or cap on residential development. The Bay Area has achieved a degree of growth limitation unequaled in any other metropolitan region in the country – evoking envy as well as criticism for the resulting 'suburban squeeze', land inflation, and chronic job/housing disjunctions. From this perspective, Southern California has only been catching up with the Bay Area precedent of how to protect and regulate the good life.

But, without denying important overlaps, crucial differences dis-tinguish the Bay Area and Southland versions of growth protest. In the first place, the slow-growth movement in the south has been overwhelmingly a movement of *homeowners*, with some environmentalists serving as organic intellectuals and apologists. Although the movement invokes the populist rhetoric of 'community control' and 'neighborhood power', tenants, with few exceptions, play no role nor are their interests usually addressed (except in opposition). The singularity of the 'People's Republic of Santa Monica' aside, there is no counterpart to the inclusive parochialism, say, of the recent Agnos coalition in San Francisco, which, while dominated by wealthy homeowners, included a significant representation of renters and urban have-nots.

Secondly, land-use politics in Southern California have tended to generate sharper contradictions and entrenched opposition than in the North. As David Dowall and other students of the Bay Area experience have discovered, large developers in Petaluma-type milieux have often mono-polized lucrative positions within growth-controlled local residential markets.[8] Although such accommodations can be found on a case-by-case basis in the south, growth issues are more commonly perceived as a zero-sum game, sowing virulent economic conflict and electoral upheaval. And the stakes are often immense, as homeowners have sought to slow down or stop billion-dollar, multi-phase projects. Indeed the assault on the development process – and, by implication, upon the rights of corporate land ownership and laissez-faire urbanization – has been sufficiently subversive at times to warrant George Will's warning of 'Sunbelt Bolshevism'.[9]

Finally, an important ideological difference. Growth control politics in the Bay Area have been incubated in a specific regional tradition of patrician conservationism represented by the Sierra Club, the Bay Conser-vation and Development Commission, and California Tomorrow. 'Responsible environmentalism' constitutes a hegemonic discourse in which all sides, developers and their community opponents, must formulate their arguments. The tap-root of slow growth in the South, however, is an exceptionalistic local history of middle-class interest formation around home ownership. Environmentalism is a congenial discourse to the extent that it is congruent with a vision of eternally rising property values in secure bastions of white privilege. The master discourse here – exemplified by the West Hills secessionists – is homestead exclusivism, whether the immediate issue is apartment construction, commercial encroachment, school busing, crime, taxes or simply community designation.[10]

Slow growth, in other words, is about homeowner control of land use and much more. Seen in the context of the suburban sociology of Southern California, it is merely the latest incarnation of a middle-class political subjectivity that fitfully constitutes and reconstitutes itself every few years around the defense of household equity and residential privilege. These diverse 'movements' have been notoriously volatile, but their cumulative impact upon the shaping of the socio-spatial structure of the Los Angeles region has been enormous.

Any serious analysis, therefore, of Southern California's current 'growth wars' must take careful account of this ramified heritage of homeowner mobilization in all of its guises. But the reader must be warned that this means entering a labyrinth of micro-history – a dark chronicle of the tractlands – whose perplexing passageways sometimes lead to places even stranger than West Hills or the 'Open Zone'. Like Orson Welles's Lady from Shanghai, the slow-growth movement has a checkered past that conceals ominous clues about how it will behave in the future. The starting-point is to reconstruct the white-supremacist genealogy of its essential infrastructure: the *homeowners' association.*

THE WHITE WALL

If we can't enforce restrictive covenants in this area then pretty soon the whole Westside will be gone and be worth nothing for people of our class. *1940s homeowners' leader*[11]

For most of the twentieth century, homeowners' associations (HAs) have been the 'trade unions' of an important section of the middle class. Yet they remain largely a *terra incognita*, neglected by urban historians and sociologists alike. The sparse academic literature on the subject focuses almost entirely on the recent proliferation (over 16,000 in California alone) of so-called 'common interest' homeowners' associations (CIHAs) mandatorily tied to condominium and planned unit developments.[12] The traditional HA – organizing owners of detached, single-family homes (usually without the common property component of CIHAs) – has a bibliography only in land law case studies. However familiar a feature on the landscape of Los Angeles (and the suburban fringes of other American cities), it remains an invisible object in social science.

Before meeting the earliest local examples of this neglected species, it is useful to make some primitive taxonomic distinctions. Some homeowners' associations are entirely voluntary coalescences of perceived common interest; many others are mandatory enrolments (*preorganized* by developers) of all residents of a tract or planned unit development. Amongst the former, HAs banded together against an external threat tend to be more cohesive than those organized merely for self-improvement. Amongst the latter it is important to distinguish the new-fangled CIHAs – with their quotidian, quasi-governmental responsibilities for common property – from older HAs organized around the enforcement of legally binding subdivision deed restrictions.

The first HAs in Los Angeles, beginning with the Los Felix Improvement Association in 1916, were the children of deed restrictions in a new kind of planned subdivision.[13] As Marc Weiss has pointed out in *The Rise of Community Builders*, early-twentieth-century Los Angeles established the national legal precedent for zoning districts exclusively for upscale, single-family residences. Moreover, the local real-estate industry, dominated by 'highend' builders exploiting economies of scale, specialized in the creation of large planned subdivisions on the urban fringe. Together with exclusionary zoning and stringent subdivision regulation, deed restrictions, that 'both mandated and prohibited certain types of behavior on the part of the present and future property owner', constituted 'the main method by which community builders implemented their planning and design vision'. Although deed restrictions also specified details of lot and home design, their overriding purpose was to ensure social and racial homogeneity. 'Private restrictions, for example, normally included such provisions as minimum required costs for home construction, and exclusion of all non-Caucasians [and sometimes non-Christians as well] from occupancy, except as domestic servants.'[14]

By World War One, deed restrictions (or restrictive covenants), enforced by tract HAs, were helping to define the insulated, middle-class world of Los Angeles's Westside. At the same time, acting as private Jim Crow legislation, deed restrictions were also building a 'white wall' around the Black community on Central Avenue. Homeowners' associations first appeared on the *political* scene in the 1920s as instruments of white mobilization against attempts by Blacks to buy homes outside the ghetto. Where tracts were not already legally bound by subdivision deeds, white homeowners banded together as 'protective associations' to create racially specified 'block restrictions'. Some neighborhoods carried both deed and block racial restrictions. In this fashion 95 per cent of the city's housing stock in the 1920s was effectively put off limits to Blacks and Asians.[15]

In her 1929 study of the 'University Addition' neighborhood near the University of Southern California, sociologist Bessie McClenahan described how the arrival of a single Black family east of Budlong Avenue in the summer of 1922 sowed panic that home values would collapse in the wake of an imminent 'Negro Invasion'. Whites quickly formed the 'Anti-African Housing Association' (limited to homeowners) to campaign for a restrictive agreement to exclude non-whites (Japanese as well as Blacks) from the neighborhood. Although the Anti-African Association (later renamed the University District Property Owners Association) also sponsored street paving and school construction, its main purpose continued to be the defense of the white *laager* between Vermont and Budlong avenues.[16]

As industrial conversion in the 1930s consumed hundreds of Black homes in the Central Avenue corridor, overcrowding became critical. But every foray by Black homebuyers into an outside residential area was met by the immediate wrath of white homeowners. Sometimes, as in the case of the White Homeowners Association, formed under the auspices of the Broadway Business Association, local chamber of commerce elements played a key instigating role. In other cases, homeowner protective groups overlapped with Ku Klux Klan vigilantism, for example in beach communities where Blacks were harassed and driven out in a series of incidents in the 1920s and 1930s. (Los Angeles's satellite suburbs in the 1920s have been described by one historian as a 'happy hunting ground of the Klan'.)[17] White homeowners' associations were also frequently used as springboards for demagogic political ambitions. Thus Harry Burker, the erstwhile president of the White Home Owners Protective Association (covering a vast residential area bounded by Santa Barbara, Main, Manchester and Vermont) ran for various municipal offices on a platform of Black and Mexican exclusion.[18]

Until the US Supreme Court finally ruled against restrictive covenants in 1948, white homeowner groups in Los Angeles had ample sanction in the law. The California Supreme Court first established the doctrine in the Gary case of 1919, extended it to *post facto* 'block' restrictions in *Wayt versus Patee* (1928), and continued to reaffirm it as late as 1947. As a result white homeowners were able to file more than a hundred suits against non-white homebuyers (including even Hollywood celebrities like Hattie McDaniel and Louis Beavers), while a compliant Superior Court regularly found

Blacks as well as Filipinos and Native Americans in contempt for occupying homes within restricted subdivisions or blocks. Lest Blacks cling to any illusion about the benevolence of the New Deal, Roosevelt's Federal Housing Authority not only sanctioned restrictions, but developed a recommended formula for inclusion in subdivision contracts.[19]

Restrictionism, moreover, was a lucrative business. It has been estimated that $17 out of every $20 subscribed by white homeowners to join a 'protective association' ended up as profit in the hands of organizers and allied title companies.[20] Thus the upscale Southwest Wilshire Protective Association generated handsome commissions for its founder, Charles Shattuck (brother of Republican leader Ed Shattuck), and its president, W.W. Powell, whose Title Insurance and Trust Company processed 90 per cent of Los Angeles's restrictive covenant agreements. Los Angeles's largest and most prestigious law firm – Gibson, Dunn and Crutcher – also reaped generous rewards from its long service fighting open housing on behalf of realtors' groups.[21]

The wartime housing shortage only exacerbated racial conflict. The immigration of tens of thousands of Black war workers from the Southwest imposed intolerable strains on the confined housing stock of the Los Angeles ghetto. As Blacks tried to jump over the 'white wall' to buy shelter in outlying suburban or rural fringes, they were met by a new wave of homeowner hostility. As Lawrence de Graaf observes, the San Gabriel Valley was a particularly notorious citadel of restrictionism:

Residential segregation was steadily tightened during the early 1940s as white property owners secured the limited supply of housing outside existing Negro areas for white occupancy only by attaching race restrictive covenants to the titles. In several areas . . . 'home improvement' associations led vigorous campaigns to cover all standing residential structures with covenants. Much of the San Gabriel Valley and Pasadena was thus closed to Negroes in 1941.[22]

In the immediate postwar period, local chambers of commerce and homeowners' groups, supported by developers, attempted to restrict the entire western half of the San Fernando Valley to Black immigration. The Huntington Park Homeowners Association became the model for a comparable effort to keep Blacks out of the white industrial suburbs east of

Alameda Avenue's 'Cotton Curtain'. On the Westside, Black entry was blocked by powerful middle-class housing associations with ironclad covenants.[23] The only conceivable *lebensraum* was south and southwest, where lower-middle-class white homeowners bitterly contested housing integration, block by block.[24]

Veteran Black newspaper publisher Charlotta Bass recalled some of these now forgotten battles in her memoirs. On the eve of Pearl Harbor, for example, whites in the West Jefferson area sued to evict five Black homeowners, while the local Klan burnt 'Keep Slauson White!' crosses a few blocks away. The gradually increasing Black presence in the old railroad town of Watts was contested by the virulent South Los Angeles Home Owners Association, whose spores later became the core of white resistance in Willowbrook and Compton further south. A Black home was blown up (presumably by the Klan) on 30th Street, crosses were burnt in Crenshaw and on the USC campus, and white homeowners rioted against sales to Blacks on East 71st Street.[25] Finally, just before Christmas 1945, Southland residential racism reached its gruesome climax with the Fontana *auto da fe* discussed in chapter seven below.

If white homeowner resistance in Southcentral Los Angeles gradually dissipated after the Korean War, although continuing ferociously along the ghetto's western and eastern edges,[26] it was largely because Southside whites were fleeing to the new suburbs in the San Fernando Valley and across the southeastern tier of Los Angeles County. Despite the 1948 Supreme Court ruling against restrictive covenants and the 1950 repeal of California's Alien Land law, suburban developers continued to exclude Blacks, Chicanos and Asians.[27] Moreover the growth of the suburban population outside the Los Angeles city limits (a majority of the County's population by 1950) offered a new terrain for homeowner separatism: this time with the aim of putting the more permanent barriers of independent incorporation and exclusive land-use zoning between themselves and non-white, or non-homeowning, populations. The emergence of suburban Southern California as a 'metrosea' of fragmented and insular local sovereignties – often depicted in urbanist literature as an 'accident' of unplanned growth – was in fact the result of deliberate shaping. A second wave of homeowner activists collaborated with realtors and developers to plan postwar racial and class segregation in the *Leave It to Beaver* suburbs.

SUBURBAN SEPARATISM

The municipal incorporation of the Lakewood Plan cities was a revolt
of the rich against the poor . . . *Gary Miller*[28]

To understand the role of homeowners as potent agents of metropolitan
fragmentation, it is first necessary to explain how the ground rules of
separatism evolved. Prior to the 1950s, the separate incorporation of small
populations had been a game only a handful of special interests could afford
to play. On the one hand, aristocratic incorporations like Beverly Hills and
San Marino were the first to realize the full potential of zoning law as
barbed-wire social fencing around home values. On the other hand,
powerful industrial landowners created the 'phantom city' of Vernon to
exploit land-use control and hoard their lucrative tax base. But in most
cases incorporation-minded homeowners or industrialists were deterred by
the tax burdens involved in establishing new muncipal services. Many
preferred to be 'free-riders' in undertaxed, unincorporated county areas –
a situation that maximized fiscal advantage even if it ceded local control
over zoning.[29]

Separate incorporation, however, acquired new momentum after the
Korean War. The instigators (whom we met in the last chapter) were the
'merchant builders' who were mass-producing, with the aid of the
burgeoning savings-and-loan industry, scores of new suburban communities
out of raw farm land. Lakewood, just north of Long Beach, was twice the
size of Long Island's more famous Levittown, and contained the nation's
pioneer regional shopping center. Threatened with annexation by Long
Beach, its developers, Weingart, Boyar and Taper, hired consultants to
explore options for incorporation without the traditional cost of creating
city government out of whole cloth.

The result was the famous 'Lakewood Plan'. Anxious to avoid shrinkage
of their budget and workforce through suburban municipalization, and
equally opposed to any form of metropolitan consolidation, the Los Angeles
County Supervisors agreed to let Lakewood contract its vital services (fire,
police, library, and so on) at cut-rate prices determined by the county's
economy of scale (i.e., indirectly subsidized by all county taxpayers). This
allowed suburban communities to reclaim control over zoning and land use

without the burden of public expenditures proportionate to those of older cities.

A few years later the Legislature stepped in to sweeten the Lakewood Plan even more. The 1956 Bradley–Burns Act allowed all local governments in the state to collect a uniform 1 per cent sales tax for their own use. This meant that fringe areas with new-fangled shopping centers or other commercial assets could finance city government without resorting to a property tax. In other words, Sacramento licensed suburban governments to pay for their contracted county services with regressive sales revenues rather than progressive property taxes – a direct subsidy to suburban separatism at the expense of the weakened tax bases of primate cities.[30]

In his brilliant study of the twenty-six new 'minimal cities' formed along Lakewood lines in Los Angeles County between 1954 and 1960, Gary Miller has shown that it was not 'municipal efficiency' (as claimed by 'Public Choice' theorists) but self-seeking economic advantage that impelled incorporation. 'The reasons for creating or moving to a . . . minimal city was not to signal something unique about one's demand for public goods, but to insulate one's property from the burden of supporting public services.' This 'exit privilege' – subsidized by the County and State – was enhanced by the other advantages of local control. Residents of minimal cities could zone out service-demanding low-income and renting populations, eliminate (through service contracting) homegrown union or bureaucratic pressures for service expansion, and, perhaps most importantly, safeguard their property from potential utilization as a resource for government expansion or fiscal redistribution.[31] Needless to say, by providing such an attractive escape hatch from ordinary municipal citizenship, the Lakewood Plan fueled white flight from Los Angeles, while at the same time reducing the city's capacity to deal with the needs of increasing low-income and renter populations.[32]

Although a galaxy of different interest groups, ranging from public-sector unions to industrialists, supported the 'Lakewoodization' of Southern California's suburban fringe, the major social impetus came from organized homeowners. Miller skilfully demonstrates how the ideology of the 1970s tax revolt (as well as, by extension, the 1980s slow-growth protests) was prefigured by the 1950s and early 1960s movements for suburban incorporation, which unified 'middle-class and upper-class home-owners . . . around an anti-bureaucratic, anti-welfare ideology'. Typical pro-incorporation literature luridly depicted homes threatened by 'exorbitant taxes to pay for redistributional services and bureaucratic salaries'. 'Long before this theme was being sounded by Howard Jarvis, it was being consciously articulated as the rationale for new jurisdictions, where the evils of bureaucracy could be forever exorcised.'[33]

The role of homeowners in these separatist struggles, however, differed markedly as a function of economic status. Wealthy homeowners were typically the leaders in local incorporation, while middling home-owners – to the extent that they were not the group being incorporated *against* – were usually the led. The most famous movement of affluent surburbanites in this period was the campaign by Palos Verdes homeowners to turn that peninsula into a congerie of walled, privatized residential 'cities'. In the process, home values and organizational capacity seemed directly correlated. Thus the very wealthy Rolling Hills area had a single, powerful homeowners' association that engineered its incorporation. Partially to ensure a protective single-family barrier around themselves, the Rolling Hillsites supported the anti-development incorporation of affluent, but less resplendent, Rancho Palos Verdes (after, however, deliberately excluding the lower-middle-class homeowners in the San Pedro Hills tract). Rolling Hills and Rancho Palos Verdes then combined forces to promote the incorporation of Rolling Hills Estate. Incorporation expert Johnny Johnson – the Mephistopheles of a dozen Lakewood Plan cities – was brought in to consolidate the Estate's two dozen contentious homeowners' associations into a single federation on the Rolling Hills model. [34]

The basis of almost every residential incorporation in this era was the existence of a sharp gradient of home values between the inclusive community and the area intended for exclusion. South El Monte, for instance, was scarcely a Shangri-la like Rolling Hills, but its incorporation allowed its middle-income homeowners to separate themselves from nearby apartment dwellers and welfare recipients. In other cases, the insulation of home values went hand in hand with the definition of communal lifestyles. Thus the incorporation of La Habra Heights enabled its homeowners' associations to restrict development and impose a one-acre minimum zoning law to ensure the maintenance of a 'horse-oriented community'.

Other minimal cities have anchored home values in amenities as varied as golf courses, beach fronts, universities, and country clubs.

These myriad local manipulations of the 'exit option' by homeowners' groups and business cliques have generated the current nonsense-jigsaw map of Southern California. One consequence of this ongoing process – Lakewood Plan populations now exceed one and a half million in Los Angeles County – has been the extension of residential segregation across a vast metropolitan space. According to the 1980 Census, Los Angeles County was nearly 13 per cent Black, but 53 of its 82 cities (including 30 Lakewood Plan incorporations) had Black populations of 1 per cent or less.[35] Moreover, Orange County – conceived, as Miller suggests, as 'perform[ing] the same function for middle-class taxpayers that the Lakewood Plan cities were originally intended to perform, but. perform[ing] that function more effectively' – reproduces the same result: with 0.6 per cent Black housing units compared to 10 per cent in Los Angeles County. Overall, while established Black and Chicano neighborhoods were losing several thousand units a year to freeway construction, non-Anglos were able to purchase only 3.3 per cent of the new housing stock constructed during the 1950s boom.[36]

'Lakewoodism', combined with a widening homeownership gap since the 1960s, has also accelerated the sorting out of the county's population between zones of single-family homeowners (the majority in low-tax-rate minimal cities) and renters (the increasing majority in higher-tax older cities). 'Between 1960 and 1970 home ownership in the county as a whole dropped dramatically, but homeowners continued to be attracted to the Lakewood Plan cities.' At the same time, homeowners in some older, 'independent cities' – like Whittier, Culver City, Manhattan Beach, Torrance and Glendora – gentrified themselves by 'fiscal zoning': by restricting construction of multi-family dwellings, raising the threshold value (or lot size) of new housing, and competing for commercial centers.[37]

Miller argues that the 1970s explosion in property values – which, as we shall see, spurred both the tax revolt and slow-growth protests – was directly related to limitations on housing expansion and residential densification brought about by the 'fiscal zoning' practices of the Lakewood cities and their older imitators. The affluent enclaves with their gold-plated, ever-rising property values tend to steal higher-income taxpayers as well as shopping malls from primate cities and needier suburbs, thus intensifying the spiraling conflict between rich and poor cities over revenue-generating resources. The huge magnet of fiscal zoning has also sucked hundreds of industries out of the heart of Los Angeles. In 1977 the *Times* reported that the city was losing up to fifty firms a year to the suburbs and Orange County, a trend that only increased in the 1980s with the flight of industry and warehousing to the Inland Empire. Not surprisingly Black workers, less mobile than their jobs because of de facto residential segregation, have suffered disproportionately from this relocation of industry.[38]

To summarize: the Lakewood Plan and the Bradley–Burns Act gave suburban homeowners a subsidized 'exit option' as well as a powerful new motive for organizing around the 'protection' of their home values and lifestyles. The ensuing maximization of local advantage through incorporation and fiscal zoning – whether led by affluent homeowners or business fractions – inevitably produced widening racial and income divides. And, by eroding the tax base of the city of Los Angeles, this fiscal-driven spatial restructuring precipitated more bitter, zero-sum struggles between the affluent homeowner belts of the Westside and Valley, and a growing inner-city population dependent upon public services. As we shall see later, part of the logic of the 1978 tax revolt, which burned over the Valley in particular, was to equalize advantages between Los Angeles's 'captive' white suburbanites and the residents of the Lakewoodized periphery.

DEFENDING THE FAT LIFE

It is Nature's contours versus Man's ever stronger bulldozers, the historic past versus the politically expedient, the private vale versus the public highway, the orchard versus the subdivision, . . . the person versus the populace. . . . *Richard Lillard, 1966*[39]

The history of homeowner activism in Southern California divides into two epochs. In the period we have examined so far – roughly the forty years between 1920 and 1960 – homeowners' associations were overwhelmingly concerned with the *establishment* of what Robert Fishman has called 'bourgeois utopia': that is, with the creation of racially and economically homogeneous residential enclaves glorifying the single-family home.[40] In the subsequent period – roughly since the beginning of the Kennedy–Johnson boom – homeowner politics have focused on *defense* of this suburban dream against unwanted development (industry, apartments and offices) as well as against unwanted persons. The first epoch saw only episodic conflicts between developers and homeowners; indeed the former were frequently the mobilizers of the latter in the common cause of exclusionism. Homeowners had little material interest in opposing home-value-raising 'growth', except in occasional cases where it threatened to dump noxious uses on their doorsteps.

After 1965 the structural context of homeowner interests dramatically changed. On one hand, the open space amenities that supported the life-styles and home values of wealthy hillside and beach dwellers were threatened by rampant, large-scale development; on the other, traditional single-family tracts were suddenly inundated by waves of apartment construction. New development was perceived as a categorical threat to the detached culture of low-density residential life. However reluctantly, in the face of entrenched conservative stereotypes and prejudices, elements of the environmental critique advanced by the Sierra Club and California Tomorrow gained currency amongst homeowner activists, who grasped at the notion that the endangered open spaces around their homes – even the 'pastoral scatteredness' (aka sprawl) of their subdivisions – were conservation values as much as rock piles in Yosemite or wild rivers on remote coasts.

This 'new urban environmentalism' is usually recalled as a Bay Area invention associated with the 1960s movements to save the Bay and preserve hillside open space, which subsequently spilled over into statewide efforts at coastal conservation in the Jerry Brown era. In fact, identical concerns about deteriorating amenities produced parallel backlashes against growth in a number of wealthy Southern California communities. By the early 1970s, for example, environmental regulation of land use had become a potent, sometimes explosive, issue in the archipelago of 'redtile' communities from Coronado and Point Loma (in San Diego), to San Clemente, San Juan Capistrano, Newport Beach, Riverside, Redlands and Santa Barbara. These old-money resorts and retirement centers, built out of restrictive covenants and Spanish Colonial architecture, contained influential constituencies of retired admirals, landscape artists, horse ranchers, professors, yachtsmen, and the like – all determined to see that disruptive development went somewhere else.

But the best southern analogue to Bay Area patrician environmentalism was the broad-based homeowners' movement that emerged in the 1960s to 'save' the Santa Monica Mountains. This famous range, from the movie colony at Malibu to the Griffith Observatory (including the Hollywood Hills), contains one of the largest concentrations of affluence on the planet: a unique ecology which Reyner Banham memorably described as the 'fat life of the delectable mountains'. Thousands of rambling split-levels, mansard-roofed mansions and mock Greek temples shelter in the artificial lushness of dozens of arroyos and canyons with world-famous names. But, as Banham pointed out, it is an ecology imperiled by its own desirability: on the one hand, by overdevelopment and 'hill cropping'; on the other, by man-made disasters like slides and fires.[41] With lifestyles and property values so dependent upon the preservation of a delicate balance, it is not surprising that wealthy homeowners emerged from their 'thickets of privacy' to organize the earliest and most powerful coalition of homeowners' associations in the country.

Already in the early 1950s, the pioneer Federation of Hillside and Canyon Homeowners, founded in the gated movie colony of Bel-Air, was crusading against hotrodding on Mulholland Drive and lobbying for slope-density down-zoning and the establishment of minimum lot sizes to control new hillside development. With a dozen affiliated associations by the mid 1960s (grown to fifty in 1990), and armed with volunteer expertise in land-use law and planning, the Federation was an evolutionary leap beyond any homeowners' group in existence.[42]

Moreover, at a time when academic opinion still visualized the typical Southern California homeowner as a yahoo with a power mower and a Goldwater bumpersticker, the Federation's world view was being represented by Richard Lillard's acclaimed *Eden in Jeopardy (Man's prodigal meddling with his environment: The Southern California experience)* (1966). A founder of the Federation and first president of the Residents of Beverly Glen, Inc., Lillard polemicized passionately (and at times almost radically) against a mechanized capitalism that seemed determined to turn nature into 'one big parking lot' and to erase the past with a 'quickened destruction more exact than wartime bombing'. In an extraordinary epilogue, which remains an eloquent summary of the Federation's ideology, he described the opposed value systems locked in struggle over the future of Los Angeles:

Allied on the one side have been love for unspoiled nature and adjustment to it, respect for the past, conservationism and conservatism, single-dwelling home life, agriculture, Utopianism, the status quo, individual character, established wealth, traditional legality, privacy and private property, and nostalgia. . . . On the other side are concentration on development and alteration, immediate use and exploitation of nature or improvement on nature, emphasis on repetitive recreation for masses of people, the inalienable rights of all to the pursuit of happiness, adulation of novelty and the doings of the newly prominent, and a faith in force, machinery and progress.[43]

For Lillard and the Federation, Eden's last-ditch defense was in the Santa Monicas, where a handful of large landowners – including Hilton Hotels, the Lantain Corporation, Castle and Cooke, Gulf-America and the Tucker Land Company – were threatening to 'despoil' the hillsides west of Sepulveda Pass. They had capitalized the Las Virgenes and Triunfo water districts with the aim of bringing as many as 450,000 new residents into mountain tracts (including Lantain's proposed '20-square-mile Trousdale Estates' nightmare). Development, however, hinged on a plan by the State Division of Highways to cut four new freeways through wild canyons and to convert scenic Mulholland Drive, on the crestline of the Santa Monicas, into a four-lane, 120-foot-wide expressway. The Federation, in alliance with the Sierra Club and Friends of the Santa Monica Mountains, mobilized ten thousand homeowners to oppose this 'lunatic' mountain freeway scheme. Their petition counterposed the creation of a regional park to permanently conserve open space.[44]

The first chairperson of the resulting Santa Monica Mountain Regional Park Association was a wealthy electronics entrepreneur, Marvin Braude, who presided over the Crestwood Hills Homeowners Association, a Federation affiliate in Brentwood. Braude – who today relishes his reputation as 'the sage of the slow-growth movement' – was the first standard-bearer for homeowners on the Los Angeles city council. With the ardent support of the Federation and the Santa Monicas movement, he ousted the bribe-tainted incumbent in the ritzy eleventh councilmanic district (which included the Reagans' ould sod of Pacific Palisades) in 1967 and began his long, unbroken representation of the interests of Westside canyon and hill dwellers.[45]

To veteran politicos, however, Braude's election was a fluke. Although the protracted struggle against the corporate exploitation of the mountains (and the related issue of offshore oil drilling in Santa Monica Bay) had injected environmental issues into city politics, the hillside homeowners were still caricaturable as 'limousine conservationists'. The 'greening' of the Santa Monicas, like growth-control initiatives in redtile beach towns or Marin County villages, was widely seen as a hypocritical attempt by the rich to use ecology to detour Vietnam-era growth around their luxury enclaves. By 1972, however, this first wave of preservationist protest was reinforced by populist outbursts in dozens of flatland white-collar communities. Suddenly 'slow growth' no longer seemed so socially precious or, for that matter, politically containable.

REVOLT AGAINST DENSITY

> Those immortal ballads, *Home Sweet Home*, *My Old Kentucky Home*, and
> *The Little Gray Home in the West*, were not written about apartments
> ... they never sang songs about a pile of rent receipts.
> *Herbert Hoover*[46]

The explicit issue of this shortlived prefigurative revolt was 'density', especially the Vietnam-boom apartment and condominium construction that was perceived to be drowning Edenic landscapes of detached, single-family homes on quiet streets. Although the suburban wrath of 1972–3 caught many politicians by surprise, it had a distant direct ancestor in a 1956 uprising of Valley homeowners against the so-called 'Simons' Resurvey', that threatened to dump 2,600 acres of industry into single-family subdivisions.[47] As in the 1970s, homeowners had rallied to prevent the 'contamination' of their lifestyles. But whereas in the 1950s the issue had simply concerned zoning, in the 1970s it had overtones of an emerging Darwinian struggle between homeowners on one hand, and developers and renters on the other.

The new, deeper causality was an epochal change in the regional political economy, an unexpected clouding of the California dream. The postwar virtuous circle of good jobs, rising incomes, cheap land, and quality public services was beginning its slow disintegration into the present vicious circle of social polarization, expensive land and a declining public sector. The Watts Rebellion of 1965, and the subsequent 'Chicano Power' protests, had already registered non-Anglo anger at exclusion from boom times and decent housing; after 1970 new class contradictions began to surface in white suburbia as well.

Orange County – the home rush frontier of the 1950s – provides a vivid illustration of this historic transition. In 1960 over two-thirds of the new housing units constructed in the county had been detached single-family homes. By the end of the decade the proportions were almost reversed: 60 per cent of new construction consisted of apartments and condominiums. Higher interest rates in the late sixties, combined with a disappearing supply of cheap farm land and the entry into the housing market of younger and poorer 'baby boom' families, drastically altered the equation of housing affordability. Starter homes for under $20,000 (in real terms) – the basis for family formation in the 1950s – became extinct, while the percentage of Southern California households with incomes at the minimum mortgage threshold fell from over half to barely a quarter.[48]

The development industry, evolving into the 'new Octopus' discussed previously, adapted to this structural change with a combination of strategies. On the one hand, it applied tremendous pressures on planning agencies in the six Southern California counties to open up virgin home-building frontiers in the mountains, desert and interior basins.[49] Although the Federation blocked the juggernaut in the western Santa Monicas, compliant county supervisors sacrificed a million acres of open space for breakneck single-family development in the Agoura and La Puente hills, the Conjeo, Santa Clarita, Simi and Saddleback valleys, the San Bernardino and San Jacinto basins, and the Mojave Desert around Palmdale. The developers neglected to calculate, however, that the first generation of arriving home-owners would have a powerful interest in trying to pull up the gangplanks to prevent further urbanization and loss of rural amenities.

Meanwhile developers were also busy infilling the single-family belts of the urban coastal plain with multi-unit housing , carefully segmented to take

LAND INFLATION

optimum advantage of land values and market demand. At the upscale end
they introduced planned communities of condos and 'townhouses' (i.e. row
houses for the middle class); at the lower end, they constructed seeming
infinities of 'dingbat' stucco tenements.[50] Planners and politicians accommodated the new density by re-zoning single-family zones. In some older
urban areas – East San Diego, parts of Santa Monica, Long Beach, and so on
– whole neighborhoods of 1920s bungalows were ripped out and replaced
by rows of badly built dingbats. A stratum of homeowners (primarily elderly
people who owned a second home, rental unit or developable lot), as well
as wealthy 'tax investors' attracted to the lucrative write-offs of multi-unit
housing, were instant beneficiaries of densification. Most homeowners,
however, were angered by the rate of infill, the deterioration of the physical
aspect of their communities, increasing traffic congestion, rising numbers
of poorer people (and sometimes minorities), perceived tax costs, and the
dilution of their political clout.

Accumulated resentments against apartment construction and
suburban 'deruralization' vented themselves in the April and June 1972
local elections. The *Times* Orange County edition noted that 'disaffected
homeowners and environmental groups turned out in large numbers in
South Coast cities to unseat incumbents'. In Tustin, Brea, Yorba Linda,
Orange and Fullerton simmering grievances over apartment infill boiled
over into bitter council contests. In unincorporated Laguna Niguel,
residents appealed to county supervisors to prevent further increases in
density, while the homeowners' associations of the Saddleback Valley
banded together to seek federal funding for a study of how to restrict
density and preserve open space. In Irvine the slow-growth realignment of
the 1980s was prefigured by the Citizens' Coalition which united
homeowners and environmentalists to protest the city's repeated failure to
keep faith with its promise of responsible growth management. Finally, in
redtiled Newport Beach and San Juan Capistrano, irate homeowners tossed
out pro-growth mayors and their supporters.[51]

Further up the coast, Torrance, Hermosa Beach and Redondo Beach –
launching their careers as upwardly-mobile fiscal zoners – passed new
limitations on apartment construction, while the 'Save Our Coastline'
coalition crusaded to incorporate Rancho Palos Verdes as a further rampart
against apartment encroachment on the peninsula. Within Los Angeles

itself (in subsequent months), the Hillside Federation campaigned to stop the sprawling Allied Canon project in Benedict Canyon, while a dozen Valley homeowners' associations tangled with the city over pro-apartment zoning revisions.[52]

Far out on the subdivision frontier of eastern Los Angeles County, homeowners' associations from Hacienda Heights, Diamond Bar and Rowland Heights united as the Puente Hills Community Coalition to petition supervisors to roll back apartment zoning, restrict development to one-acre lots, and provide more recreational land (demands echoed a few miles away by a La Habra Heights homeowners' coalition). Anti-density tremors continued eastward through redtiled Riverside and Redlands before reaching a crescendo in Palm Springs where Desert People United confronted voters in the fall elections with the choice, 'Carmel versus Las Vegas!'. The first act of the newly elected slow-growth council majority was to impose a tough 120-day moratorium on multiple-unit construction.[53]

The significance of these Southland skirmishes was amplified statewide by the parallel progress of local growth control in Northern California and, especially, by the passage in November of Proposition 20, which provided for coastal commissions to control beachfront development. In the course of the battle over Proposition 20, the Sacramento *Bee* revealed that Jack Crose, formerly Jesse Unruh's chief aide and now nemesis to the Hillside Federation as lobbyist for the Santa Monica Mountain landowners, had organized thirty-four capital lobbyists into the so-called 'Committee to Kill Ecology Legislation'.[54] Faced with a spreading homeowners' revolt, the development industry suddenly sang the praises of regional government and housing the poor. In a revealing *Times* op-ed piece, super-developer Eli Broad, posing the issue of the 1970s as 'no growth versus low-income housing', argued that the region needed 'larger-scale decision-making . . . less subject to local prejudice'.[55]

But the 1972–3 Los Angeles mayoral campaign resounded with a cacophony of 'local prejudices'. Although Broad and the building-trades unions rallied around the pro-growth carpetbagging of 'Big Daddy' Unruh, a majority of developers clung to incumbent Mayor Yorty. Originally elected in 1961 on a wave of Valley homeowner resentment against Downtown – Yorty now became the hammer of growth control. Torquing up Broad's pseudo-proletarian rhetoric, he churlishly denounced City

Planning Director Calvin Hamilton's proposal to safeguard single-family areas by rolling back some of the multiple unit zoning – a move Yorty claimed would create a city 'that only the rich could afford to live in'. On another occasion he stupefied observers by demanding that leaders of homeowners' associations be forced to register themselves as political lobbyists. Finally, at a 'Yorty Years Dinner', he 'attacked Communists, environmentalists, opponents of city oil drilling and concluded the speech by [again] denouncing Hamilton's zoning rollback plan'.[56]

On the other side, Councilmember Tom Bradley – Yorty's opponent in the racially polarized 1969 election – wooed homeowners with his support for down-zoning and opposition to Palisades oil-drilling. But the leadership of the density revolt, uneasy about supporting a Black and worried that labor's defection to Unruh had fatally wounded Bradley, preferred to coin their own candidate. Over Thanksgiving 1972, representatives of fifty Valley and hillside homeowners' associations, led by Shirley Solomon of No Oil Inc. and Elliot Blinderman of the Benedict Canyon Homeowners (a Federation affiliate), rallied to endorse Joel Wachs, junior councilmember from the Valley. The Hillside Federation had helped to engineer Wachs's election in 1981 after his predecessor, James Potter, had been implicated in the 'Beverly Ridge' scandal involving a mountain land scheme financed by a Teamster pension fund with Mafia undertones. Running on an anti-apartment, 'neighborhood protection' platform, Wachs boasted that he would 'be able to unite homeowner groups in the Valley, mountains, the Westside, the Wilshire District and other areas, "making each one see they have something in common" '.[57]

Meanwhile Councilmember Braude, the original champion of growth limitation, had vaulted into the county supervisors' race, challenging a Reagan appointee in the fourth district along Santa Monica Bay and the Palos Verdes Peninsula. Campaigning as ardent conservationist, he mobilized a core support which the *Times* described as 'the middle- and upper-middle-class people who live in coastal neighborhoods, feel settled, and are deeply concerned about preserving and improving the environment around them'. Braude told audiences that the recent 'Friends of Mammoth' court decision, extending California's 1970 Environmental Quality Act to private developments, armed office-holders with new powers to implement environmentalist land planning. Braude's threat to developers' hegemony over county government was reinforced by the maverick candidacy of newscaster Baxter Ward in the Valley and North County. Although not a *soi-disant* environmentalist, Ward was nonetheless attuned to the concerns of insurgent homeowners and unbeholden to any corporate interest.[58]

In the event, the 1973 elections had mixed, and not entirely happy, results for the emerging politics of slow growth. In the mayoral race, Yorty's silly, McCarthyite fulminations against commie-environmentalists estranged many of the same Westside and Valley homeowners who had once warmed to his 'just plain white folks' style. But the Unruh and Wachs forces underestimated the centrality of the Black Southcentral electorate to any realignment in city politics. Unruh's massive paper strength wilted into a poor third-place showing in the primary, while Wachs registered a barely discernible blip. Bradley, regrouping trade-union support and harvesting Westside homeowners, handily overcame Yorty's desperate, last-minute barrage of racist innuendo.[59] But in any inventory of Bradley's political debts, homeowners and environmentalists were far down on the list, behind his outstanding obligations to growth-hungry unions, inner-city politicos and the Downtown development interests represented by the *Times*.

In the supervisorial races, meanwhile, Braude – despite a vigorous campaign – had minimal success carrying the gospel of affluent home-owners into industrial areas like Torrance and Compton. Baxter Ward was more fortunate in the San Fernando Valley, but his victory was counter-balanced by the confirmation of Pete Schabarum, a former pro football player and real-estate developer, in the San Gabriel Valley. With a huge warchest from developers, Schabarum began to build one of the two most powerful Republican organizations in Southern California (the other being Orange County's Lincoln Club). Massively outspending the opposition, Schabarum had managed by 1980 to ensconce two protégés, Antonovich (replacing Ward) and Dana, as a three-man, right-wing supervisorial majority – the power center, so to speak, of a broad network of conservative local officials in suburban cities committed to pro-developer land use policies and the privatization of mass transit.[60]

The paradoxical result of the 1972–3 density revolt, in short, was to reinforce pro-growth coalitions at both the city and county levels. The first wave of slow-growth protest galvanized land developers as effectively as homeowners, and their redoubled campaign contributions usually overwhelmed growth-control initiatives. Moreover, as both the Wachs and Braude campaigns illustrated, opposition to apartment construction alienated renters and minorities who (quite correctly) decoded the racist subtext in 'neighborhood preservationism'. For their part, homeowners' associations, including even the Hillside Federation, lacked the coalition-building skills necessary to overcome their parochial image.

Yet if the density revolt failed to install its own cadre in office, it has had an enormous, ongoing impact on the local regulation of apartment building. Ken Baar, a well-known authority on California housing problems, has rebutted the 'self-serving argument', advanced by landlords and realtors, that rent control is largely responsible for the current, drastic shortage of affordable rental housing in California. Instead he argues that it has been intense 'homeowner opposition to multi-family construction', stemming from the mobilizations of the early 1970s, that has constrained the supply of land for multi-family housing. Moreover, like Proposition 13, the restriction of apartment construction is generally seen as a politically irreversible fact bordering on homeowner 'right':

[I]t is not politically feasible for either the legislature or courts to force localities to ease such restrictions. . . . Few homeowners want rental units in their neighborhood after struggling to buy a single family dwelling with a yard. One of the most cherished property rights in our 'free enterprise system' is not the right to do what one pleases with one's property, but the right to live in a neighborhood in which no more multi-family housing may be constructed.[61]

THE BIG BANG

It was the Watts Riot of the Middle Classes.[62]

The folk maxim that gaunt men rebel while fat men sleep was neatly reversed by the historic suburban protests of 1976–9. In face of a massive inflationary redistribution of wealth, it was the haves, not the have-nots, who raised their pikes in the great tax revolt and its kindred school and growth protests. Many of the actors in this drama were the direct beneficiaries of one of the largest mass windfalls of wealth in history. Consider, for a moment, the position of established homeowners in the older suburban areas of coastal Southern California at the end of the seventies.

In the fall of 1973 home prices in Southern California were $1000 below the national average; six years later they were $42,400 higher (fifteen years later, $143,000 higher). If in the flatlands of the Valley home values only doubled, they tripled or quadrupled in the hills or near the beach. In Beverly Hills, median home values increased $200,000 in a single year. Averaged over all of Southern California, homeowners were reported to be earning 30–40 per cent on their equity per annum, in adjusted terms, in the late 1970s, and home values increased almost three times faster than income. As 'the purpose of housing units came to be perceived more as investment and speculation than as shelter', house trading became a mass mania. In the course of the decade 164,000 new realtors' licenses were issued (bringing the total to nearly 400,000 by 1981), and homeowners were reported to be mining billions of dollars from their equity (via second trust deeds) to pay for grander lifestyles.[63]

If the infamous German inflation of 1920–23 ruined the Weimar middle class, this Southern California land inflation of 1975–9 by contrast enriched many tens of thousands of middle-class families beyond their wildest expectations. Yet the second inflation ultimately produced almost as much anxiety and political turmoil as the first. Homeowners experienced property inflation as a roller-coaster ride that unsettled traditional household accounting, raising unreasonable hopes and fears at the same time. Moreover their windfalls of wealth appeared precarious, while their bloated tax bills seemed all too real – especially for income-strapped retirees.[64] Anxieties were particularly high in the San Fernando Valley where homeowners, believing themselves to be little more than a tax colony of Downtown L.A., yearned for the kind of local control that their counterparts in the Lakewood Plan cities seemed to possess. To make matters worse, the escalated tax assessments arrived on their doorsteps in the same seasons as court-ordered school busing and a host of new growth-related complaints. It was this *fusion* of grievances in an unstable economic climate, and not just the tax crisis alone, that explains the extraordinarily high emotional temperature in the Southern California suburbs during the summer of 1978.

It is useful, however, to recall briefly the separate itineraries of these grievances before their convergence. Episodic tax revolt, for instance, as any county tax assessor could testify, had long been a malaise of prosperity in postwar suburbia. Irate Valley homeowners in late 1954 had nearly lynched County Assessor John Quinn when he appeared in San Fernando to defend tax increases of up to 1000 per cent. Although Quinn could justify the increases as reflecting actual inflation in property values, the unexpectedness of the hikes had whipped local homeowners into a frenzy of self-righteousness.[65] Tax revolt historian Clarence Lo recounts similar homeowner outbursts (including a recall campaign) against the luckless Quinn in the San Gabriel Valley in 1957, as well as a storming of the Board of Supervisors in 1964 and a taxpayers' strike in 1966.[66]

By the early 1970s – as angry taxpayers in the South Bay and San Gabriel Valley unsuccessfully attempted to secede from Los Angeles County – veteran political observers were warning of the dangers of a coalescence of suburban anti-tax protest, especially in view of right-wing efforts to direct the insurgency against social spending. Although California Democrats were able to stem the tide of Ronald Reagan's 1972 tax limitation initiative (the lineal ancestor of the successful 'Gann amendment' of 1979), they failed miserably to legislate relief for average homeowners or to decouple tax protests from attacks on the social budget. By foolishly hoarding a $4 billion state tax surplus, rather than spending it on social programs defended by mobilized constituencies, Jerry Brown yielded the stage to the demagoguery of Howard Jarvis and the behind-the-scenes machinations of landlords (for whom Jarvis was a lobbyist), realtors and commercial landowners. The Democratic leadership's last-gasp attempt to defuse the revolt with a 'circuit-breaker' bill (giving relief to medium-income and elderly homeowners) was sabotaged by Republicans under the leadership of George Deukmejian, just as homeowners were preparing to confront huge hikes in their assessments.

At this point, of course, the much lampooned 'hicks in the sticks' – the average homeowners of the San Fernando Valley and other non-aristocratic suburban fringes – suddenly materialized into Howard Jarvis's barbarian army at the gates. But the stunning success of Jarvis's California Taxpayers League in collecting 1.5 million signatures on behalf of Proposition 13 drew heavily upon the pre-existing subculture of homeowner activism, especially in its heartland of Los Angeles County. As Lo has shown, homeowners' associations, rather than single-purpose tax-reduction groups, were the preponderant local units in the revolt.[67]

Leaders of the Hillside and Canyon Federation still boast, with justice, that they effectively 'fathered' Proposition 13, supplying expertise, cadre, financing, and a captive bluechip vote. The Federation's largest affiliate, the Sherman Oaks Homeowners Association, was one of the two groups that first launched the tax revolt in the Valley in 1976, and its executives, Richard Close and Jane Nerpel, later became the leaders of Californians for Proposition 13.[68]

The hegemonic role of the Sherman Oaks Association and other upper-middle-class homeowners is a key variable in Lo's theory of how an older, more class-conscious tradition of middle-income tax protest (represented especially by the early 1960s insurgency in the San Gabriel Valley) was ultimately hijacked by the 'upwardly redistributive, pro-business' ideology of Jarvis's United Taxpayers Organization. As Lo vividly portrays it, the wealthy homeowners, stung by the 'frustrated advantage' of much money but little political power, literally came down from the hills to reclaim the tax protest tradition built by flatlands *menu peuple* :

Unable to win by themselves, upper-middle-class homeowners drove down from the scenic hills of the Palos Verdes peninsula, back through the stoplights of Hawthorne Boulevard; down from their *Sunset* magazine homes in the Santa Monica Mountains, back to the unwashed Toyota Tercels gridlocking Ventura Boulevard. . . . There, they mingled with the K-Mart shoppers in the high school auditoriums of old Van Nuys, perhaps sensing the subtle differences in bearing and in taste – realizing just what it was that they had worked so hard to escape. Joining the less affluent in mass meetings, the homeowners of Rolling Hills Estates and Sherman Oaks eventually took the lead in organizing and shaping the entire tax limitation movement.[69]

As virtually everyone recognized at the time, Proposition 13's explicit promise to roll back assessments and let homeowners pocket their capital gains was accompanied, as well, by an implicit promise to halt the threatening encroachment of inner-city populations on suburbia. In rousing their neighbors, tax protestors frequently resorted to the inflammatory image of the family homestead taxed to extinction in order to finance the integration of public education and other social programs obnoxious to white suburbanites.[70] In the Valley in particular the tax revolt overlapped and intermingled with massive resistance to school busing. After a fifteen-year-long legal battle, the courts had finally ordered the brazenly segregated Los Angeles schools to begin busing students for racial balance in 1978. Because Westside schools had possessed the foresight to sponsor token integration, the brunt of the busing was an exchange between Southcentral Los Angeles and the Valley.

As BUSTOP, the demagogic coalition led by Bobbi Fiedler and Paul Clarke, circulated petitions for Senator Alan Robbins's anti-busing Proposition 1, a more muscular, vigilante-type group, FORCE, led by Link Wyler and Assemblyman Paul Cline, organized a protracted school boycott involving more than half of the Valley's white students.[71] But it was again the Sherman Oaks Homeowners Association, acting as the universal gear of suburban anger, who most effectively meshed anti-tax and anti-density campaigns with the anti-busing movement into a unitary protest culture. Roberta Weintraub, the Valley's enduring white-backlash member of the L.A. Board of Education, has paid homage to the Association's role in educating anti-busing militants: 'We learned our political "p's" and "q's" in the Sherman Oaks Homeowners Association.'[72]

Although this explosive mixture of taxes and busing blew the top off the Valley (leading, amongst other things, to the emergence of a new homeowner-oriented Right dominated by Fiedler, Weintraub and Robbins), there was no immediate chain reaction in the region. As long as the yellow school buses only travelled over Cahuenga Pass, white homeowners in other parts of the surburban fringe could not be rallied around anti-busing in the same way they were being mesmerized by Proposition 13. In 1979, how-ever, the court began to hear testimony on a metropolitan school integration scheme that would have mandated busing over the entirety of Los Angeles County, as well as parts of Orange and Ventura counties. This gave a second wind to Valley-based efforts to create a regional movement against school integration. As new franchises sprouted up along Los Angeles's suburban rim, from La Mirada to Santa Clarita, BUSTOP's president Paul Clarke boasted that his membership had surpassed 50,000.[73] Moreover, with Beverly Hills, Santa Monica and West L.A. now proposed as candidates for metropolitan busing, powerful Westside Democratic leaders, like Howard Berman and Zev Yaroslavsky, who had previously welcomed the integration of the Valley, had sudden changes of heart. With the Democratic establishment switching sides, and Mayor

Bradley officially 'neutral', the BUSTOP juggernaut easily rolled over and crushed the bones of the few remaining liberals standing between it and control of the Board of Education.[74]

BUSTOP's victory did little, however, to slow the flight of whites from the public schools or from the older suburban parts of the city (some of which now began to take on inner-city characteristics). Just beyond the city line – in the Conejo, Simi and Santa Clarita valleys – white refugees from the San Fernando Valley were trying to reestablish the suburban Eden of the early 1950s, with low taxes and 'neighborhood' (read: white) schools. In a survey of its residents, Santa Clarita's developer, the Newhall Land Company , 'found that families who relocate in the Santa Clarita Valley cite escaping the L.A. school system as a primary reason'. The new Santa Claritans also stressed low-density, open space, low crime rates, large homes, and the 'country feel'.[75]

But the developers of this white-flight 'outer valley' had no intention of subsidizing a museum-society of suburban nostalgia. Their goal was to urbanize quickly and multiply profits. As long as plenty of open space remained, they intended to plug in more modules of housing and commerce, crowding together units as land prices soared. Not surprisingly, residents of the new valleys – some of whom had been homeowners' association activists in the old Valley – mobilized to resist development that would plunge them back into the city. Thus in Thousand Oaks – the state's fastest growing city – homeowners tried to slow urbanization by rallying against Prudential's plans for a large hillside development. Similar battles were fought in the Simi and Conejo Valleys (on the San Fernando's periphery), and in Walnut and La Habra Heights, on Los Angeles's eastern suburban border. In Santa Clarita protests against metropolitan busing and a tax-revolt proposal to secede from Los Angeles County overlapped with the first stirrings of what would become, within a decade, a powerful slow-growth movement of homeowners' associations using civic incorporation to fight the Newhall Company's development strategy.[76]

These rumblings in the outer valleys (together with another wave of growth restrictions in 'redtile' communities like San Clemente and Riverside)[77] alerted analysts that Proposition 13, by transforming the fiscal calculus of urbanization and emboldening suburban voters, had undermined pro-growth, as well as pro-welfare, politics across the state. Having voted down progressive property taxation, why shouldn't suburbanites vote down undesirable growth as well? In 1980 the California Office of Planning and Research published a study with the prophetic title: *The Growth Revolt: Aftershock of Proposition 13?* State analysts found that some thirty-two growth-control measures had been placed on the ballot in the two years since the passage of Proposition 13. Nineteen were successful 'despite being outspent by pro-growth forces by an average of four to one and in one case by fifty-five to one'. The controls passed were unprecedentedly stringent, removing powers traditionally lodged with elected officials and favoring 'established, homeowning residents'. The analysts worried whether these measures might be the harbingers of new suburban unrest, possibly as sweeping as Proposition 13 itself.[78]

HIGHRISES VERSUS HOMESTEADS

> The area is becoming a concrete jungle. The traffic, the noise, the pollution – it's just awful and ugly – and it's getting worse. What they've done is take a nice middle-class neighborhood and destroy it, block by block. *Encino homeowner*[79]

The slow-growth turmoil of the 1980s defies any single, synoptic perspective. Unlike the tax revolt there has not been a common, strategic target of protest, nor at the end of the day, any clear-cut victory or defeat. Rather, like a homeowners' version of the Tet offensive, a surprise uprising across a broad front – including guerrilla engagements, feints, and frontal assaults – has produced a confusing scoreboard of advances, losses, and inadvertent consequences. In the peak years of 1987–8, for example, control of growth was the dominant issue in nearly sixty local elections in Los Angeles and Orange counties. In each case an eccentric local history meshed with a singular balance of forces to define 'slow growth' in a specifically parochial way, from 'Glendora Pride' and 'Not Yet New York' in West L.A. (or 'Not Yet Los Angeles' in San Diego) to 'English Only' in Monterey Park.[80]

Acknowledging the geographical and political sprawl of the 1980s slow-growth movement, however, is not to deny the existence of some

DENSE-PACKED SUBURBIA
Southridge, Fontana

common objectives. Doubtless the most original – illustrating the evolution of homeowner political culture since the first regional wave of growth protest in the early 1970s – has been the widespread demand for decentralization of land-use decision-making to the neighborhood level. This was the 'hidden agenda' of the homeowners' associations supporting Proposition U – Los Angeles's 1986 slow-growth initiative – and has remained an ideological dividing line between grassroots growth protest and the political advocates of a 'managed growth' compromise.

How conservative homeowners in the age of Reagan came to advocate a structural reform implying massive regulation of one of the most sacred marketplaces (land development) is a story that has certain fascinations. Not the least of these is the fact that 'community planning' was originally less a grassroots-generated demand than a self-serving slogan that seasonally emanated from the Los Angeles city or county bureaucracy. (Our narrative here contracts to focus on events in the City of Los Angeles.)

Far back in the late 1940s, following the tumultuous recomposition of Los Angeles's social areas by wartime immigration, planners began to fret about how to reinforce communal identity in older residential neighborhoods and new outlying suburbs. They meticulously designated some four hundred 'neighborhood' areas in the hope that these identifications might become bulwalks against spreading anomie and disorientation. In a similar spirit, the County Department of Community Services in the early 1950s sponsored 'community coordinating councils' to strengthen local identity and provide focal points for the coordination of social services and charities.

This functionalist approach to neighborhood-building was later supplanted by an emphasis on reinforcing white residents' perception of local control. Thus, after the Watts Rebellion aroused suburban concerns about integration, the conservative leadership of the school board experimented with neighborhood advisory councils as a palliative to white parents. And in 1969, motivated by similar fears over 'outside' encroachments into white areas, the commission appointed by Mayor Yorty to revise the city charter recommended the legal recognition of self-defined neighborhoods (with participation of at least 30 per cent of local voters) as governmental units with elected boards and appointed executives (called 'neighbormen'). The proposal was opposed by civil rights groups, worried about the quasi-secession of white neighborhoods, and vetoed by a city council concerned about the dissipation of its powers.[81]

Despite the council's repudiation of 'neighborhood power', City Planning Director Calvin Hamilton (1968–85) embraced the concept as a basis for revision of the city's hopelessly antiquated General Plan. Gesturing in the direction of 'participatory democracy', although in fact responding to the same white homeowner pressures as the school board, Hamilton established thirty-five citizens' advisory committees to help fashion 'community plans' that would eventually be synthesized into a new master plan. Thousands participated in some phase of this populist planning experiment, including future leaders of the 1980s slow-growth revolt, who were schooled in the esoterica of planning and land law while serving as citizen advisors.

With the density rebellion of the early 1970s brewing in the background, the principal promise of Hamilton's new masterplan was widespread down-zoning to preserve the integrity of single-family residential areas. Where the old plan allowed a Manhattan density of 10 to 1 (or ten million future inhabitants), the new plan, accepting locally defined standards for development, proposed to reduce density to 4.5 to 1 by rolling back 'excessive' zoning for apartments and commerce. Furthermore, it supposedly guaranteed the traditional low-density pattern of the Westside and the Valley by assigning highrise development to a series of 'growth centers' scattered through the city.

Although the new masterplan – proclaiming peaceful coexistence between safeguarded single-family neighborhoods and sanctioned highrise centers – was welcomed as the epitome of environmentally conscious, community-involved planning, it was effectively a dead letter from the beginning. For more than a decade the pro-growth majority on the city council stubbornly prevented the Planning Department from implementing the necessary down-zoning. As a result the city's zoning map remained wildly at odds with the community plans, and developers were able to introduce one over-scaled project after another, without environmental review, into supposed sanctuaries of single-family living. As offshore investment accelerated the building boom in the late 1970s, older (1930s–1950s) suburbs found themselves choking in traffic congestion and overshadowed by new commercial development. Despite a much ballyhooed 'Downtown Renaissance' between 1975 and 1985 (26 million square feet of new office space), highrise construction actually grew three times faster in the ex-suburban belts of the Westside, South Bay and Valley (some 86 million square feet).[82]

The result was a Jekyll and Hyde transfiguration of Los Angeles's middle-class heartlands. Although property values continued to soar, neighborhoods were Manhattanized beyond recognition. Seemingly overnight, Ventura Boulevard in Encino metamorphosed from a lowrise landscape of delis and used car lots into a concrete jungle dominated by highrise Japanese banks.[83] Startled hillside homeowners above the Cahuenga Pass (between Hollywood and the Valley) found themselves looking directly into the windows of North Hollywood's and Universal City's new skyscrapers. Similarly, the affluent residents of Holmby Hills and Westwood Village watched in horror as the quaint, Spanish Colonial-style intersection of Westwood and Wilshire boulevards became a windy canyon between bizarrely configured office towers. Beach dwellers in Santa Monica and Ocean Park, despite protests to the Coastal Commissions, found Miami Beach creeping up around their doorsteps, while members of the exclusive Marina Del Rey community were stunned by the plans put forward by Howard Hughes's heirs to build one of the world's largest mixed-use projects over a nearby bird sanctuary. And in Westchester and the middle-class neighborhoods around LAX, ten commuters for every resident gridlocked formerly quiet residential streets.

Confronted with this rapid erosion of their remaining suburban amenities, homeowners were once again roused to protest. The most embittered were those who had participated in good faith in Hamilton's original community plan advisory process. As a lawyer involved in the controversy observed, 'many of the homeowner groups were surprised and amazed and dismayed when they found out that all the work they had done on community plans made no difference whatever'. Even in 1978, when the Assembly (AB 283) flatly ordered Los Angeles to bring its zoning practices into conformity with its General Plan, Mayor Bradley – acting like the Orville Faubus of pro-growth – encouraged the Planning Department to malinger in heroic fashion. Given a firm deadline of 1982 to comply with the legislative decree, the city had barely completed a quarter of the required re-zoning in 1984. In response, irate homeowners, led by the Hillside Federation, went first to the courts, then to the polls.[84]

HOMEOWNERS' SOVIETS?

> The political process has failed us. If the people don't have a voice,
> you will be in the courts and in the legislative process again and again.
> The homeowner doesn't care about the Pacific Rim, he wants to be
> able to move down the street. *Westside Slow-Growth Leader*[85]

With the assistance of the Center for Law and the Public Interest, the
Federation won a landmark court order in January 1985 giving the city a
hundred and twenty days to implement the General Plan conformity that it
had resisted for the better part of a decade. The court also mandated the
Planning Commission, under Council scrutiny, to review any project 25 per
cent or more in excess of General Plan ceilings, including those in the
Redevelopment Agency's Downtown fiefdom. Although the city managed
on appeal to protract the re-zoning process for another five years, the ruling
nonetheless precipitated a fundamental restructuring of the planning
process.[86]

On the one hand, it exposed the bankruptcy of the city's General Plan,
while, on the other hand, it opened a breach in the historic autonomy of the
powerful redevelopment agency. Political enemies of the planning
bureaucracy did not hesitate to take advantage of the opportunity. Dan
Garcia, the ambitious president of the Planning Commission, teamed up
with Pat Russell, 'dragon lady' of the city council, to get rid of the leaderships of both the Planning Department and the Redevelopment Agency:
Calvin Hamilton, under a cloud of conflict-of-interest charges, was retired,
while redevelopment chief Edward Helfeld, blamed for a 'department run
wild', was more bluntly fired.[87]

Mayor Bradley being out of sight during this 'night of the long knives',
a national planning journal worried 'who controls the city?'[88] In fact, as
veteran politicos immediately recognized, the Council under Russell's
spiked heel had shrewdly exploited the Federation's re-zoning victory to
grab a major new chunk of power – including the ability to bargain directly
with developers over density variances. As Garcia euphemistically
acknowledged, 'inevitably, developers will be spending more time with the
council, and that will make life in city hall more interesting'. He was
implying, of course, that councilmembers – the true culprits of the

re-zoning debacle – had now placed themselves in even stronger positions to squeeze campaign 'juice' out of developers.[89]

At the same time it seems that the two organizers of the coup d'état had a more strategic objective. They wanted additional political control over the planning process precisely to ensure that City Hall could deal more effectively with the negative political fallout of growth. Russell, whose district included the traffic-clogged LAX area, wanted developers to pay for more transportation improvements, while Garcia, an advocate of 'fine-tuning' conflicts in land-use interests, had been warning that City Hall would be engulfed by angry homeowners. As head of the Planning Commission, moreover, it was Garcia's responsibility to persuade the home-owners that city government was finally ready to hear their complaints.[90]

First he appointed a respected slow-growth activist, lawyer Dan Shapiro, to co-chair a new Citizens Advisory Committee to revise 'Concept L.A.' – the city's outdated statement of planning objectives. Secondly, and more impetuously, he joined with leaders of the council's 'slow-growth' minority – Marvin Braude and Zev Yaroslavsky – to sponsor the 'Initiative for Reasonable Limits on Commercial Building and Traffic Growth', which, after 100,000 registered voters signed the petition, became simply Proposition U. Its gist was a 50 per cent down-zoning of most of the commercial land in the city, with the exceptions of Downtown, Hollywood, Century City and sections of Ventura and Wilshire Boulevards. It promised not so much to stop commercial growth as to detour it from precious middle-class residences.[91]

If Garcia gambled that Proposition U's bark was worse than its bite, and that it was a harmless safety-valve for homeowner unrest, he failed to convince any of his City Hall allies. Old pols saw it as the 'opening salvo', not only of a 'land-use revolt' (as the *Times* headlined it), but also of a power struggle between Yaroslavsky and Russell over the succession to Bradley (presumed either to win the governorship or retire). Since Yaroslavsky's opening gambit was homeowners, Russell countered with the accusation that Proposition U 'would erode economic opportunity' in the inner city. She was echoed by pro-growth colleague David Cunningham, who denounced 'elitists' attempting to 'dictate growth decisions in low-income, minority areas where the community wants more jobs and development'.[92]

Garcia, now ridiculed by the *Times* for 'alternating sympathies for both homeowners and builders', was in an untenable position, and he soon retreated to the Russell camp. Having failed to coopt the slow-growth movement, he joined her in pouring gasoline on the fire. Their contrived 'Community Protection Plan' – or the 'loophole ordinance' as its detractors preferred to call it – was a brazen effort to gut Proposition U in advance by exempting an additional twenty-eight areas from its jurisdiction, including the massive Howard Hughes Center in Russell's district. When the legality of this ploy was challenged, Russell and Garcia retained counsel from Latham and Watkins – a law firm notoriously associated with the land development industry. And when Latham and Watkins didn't seem to work, they resorted to the even more desperate maneuver of reclassifying 56,000 parcels of land in a single day – a move squelched by the city attorney.[93]

A slim council majority, reluctantly endorsed by the *Times*, went along with these machinations. But the pro-growth camp had unwittingly played Russian roulette with a fully loaded gun. They had ignored the warnings of the *Times*'s urban critic Sam Hall Kaplan that by trying to sabotage 'the quite moderate' Proposition U, they risked being carried away by a true deluge: 'the sentiment welling up in the city's communities for flat out no-growth'.[94] Indeed the loophole tactic, as an expression of contempt for slow-growth homeowners, and the electorate in general, produced an overwhelming public backlash. Voters who had previously paid little attention to land-use issues now nodded their heads when critics, like the leadership of 'Not Yet New York', a Westside slow-growth coalition, charged Russell and her confederates with 'cold, calculated betrayal', 'hubris', and creating 'a disaster for our people'. Despite doomsday warnings that it would kill the boom, Proposition U carried the city – including Black and Chicano neighborhoods – with nearly 70 per cent of the vote in November 1986.[95]

Shortly after its passage, the citizens' committee Garcia had charged with reviewing the planning strategy presented its report. It urged the Planning Commission to rescue transportation planning from the morass of the City's Transportation Department and to replace Hamilton's dis-credited 'centers' strategy (which tolerated as many as *forty* highrise nodes across the city) with 'targetted growth areas' that would more effectively concentrate commercial development and guarantee that middle-class neighborhoods remained sacrosanct. Its major recommendation, however, was to institutionalize citizen participation through thirty-five community planning boards acting in an advisory capacity to the Planning Commission. The fifteen members of each board were to be balanced between political appointees and directly elected community representatives – a compromise formula reached after reportedly intense debate within the Committee.[96]

As all sides staked out new positions, the Advisory Committee's recommendations became meat for negotiation and maneuver. Although Russell was mortally wounded by the Proposition U debacle (losing her once 'impregnable' seat in November 1987 to slow-growth advocate Ruth Galanter), she and Garcia tried to deal themselves back into the game by embracing the community planning board proposal without the elected members.[97] Braude and Yaroslavsky, the slow-growth heroes of the day, countered with a detailed follow-up to Proposition U's broad plan: an ordinance that would allow the city to review any project of 50,000 square feet (the size of an ordinary supermarket) or more. Finally, Mayor Bradley, silent or acting by proxy through most of the Proposition U commotion, directed a major speech in April 1988 toward the slow-growth movement. Promising to arrest 'mini-mall blight' and protect hillside neighborhoods, he endorsed the principle of community participation in planning, but was characteristically vague about the composition of the boards and whether or not the city needed the kind of detailed environmental review powers advocated by Braude and Yaroslavsky.

For the Hillside Federation, however, empowerment of the community planning boards was *the* decisive issue. In their view, the embittering, generation-long experience of 'community participation' in impotent planning exercises had erased any doubt about the need for root-and-branch reform. The principal achievement of Proposition U was that it had 'at last produced a citizens' "planning constituency"'; the Federation rejected the 'pigmy version of participation' which appointed token homeowners to advisory boards top-heavy with developers and their agents. Instead they demanded *completely elected* community planning boards of local residents, meeting in townhall fashion, and invested with '*implementation power*' that could only be overridden by a four-fifths majority of the City Planning Commission.[98]

Twenty years of political bad faith, in other words, had driven George Wills's 'sunbelt bolsheviks' to call for homeowners' soviets. That, at least, was how it looked to horrified building industry executives, whose fears were not entirely with foundation. In advocating the devolution of land-use control to communities, the Federation was certainly raising one of the most radical demands in Southern California since the days of EPIC or Ham and Eggs in the 1930s. The Black Panther Party's famous call in the 1960s for 'community policing' seemed meek in comparison to the Federation's plan for neighborhoods to exercise the rights of screening development and regulating local real-estate markets. Moreover some hillside *enragés*, like Gerald Silver of the Homeowners of Encino, saw community planning merely as a prelude to zip-code federalism: 'break up the city into smaller, more manageable units'.[99]

But whether or not the whole Federation fully appreciated the ideological implications of its stand, it had determined to make community planning the main issue in the aftermath of Proposition U.[100] The defeat of Russell had ended the era of invincible pro-growth rule on the Council, and homeowners counted on her successor, Ruth Galanter, to become the standard-bearer of their demand for elected boards.[101] An environmental planner from a 'new left' background, but owing her election to massive support from the Federation and local homeowner groups, Galanter seemed the freshest, and most iconoclastic, face on the City Council in decades. Moreover her enthusiasm for elected boards was so much taken for granted that no one paid any heed when, at a Hillside Federation forum on community planning, she sat smiling silently through the discussion at hand.[102]

The meaning behind her Mona Lisa smile was revealed a few weeks later when she voted with the rest of the Council for appointed planning boards strictly subordinate to councilmembers. A Federation leader gasped: 'She blew us out of the water ... it was Pat Russell all over again.' Repudiating the Federation's radical vision of community sovereignty, the Council did, after a fashion, decentralize planning power, but only to itself. Grasping at the power to broker growth on a district level through puppet planning boards, individual councilmembers, however, still remained under intense pressures to deal with homeowner anger against commercial development.

By the summer of 1987 a structure of accommodation had emerged whereby Westside and Valley councilmembers were supporting each other's manipulation of the city's 'interim control' law to pacify constituents' land-use grievances. A crazy-quilt of fifty 'interim control ordinances' – temporary moratoria on specific kinds of building – gave short-term relief to complaints by homeowners' associations about minimalls, hillside development, apartment density, mobile home parks, and the like. At the same time, the ordinances acted to keep homeowners (in Los Angeles) away from the ballot-box and to demobilize city-wide protest into local supplication.[103] This was exactly what Dan Garcia, now teamed up with Citizen Advisory Committee leader Dan Shapiro, advocated:

The slow-growth movement should in the future avoid 'city-wide' solutions to all local problems, and instead should focus attention on community and neighborhood planning and controls. . . . Meat-ax approaches that stop all development or that do not permit individual community planning would simply further the polarization process.[104]

But just as the neo-feudalism of the City Council seemed on the verge of dispersing Los Angeles's slow-growth movement into benign parochialism, fifty million gallons of raw sewerage unexpectedly hit the proverbial fan.

THE HYPERION FACTOR

Hyperion – what joy the place would have brought to those passionately
prosaic lovers of humanity, Chadwick and Bentham! . . . The problem
of keeping a great city clean without polluting a river or fouling the
beaches, and without robbing the soil of its fertility, has been
triumphantly solved. Aldous Huxley[105]

As Huxley recalled it, a few months before the outbreak of World War Two he and Thomas Mann were walking along the south shore of Santa Monica Bay, 'miraculously alone' and rapt in discussion of Shakespeare, when they suddenly realized that 'as far as the eye could reach in all directions, the sand was covered with small whitish objects, like dead caterpillars'. The 'caterpillars' were, in fact, 'Malthusian flotsam' – 'ten million used condoms' Huxley estimated – washed back on shore from Los Angeles's main sewer outfall at Hyperion Beach. Without recording his famous

THE TECHNOLOGICAL FIX THAT FAILED

companion's reaction to this bizarre sight, Huxley contrasted the scene on the same beach fifteen years later: 'the sands are now clean . . . children dig, well-basted sunbathers slowly brown . . . etc.' This 'happy consummation' had been brought about by 'one of the marvels of modern technology, the Hyperion Activated Sludge Plant'.[106]

In an otherwise ironic essay about hygiene and class distinction, Huxley took for granted that Hyperion really was 'the triumphant solution' to an ancient urban problem. Indeed, other writers have evoked the 'euphoric feeling' of this Grand Coulée of sewerage plants which transforms the waste of three million people into what has been described as 'the largest freshwater stream in Southern California'.[107] All the more fitting, therefore, that the preeminent symbol of Los Angeles's supposedly infinite ability to manipulate nature for the sake of development should become the grim antihero of the city's environmental crises of the late 1980s.

The breakdown of 'marvelous' Hyperion in late May 1987 gushed millions of gallons of unspeakable waste into Santa Monica Bay, defiling beaches and inflaming local tempers. It was the first of a tragicomic succession of eco-disasters that overwhelmed the Bradley administration in 1987–8 and gave slow growth the fillip of pre-apocalyptic common sense. As shit was followed by floodwater, drought, toxics, seismic safety, smog and solid waste, the horrible penny began to drop in City Hall that the growth wars between homeowners and developers were actually being fought within the limits of a collapsing infrastructure.

At first it seemed that Los Angeles could save itself simply by sticking a gilded finger in the dike at Hyperion: a $2.3 billion renovation. But anxious engineering reports to the Mayor, immediately leaked to the press, revealed that the entire system was on the verge of collapse. As the *Times* caustically observed, 'planning procedures have been so slack that nobody made that most basic connection between population growth and the carrying capacity of a sewage system'.[108] Although the old trunk sewers were large enough to accommodate the ten million gallons of new flow added each year by urbanization, the treatment plants had exhausted their capacity. The Mayor's attempt to abate the crisis through voluntary water conservation was ignored, especially in affluent, 'slow-growth' Westside and Valley neighborhoods with their swimming pools and acre-sized lawns.

A crash program to expand the crucial Tillman sewage plant in the Sepulveda Basin of the Los Angeles River then ran foul of the Army Corps of Engineers, custodians of Los Angeles's flood control system. They warned the city that the Tillman expansion would critically reduce the Basin's capacity to retain floodwater – a serious issue in light of the Corps's recent, exhaustive 'restudy' of the city's flood control defenses. The city's original prime amenity – the lovely, meandering Los Angeles River – had been sacrificially transformed into an ugly concrete 'storm sewer' in the 1940s in order to protect adjoining real estate from the periodic flood menace. Now, the Corps study revealed, 'unforeseen levels of new development' were not only producing intolerable volumes of sewage, but – through adding tens of thousands of additional acres of road surface and rooftop – a 40 per cent increase in storm run-off that threatened new catastrophic floods. Moreover, the interconnections of the situation were such that additional sewage capacity at Tillman would encourage more growth in the Valley, which would in turn increase run-off, and by doing so, make Tillman even more susceptible to flooding.[109]

Hard on the heels of these exposés of the city's failing sewer and flood-control systems came disturbing reports of disastrous groundwater contamination potentially affecting 40 per cent of the water supply. The infiltration of industrial solvents and other toxic chemicals had already forced the closure of one hundred and fifty wells, and officials confessed that it would take three decades and at least $2 billion to flush out the polluted aquifers. Critics claimed this was a drastic under-estimate and predicted that clean-up costs could run as high as a staggering $40 billion.[110] But water, in any case, was becoming scarcer as a protracted drought escalated the water wars that pitted Southern California against Northern California and Arizona. As the withdrawal of Los Angeles aqueduct water from the Mono Basin, on the eastern flank of the Sierras, threatened a local ecological catastrophe, Los Angeles water authorities debated the unsavory last resort of purchasing water allotments from Central Valley agribusiness (now 'water ranchers').[111]

Meanwhile Los Angeles's deadline for compliance with the 1970 federal Clean Air Act expired. Pleading with Washington for a *quarter-century* extension, the city conceded defeat in its thirty-year war against air pollution, which remained by far the worst in the advanced industrial world. All the hardwon gains from the enforcement of mandatory smog-control devices had been more than offset by population growth and increased density of auto ownership. Moreover the housing affordability crisis, which was forcing hundreds of thousands of workers to commute from distant interior valleys, was inexorably driving up mileage and generating gridlock on the suburban fringes. A chilling February 1988 study from the Southern California Association of Governments warned that if population and job/housing trends continued at present levels, $110 billion in new freeway construction would be needed just to stabilize existing congestion. In lieu of this investment, growing gridlock was expected to reduce average freeway speeds to sub-horse-and-buggy velocities (about fifteen miles per hour) by the end of the 1990s. Contributing to the slowdown would be the thousands of dump trucks needed to transport the city's solid waste into the desert, or beyond, as existing landfills in a five-county area reached capacity in the early 1990s.[112]

As each crisis implied others to come, it was difficult for City Hall to pretend these were unrelated contingencies and not the falling dominoes of overdevelopment as predicted by slow-growth forces. Mayor Bradley in particular had to face inexorably mounting pressures to declare a temporary halt to new development. Even before the Hyperion spill, Assemblyman Tom Hayden (D-Santa Monica) had allied slow growth with the environmental defense of Santa Monica Bay by demanding a strict limit on new construction until sewage capacity was increased. After the May spill vindicated Hayden, he was joined by Westside Congressman Mel Levine, as well as by Proposition U authors Braude and Yaroslavsky, in threatening to call in the Environmental Protection Agency to save the Bay.[113]

The hitherto unimaginable spectre of federal environmental receivership (a threat renewed in summer 1988 after the city failed to comply with clean air standards) was the shotgun that forced Mayor Bradley into a reluctant wedding with growth-control forces. He began the courtship in July 1987 when he withdrew the city's opposition to the 'Friends of Westwood' decision. This important legal victory for slow-growth activists found that the city had erred in not requiring an environmental impact report on a 26-story Wilshire Boulevard highrise. The mayor shocked his pro-growth supporters by accepting the environmental review of all major developments – the gist of the 'follow-up' ordinance to Proposition U that Braude and Yaroslavsky had earlier proposed.[114]

Then, in early December 1987, after officially recognizing that the sewer system had reached breakdown point, Bradley boldly unveiled his own ten-point plan that included a monthly cap on new construction based on sewer capacity. (Yaroslavsky chortled, 'I'm pleased that the mayor has come around to my way of thinking.') The cap was designed to apply not only to Los Angeles, but, because of the city's authority as sewer landlord, to the thirty other municipalities contracting its sewer treatment facilities. A draconian consequence was that the cities currently pumping more sewage into the system than their quotas allowed – including Santa Monica, Burbank and San Fernando – were faced with a total growth freeze. While developers and builders watched in dismay, some of Bradley's most trenchant critics, including Tom Hayden, rallied to his side in what seemed to be a rehearsal for a major political realignment.[115]

City Hall, however, was not greened in a day (even under the influence of Mike Gage, the eco-thinking deputy mayor). During the 1988 campaigns, Bradley managed to badly undermine his credibility as a 'born-again' environmentalist – and infuriate Westside homeowners anew – by reneging on his historic opposition to Palisades oil drilling. Meanwhile his sewer cap was stalled for a half-year in the Council while jealous members – all too aware that even temporary controls could become sacred cows – wrestled with the Mayor over whether they themselves or the Board of Public Works (which he appointed) would exercise the power to ration new development and make individual exemptions. In the end the Mayor was forced to yield the prerogative to the Council, who, after excluding key megaprojects dear to their hearts and pocketbooks, finally approved (in May 1988) a nine-month trial run of the 'most restrictive growth controls since the Second World War'. Two years later a renewed version of this 'stopgap' ordinance was still in place – but now described as 'phase one of a comprehensive growth management strategy'.[116]

However prosaic a 'sewer ordinance' may seem, it constituted an important, possibly epochal, punctuation mark in the city's postwar history: the moment when the Big Boom finally had to take the Hyperion Factor into account. Land-use writer William Fulton described the ordinance as a 'stunning coup' for slow-growth activists whose cause was invested with 'mainstream, regionwide political legitimacy'. It was more significant than Proposition U because it set a precedent for '*regional* growth controls', as the Mayor of Los Angeles became the 'lever to shut off development in Santa Monica and Burbank'. [117]

Skeptical slow-growth activists like Laura Lake of Not Yet New York, inured to 'wonderful plans and laws [of the city] that it violates every day', were not so sure they had won such a historic victory and downplayed the significance of the city's new-found environmental zeal. Yet the Bradley administration – moving ever greenward as it bailed itself out from one political corruption crisis to another – continued in theory to commit itself to tougher growth-management and conservationist positions. Thus in April 1990 the mayor unveiled an official 'Environmental Primer', written in a startlingly Sierra-Club idiom, that coopted almost the entirety of mainstream eco-critiques previously directed against City Hall. Acknowledging 'a city at the limits', as it reviewed one crisis after another, the Primer declared that the days of the 'high-tech "quick fix"' are numbered' and proposed a 'tough cop' role for the city as environmental enforcer. Amongst many militant-sounding recommendations, the Primer urged an all-out municipal mobilization to support the South Coast Air Quality Management District's (AQMD) 'aggressive' Regional Air Quality Management Plan. [118]

Many developers now fear that the AQMD, with support from Los Angeles, may become the toughest slow-growth cop of them all. It is ironic that twelve white male political appointees – a majority of whom presumably espouse the Republican creed of maximum deregulation – have undertaken to impose the most comprehensive peacetime regulation of local economic activity since the days of Roosevelt's Blue Eagle. Acting in the face of a federal ultimatum, in March 1989 the AQMD's Board of Governors (which does include slow-growth patriarch Braude), adopted a sweeping twenty-year plan to restore clean air in the Los Angeles Basin by 2007.

Although developers and industrialists, led by the giant Watson Land Company (developers of L.A.'s new South Bay industrial and commercial complex), howled in protest at proposed regulations to cover every species of air pollution from refinery fumes to underarm deodorants, their real vehemence was reserved for the AQMD's decision in early 1990 to systematically review all large-scale developments in the Basin. When the AQMD leveled unprecedented criticism at developer Nathan Shapell's $2 billion Porter Ranch leviathan in the northern foothills of the Valley – the biggest single mixed-use project in Los Angeles history – the Ranch's spokesmen – ex-Planning Commission boss Dan Garcia and ex-BUSTOP leader Paul Clarke – accused the District of 'declaring war on local decision-making'. Developers, industrialists and pro-growth L.A. supervisors then retaliated by introducing a bill in the state Senate that would allow businesses to use initiative and referendum processes to veto AQMD regulations.[119]

This emergent war of position between the 'green' branches of government and the private sector (and between non-elected environmental managers and local pork-barrel politicos) is reshaping both the language in which the politics of growth are articulated, and the terrain on which different interests contend.[120] In the wake of Hyperion, a third camp – the moderate 'growth management' ideology of regional technocrats[121] – has arisen between the righteous anger of the suburbs and the haughty indifference of the developers and their political henchmen. It only remains to see how homeowner activists in the suburban valleys have risen to the challenge of this new conjuncture.

NIMBYS AND KNOW-NOTHINGS

From a handful of dog lovers with pooper-scoopers at the park, [Jane] Purse's Parkwatch has grown to a citywide group of 1,000 families with a certified accountant and enough clout to get former Vice-President Walter Mondale to support their cause. . . . In November, officials approved a pilot program to have designated times and places for dogs to run without leashes. Councilman Joel Wachs, who opposed the group from his district for years, voted for the plan. 'He had no choice', said Joan Luchs of Parkwatch, who said one hundred members of the group flooded a committee meeting. They made signs depicting Wachs as the anti-Christ, one of the Three Stooges and a 'dog Nazi'.[122]

Despite the immensity of Los Angeles's environmental crisis, it is hard to find evidence that the suburban slow-growth movement has understood its appointment with destiny. Indeed, as the tale of Parkwatch's epic struggle for a 'pooper-scooper-less dog park' in the Valley suggests, the essence of the contemporary suburban world view is precisely the inability to distinguish the historical significance of the sewage clogging Santa Monica Bay from the precious pile deposited by Rover in his favorite dogpark. A California neologism of the 1980s perfectly encapsulates this ethos of untranscendable parochialism: *nimby*. This means 'not in my back yard' although, as we shall see, 'not on my lawn' is sometimes the better translation.

In the particular case of San Fernando Valley homeowners, the big, unitary issues of the late 1970s (taxes, busing and density) were supplanted in the late 1980s by an exotic welter of 'nimby' protests: against traffic congestion, mini-mall development, airport expansion, school siting, the demolition of the Tail O'Cock restaurant, the erection of a mosque, an arts park, subdivision and apartment construction, road widening, the shaving of a hillside, 'diamond' lanes, trailers for the homeless, the disappearance of horse stables, and the construction of a tortilla factory.[123]

Not even the rich and famous could sneak a drug treatment center, or a pee behind a bush, past the vigilance of Valley homeowners. Faced with the prospect of the Lake View Terrace Homeowners Association picketing their Bel-Air mansion, the ex-first lady was forced to say no to plans for the Nancy Reagan (drug treatment) Center in a vacant medical building in the Valley neighborhood. Meanwhile the proposed Ventura Boulevard branch of a tony Beverly Hills bistro sparked a vehement homes-versus-urinals battle with the Sherman Oaks Homeowners Association. Opposing the eatery's liquor permit at a zoning hearing, the homeowners elaborated their fear: 'The urine on the street. ... People don't think that the well-to-do would urinate in public or do other crude things. It's shocking, but it's true.' To this monstrous allegation, the representative of *haute cuisine* replied:

We have been here in Beverly Hills for 25 years. We have had heads of state, movie stars, presidents, governors, princes and princesses. To even suggest that any of these would urinate on someone's lawn before they step into their Mercedes is shocking. ... I think that people who are saying those kinds of things are living in a trashy neighborhood. Our bathrooms are probably more elegant than their living rooms.[124]

When it comes to solving major urban problems, moroever, the Valley homesteaders are about as patient and constructive as Sendero Luminoso. Ironically, the one big Valley-wide issue in 1987–8 was opposition to a proposed light rail commuter line to Downtown. The Valley's nightmarish traffic problems are symptomatic of the overall crisis of L.A.'s growth infrastructures. With the smog-shrouded Ventura Freeway in *rigor mortis* due to the nation's worst congestion, excess traffic clogs arterial boulevards before spilling over into residential streets. Cal Trans engineers have warned that without a quick fix of mass transit, 'the system isn't going to break down, it's going to explode'.[125] With a traffic apocalypse imminent, it might have been expected that Valley residents would have welcomed the L.A. County Transportation Commission's plan for cheap fixed rail transit.

Instead, organized Valleyites were nimby homeowners first, and harassed commuters second. The Commission, like previous outside agencies, failed to comprehend the neighborhood geography of the Valley and the fierce localisms disguised by a superficially homogeneous landscape. The proposed light rail route was plotted along Chandler Boulevard, unwittingly through the center of an Orthodox Jewish community who protested that the line would disrupt Sabbath worship. The Hassidim were reinforced by other homeowner groups who saw the route as a conspiracy by Warner Center and Van Nuys business interests who 'want to develop, develop, develop . . . at the sacrifice of the American Dream'. Ultimately Encino Homeowners' leader Jerry Silver (whose brother Bob lives on Chandler Boulevard) pulled together a hundred other homeowners' groups into the All Valley Transit Coalition (AVTC) to oppose light rail in *anybody's* backyard.[126]

As incredulous traffic engineers looked on, the powerful Transportation Commission crumbled in the face of nimby multiplied by one hundred. Although polls indicated that potential users overwhelmingly approved the proposed line, there was no grassroots organization of commuters. (As Silver explained, 'people don't organize to fight *for* something, but they organize to fight *against* something'.) Rather than embroil themselves further with AVTC – a super-sized version of Parkwatch or West Hills – the Transportation Commission unheroically abandoned the field. Two years later, after arduous negotiations with homeowners' groups, legislators announced a 'compromise' that would extend Metro Rail underground beneath Chandler Boulevard at immensely greater cost than the original light rail proposal, but without disturbing the Sabbath.[127]

The current helter-skelter of homeowner protest in the San Fernando Valley becomes more racially charged further east in the San Gabriel Valley, where slow-growth politics act as a latter-day version of anti-immigrant Know-Nothingism. Although Los Angeles County's other great suburban valley has roughly the same population as the San Fernando (approximately 1,250,000 in 1985), it is fragmented into a complex class, ethnic and land-use mosaic of twenty-eight separately incorporated municipalities and numerous County 'holes'. Once the world's greatest citrus belt, the San Gabriel Valley, like the San Fernando, has been subjected to acute growth stress over the last generation. In the built-out western half of the Valley (dominated by Pasadena), where land values rose 30 per cent in 1987–8 alone, established homeowners' associations have fought fanatically to protect their single-family neighborhoods from desecration at the hands of apartment builders.[128] Meanwhile, in the Valley's rapidly urbanizing eastern half (especially along the growth corridor of the Pomona Freeway), which gained almost a quarter-million new residents in the 1980s, commuter-suburbanites have organized to slow development and preserve their remaining rural amenities.

Across the San Gabriel Valley, however, these stock-in-trade slow-growth issues have become hopelessly conflated with an increasingly virulent racial backlash. Once predominantly Anglo (with scattered *colonias* of Mexican citrus workers), the Valley has become a major destination for upwardly mobile Chicanos leaving East L.A. and Chinese entrepreneurs arriving from Taiwan and Hong Kong, as well as for poorer Mexicans and Vietnamese. Whereas the quarter-million Chicanos (primarily blue-collar craftsmen and professionals) are perceived primarily as a political threat to entrenched Anglo power structures, the 150,000 Chinese (businessmen and developers as well as professionals and workers) are resented for their alleged role in overdeveloping and physically degrading whole communities.

Monterey Park – a San Gabriel Valley city of 65,000 residents about eight miles east of Downtown L.A. – has for nearly a decade been the major battlefield between white homeowners and 'growth with an Asian face'.

Ninety per cent Anglo in 1960, this hilly single-family suburb evolved during the 1970s toward an uneasy triadic balance of Anglo, Chicano and Japanese-American residents until Fred Hseih, a canny real-estate promoter with offshore banking connections, conceived the idea of selling Monterey Park as the Chinese version of the California Dream. Beguiled by slick advertisements depicting a 'Chinese Beverly Hills', thousands of Mandarin-speakers from Taiwan and Cantonese-speakers from Hong Kong and Indonesia, transformed Monterey Park into North America's first Chinese-majority suburb by 1985. A half-billion dollars of diaspora capital reshaped Atlantic Boulevard into an overscaled strip of Chinese office buildings and inundated the City Planning Department with scores of applications to build mini-malls and condominiums.[129]

This extraordinary ethnic restructuring produced a nativist backlash in the form of the RAMP (the Residents Association of Monterey Park) whose self-declared aim is slow growth, particularly the restriction of new multiple-unit and commercial construction. Since most of the developers opposed by RAMP are also Chinese, RAMP has invariably assumed the alter-ego of being the main opposition to 'further Chinese take-over'. In the 1986 elections, taking advantage of the fact that the city's white minority is still a larger registered voting bloc than the new Chinese majority, RAMP swept away moderate ethnic-harmonizers (two Latinos and a Chinese-American) in favor of its own hardcore representatives. As sociologist John Horton explains, the struggle over land-use control quickly became a fight over the 'very definition of what constitutes an American community':

This nativist side of slow growth showed itself in 1985, when the City Council adopted an ordinance requiring Chinese businesses to include English translations on their signage. A year later, at 1.30 a.m., after the watchful public had gone home, the Council's slow-growth majority pushed through a resolution supporting English as the 'official language' of Monterey Park. One of the more 'patriotic' Council members even proposed that the local police cooperate with the INS in enforcing 'its American duties'.[130]

Monterey Park's slow-growth Know-Nothingism reached its lowest point in the reign of Mayor Barry Hatch, an ex-Mormon missionary, who attracted national notoriety for the table-thumping charge that a 'billion Chinese . . .

are looking for a soft place to land. There's nowhere else but here. The whole valley is what they want.'[131] Although 'Yellow Peril' Hatch was finally evicted from the Council by a 'rainbow' mobilization of Chinese, Japanese and Chicano voters in April 1990, RAMP-type groups had already spread throughout neighboring communities. For instance, one RAMP missionary had successfully lobbied conservative Republican homeowner leaders in San Gabriel, Arcadia, and six other cities facing Asian immigration to form a San Gabriel Valley 'slow-growth coalition' with exclusionary undertones.[132]

The 1990 Census will undoubtedly reveal that Alhambra – an older, more modest suburb just across the San Bernadino Freeway from Monterey Park – is on the verge of becoming the Valley's second Chinese-majority suburb. Unlike Monterey Park, however, many of its new residents are poorer ethnic Chinese from Vietnam, working in local garment shops or in Alhambra's estimated two hundred Chinese restaurants. ROC (Residents Opposing Condominiums) was Alhambra's son-of-RAMP, organizing against the lower-income Chinese influx by circulating an initiative to ban all multiple-unit construction in the city. Meanwhile Alhambra's aristo-cratic neighbor, San Marino (former national headquarters of the John Birch Society), has used a 'bedroom ordinance' to limit wealthy but large Asian families from buying into its old-money lifestyle.[133]

The young (1989) Valley city of Diamond Bar – a slow-growth incorporation inspired, like Santa Clarita, by the homeowners' associations – has also intensely debated the limitation of apartment construction, presumably with the purpose of excluding working-class non-Anglos of all kinds. Indeed the equation between apartments and crime is now so automatic in suburban consciousness that one recent Diamond Bar council candidate (financed by the owner of the Carl's Junior Restaurant chain) argued thus againt multi-family housing: 'I don't want to see graffiti, gangs and prostitution – I want safety for everyone who lives in Diamond Bar.'[134]

It would be unfair, however, to suggest that the San Gabriel Valley is the only besieged white *laager* in Southern California. In northern San Diego and southern Orange Counties – Southern California's 95 per cent white 'futuropolis' of affluent planned communities and science parks – hysterical homeowners' associations, supported by local businessmen, have begun to wage war against the very immigrant labor upon which their master-race lifestyles depend. Decrying such infamies as urination in public, homeowners in the City of Orange, Costa Mesa, San Clemente, Encinitas and elsewhere along the 'Gold Coast' have clamored for police crackdowns on street-corner labor markets and bush encampments of undocumented Mexican and Central American workers. Since there is virtually no low-income housing between the Santa Ana barrio and East San Diego (a ninety-mile distance) thousands of day-laborers and their families – Spanish-speaking Okies of the 1980s – are forced to live furtively in hillside dugouts and impromptu brush camps, often within sight of million-dollar tract homes whose owners now want the 'immigrant blight' removed.

As these examples suggest, slow-growth Know-Nothingism, by its very nature, seems to be creeping toward Malthusian final solutions. Thus, at a 1987 conference of Not Yet New York, the Westside slow-growth alliance, one group advocated a statewide 'Elbow Room' initiative that would seal the border with Mexico, drastically restrict inmigration of all kinds, and impose obligatory family planning. The irony of the situation seemed to escape the initiative's sponsors, transfixed by their blinding vision of a politically cyrogenized Ozzie-and-Harriet lifestyle: that the definitive imposition of slow growth would require the construction of a California Reich.

FRIENDS OF THE PEOPLE

> It is a universal fact that where the value of land is the highest,
> civilization exhibits the greatest luxury side by side with the most
> piteous destitution. To see human beings in the most abject, the most
> helpless and hopeless condition, you must go, not to the unfenced
> prairies, . . . but to the great cities where the ownership of a little
> patch of ground is a fortune. *Henry George, 1869*[135]

In a famous passage of the *Eighteenth Brumaire* Marx depicted the French peasantry as a 'sack of potatoes', constitutionally incapable of any large-scale coherence of interest or social action except as mobilized by a charismatic leader. From our foregoing account, it is hard to avoid a similar judgment about Southern California homeowners. Try as hard as they might to become 'sunbelt Bolsheviks', the slow-growthers remain basically peasant potatoes whose 'natural' scale of protest is disaggregated nimbyism; or would 'residential anarcho-syndicalism' be a better term? What seems exceptional was the moment of focused mass energy represented by Proposition 13 and the 'Bonapartism' of Howard Jarvis in 1978. Only the Hillside Federation, with its stable leadership and evolved program, breaks the mold of individualistic homeowners' associations, dominated by cranky personalities, consorting in temporary coalitions and then, inevitably, remolecularizing around their own back yards. It seems, in historical pespective, virtually an iron law.

Yet developers and the rest of the real-estate industry live in fear that the improbable will again occur, and that some combination of crisis and charisma will place the slow-growth equivalent of the Jarvis Amendment on the ballot. In order to forestall that particular Eighteenth Brumaire, they have devised a brilliant, if staggeringly hypocritical strategy, based on their decades of expertise in manipulating public opinion against environmentalism. Following the prescription laid down by mega-developer Eli Broad in the early 1970s, they have become 'the friends of the people', denouncing 'selfish, elitist homeowners' who prevent the 'trickle down' of growth dividends and low-income housing to the bottom of society.

The 1988 campaign against slow-growth Measure A in Orange County was something of a *déjà vu* landmark in the history of special-interest electioneering in California. Under the direction of New Right political consultant Lynn Wessell ('Weasel' to his opponents), a $2.5 million advertising onslaught financed by the Irvine and Mission Viejo companies was repackaged as a broad-based response by unions and minority groups. Pro-growth mailings in the blue-collar suburbs of northern Orange County falsely claimed that every household faced paying $1,800 tribute to 'some south county elitists'. A few months later, Riverside County developers, fighting 'Yes on Residents Controlling Growth' (Measure B), repeated the Weasel's strategy with 'Residents for Responsible Planning', depicted as 'a broad-based coalition with representation from organized labor, the Hispanic Chamber of Commerce [and] affordable housing advocates'. Although some building trades unions and minority groups did endorse this developers' front, the money (or at least 83 per cent of it) came from the *latifundistas*, especially the 97,000-acre Rancho California Company. If in both counties slow-growth measures that early polls judged highly popular were defeated by scare tactics aimed at blue-collar voters, it was only the revival of an ancient ploy. Long before the Weasel, the old (SP) Octopus routinely bought elections in the name of popular anti-elitism.[136]

As in the early 1900s, moreover, the façade of populism dissimulates the operation of an ultra-elite power structure – in the contemporary case, of a statewide alliance of developers, builders, realtors and banks opposed to growth controls. This newer, bigger 'Octopus', as we saw in the last chapter, possesses extraordinary bipartisan leverage over both parties at all levels of government. Bleating loudly about the plight of the proletariat and 'affordable housing', the pro-growth camp (led by the California Building Industry Foundation) comprises developers opposed to inclusionary housing, builders opposed to unions, realtors opposed to housing integration and landlords opposed to rent control. While professing to be the cause of 'responsible planning', they have in fact sponsored a sweeping legal offensive – the second prong of their strategy – to reaffirm the untrammeled rights of private development against any communitarian regulation. Ominously, this initiative has found powerful philosophical allies in rightward-moving state and federal supreme court majorities, ready to restore nineteenth-century doctrines of 'absolute property'.[137]

And, as in the bad old days at the beginning of the century, the labor and civil rights groups allied with the Octopus are being led from behind. Minority groups, rightly distrustful of white-supremacist homeowners, have jumped from the frying pan into the fire to support developers responsible for the creation of the monochromatic suburban fringes in northern Los Angeles and southern Orange counties. Powerful building-trades bosses for the most part continue to lock local labor federations (as in the City of Los Angeles, Riverside, San Bernardino and Orange counties) into supine coalitions with big developers, even when the latter are major backers of union-busting. (One pathbreaking exception to this dreary tradition was the 1988 initiative by the giant L.A. county employees Local of the Service Employees International Union (SEIU) to band together with environmentalists and Valley homeowners to oppose Mike Antonovich, the anti-union, pro-growth supervisor for northern Los Angeles County.)

To legitimate their popular mandate, pro-growth forces regularly unveil polls to prove that inner-city residents and blue-collar workers are strongly opposed to the slow-growth movement. The *Times* interpreted one poll in a front-page story to allege that growth was the major new ethnic divide in the city, threatening to unravel Mayor Bradley's historic Westside–Southcentral coalition. In fact, the evidence is far more complex and ambiguous. Despite its demonization as the 'end of the boom', Black and Latino voters overwhelmingly endorsed Proposition U, and in other polls, 56 per cent of Latinos and 40 per cent of Blacks have indicated support for a slowdown of development. Other research from Orange County and across the country has failed to find a clear class polarization over growth issues.[138]

Possibly there is a significant internal divide in non-Anglo communities between renters and homeowners, with the latter more inclined toward slow growth. But the crucial point is that the polls themselves, by the exclusive way they frame questions (pro and contra economic development, for instance), simply reproduce the distorted dichotomies of growth war ideology. It is not surprising that poor people, especially renters, will choose jobs over environmental quality when the two are artificially counterposed. If it were the only choice offered, most people would also opt to cut their toe off rather than their leg. Such dubious, but ubiquitous survey methods only reveal people's relative anxieties, not their substantive opinions.

Like all ideology, 'slow growth' and its 'pro-growth' antipode must be understood as much from the standpoint of the questions *absent*, as those posed. The debate between affluent homeowners and mega-developers is, after all, waged in the language of *Alice in Wonderland*, with both camps conspiring to preserve false opposites, 'growth' versus 'neighborhood quality'. It is symptomatic of the current distribution of power (favoring both capital *and* the residential upper-middle classes) that the appalling destruction and misery within Los Angeles's inner city areas (see chapters five and six below) became the great non-issue during the 1980s, while the impact of growth upon affluent neighborhoods occupied center-stage. The silent majority of non-affluent homeowners and renters have remained mere pawns in the growth power struggles, their independent social interests (for instance, economic justice *and* environmental protection, jobs *and* clean air, and so on) suppressed in civic controversy.

If the slow-growth movement, in other words, has been explicitly a protest against the urbanization of suburbia, it is implicitly – in the long tradition of Los Angeles homeowner politics – a reassertion of social privilege. Ironically, at the very moment when the Anglo middle classes have demographically declined to a minority within the city, their organized social power waxes at a maximum, even if dispersed into nimby-type protests. Growth politics, in general, seem to militate against class politics. Yet, as we shall see in the next chapter, a one-sided class struggle, ironically uniting homeowners and developers, rages fiercely at the level of Los Angeles's built environment.

NOTES

1. See *Daily News*, 18 October 1987.
2. Benjamin Zycher, 'She Should Have Said "No" ', Los Angeles *Times* (op-ed), 4 September 1987.
3. See *Daily News*, 29 November 1987.
4. Paraphrased in *Times*, 6 March 1988.
5. *Times*, 12 October 1986.
6. According to the California Association of Realtors, 76 growth-control ballot measures were put to the vote throughout the state in 1986–8. Nearly half originated in Los Angeles, Orange or San Diego counties, and 70 per cent were successful. (*Times*, 31 July 1988; and my compilation of Southern California growth measures.)
7. See the premature obituary: 'Decisive Defeats Leave State's Slow-Growth Movement in Disarray', *Times*, 10 November 1988.
8. David Dowall, *The Suburban Squeeze: Land Conversion and Regulation in the San Francisco Bay Area*, Berkeley 1984, pp. 139–42.
9. George Will, ' "Slow Growth" Is the Liberalism of the Privileged', *Times*, 30 August 1987.
10. Of course, both ideological positions – environmentalist *noblesse oblige* and crabgrass xenophobia – end up defending substantially the same conservative interests. As George Will explains: 'The "slow growth" movement here and elsewhere represents the growing desire of the possessing classes for "conserving government", for laws to protect the value of the positional goods in a choice location. Conserving government is the liberalism of the privileged, it is activist government protecting the well-positioned from inundation by change and competition.' Ibid.
11. Quoted in the *Eagle*, 25 September 1947.
12. See Stephen Barton and Carol Silverman, 'Common Interest Homeowners' Associations: Private Government and the Public Interest Revisited', *Public Affairs Report*, May 1988, p. 5.
13. On Los Felix Improvement Association, see *Times*, 26 January 1989. The oldest HA in Los Angeles *County* is probably the Arroyo Seco Improvement Association in Pasadena (circa 1905).
14. Marc Weiss, *The Rise of the Community Builders: The American Real Estate Industry and Urban Land Planning*, New York 1987, pp. 3–4, 11–12. Robert Fogelson points out, however, that deed restrictions were not usually in perpetuity – a consideration that provided continuing impetus to restriction through public zoning. (See *The Fragmented Metropolis*, Cambridge, Mass. 1967, p. 248.)
15. J. Max Bond, *The Negro in Los Angeles*, PhD thesis, USC 1936, p. 41; and Charlotta Bass, *Forty Years*, Los Angeles 1960, p. 56.

16. Bessie McClenahan, *The Changing Urban Neighborhood: From Neighbor to NightDweller*, USC, Los Angeles 1929, pp. 83, 90–93. Intriguingly, the main thesis of McClenahan's monograph was the obsolescence of the 'traditional American neighborhood and small community' and its replacement by a mere convergence of interest around home values and social exclusivity, as represented by the formation of the Anti-African Association. (See especially p. 107.)

17. David Chalmers, *Hooded Americanism*, New York 1976, p. 118.

18. Bass, pp. 95–113. Los Angeles Blacks did not submit meekly to expulsion from their homes. As early as 1924, Black homeowners were reported defending their families with guns in hand. (See E. Frederick Anderson, *The Development of Leadership and Organization Building in the Black Community of L.A. from 1900 through World War II*, Saratoga, Calif. 1980, p. 70.)

19. Bond, p. 41; John Denton, *Apartheid American Style*, Berkeley 1967, pp. 60, 69; Weiss, p. 151; Anderson, p. 69.

20. Interview with anti-restriction lawyers Loren Miller and John McTernan, *Eagle*, 16 October 1947.

21. See *Eagle*, 25 September 1947; Denton, ibid., As spokesman for the California Real Estate Association, Charles Shattuck continued to organize the fight against housing integration through the 1950s and early 1960s.

22. Lawrence de Graaf, *Negro Migration to Los Angeles, 1930–1950*, PhD History, UCLA 1962, pp. 199–200.

23. Nat King Cole was the pioneer Black homeowner in the exclusive Hancock Park section of the old Westside in the early 1950s. His wealthy white neighbors burnt crosses on his lawn and generally refused to speak to him for more than a decade. Mayor Bradley now lives in the neighborhood.

24. *Eagle*, 22 August and 16 October 1947. In the early 1920s the southern edge of the Central Avenue ghetto met the 'white wall' at Santa Barbara Blvd.; later in the 1930s it moved to Vernon Blvd.; and finally, in the 1940s, to Slauson Blvd.

25. Bass, ibid.; *Eagle*, 7 May 1946, 20 January and 8 September 1949.

26. Thus Los Angeles's future mayor – then police sergeant Tom Bradley – was initially prevented from buying a home in Leimert Park in 1950.

27. A 1951 study of the problems of rehousing Black and Chicano families projected to be displaced by redevelopment advocated public housing since 'new housing for sale is [still] restricted to "white" families only'. (See Robert Alexander and Drayton Bryant, *Rebuilding a City: A Study of Redevelopment Problems in Los Angeles*, Los Angeles 1951, p. 58.) Many luxury enclaves, like Rancho Santa Fe (the hideout of Howard Hughes and various movie stars) in northern San Diego County, continued to have racial restrictions until the middle 1970s. (*Times*, 15 June 1980.)

28. Gary Miller, *Cities By Contract: The Politics of Municipal Incorporation*, Cambridge, Mass. 1981, p. 9.

29. Since city taxpayers paid *both* municipal and county rates, they substantially subsidize residents and businesses in unincorporated areas.

30. California in 1914 was the first state to provide constitutional approval for counties to provide services to municipalities. For a classic overview of the evolution of Southern California's fragmented metropolitan political system, see Winston Crouch and Beatrice Dinerman, *Southern California Metropolis*, Berkeley 1964.

31. Miller, p. 9.

32. Ibid., p. 176.

33. Ibid., p. 85.

34. Ibid., pp. 87–95, 150–51.

35. Amongst the larger cities with virtually no Black population in 1980: Arcadia, Burbank, El Monte, Glendale (0.06%!), Norwalk, and Torrance.

36. Ibid., p. 192; Frank Mittelbach, 'The Changing Housing Inventory: 1950–59', in Leo Grebler, ed., *Metropolitan Contrasts*, UCLA 1963, pp. 5–6, 19.

37. Ibid., p. 159. Fiscal zoning is too often imagined simply as a survivalist adaptation to Proposition 13. In fact, it is often a municipal mini-imperialism by which 'have' communities aggressively redistribute resources from the 'have-nots'.

38. Ibid., p. 151.

39. *Eden in Jeopardy (Man's prodigal meddling with his environment: The Southern California experience)*, New York 1966, p. 314.

40. Fishman, *Bourgeois Utopias*, New York 1987.

41. Reyner Banham, *Los Angeles: The Architecture of Four Ecologies*, London 1971, pp. 100–2.

42. See The Federation of Hillside and Canyon Associations, Inc., 'History of the Hillside Federation: 1952–1986', n.d.

43. Lillard, pp. 314–15.

44. Cf. *Times*, 8 June 1972, 5 February 1978.

45. See profile of Braude, *Times*, 6 March 1988.

46. Quoted in Bernard Frieden, *The Environmental Protection Hustle*, Cambridge, Mass. 1979, p. 2.

47. See Wesley Jackson, 'How Pleasant Was Our Valley?', *Frontier*, April 1956.

48. Cf. *Times*, 27 February 1972 (on Orange County housing trends); 1970 *Census*, Los Angeles–Orange County SMSA; Max Nutze, *The Suburban Apartment Boom: Case Study of a Landuse Problem*, Baltimore 1968. The first year that Southern California, as a whole, built more apartments than single-family homes was 1962.

49. In the Los Angeles County case, developer influence was most obvious in the supervisors' brazen efforts to ditch the Environmental Development Guideline – drawn up by a fifty-member Citizens Planning Council – which designated priority open spaces for preservation. The subversion of the Guideline 'liberated' a million acres for development and postponed for a generation the extinction of the traditional detached home style; at the same time, it inflicted incalculable environmental damage and exported the problems of sprawl another 20 to 50 miles further inland.

50. Reyner Banham, who popularized the term 'dingbat', suggested that it was a 'true symptom of Los Angeles's urban Id trying to cope with the unprecedented appearance of residential densities too high to be subsumed within the illusion of homestead living'. Banham, p. 177.

51. *Times* (Orange County edition), 13 April, 2 July, 14 September, 20 October, and 7 December 1972.

52. *Times*, 22 July, 19 October, 1, 19, and 22 December 1972. For Torrance, also see 27 December 1973.

53. *Times*, 23 November and 7 December 1972.

54. *Bee*, 19 April 1972.

55. *Times*, 23 September 1972.

56. *Times*, 19 and 26 October 1972.

57. *Times*, 30 November 1972 and 18 March 1979.

58. *Times*, 12 and 29 October 1972.

59. The secret to Bradley's victory was his ability to carry both the Palisades and Watts, while undercutting Yorty's historic majority amongst Valley homeowners. (Cf. *Times*, 31 May 1973; and J. Gregory Payne and Scott Ratzan, *Tom Bradley: the Impossible Dream*, Santa Monica 1986, chapter nine).

60. For one example of how Schabarum connived to undermine state law protecting open space in order to favor the land speculation of one of his corporate contributors (in this case, Transamerica), see *Times*, 16 May 1979.

61. Ken Baar, 'Facts and Fallacies in the Rental Housing Market', *Western City*, September 1986, p. 57.

62. This, I believe, was how the now defunct Los Angeles *Herald-Examiner* once headlined the tax revolt.

63. Daniel Durning and Michael Salkin, 'The House as an Investment', *Mortgage Banking*, January 1987; *Times*, 8 January and 21 May 1978, 17 September and 16 November 1979, 15 February 1987; Alan Mallach, *Inclusionary Housing Programs*, New Brunswick, N.J. 1984, p. 148.

64. Social scientists analyzing the voter base of the tax revolt, however, have discovered that 'Proposition 13 drew its support more from fairly affluent people attracted to a large cash bonus' than from 'vulnerable' low-income or retired homeowners. See David Sears and Jack Citrin, *Tax Revolt: Something for Nothing in California*, Cambridge, Mass. 1985, pp. 123–4.

65. See Frank Sherwood, 'Revolt in the Valley', *Frontier*, February 1955.

66. Clarence Lo, *Small Property, Big Government: The Property Tax Revolt*, Berkeley 1990, p. 21. The 1964–6 San Gabriel Valley tax protest movement was led by Mike Rubino, a beer truckdriver from Alhambra. See interview, *Times*, 27 September 1979.

67. Thus at the beginning of the tax revolt in 1976 a Valley anti-tax newsletter listed seven single-purpose tax reduction groups and eighteen homeowners' associations. A later, post-13, key-list of anti-tax groups in Los Angeles County included twelve single-purpose groups and 28 homeowners' associations. See Lo, pp. 53–5.

68. Talk by Brian Moore, chairman of the Hillside Federation, UCLA, 1988; *Times*, 9 March 1978 (for Close's role).

69. Lo, p. 154. Jarvis, of course, brought not only his boilerplate 'charisma'', but also his social base: the landlord class, several hundred-thousand strong in Los Angeles and Orange counties. See ibid., p. 172.

70. Reciprocally, anti-busing leaders like Richard Ferraro and Bobbi Fiedler argued that supporting Proposition 13 would fiscally cripple busing for integration. See *Times*, 20 March 1978.

71. *Times*, 4 March and 23 November 1978.

72. Quoted in *Times*, 22 June 1989.

73. *Times*, 28 January 1979.

74. *Times*, 3 May and 7 October 1979. Looking back on the conjoint tax and busing protests of the late 1970s, it is clear that one of their main political consequences was to provide a political mobility for ambitious suburban Republicans outside the party's power-structures in Los Angeles and Orange County.

75. *Times*, 16 November 1978.

76. *Times*, 7 January 1978 and 22 December 1979 (Thousand Oaks), 17 June 1979 (Simi), 5 March 1979 (Conejo Valley), 27 April 1978 (La Habra Heights), 17 June and 18 November 1979 (Walnut), 22 April and 8 November 1979 (Santa Clarita).

77. In 1979, for example, Riverside approved Proposition R which established an urban greenbelt and drastically restricted hillside development. See *Times*, 3 August 1988.

78. California, Office of Planning and Research, *The Growth Revolt: Aftershock of Proposition 13?*, Sacramento 1980.

79. *Times*, 31 May 1979. In response a local realtor noted that home values near Ventura Boulevard had increased nearly $200,000 in the decade-and-a-half of highrise development.

80. Cf. *Times*, 5 November 1987 and (San Gabriel Valley edition) 3 April 1988.

81. Cf. *National Civic Review*, March and December 1971 (on neighborhoods in draft charter). The revised charter itself was defeated in November 1970 and again in May 1971.

82. *Times*, 12 October 1986; Grubb and Ellis, *Los Angeles Basin Real Estate – 1989*, Los Angeles 1989.

83. 'My daughter just got back from a year away and can't believe the change the development along the boulevard has brought.' See *Times*, 31 May 1979.

84. John Chandler, 'Who's Who: Big Names on the L.A. Planning Scene', *Planning*, February 1986, pp. 9–10.

85. Ron Rosen of the Westside Civic Federation quoted in the *Downtown News*, 6 July 1987.

86. Hillside Federation Chairperson Brian Moore described the court victory as 'the most significant event in city planning in a half-century'. (Talk, UCLA, 1988.)

87. Ibid.; *Times*, 21 January 1986.

88. *Planning*, p. 10.

89. Ibid. Although Bradley deported himself throughout the planning purges as a rather remote Pontius Pilate, the *Times* emphasized that the two 'potential political rivals', Russell and Garcia, 'would not have acted without his blessing'. (Ibid.)

90. *Times*, 21 November 1986.

91. See Yaroslavsky and Braude, op-ed., *Times*, 1 April 1986.

92. *Times*, 30 March; 12 and 30 October 1986. Garcia was undoubtedly also testing the Westside political waters for his own rival purposes.

93. *Times*, 10, 18 and 25 September, 2, 5, 19, and 22 October, 21 November 1986; *Herald-Examiner*, 25 September 1986.

94. *Times*, 5 October 1986.

95. Cf. *Times*, 24 and 29 October 1986 (editorial: 'No on Proposition U'); *Los Angeles Business Journal*, 26 January 1987.

96. Cf. urban critics' views: *Times*, 23 November 1986 (Sam Hall Kaplan); *Herald-Examiner*, 19 October 1986 (Leon Whiteson).

97. The *Times*, 21 November 1986, described Garcia's 'example of compromise' in embracing the planning boards, 'a plan he only half-heartedly supports'.

98. Through elections, the Federation particularly wanted to preclude the *ex-officio* parity of developer representation which the Council wanted to establish after the model of mediation boards. Cf. 'Community Planning Boards', a press release of the Hillside Federation, December 1986; Moore talk, 1988.

99. Gerald Silver, 'If you like L.A. today, you'll love it tomorrow', Los Angeles *Business Journal*, 26 March 1990.

100. Apparently there had been a fascinating debate before the Hillside Federation unanimously adopted its community planning board resolution. According to Federation President Brian Moore, 'some conservatives worried that the unions might take over elected boards'(!). (Talk, UCLA, 1988.)

101. Russell's fall equalized the solid pro-growth strength on the Council (Alatorre, Bernson, Farrell, Ferraro, Lindsay, Milke-Flores) with the moderate 'slow-growth' bloc (Picus, Braude, Yaroslavsky, Galanter, Wachs, Bernardi), leaving a 'swing vote' of three members (Woo, Holden, Molina). Picus, it should be noted, was a 'born-again' slow-growth supporter. See analysis in *Times*, 15 June 1987.

102. 7 November 1987 in Westwood.

103. *Times*, 1 August 1987.

104. *Times*, 8 September 1987. Shapiro, however, found it difficult to confine himself to purely local issues. Two months later he was organizing a citywide initiative to prevent the extension of an all-year school schedule – an austerity measure previously borne solely by inner-city schools – to other parts of the city. In the Valley the all-year controversy rekindled the embers of BUSTOP and the school busing battles, with approximately the same racist connotations.

105. 'Hyperion to a Satyr', in *Tomorrow and Tomorrow and Tomorrow*, New York 1956, pp. 149, 165.

106. Ibid.

107. Howard Nelson, *The Los Angeles Metropolis*, Dubuque 1983, pp. 101–2.

108. *Times*, 27 April 1988.

109. *Daily News*, 30 November 1987.

110. Cf. *Times*, 18 February 1988; 10 December 1989 (special Southern California Environment supplement); *Daily News*, 28 and 29 November 1987.

111. *Times*, 14 August 1986. The commanding account of contemporary California water politics is Robert Gottlieb, *A Life of Its Own: The Politics and Power of Water*, Berkeley 1989.

112. *Times*, 3 and 8 February 1988.

113. *Times*, 21 July 1987.
114. Previously Dan Garcia had advised against discretionary environmental review because it gave more power to the City Council. See *California Planning and Development Report*, August 1987, p.3. (It took two years for the Council to translate *Friends of Westwood* into an environmental review ordinance.)
115. *Times*, 10 December 1987.
116. The law requires developers to line up for permits to hook into the Hyperion Treatment System and reserves 65% of the sewage allotment for housing – especially moderate and low-income. Cf. City Ordinance 165615 (renewed 16 March 1990); David Salvesen and Terry Lassar, 'L.A.'s Sewer Moratorium Curbs Growth', *Urban Land*, August 1988; *Times*, 4 May 1988.
117. *Times*, 27 March 1988.
118. City of Los Angeles, Board of Environmental Quality Commissioners, *State of the City's Environment – Primer*, Los Angeles 1990.
119. Cf. Alan Weissman, 'L.A. Fights for Breath', *The New York Times Magazine*, 30 July 1989; *Los Angeles Business Journal*, 19 February and 19 March 1990; *Downtown News*, 5 February 1990.
120. Another vector of growth management, in lieu of some all-embracing regional authority, is through the power of Cal Trans or regional transportation planning agencies. In January 1990 Assemblyperson Richard Katz (D-San Fernando Valley) proposed legislation that would ration growth via 'traffic flow standards' in much the same way that Los Angeles's sewer ordinance tied development rights to sewer capacity. See *Los Angeles Business Journal*, 20 January 1990.
121. The *L.A. 2000 Report* is a paradigmatic instance of this mentality.
122. *Daily News*, 3 January 1988.
123. See Greg Baer, 'Slow/Planned Growth Movements in the San Fernando Valley', unpublished manuscript, 1988.
124. *Times*, 25 September 1988.
125. Tom Johnson, 'Stop That Train', *Los Angeles Magazine*, 10 January 1988.
126. Another 'rising star in the middle of the [light rail] acrimony' was former BUSTOP leader and conservative Congresswomen, Bobbi Fielder 'whose attention has moved on from little yellow school buses to silver Metro Rail trains'. (Johnson, ibid.)
127. My account compresses very arcane maneuverings and realignments of contending forces. For the full story, see Johnson, and Elaine Litster, 'The Political Development of the San Fernando Light Rail System', unpublished manuscript, 1989. See also *Daily News*, 29 November 1987.
128. Despite outspending slow-growth forces 5:1, Pasadena developers were stunned by the March 1989 victory of the PRIDE (Pasadena Residents in Defense of Our Environment) proposition capping multiple unit housing and commercial construction.
129. *Times*, 5 April 1987.
130. John Horton, 'Ethnicity and the Politics of Growth', manuscript, Department of Sociology, UCLA 1989.
131. *Times*, 27 May 1989. See also *Herald-Examiner*, 26 January 1989.
132. *Times*, 9 March 1988. In San Gabriel the growth war took on Marx Brothers overtones after Vice Mayor Frank Blaszcak, the leader of the anti-apartment forces, was accused of 'mooning' an opponent during a city council meeting. See *Times*, 30 March 1989.
133. *Times* (San Gabriel Valley edition), 30 October 1986. Alhambra should be so lucky for its young Asian immigrants. Dowdy, run-down Alhambra High (54% Asian student body) stood and delivered the nation's highest level of public high-school achievement in math and science in 1988, surpassing such famous institutions as Bronx Science. (*Times*, 17 July 1988.)
134. *Times* (San Gabriel Valley edition), 1 April 1990.
135. Quoted in Charles Barker, *Henry George*, New York 1955, p. 285.
136. *Times*, 2 August, 2 and 3 October 1988; 26 March (profile of Wessell) and 26 April 1989.

137. Two major 1987 Supreme Court decisions, *Nollan* and *First English*, eroded the land-use authority of the California Coastal Commission and local governments. On a different front, developers and landowners have started a campaign of 'SLAPPing' (strategic lawsuits against public participation) slow-growth forces. For example when the Westlake North Property Association tried to block a large development by the Lang Ranch, the company sued the homeowners for harassment and won a judgement of $750,000. In most cases residents' homes are tied up through the course of litigation (*lis pendens*), and could potentially be forfeited in damage fees. Needless to say, the compliance of courts with SLAPPs is becoming a major deterrent to public-interest actions of any kind. See Ron Galperin's article in the *Times*, 29 April 1990.

138. Cf. *Times*, 21 June 1987, 1 and 2 August 1988; Mark Baldassare, 'Predicting Local Concern About Growth', manuscript draft, University of California at Irvine, 1987; Don Albrecht, Gordon Bultena and Eric Hoiberg, 'Constituency of the Antigrowth Movement', *Urban Affairs Quarterly*, June 1986.

CHAPTER FOUR

FORTRESS L.A.

The carefully manicured lawns of Los Angeles's Westside sprout forests of ominous little signs warning: 'Armed Response!' Even richer neighborhoods in the canyons and hillsides isolate themselves behind walls guarded by gun-toting private police and state-of-the-art electronic surveillance. Down-town, a publicly-subsidized 'urban renaissance' has raised the nation's largest corporate citadel, segregated from the poor neighborhoods around it by a monumental architectural glacis. In Hollywood, celebrity architect Frank Gehry, renowned for his 'humanism', apotheosizes the siege look in a library designed to resemble a foreign-legion fort. In the Westlake district and the San Fernando Valley the Los Angeles Police barricade streets and seal off poor neighborhoods as part of their 'war on drugs'. In Watts, developer Alexander Haagen demonstrates his strategy for recolonizing inner-city retail markets: a panoptican shopping mall surrounded by staked metal fences and a substation of the LAPD in a central surveillance tower. Finally on the horizon of the next millennium, an ex-chief of police crusades for an anti-crime 'giant eye' – a geo-synchronous law enforcement satellite – while other cops discreetly tend versions of 'Garden Plot', a hoary but still viable 1960s plan for a law-and-order armageddon.

Welcome to post-liberal Los Angeles, where the defense of luxury lifestyles is translated into a proliferation of new repressions in space and movement, undergirded by the ubiquitous 'armed response'. This obsession with physical security systems, and, collaterally, with the architectural policing of social boundaries, has become a zeitgeist of urban restructuring, a master narrative in the emerging built environment of the 1990s. Yet contemporary urban theory, whether debating the role of electronic technologies in precipitating 'postmodern space', or discussing the dispersion of urban functions across poly-centered metropolitan 'galaxies', has been strangely silent about the militarization of city life so grimly visible at the street level. Hollywood's pop apocalypses and pulp science fiction have been more realistic, and politically perceptive, in representing the programmed hardening of the urban surface in the wake of the social polarizations of the Reagan era. Images of carceral inner cities (*Escape from New York, Running Man*), high-tech police death squads (*Blade Runner*), sentient buildings (*Die Hard*), urban bantustans (*They Live!*), Vietnam-like street wars (*Colors*), and so on, only extrapolate from actually existing trends.

Such dystopian visions grasp the extent to which today's pharaonic scales of residential and commercial security supplant residual hopes for urban reform and social integration. The dire predictions of Richard Nixon's 1969 National Commission on the Causes and Prevention of Violence have been tragically fulfilled: we live in 'fortress cities' brutally divided between 'fortified cells' of affluent society and 'places of terror' where the police battle the criminalized poor.[1] The 'Second Civil War' that began in the long hot summers of the 1960s has been institutionalized into the very structure of urban space. The old liberal paradigm of social control, attempting to balance repression with reform, has long been superseded by a rhetoric of social warfare that calculates the interests of the urban poor and the middle classes as a zero-sum game. In cities like Los Angeles, on the bad edge of postmodernity, one observes an unprecedented tendency to merge urban design, architecture and the police apparatus into a single, comprehensive security effort.

This epochal coalescence has far-reaching consequences for the social relations of the built environment. In the first place, the market provision of 'security' generates its own paranoid demand. 'Security' becomes a positional good defined by income access to private 'protective services' and membership in some hardened residential enclave or restricted suburb. As a prestige symbol – and sometimes as the decisive borderline between the merely well-off and the 'truly rich' – 'security' has less to do with personal safety than with the degree of personal insulation, in residential, work, consumption and travel environments, from 'unsavory' groups and individuals, even crowds in general.

Secondly, as William Whyte has observed of social intercourse in New York, 'fear proves itself'. The social perception of threat becomes a function of the security mobilization itself, not crime rates. Where there is an actual rising arc of street violence, as in Southcentral Los Angeles or Downtown Washington D.C., most of the carnage is self-contained within ethnic or class boundaries. Yet white middle-class imagination, absent from any first-hand knowledge of inner-city conditions, magnifies the perceived threat through a demonological lens. Surveys show that Milwaukee suburbanites are just as worried about violent crime as inner-city Washingtonians, despite a twenty-fold difference in relative levels of mayhem. The media, whose function in this arena is to bury and obscure the daily economic

FORTRESS L.A.
Bunker Hill

violence of the city, ceaselessly throw up spectres of criminal underclasses and psychotic stalkers. Sensationalized accounts of killer youth gangs high on crack and shrilly racist evocations of marauding Willie Hortons foment the moral panics that reinforce and justify urban apartheid.

Moreover, the neo-military syntax of contemporary architecture insinuates violence and conjures imaginary dangers. In many instances the semiotics of so-called 'defensible space' are just about as subtle as a swaggering white cop. Today's upscale, pseudo-public spaces – sumptuary malls, office centers, culture acropolises, and so on – are full of invisible signs warning off the underclass 'Other'. Although architectural critics are usually oblivious to how the built environment contributes to segregation, pariah groups – whether poor Latino families, young Black men, or elderly homeless white females – read the meaning immediately.

THE DESTRUCTION OF PUBLIC SPACE

The universal and ineluctable consequence of this crusade to secure the city is the destruction of accessible public space. The contemporary opprobrium attached to the term 'street person' is in itself a harrowing index of the devaluation of public spaces. To reduce contact with untouchables, urban redevelopment has converted once vital pedestrian streets into traffic sewers and transformed public parks into temporary receptacles for the homeless and wretched. The American city, as many critics have recognized, is being systematically turned inside out – or, rather, outside in. The valorized spaces of the new megastructures and super-malls are concentrated in the center, street frontage is denuded, public activity is sorted into strictly functional compartments, and circulation is internalized in corridors under the gaze of private police.[2]

The privatization of the architectural public realm, moreover, is shadowed by parallel restructurings of electronic space, as heavily policed, pay-access 'information orders', elite data-bases and subscription cable services appropriate parts of the invisible agora. Both processes, of course, mirror the deregulation of the economy and the recession of non-market entitlements. The decline of urban liberalism has been accompanied by the death of what might be called the 'Olmstedian vision' of public space.

Frederick Law Olmsted, it will be recalled, was North America's Haussmann, as well as the Father of Central Park. In the wake of Manhattan's 'Commune' of 1863, the great Draft Riot, he conceived public landscapes and parks as social safety-valves, *mixing* classes and ethnicities in common (bourgeois) recreations and enjoyments. As Manfredo Tafuri has shown in his well-known study of Rockefeller Center, the same principle animated the construction of the canonical urban spaces of the La Guardia–Roosevelt era.[3]

This reformist vision of public space – as the emollient of class struggle, if not the bedrock of the American *polis* – is now as obsolete as Keynesian nostrums of full employment. In regard to the 'mixing' of classes, contemporary urban America is more like Victorian England than Walt Whitman's or La Guardia's New York. In Los Angeles, once-upon-a-time a demi-paradise of free beaches, luxurious parks, and 'cruising strips', genuinely democratic space is all but extinct. The Oz-like archipelago of Westside pleasure domes – a continuum of tony malls, arts centers and gourmet strips – is reciprocally dependent upon the social imprisonment of the third-world service proletariat who live in increasingly repressive ghettoes and barrios. In a city of several million yearning immigrants, public amenities are radically shrinking, parks are becoming derelict and beaches more segregated, libraries and playgrounds are closing, youth congregations of ordinary kinds are banned, and the streets are becoming more desolate and dangerous.

Unsurprisingly, as in other American cities, municipal policy has taken its lead from the security offensive and the middle-class demand for increased spatial and social insulation. De facto disinvestment in traditional public space and recreation has supported the shift of fiscal resources to corporate-defined redevelopment priorities. A pliant city government – in this case ironically professing to represent a bi-racial coalition of liberal whites and Blacks – has collaborated in the massive privatization of public space and the subsidization of new, racist enclaves (benignly described as 'urban villages'). Yet most current, giddy discussions of the 'postmodern' scene in Los Angeles neglect entirely these overbearing aspects of counter-urbanization and counter-insurgency. A triumphal gloss – 'urban renaissance', 'city of the future', and so on – is laid over the brutalization of inner-city neighborhoods and the increasing South Africanization of its spatial relations. Even as the walls have come down in Eastern Europe, they are being erected all over Los Angeles.

The observations that follow take as their thesis the existence of this new class war (sometimes a continuation of the race war of the 1960s) at the level of the built environment. Although this is not a comprehensive account, which would require a thorough analysis of economic and political dynamics, these images and instances are meant to convince the reader that urban form is indeed following a repressive function in the political furrows of the Reagan–Bush era. Los Angeles, in its usual prefigurative mode, offers an especially disquieting catalogue of the emergent liaisons between architecture and the American police state.

THE FORBIDDEN CITY

The first militarist of space in Los Angeles was General Otis of the *Times*. Declaring himself at war with labor, he infused his surroundings with an unrelentingly bellicose air:

He called his home in Los Angeles the Bivouac. Another house was known as the Outpost. The *Times* was known as the Fortress. The staff of the paper was the Phalanx. The *Times* building itself was more fortress than newspaper plant, there were turrets, battlements, sentry boxes. Inside he stored fifty rifles.[4]

A great, menacing bronze eagle was the *Times*'s crown; a small, functional cannon was installed on the hood of Otis's touring car to intimidate onlookers. Not surprisingly, this overwrought display of aggression produced a response in kind. On 1 October 1910 the heavily fortified *Times* headquarters – citadel of the open shop on the West Coast – was destroyed in a catastrophic explosion blamed on union saboteurs.

Eighty years later, the spirit of General Otis has returned to subtly pervade Los Angeles's new 'postmodern' Downtown: the emerging Pacific Rim financial complex which cascades, in rows of skyscrapers, from Bunker Hill southward along the Figueroa corridor. Redeveloped with public tax increments under the aegis of the powerful and largely unaccountable Community Redevelopment Agency, the Downtown project is one of the largest postwar urban designs in North America. Site assemblage and clearing on a vast scale, with little mobilized opposition, have resurrected land values, upon which big developers and off-shore capital (increasingly Japanese) have planted a series of billion-dollar, block-square mega-structures: Crocker Center, the Bonaventure Hotel and Shopping Mall, the World Trade Center, the Broadway Plaza, Arco Center, CitiCorp Plaza, California Plaza, and so on. With historical landscapes erased, with mega-structures and superblocks as primary components, and with an increasingly dense and self-contained circulation system, the new financial district is best conceived as a single, demonically self-referential hyper-structure, a Miesian skyscape raised to dementia.

Like similar megalomaniac complexes, tethered to fragmented and desolated Downtowns (for instance, the Renaissance Center in Detroit, the Peachtree and Omni Centers in Atlanta, and so on), Bunker Hill and the Figueroa corridor have provoked a storm of liberal objections against their abuse of scale and composition, their denigration of street landscape, and their confiscation of so much of the vital life activity of the center, now sequestered within subterranean concourses or privatized malls. Sam Hall Kaplan, the crusty urban critic of the *Times*, has been indefatigable in denouncing the anti-pedestrian bias of the new corporate citadel, with its fascist obliteration of street frontage. In his view the superimposition of 'hermetically sealed fortresses' and air-dropped 'pieces of suburbia' has 'dammed the rivers of life' Downtown.[5]

Yet Kaplan's vigorous defense of pedestrian democracy remains grounded in hackneyed liberal complaints about 'bland design' and 'elitist planning practices'. Like most architectural critics, he rails against the oversights of urban design without recognizing the dimension of foresight, of explicit repressive intention, which has its roots in Los Angeles's ancient history of class and race warfare. Indeed, when Downtown's new 'Gold Coast' is viewed en bloc from the standpoint of its interactions with other social areas and landscapes in the central city, the 'fortress effect' emerges, not as an inadvertent failure of design, but as deliberate socio-spatial strategy.

The goals of this strategy may be summarized as a double repression: to raze all association with Downtown's past and to prevent any articulation with the non-Anglo urbanity of its future. Everywhere on the perimeter of redevelopment this strategy takes the form of a brutal architectural edge or glacis that defines the new Downtown as a citadel vis-à-vis the rest of the central city. Los Angeles is unusual amongst major urban renewal centers in preserving, however negligently, most of its circa 1900–30 Beaux Arts commercial core. At immense public cost, the corporate headquarters and financial district was shifted from the old Broadway-Spring corridor six blocks west to the greenfield site created by destroying the Bunker Hill residential neighborhood. To emphasize the 'security' of the new Downtown, virtually all the traditional pedestrian links to the old center, including the famous Angels' Flight funicular railroad, were removed.

The logic of this entire operation is revealing. In other cities developers might have attempted to articulate the new skyscape and the old, exploiting the latter's extraordinary inventory of theaters and historic buildings to create a gentrified history – a gaslight district, Faneuil Market or Ghiardelli Square – as a support to middle-class residential colonization. But Los Angeles's redevelopers viewed property values in the old Broadway core as irreversibly eroded by the area's very centrality to public transport, and especially by its heavy use by Black and Mexican poor. In the wake of the Watts Rebellion, and the perceived Black threat to crucial nodes of white power (spelled out in lurid detail in the McCone Commission Report), resegregated spatial security became the paramount concern.[6] The Los Angeles Police Department abetted the flight of business from Broadway to the fortified redoubts of Bunker Hill by spreading scare literature typifying Black teenagers as dangerous gang members.[7]

As a result, redevelopment massively reproduced spatial apartheid. The moat of the Harbor Freeway and the regraded palisades of Bunker Hill cut off the new financial core from the poor immigrant neighborhoods that surround it on every side. Along the base of California Plaza, Hill Street became a local Berlin Wall separating the publicly subsidized luxury of Bunker Hill from the lifeworld of Broadway, now reclaimed by Latino immigrants as their primary shopping and entertainment street. Because politically connected speculators are now redeveloping the northern end of the Broadway corridor (sometimes known as 'Bunker Hill East'), the CRA is promising to restore pedestrian link-ages to the Hill in the 1990s, including the Angels' Flight incline railroad. This, of course, only dramatizes the current bias against accessibility – that is to say, against *any* spatial interaction between old and new, poor and rich, except in the framework of gentrification or recolonization.[8] Although a few white-collars venture into the Grand Central Market – a popular emporium of tropical produce and fresh foods – Latino shoppers or Saturday strollers never circulate in the Gucci precincts above Hill Street. The occasional appearance of a destitute street nomad in Broadway Plaza or in front of the Museum of Contemporary Art sets off a quiet panic; video cameras turn on their mounts and security guards adjust their belts.

Photographs of the old Downtown in its prime show mixed crowds of Anglo, Black and Latino pedestrians of different ages and classes. The contemporary Downtown 'renaissance' is designed to make such hetero-geneity virtually impossible. It is intended not just to 'kill the street' as Kaplan fears, but to 'kill the crowd', to eliminate that democratic admixture on the pavements and in the parks that Olmsted believed was America's antidote to European class polarizations. The Downtown hyperstructure – like some Buckminster Fuller post-Holocaust fantasy – is programmed to ensure a seamless continuum of middle-class work, consumption and recreation, without unwonted exposure to Downtown's working-class street environments.[9] Indeed the totalitarian semiotics of ramparts and battlements, reflective glass and elevated pedways, rebukes any affinity or sympathy between different architectural or human orders. As in Otis's fortress *Times* building, this is the archisemiotics of class war.

Lest this seem too extreme, consider *Urban Land* magazine's recent description of the profit-driven formula that across the United States has linked together clustered development, social homogeneity, and a secure 'Downtown image':

HOW TO OVERCOME FEAR OF CRIME IN DOWNTOWNS

Create a Dense, Compact, Multifunctional Core Area. A downtown can be designed and developed to make visitors feel that it – or a significant portion of it – is attractive and the type of place that 'respectable people' like themselves tend to frequent. . . . A core downtown area that is compact, densely developed and multifunctional will concentrate people, giving them more activities. . . . The activities offered in this core area will determine what 'type' of people will be strolling its sidewalks; locating offices and housing for middle- and upper-income residents in or near the core area can assure a high percentage of 'respectable', law-abiding pedestrians. Such an attractive redeveloped core area would also be large enough to affect the downtown's overall image.[10]

SADISTIC STREET ENVIRONMENTS

This conscious 'hardening' of the city surface against the poor is especially brazen in the Manichaean treatment of Downtown microcosms. In his famous study of the 'social life of small urban spaces', William Whyte makes the point that the quality of any urban environment can be measured, first of all, by whether there are convenient, comfortable places for pedestrians to sit.[11] This maxim has been warmly taken to heart by designers of the high-corporate precincts of Bunker Hill and the emerging 'urban village' of South Park. As part of the city's policy of subsidizing white-collar residential colonization in Downtown, it has spent, or plans to spend, tens of millions of dollars of diverted tax revenue on enticing, 'soft' environments in these areas. Planners envision an opulent complex of squares, fountains, world-class public art, exotic shubbery, and avant-garde street furniture along a Hope Street pedestrian corridor. In the propaganda of official boosters, nothing is taken as a better index of Downtown's 'liveability' than the idyll of office workers and upscale tourists lounging or napping in the terraced gardens of California Plaza, the 'Spanish Steps' or Grand Hope Park.

In stark contrast, a few blocks away, the city is engaged in a merciless struggle to make public facilities and spaces as 'unliveable' as possible for the homeless and the poor. The persistence of thousands of street people on the fringes of Bunker Hill and the Civic Center sours the image of designer Downtown living and betrays the laboriously constructed illusion of a Downtown 'renaissance'. City Hall then retaliates with its own variant of low-intensity warfare.[12]

Although city leaders periodically essay schemes for removing indigents *en masse* – deporting them to a poor farm on the edge of the desert, confining them in camps in the mountains, or, memorably, interning them on a derelict ferry at the Harbor – such 'final solutions' have been blocked by councilmembers fearful of the displacement of the homeless into their districts. Instead the city, self-consciously adopting the idiom of urban cold war, promotes the 'containment' (official term) of the homeless in Skid Row along Fifth Street east of the Broadway, systematically transforming the neighborhood into an outdoor poorhouse. But this containment strategy breeds its own vicious circle of contradiction. By condensing the mass of the desperate and helpless together in such a small space, and denying adequate housing, official policy has transformed Skid Row into probably the most dangerous ten square blocks in the world – ruled by a grisly succession of 'Slashers', 'Night Stalkers' and more ordinary predators.[13] Every night on Skid Row is Friday the 13th, and, unsurprisingly, many of the homeless seek to escape the 'Nickle' during the night at all costs, searching safer niches in other parts of Downtown. The city in turn tightens the noose with increased police harassment and ingenious design deterrents.

One of the most common, but mind-numbing, of these deterrents is the Rapid Transit District's new barrelshaped bus bench that offers a minimal surface for uncomfortable sitting, while making sleeping utterly impossible. Such 'bumproof' benches are being widely introduced on the periphery of Skid Row. Another invention, worthy of the Grand Guignol, is the aggressive deployment of outdoor sprinklers. Several years ago the city opened a 'Skid Row Park' along lower Fifth Street, on a corner of Hell. To ensure that the park was not used for sleeping – that is to say, to guarantee that it was mainly utilized for drug dealing and prostitution – the city installed an elaborate overhead sprinkler system programmed to drench unsuspecting sleepers at random times during the night. The system was immediately copied by some local businessmen in order to drive the homeless away from adjacent public sidewalks. Meanwhile restaurants and markets have responded to the homeless by building ornate enclosures to protect their refuse. Although no one in Los Angeles has yet proposed adding cyanide to the garbage, as happened in Phoenix a few years back, one popular seafood restaurant has spent $12,000 to built the ultimate bag-lady-proof trash cage: made of three-quarter inch steel rod with alloy locks and vicious outturned spikes to safeguard priceless moldering fishheads and stale french fries.

Public toilets, however, are the real Eastern Front of the Downtown war on the poor. Los Angeles, as a matter of deliberate policy, has fewer available public lavatories than any major North American city. On the advice of the LAPD (who actually sit on the design board of at least one major Downtown redevelopment project),[14] the Community Redevelopment Agency bulldozed the remaining public toilet in Skid Row. Agency planners then agonized for months over whether to include a 'free-standing public toilet' in their design for South Park. As CRA Chairman Jim Wood later admitted, the decision not to include the toilet was a 'policy decision and not a design decision'. The CRA Downtown prefers the solution of 'quasi-public restrooms' – meaning toilets in restaurants, art galleries and office buildings – which can be made available to tourists and office workers while being denied to vagrants and other unsuitables.[15] The toiletless no-man's-land east of Hill Street in Downtown is also barren of outside water sources for drinking or washing. A common and troubling sight these days are the homeless men – many of them young Salvadorean refugees – washing in and even drinking from the sewer effluent which flows down the concrete channel of the Los Angeles River on the eastern edge of Downtown.

Where the itineraries of Downtown powerbrokers unavoidably intersect with the habitats of the homeless or the working poor, as in the previously mentioned zone of gentrification along the northern Broadway corridor, extraordinary design precautions are being taken to ensure the physical separation of the different humanities. For instance, the CRA brought in the Los Angeles Police to design '24-hour, state-of-the-art security' for the two new parking structures that serve the Los Angeles *Times* and Ronald Reagan State Office buildings. In contrast to the mean streets outside, the parking structures contain beautifully landscaped lawns or 'microparks', and in one case, a food court and a historical exhibit. Moreover, both structures are designed as 'confidence-building' circulation systems – miniature paradigms of privatization – which allow white-collar workers to walk from car to office, or from car to boutique, with minimum exposure to the public street. The Broadway Spring Center, in particular, which links the Ronald Reagan Building to the proposed 'Grand Central Square' at Third and Broadway, has been warmly praised by architectural critics for adding greenery and art (a banal bas relief) to parking. It also adds a huge dose of menace – armed guards, locked gates, and security cameras – to scare away the homeless and poor.

The cold war on the streets of Downtown is ever escalating. The police, lobbied by Downtown merchants and developers, have broken up every attempt by the homeless and their allies to create safe havens or self-organized encampments. 'Justiceville', founded by homeless activist Ted Hayes, was roughly dispersed; when its inhabitants attempted to find refuge at Venice Beach, they were arrested at the behest of the local councilperson (a renowned environmentalist) and sent back to the inferno of Skid Row.

'BUM-PROOF' BUS BENCH
Hill Street, Downtown

The city's own brief experiment with legalized camping – a grudging response to a series of exposure deaths in the cold winter of 1987[16] – was ended abruptly after only four months to make way for construction of a transit repair yard. Current policy seems to involve a perverse play upon Zola's famous irony about the 'equal rights' of the rich and the poor to sleep out rough. As the head of the city planning commission explained the official line to incredulous reporters, it is not against the law to sleep on the street per se, 'only to erect any sort of protective shelter'. To enforce this prescription against 'cardboard condos', the LAPD periodically sweep the Nickle, confiscating shelters and other possessions, and arresting resisters. Such cynical repression has turned the majority of the homeless into urban bedouins. They are visible all over Downtown, pushing a few pathetic possessions in purloined shopping carts, always fugitive and in motion, pressed between the official policy of containment and the increasing sadism of Downtown streets.[17]

FRANK GEHRY AS DIRTY HARRY

If the contemporary search for bourgeois security can be read in the design of bus benches and mega-structures, it is also visible at the level of *auteur*. No recent architect has so ingeniously elaborated the urban security function or so brazenly embraced the resulting *frisson* as Los Angeles's Pritzker Prize laureate, Frank Gehry. As we saw earlier, he has become one of the principal 'imagineers' (in the Disney sense) of the neo-boosterism of the 1990s. He is particularly adept as a crossover, not merely between architecture and modern art, but also between older, vaguely radical and contemporary, basically cynical styles. Thus his portfolio is at once a principled repudiation of postmodernism and one of its cleverest sub-limations; a nostalgic evocation of revolutionary constructivism and a mercenary celebration of bourgeois-decadent minimalism. These amphibian shifts and paradoxical nuances in Gehry's work sustain a booming cottage industry of Gehry-interpretation, mostly effused with hyperbolic admiration.

Yet, as suggested in chapter one, Gehry's strongest suit may simply be his straightforward exploitation of rough urban environments, and his

THE NEW COMMANDMENT
Vermont near Olympic

blatant incorporation of their harshest edges and detritus as powerful representational elements in his work. Affectionately described by colleagues as an 'old socialist' or 'street-fighter with a heart', much of his most interesting work is utterly unromantic and anti-idealist.[18] Unlike his popular front mentors of the 1940s, Gehry makes little pretense at architectural reformism or 'design for democracy'. He boasts of trying 'to make the best with the reality of things'. With sometimes chilling luminosity, his work clarifies the underlying relations of repression, surveillance and exclusion that characterize the fragmented, paranoid spatiality towards which Los Angeles seems to aspire.

A very early example of Gehry's new urban realism was his 1964 solution of the problem of how to insert high property values and sumptuary spaces into decaying neighborhoods. His Danziger Studio in Hollywood is the pioneer instance of what has become an entire species of Los Angeles 'stealth houses', dissimulating their luxurious qualities with proletarian or gangster façades. The street frontage of the Danziger – on Melrose in the bad old days before its current gourmet-gulch renaissance – was simply a massive gray wall, treated with a rough finish to ensure that it would collect dust from passing traffic and weather into a simulacrum of nearby porn studios and garages. Gehry was explicit in his search for a design that was 'introverted and fortress-like' with the silent aura of a 'dumb box'.[19]

'Dumb boxes' and screen walls form an entire cycle of Gehry's work, ranging from his American School of Dance (1968) to his Gemini G.E.I. (1979), both in Hollywood. His most seminal design, however, was his walled town center for Cochiti Lake, New Mexico (1973): here ice-blue ramparts of awesome severity enclose an entire community (a plan replicated on a smaller scale in the 1976 Jung Institute in Los Angeles). In each of these instances, melodrama is generated by the antithesis between the fortified exteriors, set against 'unappealing neighborhoods' or deserts, and the opulent interiors, open to the sky by clerestories and lightwells. Gehry's walled compounds and cities, in other words, offer powerful metaphors for the retreat from the street and the introversion of space that characterized the design backlash against the urban insurrections of the 1960s.

This problematic was renewed in 1984 in his design of the Loyola Law School located on the western edge of Downtown Los Angeles in the largest Central American barrio in the United States. The inner-city situation of the Loyola campus confronted Gehry with an explicit choice between the risks of creating a genuine public space, extending into the community, or choosing the security of a defensible enclave, as in his previous work. The radical, or simply idealist, architect might have gambled on opening the campus to the adjacent community, giving it some substantive stake in the design. Instead, as an admiring critic explained, Gehry chose a fundamentally neo-conservative design that was:

open, but not *too open*. The South Instructional Hall and the chapel show solid backs to Olympic Boulevard, and with the anonymous street sides of the Burns Building, form a gateway that is neither forbidding nor overly welcoming. It is simply there, like everything else in the neighborhood.[20]

(This description considerably understates the forbidding qualities of the campus's formidable steel stake fencing, concrete bloc ziggurat, and stark frontage walls.)

But if the Danziger Studio camouflages itself, and the Cochiti Lake and Loyola designs bunch frontage in stern glares, Gehry's baroquely fortified Frances Howard Goldwyn Regional Branch Library in Hollywood (1984) positively taunts potential trespassers 'to make my day'. This is undoubtedly the most menacing library ever built, a bizarre hybrid (on the outside) of dry-docked dreadnought and Gunga Din fort. With its fifteen-foot security walls of stucco-covered concrete block, its anti-graffiti barricades covered in ceramic tile, its sunken entrance protected by ten-foot steel stacks, and its stylized sentry boxes perched precariously on each side, the Goldwyn Library (influenced by Gehry's 1980 high-security design for the US Chancellery in Damascus) projects the same kind of macho exaggeration as Dirty Harry's 44 Magnum.

Predictably, some of Gehry's intoxicated admirers have swooned over this Beirutized structure as 'generous' and 'inviting', 'the old-fashioned kind of library', and so on. They absurdly miss the point.[21] The previous Hollywood Regional Branch Library had been destroyed by arson, and the Samuel Goldwyn Foundation, which endows this collection of filmland memorabilia, was fixated on physical security. Gehry accepted a commission to design a structure that was inherently 'vandalproof'. The curiosity, of course, is his rejection of the low-profile, high-tech security systems that most architects subtly integrate in their blueprints. He chose instead a high-profile, low-tech approach that maximally foregrounds the security functions as motifs of the design. There is no dissimulation of function by form; quite the opposite, Gehry lets it all hang out. How playful or mordantly witty you may find the resulting effect depends on your existential position. The Goldwyn Library relentlessly interpellates a demonic Other (arsonist, graffitist, invader) whom it reflects back on surrounding streets and street people. It coldly saturates its immediate environment, which is seedy but not particularly hostile, with its own arrogant paranoia.

Yet paranoia could be a misnomer, for the adjacent streets are a battleground. Several years ago the Los Angeles *Times* broke the sordid story about how the entertainment conglomerates and a few large landowners, monopolizing land ownership in this part of Hollywood, had managed to capture control of the redevelopment process. Their plan, still the object of controversy, is to use eminent domain and public tax increments to clear the poor (increasingly refugees from Central America) from the streets of Hollywood and reap the huge windfalls from 'upgrading' the region into a glitzy theme-park for international tourism.[22] Within this strategy, the Goldwyn Library – like Gehry's earlier walled compounds – is a kind of architectural fire-base, a beachhead for gentrification. Its soaring, light-filled interiors surrounded by bellicose barricades speak volumes about how public architecture in America is literally being turned inside out, in the service of 'security' and profit.

THE PANOPTICON MALL

In other local instances, however, the 'fortress' is being used to recapture the poor as consumers. If the Goldwyn Library is a 'shining example of the possibilities of public and private-sector cooperation', then developer Alexander Haagen's inner-city malls are truly stellar instances. Haagen, whose career began as a jukebox distributor in the honky-tonks of Wilmington, made his initial fortune selling corner lots to oil companies (since recycled as mini-malls). He now controls the largest retail

DIRTY HARRY'S LIBRARY
Goldwyn Library, Hollywood

development empire in Southern California, responsible for more than forty shopping centers. As we saw in chapter two, Haagen is a savvy political donor who swings with both Democrats and Republicans. He is also the past master at exploiting public-sector redevelopment for private gain – or, if you prefer, 'the father of the inner city's rebirth'.

He was the first major developer in the nation to grasp the latent profit potentials of abandoned inner-city retail markets. After the 1965 Watts Rebellion the handful of large retailers in Southcentral Los Angeles took flight while viable small businesses were asphyxiated by discriminatory bank 'redlining' practices. As a result, half a million Black and Latino shoppers were forced to commute to distant regional malls or bordering white areas even for ordinary grocery and prescription shopping. Haagen reasoned that a retail developer prepared to return to the inner city could monopolize very high sales volumes. Aware of the accumulating anger of the Black community against decades of benign neglect by redevelopment authorities, he also calculated that he could induce the city to subsidize this commercial recolonization. While the Community Redevelopment Agency had raced ahead to assemble land for billionaire developers Downtown, it had floundered in Watts for years, unable to attract a single supermarket to anchor a proposed neighborhood shopping center. Haagen recognized that the Bradley regime, in unprecedented hot water with its Southcentral constituency, would handsomely reward any private-sector initiative that could cut the Gordian knot of the 'anchor tenant problem'. His ingenious solution, which won national acclaim from the commercial development industry, was a comprehensive 'security-oriented design and management strategy'.[23]

The first move was made in 1979 when Haagen Development took title over an old Sears site at Vermont and Slauson, in the heart of Southcentral. Then in 1983 the redevelopment agency turned over to him the completion of its long-delayed Martin Luther King Jr. Center in Watts. A year later he won the bid for the $120 million refurbishing and expansion of the Crenshaw Plaza in Baldwin Hills, followed by a County contract to create a shopping complex in the Willowbrook area just south of Watts. In each case the guarantee of fail-safe physical security was the *sine qua non* in persuading retailers and franchises (and their insurers) to take up leases. The prototype plan shared by all four shopping centers plagiarizes brazenly from Jeremy Bentham's renowned nineteenth-century design for the 'panopticon prison' with its economical central surveillance. Consider, for example, the layout of Haagen's Watts center:

The King center site is surrounded by an eight-foot-high, wrought-iron fence comparable to security fences found at the perimeters of private estates and exclusive residential communities. Video cameras equipped with motion detectors are positioned near entrances and throughout the shopping center. The entire center, including parking lots, can be bathed in bright four-foot candle lighting at the flip of the switch.

There are six entrances to the center: three entry points for autos, two service gates, and one pedestrian walkway. The pedestrian and auto entries have gates that are opened at 6:30 a.m. and closed at 10:30 p.m. The service area located at the rear of the property is enclosed with a six-foot-high concrete block wall; both service gates remain closed and are under closed-circuit video surveillance, equipped for two-way voice communications, and operated for deliveries by remote control from a security 'observatory'. Infra-red beams at the bases of light fixtures detect intruders who might circumvent video cameras by climbing over the wall.[24]

The 'unobtrusive' panopticon observatory is both eye and brain of this complex security system. (In the Willowbrook center it is actually hidden above a public library branch.) It contains the headquarters of the shopping center manager, a substation of the LAPD, and a dispatch operator who monitors the video and audio systems as well as maintaining communication 'with other secure shopping centers tied into the system, and with the police and fire departments'. At any time of the week, day or night, there are at least four center security guards on duty: one at the observatory and three on foot patrol. They are trained and backed up by the regular LAPD officers operating from the substation in the observatory.

While these security measures may seem extraordinary, shopping center security issues have risen to the forefront of management's concerns during the last few years. With insurance carriers reviewing the security operations of shopping centers before writing new policies or even renewing existing ones, and, in some cases, insisting on upgraded security programs as a condition of insurance, centers in locations other than inner-city neighborhoods have started to focus on security operations as an integral part of their design and management strategy. Indeed protecting shopping center owners and managers from lawsuits can make a strong security program extremely profitable over the long run.[24]

These centers, as expected, have been bonanzas, averaging annual sales of more than $350 per leasable square foot, as compared to about $200 for their suburban equivalents.[25] Moreover Haagen has reaped the multiple windfalls of tax breaks, federal and city grants, massive free publicity, subsidized tenants and sixty- to ninety-year ground leases. No wonder he has been able to boast: 'We've proved that the only color that counts in business is green. There are huge opportunities and huge profits to be made in these depressed inner-city areas of America that have been abandoned.'[26]

Meanwhile the logic of 'Haagenization' has been extended to the housing as well as shopping areas of the ghetto. The counterpart of the mall-as-panopticon-prison is the housing-project-as-strategic-hamlet. The Imperial Courts Housing Project, just down the road from the Martin Luther King Jr. Center, has recently been fortified with fencing, obligatory identity passes and a substation of the LAPD. Visitors are stopped and frisked, while the police routinely order residents back into their apartments at night. Such is the loss of freedom that public housing tenants must now endure as the price of 'security'.

FROM RENTACOP TO *ROBOCOP*

The security-driven logic of urban enclavization finds its most popular expression in the frenetic efforts of Los Angeles's affluent neighborhoods to insulate home values and lifestyles. As we saw in the last chapter, new luxury developments outside the city limits have often become fortress cities, complete with encompassing walls, restricted entry points with guard posts, overlapping private and public police services, and even privatized roadways. It is simply impossible for ordinary citizens to invade the 'cities' of Hidden Hills, Bradbury, Rancho Mirage or Palos Verdes Estates without an invitation from a resident. Indeed Bradbury, with nine hundred residents and ten miles of gated private roads, is so security-obsessed that its three city officials do not return telephone calls from the press, since 'each time an article appeared . . . it drew attention to the city and the number of burglaries increased'. For its part, Hidden Hills, a Norman Rockwell painting behind high-security walls, has been bitterly divided over compliance with a Superior Court order to build forty-eight units of seniors'

PANOPTICON EYE
Police observatory above library in Haagen shopping mall,
Willowbrook district

housing outside its gates. At meetings of the city's all-powerful homeowners' association (whose membership includes Frankie Avalon, Neil Diamond and Bob Eubanks) opponents of compliance have argued that the old folks' apartments 'will attract gangs and dope' (sic).[27]

Meanwhile, traditional luxury enclaves like Beverly Hills and San Marino are increasingly restricting access to their public facilities, using baroque layers of regulations to build invisible walls. San Marino, which may be the richest, and is reputedly the most Republican (85 per cent), city in the country, now closes its parks on weekends to exclude Latino and Asian families from adjacent communities. One plan under discussion would reopen the parks on Saturdays only to those with proof of residence. Other upscale neighborhoods in Los Angeles have minted a similar residential privilege by obtaining ordinances to restrict parking to local homeowners. Predictably, such preferential parking regulations proliferate exclusively in neighborhoods with three-car garages.

Residential areas with enough clout are thus able to privatize local public space, partitioning themselves from the rest of the metropolis, even imposing a variant of neighborhood 'passport control' on outsiders. The next step, of course, is to ape incorporated enclaves like Palos Verdes or Hidden Hills by building literal walls. Since its construction in the late 1940s Park La Brea has been a bit of Lower Manhattan *chutzpah* moored to Wilshire Boulevard: a 176-acre maze of medium-rent townhouses and tower apartments, occupied by an urbane mix of singles, retirees, and families. Now, as part of a strategy of gentrification, its owners, Forest City Enterprises, have decided to enclose the entire community in security fencing, cutting off to pedestrians one of the most vital public spaces along the 'Miracle Mile'. As a spokeswoman for the owners observed, 'it's a trend in general to have enclosed communities'.[28] In the once wide-open tractlands of the San Fernando Valley, where there were virtually no walled-off communities a decade ago, the 'trend' has assumed the frenzied dimensions of a residential arms race as ordinary suburbanites demand the kind of social insulation once enjoyed only by the rich. Brian Weinstock, a leading Valley contractor, boasts of more than one hundred newly gated neighborhoods, with an insatiable demand for more security. 'The first question out of their [the buyers'] mouths is whether there is a gated community. The demand is there on a 3-to-1 basis for a gated community than not living in a gated community.'[29]

CHUTZPAH DENIED
Park La Brea

The social control advantages of 'gatehood' have also attracted the attention of landlords in denser, lower-income areas. Apartment owners in the Sepulveda barrio of the Valley have rallied behind a police program, launched in October 1989, to barricade their streets as a deterrent to drug buyers and other undesirables. The LAPD wants the City Council's permission to permanently seal off the neighborhood and restrict entry to residents, while the owners finance a guard station or 'checkpoint charlie'. While the Council contemplates the permanency of the experiment, the LAPD, supported by local homeowners, has continued to barricade other urban 'war zones' including part of the Pico-Union district, a Mid-Wilshire neighborhood, and an entire square mile around Jefferson High School in the Central–Vernon area. In face of complaints from younger residents about the 'Berlin Wall' quality of the neighborhood quarantines, Police Chief Gates reassured journalists that 'we're not here to occupy the territory. This isn't Panama. It's the city of Los Angeles and we're going to be here in a lawful manner.'[30]

Meanwhile the very rich are yearning for high-tech castles. Where gates and walls alone will not suffice, as in the case of Beverly Hills or Bel-Air homeowners, the house itself is redesigned to incorporate sophisticated, sometimes far-fetched, security functions. An overriding but discreet goal of the current 'mansionizing' mania on the Westside of Los Angeles – for instance, tearing down $3 million houses to build $30 million mansions – is the search for 'absolute security'. Residential architects are borrowing design secrets from overseas embassies and military command posts. One of the features most in demand is the 'terrorist-proof security room' concealed in the houseplan and accessed by sliding panels and secret doors. Merv Griffith and his fellow mansionizers are hardening their palaces like missile silos.

But contemporary residential security in Los Angeles – whether in the fortified mansion or the average suburban bunker – depends upon the voracious consumption of private security services. Through their local homeowners' associations, virtually every affluent neighborhood from the Palisades to Silverlake contracts its own private policing; hence the thousands of lawns displaying the little 'armed response' warnings. The classifieds in a recent Sunday edition of the Los Angeles *Times* contained nearly a hundred ads for guards and patrolmen, mostly from firms

BELLIGERENT LAWNS
Hollywood Hills

specializing in residential protection. Within Los Angeles County, the security services industry has tripled its sales and workforce (from 24,000 to 75,000) over the last decade. 'It is easier to become an armed guard than it is to become a barber, hairdresser or journeyman carpenter', and under California's extraordinarily lax licensing law even a convicted murderer is not automatically excluded from eligibility. Although a majority of patrolmen are minority males earning near the minimum wage ($4–7 per hour depending on qualifications and literacy), their employers are often multinational conglomerates offering a dazzling range of security products and services. As Michael Kaye, president of burgeoning Westec (a subsidiary of Japan's Secom Ltd), explains: 'We're not a security guard company. We sell a *concept* of security.'[31] (This quote, as aficionados will immediately recognize, echoes the boast of Omni Consumer Products' Dick Jones – the villain of Paul Verhoeven's *Robocop* – that 'everything is security concepts . . . sometimes I can just think of something and it makes me so horny'.)

What homeowners' associations contract from Westec – or its principal rival, Bel-Air Patrol (part of Borg-Warner's family of security companies, including Burns and Pinkerton) – is a complete, 'systems' package that includes alarm hardware, monitoring, watch patrols, personal escorts, and, of course, 'armed response' as necessary. Although law-enforcement experts debate the efficiency of such systems in foiling professional criminals, they are brilliantly successful in deterring innocent outsiders. Anyone who has tried to take a stroll at dusk through a strange neighborhood patrolled by armed security guards and signposted with death threats quickly realizes how merely notional, if not utterly obsolete, is the old idea of the 'freedom of the city'.

THE L.A.P.D. AS SPACE POLICE

This comprehensive urban security mobilization depends not only upon the imbrication of the police function into the built environment, but also upon an evolving social division of labor between public- and private-sector police services, in which the former act as the necessary supports of the latter. As *Police Chief* magazine notes, 'harsh economic realities of the 1980s' – for instance, the tax revolt, rising rates of crime against property, and burgeoning middle-class demands for security – have catalyzed 'a realignment of relationships between private security and law enforcement'.[32] The private sector, exploiting an army of non-union, low-wage employees, has increasingly captured the labor-intensive roles (guard duty, residential patrol, apprehension of retail crime, maintenance of security passages and checkpoints, monitoring of electronic surveillance, and so on), while public law enforcement has retrenched behind the supervision of security macro-systems (maintenance of major crime data bases, aerial surveillance, jail systems, paramilitary responses to terrorism and street insurgency, and so on). The confusing interface between the two sectors is most evident in the overlapping of patrol functions in many neighborhoods and in the growing trend to subcontract jailing (with the privatized supervision of electronic home surveillance as another potentially lucrative market).

In many respects this division of labor is more elaborated in Los Angeles than elsewhere, if only because of the LAPD's pathbreaking substitutions of technological capital for patrol manpower. In part this was a necessary adaptation to the city's dispersed form; but it has also expressed the department's particular definition of its relationship to the community. Especially in its own self-perpetuated myth, the LAPD is seen as the progressive antithesis to the traditional big-city police department with its patronage armies of patrolmen grafting off the beat. As reformed in the early 1950s by the legendary Chief Parker (who admired above all the elitism of the Marines), the LAPD was intended to be incorruptible because unapproachable, a 'few good men' doing battle with a fundamentally evil city. *Dragnet*'s Sergeant Friday precisely captured the Parkerized LAPD's quality of prudish alienation from a citizenry composed of fools, degenerates and psychopaths.

Technology helped insulate this paranoid *esprit de corps*. In doing so, it virtually established a new epistemology of policing, where technologized surveillance and response supplanted the traditional patrolman's intimate 'folk' knowledge of specific communities. Thus back in the 1920s the LAPD had pioneered the replacement of the flatfoot or mounted officer with the radio patrol car – the beginning of dispersed, mechanized policing. Under Parker, ever alert to spinoffs from military technology, the LAPD introduced the first police helicopters for systematic aerial surveillance. After the Watts Rebellion of 1965 this airborne effort became the cornerstone of a policing strategy for the entire inner city.[33] As part of its 'Astro' program LAPD helicopters maintain an average nineteen-hour-per-day vigil over 'high crime areas', tactically coordinated to patrol car forces, and exceeding even the British Army's aerial surveillance of Belfast. To facilitate ground-air synchronization, thousands of residential rooftops have been painted with identifying street numbers, transforming the aerial view of the city into a huge police grid.

The fifty-pilot LAPD airforce was recently updated with French Aerospatiale helicopters equipped with futuristic surveillance technology. Their forward-looking infra-red cameras are extraordinary night eyes that can easily form heat images from a single burning cigarette, while their thirty-million-candlepower spotlights, appropriately called 'Nightsun', can literally turn the night into day. Meanwhile the LAPD retains another fleet of Bell Jet Rangers capable of delivering complete elements of SWAT personnel anywhere in the region. Their training, which sometimes includes practice assaults on Downtown highrises, anticipates some of the spookier Hollywood images (for example, *Blue Thunder* or *Running Man*) of airborne police terror. A few years ago a veteran LAPD SWAT commander (apparently one of the principals in the infamous SLA holocaust in Southcentral Los Angeles) accidentally shot his own helicopter out of the sky while practicing a strafing run with a machine-gun.

But the most decisive element in the LAPD's metamorphosis into a technopolice has been its long and successful liaison with the military aerospace industry. Just in time for the opening of the 1984 Los Angeles Olympics, the department brought on line ECCCS (Emergency Command Control Communications Systems), the most powerful, state-of-the-art police communications system in the world. First conceptualized by Hughes Aerospace between 1969 and 1971, ECCCS's design was refined and updated by NASA's Jet Propulsion Laboratory, incorporating elements of space technology and mission control communications. After the passage of a $42 million tax override in May 1977, the City Council appoved Systems Development Corporation of Santa Monica as prime contractor for the system, which took more than seven years to build.

The central hardware of ECCCS is encased in security comparable to a SAC missile silo in Montana. Bunkered in the earthquake-proofed and security-hardened fourth and fifth sublevels of City Hall East (and interconnecting with the Police pentagon in Parker Center), Central Dispatch Center coordinates all the complex itineraries and responses of the LAPD using digitalized communication to eliminate voice congestion and guarantee the secrecy of transmission. ECCCS, together with the LAPD's prodigious information-processing assets, including the ever-growing databases on suspect citizenry, have become the central neural system for the vast and disparate, public and private, security operations taking place in Los Angeles.

But this is hardly the ultimate police sensorium. As gang hysteria and the war on crack keep the city's coffers open to police funding requests, it is likely the LAPD will continue to win political support for ambitious capital investment programs in new technology. Having brought policing up to the levels of the Vietnam War and early NASA, it is almost inevitable that the LAPD, and other advanced police forces, will try to acquire the technology of the Electronic Battlefield and even Star Wars. We are at the threshold of the universal electronic tagging of property and people – both criminal and non-criminal (small children, for example) – monitored by both cellular and centralized surveillances. Of the latter, ex-Los Angeles police chief, now state senator, Ed Davis (Republican – Valencia) has proposed the use of a geosynclinical space satellite to counter pandemic car theft in the region. Electronic alarm systems, already tested in New England, would alert police if a properly tagged car was stolen; satellite moitoring would extend coverage over Los Angeles's vast metropolitan area. Once in orbit, of course, the role of a law enforcement satellite would grow to encompass other forms of surveillance and control.

The image here is ultimately more important than the practicality of the proposal, since it condenses the historical world view and quixotic quest of the postwar LAPD: good citizens, off the streets, enclaved in their high-security private consumption spheres; bad citizens, on the streets (and therefore not engaged in legitimate business), caught in the terrible, Jehovan scrutiny of the LAPD's space program.

THE CARCERAL CITY

All this airborne surveillance and engridding, endless police data-gathering and centralization of communications, constitutes an invisible

'Haussmannization' of Los Angeles. No need to clear fields of fire for cannon when you control the sky; less need to hire informers on every block when surveillance cameras are universal ornaments on every building. But the police also reorganize space in far more straightforward ways. We have already seen their growing role as Downtown urban designers, indispensable for their expertise in 'security'. But they also lobby incessantly to enlarge law-and-order land use: additional warehouse space for a burgeoning inmate population, and administrative-training facilities for themselves. In Los Angeles this has taken the form of a de facto urban renewal program, operated by the police agencies, that threatens to convert an entire salient of Downtown-East Los Angeles into a vast penal colony.[34]

Nearly 25,000 prisoners are presently held in six severely overcrowded county and federal facilities – not including Immigration and Naturalization Service (INS) detention centers – within a three-mile radius of City Hall – the largest incarcerated population in the nation. Racing to meet the challenge of the current 'War on Drugs' (which will double detained populations within the decade), authorities are forging ahead with the construction of a new state prison in East Los Angeles as well as a giant expansion of the County Jail near Chinatown. Both projects are vigorously contested by community coalitions opposed to further dumping of jail space in the inner city. Yet at the same time agencies like the Bureau of Prisons and County Jail, together with the innumerable private security companies, have become major community employers in the wake of plant closures and deindustrialization in East Los Angeles during the 1970s and early 1980s. Jails now vie with County/USC Hospital as the single most important economic force on the Eastside.

The conflict of interest between community and law enforcement land use is also sharply focused on the fate of Elysian Park, the home of Dodger Stadium and the Police Academy. Consisting of steep hillsides and ravines immediately northwest of the original El Pueblo de Los Angeles, Elysian Park was once upon a time a prime tourist attraction, one of the foremost 'City Beautiful' parks in the country. Through an extraordinary circumvention of local government, the police department has managed to turn its occupancy of the 1932 Olympic pistol range (under temporary lease to the Police Athletic and Gun Club) into an occupation of the entire park. Although lawyers for 'Friends of Elysian Park' were able to prove that the

NEIGHBORHOOD PRISON
INS Detention Center, MacArthur Park district

development of the Police Academy was an unauthorized, even illegal appropriation of public land, the LAPD cowed the City Council into ratifying the status quo. Then in 1989 fine print attached to a larger police bond issue, fueled by the gang and drug crisis, provided authority and funds for the three-fold expansion of the Academy in the park. To suggest an analogy, it is almost as if the San Francisco police were to occupy Golden Gate Park or the New York Police Department to commandeer half of Central Park.

The INS, meanwhile, has been trying to shoehorn privatized 'microprisons' into unsuspecting inner-city neighborhoods. Facing record overcrowding in its normal facilities, *La Migra* has commandeered motels and apartments for operation by private contractors as auxiliary jails for detained aliens – many of them Chinese and Central Americans seeking asylum. The disclosure of one of these centers caused a community uproar in Hollywood in 1986, and again in early 1990 in the MacArthur Park neighborhood after an audacious escape by eight female detainees led by a Chinese political dissident. The women claimed that the detention center (an anonymous, barred storefront on the area's main shopping street) lacked basic hygiene and that male guards spent the night in the women's cells.[35]

The demand for law enforcement *lebensraum* in the central city, however, will inevitably bring the police agencies into conflict with more than mere community groups. Already the plan to add two highrise towers, with 2,400 new beds, to County Jail on Bauchet Street downtown has raised the ire of planners and developers hoping to make nearby Union Station the center of a giant complex of skyscraper hotels and offices. If the jail expansion goes ahead, tourists and prisoners could end up ogling one another from opposed highrises. One solution to the conflict between carceral and commercial redevelopment is to use architectural camouflage to finesse jail space into the skyscape. If buildings and homes are becoming more prison- or fortress-like in exterior appearance, then prisons ironically are becoming architecturally naturalized as aesthetic objects. Moreover, with the post-liberal shift of government expenditure from welfare to repression, carceral structures have become the new frontier of public architecture. As an office glut in most parts of the country reduces commissions for corporate highrises, celebrity architects are rushing to design jails, prisons, and police stations.[36]

An extraordinary example, the flagship of an emerging genre, is Welton Becket Associates' new Metropolitan Detention Center in Downtown Los

Angeles, on the edge of the Civic Center and the Hollywood Freeway. Although this ten-story Federal Bureau of Prison's facility is one of the most visible new structures in the city, few of the hundreds of thousands of commuters who pass it by every day have any inkling of its function as a holding and transfer center for what has been officially described as the 'managerial elite of narco-terrorism'. Here, 70 per cent of federal incarcerations are related to the 'War on Drugs'. This postmodern Bastille – the largest prison built in a major US urban center in generations – looks instead like a futuristic hotel or office block, with artistic charms (like the high-tech trellises on its bridge-balconies) comparable to any of Downtown's recent architecture. But its upscale ambience is more than mere facade. The interior of the prison is designed to implement a sophisticated program of psychological manipulation and control: barless windows, a pastel color plan, prison staff in preppy blazers, well-tended patio shubbery, a hotel-type reception area, nine recreation areas with nautilus workout equipment, and so on.[37] In contrast to the human inferno of the desperately overcrowded County Jail a few blocks away, the Becket structure superficially appears less a detention than a convention center for federal felons – a 'distinguished' addition to Downtown's continuum of security and design. But the psychic cost of so much attention to prison aesthetics is insidious. As one inmate whispered to me in the course of a tour, 'Can you imagine the mindfuck of being locked up in a Holiday Inn?'[38]

THE FEAR OF CROWDS

Ultimately the aims of contemporary architecture and the police converge most strikingly around the problem of crowd control. As we have seen, the designers of malls and pseudo-public space attack the crowd by homogenizing it. They set up architectural and semiotic barriers to filter out 'undesirables'. They enclose the mass that remains, directing its circulation with behaviorist ferocity. It is lured by visual stimuli of all kinds, dulled by musak, sometimes even scented by invisible aromatizers. This Skinnerian orchestration, if well conducted, produces a veritable commercial symphony of swarming, consuming monads moving from one cashpoint to another.

Outside in the streets, the police task is more difficult. The LAPD, true to its class war background, has always hated certain kinds of public gatherings. Its early history was largely devoted to bludgeoning May Day demonstrators, arresting strikers and deporting Mexicans and Okies. In 1921 it arrested Upton Sinclair for reading the Declaration of Independence in public; in the 1960s it indiscriminately broke up love-ins and family picnics in battles to control Griffith and Elysian Park. Subconsciously it has probably never recovered from the humiliation of August 1965 when it temporarily was forced to surrender the streets to a rebellious ghetto.

Whatever the reasons, the LAPD (and the County Sheriffs as well) continue relentlessly to restrict the space of public assemblage and the freedom of movement of the young. In the next chapter we will examine in some detail the history of 'Operation HAMMER' and other Vietnam-style police tactics in Southcentral L.A.[39] But long before the LAPD and the Sheriffs launched their famous anti-gang dragnets, they were operating extensive juvenile curfews in non-Anglo areas and barricading popular boulevards to prevent 'cruising' (in Hollywood this directly abets the current gentrification strategy). And now, of course, they are sealing off entire neighborhoods and housing projects under our local variant of 'pass law'. Even gilded white youth suffer from this escalating police regulation of personal mobility. In the erstwhile world capital of teenagers, where millions overseas still imagine Gidget at a late-night surf party, the beaches are now closed at dark, patrolled by helicopter gunships and police dune buggies.

A watershed in the dual architectural and police assault on public space was the rise and fall of the 'Los Angeles Street Scene'. Launched in 1978 the two-day festival at the Civic Center was intended to publicize Downtown's revitalization as well as to provide Mayor Bradley's version of the traditional Democratic barbecue. The LAPD were skeptical. Finally in 1986, after the failure of the Ramones to appear as promised, the youthful audience began to tear up the stage. The LAPD immediately sent in a phalanx of one hundred and fifty helmeted officers and a mounted unit. In the two-hour melée that followed, angry punks bombarded the police cavalry with rocks and bottles, and fifteen officers and their horses were injured. The producer of the Street Scene, a Bradley official, suggested that 'more middle-of-the-

FEAR OF CROWDS
Downtown

road entertainment' might attract less boisterous crowds. The prestigious *Downtown News* counter-attacked, claiming that the 'Street Scene gives Downtown a bad name. It flies in the face of all that has been done here in the last thirty years.' It demanded 'reparations' for the wounded 'reputation of Downtown'. The Mayor's office cancelled the Scene.[40]

Its demise suggests the consolidation of an official consensus about crowds and the use of space in Los Angeles. Since the restructuring of Downtown eliminated the social mixing of crowds in normal pedestrian circulation, the Street Scene (ironically named) remained one of the few carnival-like occasions or places (along with redevelopment-threatened Hollywood Boulevard and Venice Boardwalk) where pure heteroglossia could flourish: that is to say, where Chinatown punks, Glendale skinheads, Boyle Heights lowriders, Valley girls, Marina designer couples, Slauson rappers, Skid Row homeless and gawkers from Des Moines could mingle together in relative amity.

Until the final extinction of these last real public spaces – with their democratic intoxications, risks and unscented odors – the pacification of Los Angeles will remain incomplete. And as long as this is the case, the various insecure elites, like the yuppie-aliens in John Carpenter's *They Live!*, will never know when some revolt may break out, or what strange guise it may wear. On Halloween eve 1988 – a week before the law-and-order climax of the Bush campaign – the LAPD attempted to disperse 100,000 peaceful revelers on Hollywood Boulevard. Police horses charged into crowds while squad cars zigzagged onto curbs, pinning terrified onlookers against storefront windows. Displaying what the police would later characterize as 'a complete lack of respect for the spirit of the holiday', part of the crowd angrily fought back, tossing bottles and smashing the windows of the Brown Derby. By midnight the rioters, mainly costumed, were looting storefronts. The next morning's *Times* carried the following description, evocative of Nathanael West:

At one souvenir store, the Holly Vine Shoppe, looters smashed windows and took stuffed animals, Hollywood postcards, Hollywood pennants and baseball caps emblazoned 'LAPD'.[41]

NOTES

1. See National Committee on the Causes and Prevention of Violence, *To Establish Justice, To Ensure Domestic Tranquility (Final Report)*, Washington D.C. 1969.
2. 'The problems of inversion and introversion in development patterns, and ambiguity in the character of public space created within them, are not unique to new shopping center developments. It is commonplace that the modern city as a whole exhibits a tendency to break down into specialised, single-use precincts – the university campus, the industrial estate, the leisure complex, the housing scheme . . . each governed by internal, esoteric rules of development and implemented by specialist agencies whose terms of reference guarantee that they are familiar with other similar developments across the country, but know almost nothing of the dissimilar precincts which abut their own.' (Barry Maitland, *Shopping Malls: Planning and Design*, London 1985, p. 109.)
3. Cf. Geoffrey Blodgett, 'Frederick Law Olmsted: Landscape Architecture as Conservative Reform', *Journal of American History* 62: 4 (March 1976); and Manfredo Tafuri, 'The Disenchanted Mountain: The Skyscraper and the City', in Giorgio Ciucci, et. al., *The American City*, Cambridge, Mass. 1979.
4. David Halberstam, *The Powers That Be*, New York 1979, p. 102.
5. *Los Angeles Times*, 4 November 1978, X, p. 13. See also Sam Hall Kaplan, *L.A. Follies: A Critical Look at Growth, Politics and Architecture*, Santa Monica 1989.
6. Governor's Commission on the Los Angeles Riots. *Violence in the City – An End or Beginning?*, Los Angeles 1965.
7. In the early 1970s the police circularized members of the Central City Association about an 'imminent gang invasion'. They urged businessmen 'to report to the police the presence of any groups of young Blacks in the area. These are young people between the ages of twelve and eighteen, both boys and girls. One gang wears earrings and the other wears hats. When encountered in groups of more than two they are very dangerous and armed.' (*Los Angeles Times*, 24 December 1972, I, p.7.)
8. Gentrification in this case is 'Reaganization'. In a complex deal aimed at making the north end of the Broadway corridor an upscaled 'bridge' linking Bunker Hill, the Civic Center and Little Tokyo, the CRA has spent more than $20 million inducing the State to build the 'Ronald Reagan Office Building' a block away from the corner of Third and Broadway, while simultaneously bribing the Union Rescue Mission $6 million to move its homeless clientele out of the neighborhood. The 3,000 civil servants from the Reagan Building are intended as shock troops to gentrify the strategic corner of Third and Broadway, where developer Ira Yellin has received further millions in subsidies from the CRA to transform the three historic structures he owns (the Bradbury Building, Million Dollar Theater and Grand Central Market) into 'Grand Central Square'. The 'Broadway-Spring Center' – discussed in the text – provides 'security in circulation' between the Reagan Building and the Square.
9. In reflecting on the problem of the increasing social distance between the white middle classes and the Black poor, Oscar Newman, the renown theorist of 'defensible space', argues for the federally ordered dispersion of the poor in the suburban residential landscape. He insists, however, that 'bringing the poor and the black into the fold' (sic) must be conducted 'on a tightly controlled quota basis' that is non-threatening to the middle class and ensures their continuing social dominance. (*Community of Interest*, Garden City 1981, pp. 19–25.) Such 'tightly controlled quotas', of course, are precisely the strategy favored by redevelopment agencies like Los Angeles's as they have been forced to include a small portion of low or very-low income housing in their projected 'urban villages'. It seems inconceivable to Newman, or to these agencies, that the urban working class is capable of sustaining their own decent neighborhoods or having any voice in the definition of public interest. That is why the working poor are always the 'problem', the 'blight' in redevelopment, while the gilded middle classes always represent 'revitalization'.

10. N. David Milder, 'Crime and Downtown Revitalization', in *Urban Land*, September 1987, p. 18.

11. *The Social Life of Small Spaces*, New York 1985.

12. The descriptions that follow draw heavily on the extraordinary photographs of Diego Cardoso, who has spent years documenting Downtown's various street scenes and human habitats.

13. Since crack began to replace cheap wine on Skid Row in the mid 1980s, the homicide rate has jumped to almost 1 per week. A recent backpage *Times* story – 'Well, That's Skid Row' (15 November 1989) – claimed that the homeless have become so 'inured to street violence' that 'the brutal slayings of two people within two blocks of each other the night before drew far less attention than the taping of an episode of the television show, "Beauty and the Beast" '. The article noted, however, the homeless have resorted to a 'buddy system' whereby one sleeps and the other acts as 'spotter' to warn of potential assailants.

14. For example, the LAPD sits on the Design Advisory Board of 'Miracle on Broadway', the publicly funded body attempting to initiate the gentrification of part of the Downtown historic core. (*Downtown News*, 2 January 1989.)

15. Interviews with Skid Row residents; see also Tom Chorneau, 'Quandary Over a Park Restroom', *Downtown News*, 25 August 1986, pp. 1, 4. In other Southern California communities the very hygiene of the poor is being criminalized. New ordinances specifically directed against the homeless outlaw washing oneself in public 'above the elbow'.

16. See 'Cold Snap's Toll at 5 as Its Iciest Night Arrives', *Times*, 29 December 1988.

17. See my '*Chinatown*, Part Two? The Internationalization of Downtown Los Angeles', *New Left Review*, July–August 1987. It is also important to note that, despite the crack epidemic on Skid Row (which has attracted a much younger population of homeless men), there is no drug treatment center or rehabilitation program in the area. Indeed within the city as a whole narcotic therapy funding is being cut while police and prison budgets are soaring.

18. 'Old socialist' quote from architect and 'Gehry Kid' Michael Rotundi of Morphosis; Gehry himself boasts: 'I get my inspiration from the streets. I'm more of a street fighter than a Roman scholar.' (Quoted in Adele Freedman, *Progressive Architecture*, October 1986, p. 99.)

19. The best catalogue of Gehry's work is Peter Arnell and Ted Bickford, eds, *Frank Gehry: Buildings and Projects*, New York 1985. Also cf. Institute of Contemporary Art, *Frank O. Gehry, An Exhibition of Recent Projects*, Boston 1982; and University of Southern California, *Frank Gehry: Selected Works*, Los Angeles 1982.

20. Mildred Friedman, ed., *The Architecture of Frank Gehry*, New York 1986, p. 175.

21. Pilar Viladas, 'Illuminated Manuscripts', *Progressive Architecture*, October 1986, pp. 76, 84.

22. See David Ferrell's articles in the Los Angeles *Times*, 31 August and 16 October 1987. In a letter to the *Times* (16 September 1987) the former Los Angeles Director of Planning, Calvin Hamilton, corroborated that the Hollywood Chamber of Commerce 'dominated and aggressively manipulated for their own purposes the decision process. In most areas of planning concern, in my opinion, they were only interested in maximizing their own profit, not in doing a comprehensive, balanced plan for the improvement and long-term benefit of all the people in Hollywood.'

23. See portrait in *Times*, 7 October 1987.

24. Jane Buckwalter, 'Securing Shopping Centers for Inner Cities', *Urban Land*, April 1987, p. 24.

25. Richard Titus, 'Security Works', *Urban Land*, January 1990, p. 2.

26. Buckwalter, p. 25. As some longtime community activists have pointed out, there is rich irony in all this: namely, that the same forces (redlining banks, negligent politicians, discriminatory insurance companies, etc.) who share responsibility for the lunar retail landscape of Southcentral Los Angeles are now celebrating its reoccupation by security-concept entrepreneurs like Haagen. Having allowed the public spaces and shopping streets of the inner city to deteriorate to the point where the only extant enterprises are storefront churches and a few heavily fortified liquor stores, the city suddenly gushes subsidies to create private shopping fortresses whose profits flow outside the community.

27. Cf. *Daily News*, 1 November 1987; and television interview, Fox News, March 1990.

28. Los Angeles *Times*, 25 July 1989, II, p. 2.

29. Quoted in Jim Carlton 'Walled In', Los Angeles *Times*, 8 October 1989, II, p. 1. The mania for walls has also caught up with the Hollywood Chamber of Commerce who are planning to wall off the base of the famous 'Hollywood Sign' on Mount Lee, as well as installing motion detectors and video surveillance.

30. *Times*, 15 November 1989.

31. Quoted in Linda Williams, 'Safe and Sound', Los Angeles *Times*, 29 August 1988, IV, p. 5.

32. William Cunningham and Todd Taylor, 'A Summary of the Hallcrest Report', *The Police Chief*, June 1983, p. 31.

33. The following section is based on LAPD publicity and interviews with personnel. (See also, Don Rosen, 'Bleu Thunder', *Herald-Examiner*, 28 May 1989, pp. 1, 12.) During February of 1989, elite Army anti-terrorist units from the First Special Operations Command in Fort Bragg, North Carolina, conducted a series of simulated helicopter assaults and battles over Bunker Hill skyscrapers. 'The Army declined to give any further details about the troops and equipment involved or the nature and purpose of the training.' (Los Angeles *Times* 18 February 1989, I, p. 23.)

34. In the exact words of Aurora Castillo, leader of *Las Madres* (the East Los Angeles group fighting further prison construction): 'It seems like they're making our area into a penal colony'. (Los Angeles *Times*, 3 August 1988, II, p. 1.)

35. *Times*, 23 January 1990.

36. Aside from the Welton Becket example discussed here, another flamboyant local instance is the new Pasadena Police and Jail facility designed by Robert Stern, one of the conservative high priests of 'postmodernism'.

37. The Detention Center's upbeat 'Fact Sheet' seems designed with federal tourists in mind: 'The institution is of a modern architectural design with no external characteristics of the traditional jail. . . . Program services . . . emphasize an intensive short-term education experience and supervised recreational activities for all inmates. . . . The mission is to provide the pretrial detainee with safe and humane care, custody, and control; to maintain a positive environment for detainees and staff. . . .'

38. Thanks to Lynden Croasmun, Executive Assistant to the Warden, I was able to tour the Metropolitan Detention Center in October 1989.

39. The 'HAMMER' may only be a mild prefiguration of draconian measures yet to be introduced in the war on drugs. For years the alternative press has reminded us that extreme martial law plans, devised by the Pentagon in the aftermath of the 1967 Detroit Rebellion, are still alive, cultivated by the Armed Forces as well as by national guard and local law enforcement. As Tim Redmond of the *Bay Guardian* explains: 'California was one of the most enthusiastic participants in the national program. Between 1968 and 1973 , three major exercises, code-named Cable Splicer I, II and III, took place in California, bringing together police and military officials from across the state for seminars and war games at a special "anti-terrorist" training center near San Luis Obispo.' (9 September 1987, p. 17.) A variant of these plans, labeled Garden Plot, was recently revealed as part of the contingency planning for civil disturbances in the wake of the homeporting of the battleship Missouri in San Francisco (ibid.). Students of the LAPD generally believe that similar, comprehensive planning has long existed to deal with civil disturbances in the ghetto or barrios, and, possibly now, to assert a virtual military occupation over areas of high gang density.

40. Cf. Los Angeles *Times*, 22 September, II, p. 1, and 25 September, II, p. 1, 1986; and reprint of 'best editorial', 'Trouble at Street Scene', *Downtown News*, 2 March 1987, p. 12.

41. George Ramos, 'Hollywood Halloween: Some Came as Vandals and Looters', Los Angeles *Times*, 2 November 1988, II, pp. 1, 8. Also interviews with eyewitnesses.

CHAPTER FIVE

THE HAMMER AND THE ROCK

Perhaps 6 April 1989 will go down in history as the first 'designer drug raid'. As heavily armed and flak-jacketed SWAT commandoes stormed the alleged 'rock house' near 51st and Main Street in Southcentral L.A., Nancy Reagan and Los Angeles Police Chief Daryl Gates sat across the street, nibbling fruit salad in a luxury motor home emblazoned 'THE ESTABLISHMENT'. According to the *Times*, the former first lady 'could be seen freshening her make-up' while the SWATs roughly frisked and cuffed the fourteen 'narco-terrorists' captured inside the small stucco bungalow. As hundreds of incredulous neighbors ('Hey, Nancy Reagan. She's over here in the ghetto!') gathered behind police barriers, the great Nay-sayer, accompanied by Chief Gates and a small army of nervous Secret Service agents, toured the enemy fortress with its occupants still bound on the floor in flabbergasted submission. After frowning at the tawdry wallpaper and drug-bust debris, Nancy, who looked fetching in her LAPD windbreaker, managed to delve instantly into the dark hearts at her feet and declare: 'These people in here are beyond the point of teaching and rehabilitating.' This was music to the ears of the Chief, whose occupation thrives on incorrigibility. 'Gates fairly beamed as television cameras pressed in: "We thought she ought to see it for herself and she did. . . . She is a very courageous woman".'[1]

It was a heck of a heavy date, even if Nancy's press secretary Mark Weinberg complained obnoxiously the next day about the media's failure to take better advantage of the photo opportunity. In the larger picture, however, Nancy Reagan – who had lived in Southern California for nearly fifty years – had made her first visit to the ghetto, and Chief Gates, who dreams of becoming governor, had his perfect drug bust. It was an easy victory in a drug 'war' that the LAPD secretly loves losing.

VIETNAM HERE

> Tonight we pick 'em up for anything and everything.
> *LAPD spokesman (9 April 1988)*[2]

Flashback to the previous April. A thousand extra-duty patrolmen, backed by elite tactical squads and a special anti-gang taskforce, bring down the first act of 'Operation HAMMER' upon ten square miles of Southcentral Los Angeles between Exposition Park and North Long Beach, arresting more Black youth than at any time since the Watts Rebellion of 1965. Like a Vietnam-era search-and-destroy mission – and many senior police are proud Vietnam veterans – Chief Gates saturates the street with his 'Blue Machine', jacking up thousands of local teenagers at random like so many surprised peasants. Kids are humiliatingly forced to 'kiss the sidewalk' or spreadeagle against police cruisers while officers check their names against computerized files of gang members. There are 1,453 arrests; the kids are processed in mobile booking centers, mostly for trivial offences like delinquent parking tickets or curfew violations. Hundreds more, un-charged, have their names and addresses entered into the electronic gang roster for future surveillance.[3]

Gates, who earlier in the year had urged the 'invasion' of Colombia (in 1980 he offered Jimmy Carter the LAPD SWAT team to liberate the hostages in Tehran), derided civil libertarian protests: 'This is war . . . we're exceedingly angry. . . . We want to get the message out to the cowards out there, and that's what they are, rotten little cowards – we want the message to go out that we're going to come and get them.' To reinforce the metaphor, but meaning it literally, the chief of the DA's Hardcore Drug Unit added: 'This is Vietnam here.'[4]

The 'them' – what a local mayor calls 'the Viet Cong abroad in our society'[5] – are the members of local Black gangs, segmented into several hundred fighting 'sets' while loosely aligned into two hostile super-gangs, the 'Crips' and the 'Bloods' – universally distinguished, as every viewer of Dennis Hopper's *Colors* now knows, by their color-coding of shoelaces, T-shirts and bandannas (red for Bloods, blue for Crips). In the official version, which Hollywood is incessantly reheating and further sensationalizing, these gangs comprise veritable urban guerrilla armies organized for the sale of crack and outgunning the police with huge arsenals of Uzi and Mac-10 automatics. Although gang cohorts are typically hardly more than high-school sophomores, local politicians frequently compare them to the 'murderous militias of Beirut'.[6]

Across town, or increasingly in Southcentral itself, there is another large, traditional constituency of Latino gang membership, frequently depicted in the same lurid images. Indeed the primary focus of gang hysteria

VIETNAM IN THE STREETS

in the 1970s was the rising violence amongst the third generation of East L.A. *vatos locos*. But a major community counter-offensive, unabetted by the police, and led instead by priests, parents and gang *veteranos* appealing to 'Chicano unity', managed to dramatically reduce Eastside gang killings from 24 in 1978 to zero in 1988.[7] A major recrudescence of Latino gang warfare in recent days may be directly attributable to new liaisons with the crack trade.

If anything made ghetto turf rivalries so much more deadly than the Eastside's during the 1980s, it was the incomparably higher economic stakes involved in control of the retail cocaine trade. 'Gangbangin'' rose in a murderous arc from 1984 in rough synchronization with the emergence of crack as the narcotic equivalent of fast food and the rerouting of the main cocaine trail from Florida to Southern California via Mexico. Since the beginning of 1987, 'gang-related' slayings, principally in Southside city and county areas, have averaged over one per day.[8]

This very real epidemic of youth violence, with its deep roots (as we shall see) in exploding youth poverty, has been inflated by law enforcement agencies and the media into something quite phantasmagoric. In a numbers game that ceases to distinguish the authentic 'high rollers' and 'stone killers' of the gang world from the 'claimers' and 'wannabees', the city attorney's office has steadily escalated its estimates of hardcore gang membership from 10,000 to 50,000. Local media have amplified this figure to 70,000–80,000, while Sheriff's 'gang experts' have invoked the spectre of 100,000 'rotten little cowards' overrunning Los Angeles County. Meanwhile an Andromeda Strain of Crips and Bloods is reported to have infected the entire West, from Tucson to Anchorage, before invading Middle America itself (with new sightings from Kansas City to Buffalo).[9]

Like the Tramp scares in the nineteenth century, or the Red scares in the twentieth, the contemporary Gang scare has become an imaginary class relationship, a terrain of pseudo-knowledge and fantasy projection. But as long as the actual violence was more or less confined to the ghetto, the gang wars were also a voyeuristic titillation to white suburbanites devouring lurid imagery in their newspapers or on television. Then in December 1987 *frisson* became fear as Southside gang hitmen mistakenly gunned down a young woman outside a theater in the posh Westwood Village entertainment district near UCLA. Westwood's influential merchants, who had recently induced the LAPD to enforce curfew ordinances to repel non-white youth from the Village, clamored for extra police protection, while local Councilmember Zev Yaroslavsky, then essaying a Koch-like challenge to Mayor Bradley, posted a huge reward for apprehension of the 'urban terrorists'.

The dramatically different press coverage of, and preferential police response to, the Westwood shooting ignited the simmering resentment of Black community leaders, who blasted Yaroslavsky, Bradley and the LAPD for failing to respond comparably to the mayhem in their neighborhoods. For several weeks the council chambers resounded to an arcane debate over relative police response times in different divisions and the comparative allocations of department personnel. This ideologically circumscribed and loaded debate, focusing exclusively on the demand for a more equal and vigorous prosecution of the war against gangs, was a cue for the ambitious and media-hungry Chief to reclaim center-stage.

GANGBUSTERS

This is the era of the police. If I were chief, I'd ask for as many as I could. *Councilmember Richard Alatorre*[10]

Since the days of the legendary Chief William Parker in the early 1950s, the LAPD has been regarded by L.A.'s Black community as a redneck army of occupation. On the eve of Daryl Gates's appointment as chief in 1978, the so-called 'Masked Marvel', a white ex-cop who had served five years in 77th Street's 'Fort Apache', appeared in disguise on a series of local television shows to luridly chronicle the pathological racism and trigger-happiness of the 'blue knights' towards ordinary Blacks.[11] Gates, the third Parker protégé in a row to command the LAPD, ridiculed these charges and the 'liberals' who listened to them. Soon afterwards came the police killing of Eulia Love, a 39-year-old Black widow in default of her gas bill. Community outrage was so great that Watts Assemblymember Maxine Waters demanded, 'Chief Gates, we want you out!' As Gates defended the twelve 38-caliber holes in Mrs Love's body before a cowed Police Commission, several hundred Black clergymembers petitioned the Carter administration to intervene. They asked the Justice Department to probe a pattern of systematic abuse of non-whites, including 'more than 300 police shootings of minority citizens in the last decade'. Meanwhile, the Coalition Against Police Abuse (CAPA) collected tens of thousands of signatures calling for the establishment of a civilian police review board.[12]

The LAPD rode out this storm in alliance with a silent Mayor Bradley, whose gubernatorial ambitions seemed to preclude any stance that could be interpreted by white voters as 'anti-police'. Thus insulated from political accountability, Chief Gates was only emboldened to taunt the Black community with increasingly contemptuous or absurd excuses for police brutality. In 1982, for example, following a rash of LAPD 'chokehold' killings of young Black men in custody, he advanced the extraordinary theory that the deaths were the fault of the victims' racial anatomy, not excessive police force: 'We may be finding that in some Blacks when [the carotid chokehold] is applied the veins or arteries do not open up as fast as they do on normal [sic] people.'[13]

By 1987, however, after the crack blizzard had hit Southcentral in full force, some Black leaders began to weigh police misconduct as a 'lesser evil' compared to drug-dealing gangs. Groups like the Urban League and SCLC redefined the community's problem as 'too little policing' instead of 'too much', and repudiated attempts to restrain the LAPD. The 'equal policing' furor after the Westwood shooting gave Gates an unexpected opportunity to convert some of these former critics into born-again fans of his aggressive policing. While politicians merely worked their jaws, he was seen to respond dramatically to Southcentral's urgent outcry for police protection. With a typical eye for media exposure, the Chief launched the first of his heavily hyped anti-gang sweeps. (The LAPD already conducted regular sweeps to drive homeless people off the streets of Downtown.) This so-called Gang Related Active Trafficker Suppression program (GRATS) targeted 'drug neighborhoods' for raids by 200–300 police under orders to 'stop and interrogate anyone who they suspect is a gang member, basing their assumptions on their dress or their use of gang hand signals'.[14] Thus, on the flimsy 'probable cause' of red shoelaces or high-five handshakes, the taskforces in February and March mounted nine sweeps, impounded five hundred cars and made nearly fifteen hundred arrests. By Good Friday, Gates was gloating over the success of GRATS in drastically curtailing street

WEATHER REPORT
Belmont Tunnel

violence. A few hours after his self-congratulatory speech, however, some rogue Crips mowed down a crowd on a Southcentral street corner, killing a 19-year-old woman.

Hysteria again took command in the Civic Center. County Supervisor Kenneth Hahn called for the mobilization of the National Guard, while Yaroslavsky claimed that the city was 'fighting a war on gang violence . . . that's worse than Beirut'.[15] Gates, frantic to keep the LAPD in command of events, announced that the full manpower reserves of the Department would be thrown into the super-sweeps called the HAMMER. Although one high-ranking LAPD veteran would later admit that the catch-as-catch-can strategy was just 'a hokey publicity deal', it was billed as L.A. law enforcement's 'D-Day'.[16] And like the Marines hitting the beach at Danang in the beginning of LBJ's escalations in Vietnam, the first of the thousand-cop blitzkriegs made the war in Southcentral L.A. look deceptively easy.

Black politicians generally applauded Gates, even if that put some 'civil rights leaders' in the awkward position of undermining the civil rights of Black youth. But as state Senator Diane Watson's press secretary rationalized it, 'when you have a state of war, civil rights are suspended for the duration of the conflict'. The local peasantry, on the other hand, were wary and even belligerent. As an LAPD spokesperson complained: 'People in the neighborhood instead of being on our side, make all kinds of accusations.' Indeed the NAACP reported an unprecedented number of complaints, in the hundreds, about unlawful police conduct.[17] Community members also claimed that the police were deliberately fueling gang violence by leaving suspects on enemy turfs, writing over Crip graffiti with Blood colors (or vice versa) and spreading incendiary rumors.[18]

Given an open season to terrorize gang members and crack dealers, the LAPD predictably began to exceed the call of duty. On 5 April they shot down an unarmed teenager cowering behind a small palm tree on Adams Boulevard. He was alleged to be reaching suspiciously into his pants; more importantly, he was a 'suspected gang member' – a category that now seemed to justify abuse or even execution. A few weeks later, HAMMER forces, storming one of the nearly five hundred 'rock houses' that they claim to have put out of business in 1988, poured double-ought buckshot into an 81-year-old retired construction worker. No drugs were actually found, there was strong suspicion that the police had an incorrect address, and the victim's niece, a witness, testified that he was killed with his hands held up. The LAPD merely replied that gangs were now paying off elderly people to use their homes as sales points. No disciplinary action was taken.[19]

In a year when every gang murder had become a headline atrocity, these two police homicides caused barely a blip. With most of the Black political family arrayed behind the LAPD, civil libertarians spoke in tiny voices. Looking back on the beginning of the HAMMER, journalist Joe Domanick would later ask: 'Where was L.A.'s liberal community? A community that boasts the largest American Civil Liberties Union (ACLU) chapter in the nation . . . ?' In fact the Southern California chapter of the ACLU, an organization that in past decades had been frequently spied on and victimized by the LAPD, did condemn the HAMMER. ACLU attorney Joan Howarth, who specializes in defending youth civil liberties ('an endangered species'), was eloquent in exposing the hypocrisy of Chief Gates's Rambo-style gimmicks. But Howarth was soon transferred to other responsiblities, while the ACLU shifted the bulk of its energies to confront the right-to-life movement. Meanwhile another group of prominent liberal attorneys, who had been carefully preparing a class action suit against the police based on affidavits taken from victims of the HAMMER, suddenly dropped the project. It was latter revealed that they had been hectored and even redbaited by one of the city's most notable 'civil rights' leaders, now a crusader for police saturation of the streets.[20]

With legal opposition thus chilled out, the gangbusters had little reason to look over their shoulders as they started ronsoning hootches and boosting body counts in the rice paddies of Southcentral. The raid on Dalton Street in August 1988, if not quite the My Lai of the war against the underclass (an infamy that better attaches to the 1985 MOVE holocaust in Philadelphia so much admired by Chief Gates),[21] was nonetheless a grim portent of what 'unleashing the police' really means. A company-sized detachment of eighty-eight police from the Southwest Division – an outpost wracked internally by charges of racial abuse against Black officers – swooped down on a group of apartments in the 3900 block of Dalton Avenue, near Exposition Park and not far from the infamous 'Black Dahlia' murder site of 1946. Wielding shotguns and sledgehammers, as well as racist epithets and a search warrant, the assault force, as Chief Gates would later admit, 'got out of hand'.

Residents . . . said they were punched and kicked by officers during what those arrested called 'an orgy of violence'. Residents reported the officers spraypainted walls with slogans, such as 'LAPD Rules'.

They also accused the officers of throwing washing machines into bathtubs, pouring bleach over clothes, smashing walls and furniture with sledgehammers and axes, and ripping an outside stairwell away from one building.

Damage to the apartments was so extensive that the Red Cross offered disaster assistance and temporary shelter to displaced residents – a service normally provided in the wake of major fires, floods, earthquakes or other natural disasters.[22]

At Southwest Division the thirty-two terrified captives of the raid were forced to whistle the theme from the 1960s Andy Grifith TV show (apparently the *Horst Wessel* song of the LAPD) while they ran a gauntlet of cops beating them with fists and long steel flashlights. (At least they did not have to meet Nancy Reagan.) When it was all over, lives and homes were devastated, and the LAPD had two minor drug arrests. Despite allegations in the search warrant, the police found neither wanted gang members nor weapons, just a small quantity of dope belonging to two non-resident teenagers. Moreover for the first time in memory the LAPD blew the cover-up. The cyclone-like destruction at Dalton Street was too extreme to tally with initial police accounts of the incident; the many victims all told the same horror story; and the Dalton Raiders stumbled over their alibi that the damage had been gang-inflicted. With its dirty linen waving in the breeze and the FBI investigating possible civil rights violations, the LAPD initiated disciplinary or criminal action against thirty-eight officers. These included former Southwest Division Captain Thomas Elfmont – the Lt. Calley of this incident – who was accused of ordering his raiders 'to "level" and "make uninhabitable" the targeted apartments', and Sgt. Charles Spicer who reiterated Elfmont's orders in the field ('This is a Class-A search – that means carpets up, drywall down').[23]

But 'physician heal thyself' is not Chief Gates's favorite motto. Within months of the Dalton Street raid, the Chief was again blustering away in apparent defense of police brutality. After being called to testify in the case of the Larezes – a Chicano family beaten by other police raiders – he told reporters that 'Mr Larez was lucky to have only his nose broken'. The jurors in the Larez suit were so outraged by this remark that they raised the victims' damages by $200,000, which they ordered Gates to pay out of his own pocket – an unprecedented attempt to hold the Chief liable for his incitements. (At Mayor Bradley's urging, the City Council paid the fine – as it will the $3 million in damages for the Dalton Street outrage.)[24]

In the meantime, as the HAMMER mercilessly pounded away at Southcentral's mean streets, it became increasingly apparent that its principal catch consisted of drunks, delinquent motorists and teenage curfew violaters (offenders only by virtue of the selective application of curfews to non-Anglo neighborhoods). By 1990 the combined forces of the LAPD and the Sheriffs (implementing their own street saturation strategy) had picked up as many as 50,000 suspects. Even allowing for a percentage of Latino detainees, this remains an astonishing figure considering there are only 100,000 Black youths in Los Angeles. In some highly touted sweeps, moreover, as many as 90 per cent of detained suspects have been released without charges – an innocent victim rate that belies LAPD demonology as well as evoking an analogy with inflated VC bodycounts in Vietnam.[25]

As we saw in the last chapter, Chief Gates's response to the declining shock value of the HAMMER was to institutionalize the sweeps as semi-permanent community occupations, 'narcotic enforcement zones' acting as the urban equivalents of strategic hamlets. (Actually what the Chief *really* wanted was to intern gang members in 'abandoned military bases with landmines planted behind barbed wire fences'.) Claiming that the Pico-Union neighborhood had become 'a veritable flea market for drug dealers', the Chief ordered a 27-square-block area sealed off with barricades and police checkpoints in October 1989. The next month, while the Berlin Wall was being spontaneously dismantled, the LAPD extended the barricades ('Operation Cul-de-Sac') to a barrio in the Valley and then to a huge stretch of Central Avenue in Southcentral.[26] But the real bite in this new escalation came less from LAPD's visible barriers than from the invisible legal partitioning of the city instigated by Los Angeles's aggressive young city attorney, James Hahn.

LITTLE JIMMY VERSUS THE PLAYBOY GANGSTERS

The continued protection of gang activity under the guise of upholding our constitution is causing a deadly blight on our city. *City Attorney Hahn*[27]

'Hahn' is a strangely magical name in the flatlands of Southcentral Los Angeles. For nearly forty years, Kenneth Hahn, a white Democrat, has been one of the 'five little kings' on the Los Angeles County Board of Supervisors thanks to his impregnable support from Black voters. In return, Supervisor Hahn, who has more personally disposable power than any of Los Angeles's Black politicans (including Mayor Bradley), has engraved his name across a series of showpiece government projects in the ghetto, ranging from a fortress shopping mall in Willowbrook (described in the last chapter) to the new General Post Office on Central Avenue. He also receives a lion's share of credit for the integration of the County's 90,000-strong civil service, the major employer in otherwise deindustrialized Black neighborhoods. Perpetually attuned to the complaints of his older, more conservative constituents, he has always been a 'hawk' on the gang question. As far back as 1972 when the first sagging pants and blue bandannas announced the advent of 'Crippin'' in ghetto high schools and playgrounds, Hahn was off the mark with a 48-point plan to 'quarantine . . . juvenile *terrorism*' – indeed, he was one of the first politicians in the 1970s to apply that most loaded of terms to inner-city thirteen-year-olds.[28]

James Hahn is a chip off the old block who used his father's clout (including Southside patronage) to win the city attorneyship in a bloody battle with a Manatt Phelps protégé from the Westside (no mean feat, as we saw in chapter two). Like his predecessor, the current County District Attorney, Ira Reiner, Hahn is an ambitious, younger Democrat trying to turn the law-and-order tables on older Republicans (like Chief Gates and ex-Chief, now state Senator, Ed Davis) by being an even tougher cop in the courtroom. This is not to say that the younger Hahn is without liberal scruples; in fact, he has compiled an extraordinary record prosecuting slumlords and other vampires of the poor. But since the scalps of gang members, not slumlords, are the current wampum of political fortune, Hahn has determined to make Los Angeles the showpiece of an unprecedented attempt (since emulated nationally by Drug Czar Bennett and HUD Secretary Kemp) to *criminalize gang members and their families as a class*. If Chief Gates sometimes seems too much like a Barnum playing at *Dragnet*, with his trick-bag of rockhouse raids and mega-sweeps, Jim Hahn is, as they say on the street, 'serious as a heart attack'. Liberal conscience aside, he has probably traveled further than any metropolitan law enforcement official in the country towards establishing the legal infrastructure of an American police state.

NO OUTLET
MacArthur Park district

Hahn ingeniously reworked his dad's old 'juvenile terrorism quarantine' as the opening gambit in his own war on gangs. In the fall of 1987 he surprised the legal establishment by filing a *civil* lawsuit against the 'Playboy Gangster Crips – an unincorporated association'. The Playboy Gangsters, one of the countless neighborhood isotopes of the Crip subculture, were singled out because of their unusual proximity – in the 26-square-block Cadillac-Corning area, just south of Beverly Hills and east of Beverlywood – to rich white neighborhoods. An amalgam of gang members from several Westside high schools (Hamilton, University and even Palisades), the Playboy Gangsters moved into the Cadillac-Corning neighborhood around 1981. Originally peddling marijuana, they shifted into the more lucrative rock-cocaine or 'crack' trade as it appeared in 1983–4. Because of its adjacency to the world of Rodeo Drive, Cadillac-Corning is an ideal drive-in drug market, catering to rich white youth and giving the Playboy Gangsters an enviable locational advantage over other Southside gangs.[29]

No individual was specifically cited in Hahn's suit, only 'Does 1 to 300'. The court was requested to issue a temporary restraining order with twenty-four separate provisions, spelling out a range of activities that would become illegal. These included 'congregating in groups of two or more', 'remaining in public streets for more than five minutes at any time of day or night', and 'having visitors in their homes for *less* than ten minutes' (an allusion to drug sales). Hahn also demanded the banning of gang colors and the imposition of a dusk-to-dawn curfew for juvenile members.[30] Finally he asked for a 'pass law' provision: within the 26 square blocks of Cadillac-Corning, any 'Doe' would be subject to arrest unless they could produce a signed letter from a 'lawful property owner or employer' authorizing their presence.[31]

As the ACLU was not slow to point out, Hahn's inversion of the usual corporate immunity, that is, his demand for collective liability for gang offensives, mirrored the reasoning of the contemporary South African court that sentenced the 'Sharpeville Six' to death for mere 'membership' in a mob that lynched an informer. Joan Howarth icily observed that the City Attorney's proposed remedies – a 'dress code', a curfew, contempt citations, and so on – were 'weak trade-offs' for the suspension of the Constitution. Superior Court Judge Deering, hearing the case, agreed with the ACLU that abatement actions were only constitutional if applied against named and served individuals.[32]

Although Hahn was upbraided in court, the debate continued in the pages of the *Times*. The ACLU's new chairperson, Danny Goldberg, stellar rock producer and leading Democratic fundraiser, accused fellow Democrat Hahn of being a 'headline hunter with simplistic solutions'. The unabashed City Attorney slashed back at the ACLU's 'silent surrender to misplaced notions' about civil liberties of gang members 'in a city under siege'. Maintaining that 'no constitutional rights are absolute' and evoking the precedent of war, Hahn virtually accused the ACLU of being responsible for the perpetuation of gang violence.[33]

Despite the setbacks in the Playboy Gangster lawsuit, the City Attorney's office redoubled its search for a means to outlaw gang membership. In November 1987 they dusted the cobwebs off California's 1919 Criminal Syndicalism Act to indict Michael 'Peanut' Martin, an eighteen-year-old high-school dropout alleged to be the ringleader of seven self-proclaimed 'working-class Aryan youth' from the San Fernando Valley. This tiny skinhead malignancy, accused of harassing Latino immigrants, was obviously the legal *in locum* for gangs in general. The Criminal Syndicalism Act, enacted specially to destroy the IWW and the fledgling Communist Party, is an ancient horror. Last utilized, unsuccessfully, against two organizers of the Maoist Progressive Labor Party in the 1960s, most reporters and civil libertarians were surprised that it still remained on the books, much less that any prosecutor would brashly attempt to resuscitate it. In the event, Hahn was predictably stymied by constitutional considerations, and forced to reindict Martin under more prosaic misdemeanor statutes.[34]

Still, Hahn had made his point. He could now claim that he had exhausted available legal remedies and that only the legislature could rescue Los Angeles from the 'gang siege'. His position was neatly echoed by his predecessor, County D.A. Ira Reiner, another candidate yearning for higher office. While at Hahn's post in 1982, Reiner had anticipated the principle of collective liability by getting the court to order gang members (whether or not they were individually responsible) to remove graffiti or face jail. Now, at a histrionic press conference he announced that he was no longer concerned with the rehabilitation of street criminals but only with 'putting every one of these little murderous hoodlums in jail for as long as possible'. To achieve this objective he promised that his office would abandon plea-bargaining in gang-related cases and instead fight for maximum sentences regardless of extenuations. 'The objective is to use each occasion that a gang member is arrested for a crime, no matter how minor, as a means to remove them from the streets for as long as possible.'[35] Together with Hahn he also called for decisive action in Sacramento.

Governor Deukmejian's special state taskforce on gangs and drugs attempted to oblige Hahn and Reiner by proposing legislation to try sixteen-years-olds as adults, impose life sentences in cases involving Uzis and other automatic weapons, and reopen vacant military bases as gang detention centers. State Attorney General John Van de Kamp – another Los Angeles law-and-order liberal – called for massively augmented state aid for Los Angeles's gangbusters as well as an 8,000 capacity prison for gang offenders in the Mojave Desert. He also brightened the day for a particular group of ethnic entrepreneurs by announcing that, compared to the Crips and Bloods, 'the Mafia have become the least of our problems'. Meanwhile Los Angeles's new FBI chief Lawrence Lawler, taking over a scandal-ridden regional office, promised that street gangs would be his chief priority and hinted at new applications of the all-encompassing federal Racketeer-Influenced and Corrupt Organizations Act (RICO), which the Feds had already invoked against L.A. Crip 'infiltrators' in Seattle.[36]

But the new iron heel of the war against the gangs, crafted by Reiner's and Hahn's staffs, and co-sponsored by two L.A. Democrats – state Senator Alan Robbins from the Valley and Assemblywoman Gwen Moore from Southcentral – is a state-level 'son of RICO'. Although state Senator Bill Lockyer (D-Hayward) warned that the bill 'would have justified the internment of the Japanese in World War Two', the 'Street Terrorism Enforcement and Prevention Act of 1988' (STEP) was passed with frenetic bipartisan support from Southern California. In the spirit of the original Playboy Gangster suit, STEP makes membership in a 'criminal gang' a felony. The law allows prosecution of 'any person who actively participates in a criminal street gang with knowledge that its members have engaged in a pattern of criminal gang activity and who willfully promotes or assists any felonious conduct by members of that gang'. In explaining the implementation of the law, Reiner noted that a gang member would now face three years in prison for loaning a car used in commission of a crime – 'even if he had not otherwise participated in the act'. What Reiner did not emphasize was that the fine print of the law also provides for the prosecution of *parents* of gang members who do not exercise 'reasonable care' to prevent their children's criminal activities.[37]

In Spring of 1989 (Year Two of the HAMMER) Hahn's office tested STEP's 'bad parent' provision with the sensationalized arrest of a 37-year-old Southcentral woman whose 15-year-old son had earlier been arraigned for participation in a gang rape. In an elaborately contrived exposé for the press, detectives and city attorneys feigned horror at discovering the Oedipal command post of the gang conspiracy:

Authorities said they were stunned at the pervasive atmosphere of gang activity within the household. 'It looks like the headquarters for the local gang', said Robert Ferber of the city attorney's gang unit. 'There was graffiti all over the walls'. 'I was amazed. I couldn't believe my eyes,' said Southwest LAPD Detective Roy Gonzaque. 'In all my 20 years on the police force I have never seen anything like this. It was obvious that the mother was just as much a part of the problem because she condoned this activity.'[38]

Unsurprisingly anti-gang crusaders avidly latched onto this image of 'Mama Crip' in order to villify inner-city 'welfare queens' supposedly breeding a generation of baby street terrorists. But as Hahn's assistant Robert Ferber meditated on the severity of her penalty ('I certainly don't think she is the type of woman who will benefit from counseling'), and Southwest Division Detective Commander Nick Bakay promised that he would keep arresting the parents of gang members ('as many as necessary'), the contrived portrait of maternal malevolence began to disintegrate. Instead of a 'gang mother', reporters discovered a hard-working single parent of three, coping as best she could with overwhelming problems. They also found that the police investigation into her background was hasty and error-ridden. In their race to apply STEP against ghetto parents, Hahn's office and the LAPD anti-gang unit had only managed to reenact the moral equivalent of the Dalton Street raid against an innocent woman. After smearing her name in the press for weeks, the STEP charges were quietly dropped.[39]

Although the ACLU temporarily reentered the fray to denounce the use of 'headline justice to whitewash ineffective and constitutionally indefensible laws', City Attorney Hahn was undeterred. While STEP allowed his office to add centuries of additional jail time to sentences, new abatement laws – patterned after the 1912 Red Light Abatement Act – authorized the City Attorney to drain 'cesspools of drug dealing' by suing landlords, evicting tenants and even bulldozing houses suspected of being 'drug nuisances' ('Operation Knockdown'). Patterned after HUD Secretary Kemp's controversial national policy of expelling from public housing the *families* of those *arrested* (not necessarily convicted) for drug dealing, these new abatement regulations, acting in concert with STEP and barricaded 'Narcotics Enforcement Zones', imply a 'West Bank' strategy towards the troubled neighborhoods of Southcentral L.A.[40] The 'terrorism' metaphor has metastasized as Hahn and Reiner have criminalized successive strata of the community: 'gang members', then 'gang parents', followed by whole 'gang families', 'gang neighborhoods', and perhaps even a 'gang generation'.

A GENERATION UNDER CURFEW

> I think people believe that the only strategy we have is to put a lot of
> police officers on the street and harass people and make arrests for
> inconsequential kinds of things. Well, that's part of the strategy, no
> question about it. *Chief Gates*[41]

As a result of the war on drugs every non-Anglo teenager in Southern California is now a prisoner of gang paranoia and associated demonology. Vast stretches of the region's sumptuous playgrounds, beaches and entertainment centers have become virtual no-go areas for young Blacks or Chicanos. After the Westwood gang shooting, for example, Don Jackson, an off-duty Black policeman from Hawthorne, precisely in order to make a point about de facto apartheid, led some ghetto kids into the Village. They carefully observed the law, yet, predictably, they were stopped, forced to kiss concrete, and searched. Jackson, despite police identification, was arrested for 'disturbing the peace'. Afterwards at a press conference, Chief Gates excoriated him for 'provocations' and a 'cheap publicity stunt', descriptions more aptly applied to the LAPD.[42] Similarly, a few weeks later, a busload of well-dressed Black members of Youth for Christ were

FAST FOOD
MacArthur Park district

humiliatingly surrounded by security guards and frisked for 'drugs and weapons' at the popular Magic Mountain amusement park. Park managers adamantly defended their right to search 'suspicious' (i.e., Black) youth as a matter of policy.[43] More recently twenty-four Black and Latino kids out to play baseball at Will Rogers State Park were arrested for violating some white cops' personal Jim Crow law. The *Times* reported the kids' account of how they 'spent 90 terrifying minutes held face down on the polo field . . . while a group of LAPD taunted and brutalized them. . . . One officer was quoted as having told them that the scenic park in Pacific Palisades was "for rich white people" only.' (The NAACP and the Mexican American Political Association have jointly filed suit against the LAPD for this incident.)[44]

As we saw in the last chapter, curfews have become essential weapons in the LAPD's campaign against the subversive crowd. Residential curfews are deployed selectively and almost exclusively against Black and Chicano neighborhoods. As a consequence, thousands of youth in Southcentral acquire minor records for behavior that would be legal or inoffensive on the Westside. During daylight hours, moreover, the post-Bird California Supreme Court has given police *carte blanche* to stop and search any youthful person for suspicion of truancy. As with the random drunk-driver checkpoints that the Lucas court has also authorized, or the random car weapons searches that the legislature has enacted as part of anti-gang legislation – the 'probable cause' safeguard against capricious stop-and-search is rendered practically extinct. Police now have virtually unlimited discretion, day or night, to target 'undesirables', especially youth.

One of the most disturbing instances of such police 'targeting' has been the LAPD Ramparts Division's relentless campaign against Salvadorean youth in the MacArthur Park district just west of Downtown. Community workers in this poor and overcrowded neighborhood, the home of tens of thousands of refugees from US-financed state terrorism in Central America, tell bitter tales of police brutality. Ramparts cops were particularly incensed by church efforts to work with members of *Mara Savatrucha* (MS) (liberally translated: 'cool Salvadorean dudes', but also known as 'Crazy Riders'), a vast, loosely organized gang grouping. When the Joffrey Ballet in 1988 offered some free seats to Salvadorean youngsters studying dance at a local church center, Ramparts Division warned the Ballet that the kids were the most 'ruthlessly violent in the city' and that the church was basically a gang hangout. The terrified Ballet withdrew the tickets. Meanwhile, coincident with the HAMMER sweeps in Southcentral, the LAPD's CRASH (Community Resources Against Street Hoodlums) program launched a new offensive to 'decimate' the leadership of MS. Howard Ezell, Western regional commissioner for the INS (whom we shall meet again in the next chapter), assigned eight teams of federal immigration agents to work with the LAPD identifying and deporting gang members. As the leader of the INS agents explained, gang *membership*, not necessarily criminal activity, was the qualification for deportation. 'If a gang member is out on the street and the police can't make a charge, we will go out and deport them for being here illegally if they fit that criterion.' Fifty-six of the 175 youth deported were returned to El Salvador, to uncertain fates at the hands of the military and death squads.[45]

But the growing authoritarian reach of police control is nowhere as disturbingly evident as in Los Angeles schools. Another of Chief Gates's publicity-generating 'body count' projects is the so-called 'School Buy' program. As ACLU attorney Joan Howarth describes it, 'up to high school, kids are taught to look on cops as friends; after the eighth grade, "School Buy" cops are trying to entrap them into drug deals'. Youthful undercover cops, in fact, infiltrate high schools, enticing students to sell them drugs. Howarth particularly denounces 'the exploitation of peer pressure to create narcotic offenses; in many cases the undercover police (male and female) exploit sexuality and attractiveness. For this reason, "special education" [educationally handicapped] students, approached for possibly the first time in their life by an attractive member of the opposite sex, are especially likely to become entrapped. The program is a complete fraud.' With little impact on the actual volume of drug sales and negligible success in capturing adult suppliers, the School Buy program is primarily a cheap source of the felony arrests that make the Chief look heroic in the media.[46]

Thanks partially to such police 'vigilance', juvenile crime in Los Angeles County is increasing at 12 per cent annually. One out of twelve kids in Los Angeles, aged eleven to seventeen, will be arrested, half for serious felonies. For older juveniles tried as adults, moreover, conviction rates have soared ominously over the last decade as prosecutors routinely overcharge suspects, threatening them with long sentences, in order to force them to 'cop pleas' to lesser charges. Public defenders and civil libertarians alike have denounced this practice of railroading thousands of poor and frightened teenagers into undeserved criminal convictions.[47]

At the same time, the new punitive increments that STEP and federal and state anti-drug laws have added to sentencing expose a terrible class and racial bias. As the *Times* points out:

Under new federal statutes, defendants convicted of selling 5 grams or more of crack cocaine, worth perhaps $125, receive a mandatory minimum of five years in prison. However, it takes 500 grams of the powdered drug, nearly $50,000 worth of 'yuppie cocaine', to receive an equivalent sentence. Consequently, someone caught in a drug bust with a relatively small amount of cocaine can receive a sentence that is two to three years longer than a person convicted of selling nearly 100 times that amount.[48]

A few illustrations of this new, Kafkaesque class justice: in Southcentral L.A. a young Black three-time loser, never charged with violent crime, but holding a weapon, was sentenced to life imprisonment *without possibility of parole* for the possession of 5.5 grams of crack. A 20-year-old Chinese man received *two* life terms (parole in forty years) for being accessory to the murder of federal agents even though he was not at the scene, did not know that the murders would occur, and was described by the judge as playing 'only a minor role'. Meanwhile, a 21-year-old Baldwin Park Chicano, high on PCP, who ran into the back of a truck and killed his passenger, was charged with murder because he was a suspected gang member. Finally, an elite LAPD stake-out team that the *Times* had exposed as a virtual police death squad, ambushed four young Latinos who had just robbed a MacDonalds in Sunland with a pellet gun. Three of the Latinos were killed by the cops, while the fourth, seriously wounded, was charged with murder, for the deaths of his companions![49]

Processed by such 'justice' (which since 1974 has arrested *two-thirds* of all younger Black males in California), a flood of captives, four-fifths of whom are substance addicted and less than half of whom have committed violent crimes, overwhelm the state prisons – 84,000 inmates in a system with room for 48,000. With the prison population expected to continue to soar, as a result of the 'victories' of the war on drugs and gangs, to 145,000 by 1995, California is creating a time-bomb of multiple-Attica potential. Lacking minimal educational, job-training or drug-treatment resources, the prisons of today have all but abandoned the pretense of 'rehabilitation'.[50] Some are merely minimum security warehouses, where the inmate populations are turned over to endless television gameshow viewing; others, especially designed to accommodate the hardcore gangsters from Los Angeles's ghettoes and barrios, are Orwellian hells.

The ultimate destination for a damned generation is an Antarctica of solitude moored to the picturesque Redwood Coast, just south of the Oregon border. The prison's name 'Pelican Bay' evokes a nature reserve or peaceful sanctuary, but this is only a cruel joke in face of the incredible social isolation and sensory deprivation contained inside. As journalist Miles Corwin describes it:

Pelican Bay is entirely automated and designed so that inmates have virtually no face-to-face contact with guards or other inmates. For twenty-two and a half hours a day, inmates are confined to their windowless cells, built of solid blocks of concrete and stainless steel so that they won't have access to materials they could fashion into weapons. They don't work in prison industries; they don't have access to recreation; they don't mingle with other inmates. They aren't allowed to smoke because matches are considered a security risk.

The justification for this kind of isolation – 'unprecedented in modern prisons' according to one authority whom Corwin interviewed – is simply that 'these inmates are the worst of the worst'. As a prison officer elaborates:

Prisons are representative of what's going on in the streets. . . . You've got more gangs and violence on the streets, so you've got more gangs and violence in the prisons. You need a place to put these people . . . that's why a place like Pelican Bay is necessary.[51]

THE 'BLACK-LASH'

We have to learn to fight Black oppression as much as we fight white oppression. *Earl Caldwell*

I challenge you because I love you. *Jesse Jackson*[52]

As the high-tech gulag of Pelican Bay suggests, the spectre of the Black criminal underclass has begun to augment, even replace, the Red Menace as the satanic 'Other' which justifies the trampling of civil liberties. George Bush's notorious 1988 'Willie Horton' television spot, which destroyed Michael Dukakis's commanding lead, has terrified a whole generation of Democrats into believing that their political survival depends on being even more bloodthirsty than Republicans (for instance, witness the role of death row in California's 1990 gubernatorial campaign). In California, Hahn, Reiner and Van de Camp are exemplars of younger Democrats trying to ride the gibbet (or, more literally, the gas chamber) to higher office. Moreover, as we noted earlier, there has been little effective opposition from their left.

In a 1988 interview, Joan Howarth of the ACLU complained, more in sadness than bitterness, that

progressives have virtually deserted us on this issue . . . the Left has been largely shut out of the policy debate which is now totally framed by the Reaganite Right and its Democratic shadow. There is no progressive agenda on crime, and consequently, no challenging of the socio-economic forces that have produced the burgeoning counterculture of gang membership.[53]

The LAPD likes to rub the ACLU's face in the new, post-liberal balance of power. In June 1988 the police easily won Police Commission approval for the issuing of flesh-ripping hollow-point ammunition: precisely the same 'dum-dum' bullets banned in warfare by the Geneva Conventions and previously kept out of their hands by ACLU lobbying. At the press conference a gloating LAPD spokesperson told the civil libertarians 'to eat your hearts out'.[54]

In philosophically justifying the HAMMER, STEP and other encroachments on the Constitution, the gangbusters have had to look no further than Moynihanized recapitulations of traditional white prejudice. 'Family failure' in the ghetto, abetted by indulgent welfarism, the decline of paternal role models, and the flight of the Black middle class, have connived to create a feral population of grave social menace. Thus once-and-future mayoral challenger Yaroslavsky, in his student days McGovern's UCLA organizer, snarls when asked about the 'economic roots of the gang problem' and tells a nasty little story – of doubtful accuracy – about a drunken welfare mother in the ghetto abusing police for arresting her gang-member son.[55] As head of the Council committee overseeing the police budget, Yaroslavsky has made it clear that gangbusting deserves a blank check. In a city where emergency medical care for the poor has virtually collapsed, where 100,000 sleep without beds, and where infant mortality levels are inching upwards toward third-world levels, Yaroslavsky has put police firepower above all: 'A budget is a statement of priorities and if fighting gang violence in this city is our highest priority, it should be reflected in our budget and it will be at the expense of virtually anything else.'[56]

In past years this pitiless approach to juvenile crime might simply have been dismissed as the venom of white backlash, racism in its law-and-order guise. But this time there is an unprecedented 'Black-lash' as well. The qualitatively new and disturbing dimension of the war on the underclass is the swelling support of Black leadership for the approaches of Gates, Hahn and Reiner. Thus the NAACP endorsed Hahn's attempt to impose martial law on the Playboy Gangsters, while the influential South Central Organizing Committee (SCOC) – the church-supported local affiliate of the Industrial Areas Foundation (IAF) – has been a major voice calling for greater police deployment against street youth.[57] Even Maxine Waters, a respected legislator from Watts-Willowbrook and co-chair of the California Rainbow Coalition, has reluctantly endorsed police sweeps and 'street terrorism' laws.

The trend is national. Although Jesse Jackson continues to campaign for the rescue of ghetto youth, including hardcore gang members, others argue that vigilantism has become the order of the day. In an essay written from Oakland 'ground zero', the novelist Ishmael Reed predicts that the time is fast approaching when the Black working class – 'people who've put in time at stupid dull jobs all their lives and suffered all manner of degradation so that their children might become achievers' – will have to take the offensive against 'Black terrorists . . . the brutal crack fascists'. Comparing daily existence in East Oakland or Watts to the oppression in Haiti under the Tontons Macoutes, Reed scorns white liberals from the hills 'who have "Out of Nicaragua" bumper stickers on their Volvos but are perfectly willing to tolerate drug fascists who prey upon the decent citizens of Oakland'.[58]

In order to save Black America, Reed canvasses the idea of a curfew for 18-to-24-year-olds and a much sterner community invigilation of youth. But Harry Edwards, organizer of the famous Black Power protests at the 1968 Olympics and former Minister of Propaganda for the Black Panther Party, doubts the efficacy of anything short of the permanent removal of a large stratum of youth from the streets. Now a professor of sociology at U.C. Berkeley and a highly paid consultant to professional sports, Edwards gave a chilling account of his views to an interviewer from a San Francisco magazine. When asked how he would 'turn around' a 13-year-old kid selling crack in the streets, he replied:

Edwards: The reality is, you can't.
S.F. Focus: So then what?
Edwards: You gotta realize that they're not gonna make it. The cities, the culture and Black people in particular have to begin to move to get that garbage off the streets.
S.F. Focus: How?
Edwards: It means we have to realize that there are criminals among us and we have to take a very hard line against them, if we're to preserve our next generation and future generations. Even if they are our children.
S.F. Focus: So what do you do if you're a parent and you discover your 13-year-old kid is dealing crack?
Edwards: Turn him in, lock him up. Get rid of him. Lock him up for a *long* time. As long as the law will allow, and try to make it as long as possible. I'm for locking 'em up, gettin 'em off the street, put 'em behind bars.[59]

Black middle-class revulsion against youth criminality – indeed the perception that dealers and gangs threaten the very integrity of Black culture – is thus translated, through such patriarchal bluster, into support for the exterminist rhetoric of the gangbusters. It is a dismal sign of the times that once fiery nationalist intellectuals, like Reed and Edwards, can openly float the idea that a 'sacrifice' or 'triage' of criminalized ghetto youth (i.e., 'the garbage') is the only alternative to the dissolution of a community fabric heroically built up over generations of resistance to racist white America. How is it that inter-generational relations within the Black community have suddenly grown so grimly foreboding?

THE REVOLUTIONARY
LUMPENPROLETARIAT

The drug-taking, apathetic young Black people we bemoan today are
the result of our failure to protect and cherish the Black Panthers
during the Sixties. *Sonya Sanchez*[60]

It is time to meet L.A.'s 'Viet Cong'. Although the study of barrio gangs is
a vast cottage industry, dating back to Emory Bogardus's 1926 monograph,
inspired by the Chicago school, *The City Boy and His Problems*, almost
nothing has been written about the history of Southcentral L.A.'s
sociologically distinct gang culture. The earliest, repeated references to a
'gang problem' in the Black community press, moreover, deal with gangs of
white youth who terrorized Blacks residents along the frontiers of the
southward-expanding Central Avenue ghetto (see chapter three). Indeed,
from these newspaper accounts and the recollections of oldtimers, it seems
probable that the first generation of Black street gangs emerged as a
defensive response to white violence in the schools and streets during the
late 1940s. The *Eagle*, for example, records 'racial gang wars' at Manual
Arts High in 1946, Canoga Park High (in the Valley) in 1947, and John
Adams High in 1949, while Blacks at Fremont High were continuously
assaulted throughout 1946 and 1947. Possibly as a result of their origin in
these school integration/transition battles, Black gangs, until the 1970s,
tended to be predominantly defined by school-based turfs rather than by the
microscopically drawn neighborhood territorialities of Chicano gangs.[61]

Aside from defending Black teenagers from racist attacks (which
continued through the 1950s under the aegis of such white gangs as the
'Spookhunters'), the early Southcentral gangs – the Businessmen, Slausons,
Gladiators, Farmers, Parks, Outlaws, Watts, Boot Hill, Rebel Rousers, Roman
Twenties, and so forth – were also the architects of social space in new and
usually hostile settings. As tens of thousands of 1940s and 1950s Black
immigrants crammed into the overcrowded, absentee-landlord-dominated
neighborhoods of the ghetto's 'Eastside', low-rider gangs offered 'cool worlds'
of urban socialization for poor young newcomers from rural Texas, Louisiana
and Mississippi. Meanwhile, on the other side of Main Street, more affluent
Black youngsters from the 'Westside' bungalow belt created a status-oriented

simulacrum of the ubiquitous white 'car club' subculture of Los Angeles in the 1950s. As J.K. Obatala would recall, 'besides the territorial factor, there was an element of class warfare in the 1950s':

Members of gangs such as the Flips and the Slausons were Westsiders whose families usually had a little more money and who considered themselves more socially sophisticated than their Eastside counterparts. The Eastsiders, in turn, looked upon their rivals to the West as snobs and sometimes deliberately ventured into their sphere of influence to break up parties or other social events.[62]

While 'rumblin' ' (usually non-lethally) along this East–West socio-economic divide, or sometimes simply in extension of intermural athletic rivalries, the Black gangs of the 1950s also had to confront the implacable (often lethal) racism of Chief Parker's LAPD. In the days when the young Daryl Gates was driver to the great Chief, the policing of the ghetto was becoming simultaneously less corrupt but more militarized and brutal. Under previous police chiefs, for example, Central Avenue's boisterous, interracial night scene had simply been shaken down for tribute; under Parker – a puritanical crusader against 'race mixing' – nightclubs and juke joints were raided and shuttered. In 1954 John Dolphin, owner of Los Angeles's premier R&B record store near the corner of Vernon and Central, organized a protest of 150 Black business people against an ongoing 'campaign of intimidation and terror' directed at interracial trade. According to Dolphin, Newton Division police had gone so far as to blockade his store, turning away all white customers and warning them that 'it was too dangerous to hang around Black neighborhoods'.[63]

After smashing interracial 'vice' on Central Avenue, Chief Parker launched his own 'all-out war on narcotics' in Southcentral and East L.A., alleging that heroin and marijuana were being exported to white neighborhoods. He charged in the press that 'the Communists furthered the heroin and marijuana trade, because drug use sped the moral degeneration of America'. Prefiguring Gates's call years later for the invasion of Colombia, Parker demanded the closing of the Mexican border, while his principal newspaper supporter, the *Herald-Express*, called for the execution of drug dealers.[64]

Chief Parker also did his bit to support the *Times*'s crusade against 'socialistic' public housing (see chapter two) by using phoney crime statistics to paint lurid images of 'jungle life' in the projects – a political manipulation of police data which some critics feel has continued through the present. Like his protégé-successors, Chief Parker invoked racialized crime scares to justify his tireless accumulation of power. As one of his retiring subordinates observed in 1981, Parker constantly and self-servingly projected the specter of a vast criminal reservoir in Southcentral L.A. ('all Blacks as bad guys'), held in check by an outnumbered but heroically staunch 'Blue line'. Accordingly, any diminution of the police budget or questioning of Parker's authority would weaken the dike and release a Black crime deluge on peaceful white neighborhoods.[65] Consider, for example, the Chief's extraordinary testimony before the US Commission on Civil Rights in early 1960:

A belligerent Parker characterized the LAPD as the real 'embattled minority' and argued that the tensions between L.A.'s minority communities and the cops had simply to do with the fact that Blacks and Latinos were statistically many times more likely than Whites to commit crimes. Indeed Parker assured the Commission that the 'established [read White] community thinks cops aren't hard enough on Black vice'. Parker sparked a 500-strong protest rally in East Los Angeles when he went on to offer his insight into the high crime rate in the *barrios*, explaining that the people who lived there were only one step removed from 'the wild tribes of Mexico'.[66]

Since 'wild tribes' and gang perils were its golden geese, it is not surprising that Parker's LAPD looked upon the 'rehabilitation' of gang youth in much the same way as the arms industry regarded peace-mongering or disarmament treaties. Vehemently opposed to the extension of constitutional rights to juveniles and loathing 'social workers', Chief Parker, a strict Victorian, 'launched a concerted attack on the Group Guidance Unit of the Probation Department', a small program that had emerged out of the so-called 'Zoot Suit Riots' of 1943. The original sin of Group Guidance, in the Chief's opinion, was that they 'gave status to gang activity' by treating gang members as socially transformable individuals. Like the contemporary rhetoric of the HAMMER or 'Black-Lash', the LAPD in the 1950s and early 1960s dichotomized youth offenders into two groups. On one hand, were mere 'delinquents' (mainly white youth) susceptible to the shock treatment of juvenile hall; on the other hand, were 'juvenile criminals' (mainly Black and Chicano) – miniature versions of J. Edgar Hoover's 'mad dogs' – destined to spend their lives within the state prison system. Essential to the LAPD worldview was the assertion that ghetto gang youth were composed of the latter: a residuum of 'hardcore', unrehabilitable criminality. Moreover, as Black nationalist groups, like the Muslims, began to appear in the ghetto in the late 1950s, Parker, like Hoover, began to see the gang problem and the 'militant threat' as forming a single, overarching structure of Black menace.[67]

The LAPD's own abuses, in fact, were a self-fulfilling prophecy, radicalizing gang subculture in Southcentral. After the LAPD's unprovoked attack on a Nation of Islam Mosque in April 1962, which left one Muslim killed and six wounded, a community uprising against Parker's 'army of occupation' became envisioned as justified and virtually inevitable. Thus in May 1964 Howard Jewel memoed his boss, California Attorney General Stanley Mosk, that 'soon the "long, hot summer" will be upon us. The evidence from L.A. is ominous'. Jewell blamed Chief Parker for inciting racial polarization and predicted widespread violence.[68]

At the same time the Black version of the Southern California Dream, which had lured hundreds of thousands of hopeful immigrants from the Southwest, was collapsing. Excluded from lucrative construction and aerospace jobs, Black youth experienced the 1959–65 period – the white kids' 'endless summer' – as a winter of discontent. The absolute income gap between Black and white Angelenos dramatically widened. Median incomes in Southcentral L.A. declined by almost a tenth, and Black unemployment skyrocketed from 12 per cent to 20 per cent (30 per cent in Watts). Despite deceptive palm-lined streets and cute bungalow exteriors, the housing stock of Southcentral was dilapidated: the 'largest blighted area of any US city' according to the Regional Planning Commission.[69] But every attempt by civil rights groups to expand job or housing opportunities for Blacks was countered by fierce white resistance, culminating in the 75 per cent white vote in 1964 (Proposition 14) to repeal the Rumford Fair Housing Act.

Yet, unlike today's social polarization, this was also the heroic age of the Civil Rights Movement, of epic debates about strategies of liberation. Southcentral gang youth, coming under the influence of the Muslims and the long-distance charisma of Malcolm X, began to reflect the generational awakening of Black Power. As Obatala describes the 'New Breed' of the

1960s, 'their perceptions were changing: those who formerly had seen things in terms of East and West were now beginning to see many of the same things in Black and White'. As the gangs began to become politicized, they became 'al fresco churches whose ministers brought the gospel [of Black power] out into the streets'.[70]

Veteran civil rights activists can recall one memorable instance, during a protest at a local whites-only drive-in restaurant, when the timely arrival of Black gang members saved them from a mauling by white hotrodders. The gang was the legendary Slausons, based in the Fremont High area, and they became a crucial social base for the rise of the local Black Liberation movement. The turning-point, of course, was the festival of the oppressed in August 1965 that the Black community called a rebellion and the white media a riot. Although the 'riot commission' headed by old-guard Republicans John McCone and Asa Call supported Chief Parker's so-called 'riff-raff theory' that the August events were the work of a small criminal minority, subsequent research, using the McCone Commission's own data, proved that up to 75,000 people took part in the uprising, mostly from the stolid Black working class.[71] For gang members it was 'The Last Great Rumble', as formerly hostile groups forgot old grudges and cheered each other on against the hated LAPD and the National Guard. Conot cites examples of old enemies, like the Slausons and the Gladiators (from the 54th Street area), flashing smiles and high signs as they broke through Parker's invincible 'blue line'.[72]

This ecumenical movement of the streets and 'hoods lasted for three or four years. Community workers, and even the LAPD themselves, were astonished by the virtual cessation of gang hostilities as the gang leadership joined the Revolution.[73] Two leading Slausons, Alprentice 'Bunchy' Carter (a famous 'warlord') and Jon Huggins became the local organizers of the Black Panther Party, while a third, Brother Crook (aka Ron Wilkins) created the Community Alert Patrol to monitor police abuse. Meanwhile an old Watts gang hangout near Jordan Downs, the 'parking lot', became a recruiting center for the 'Sons of Watts' who organized and guarded the annual Watts Festival.[74]

It is not really surprising, therefore, that in the late 1960s the doo-ragged, hardcore street brothers and sisters, who for an extraordinary week in 1965 had actually driven the police out of the ghetto, were visualized by

Black Power theorists as the strategic reserve of Black Liberation, if not its vanguard. (A similar fantasy of a *Warriors*-like unification of the gangs was popular amongst sections of the Chicano Left.) There was a potent moment in this period, around 1968–9, when the Panthers – their following soaring in the streets and high schools – looked as if they might become the ultimate revolutionary gang. Teenagers, who today flock to hear Eazy-E rap, 'It ain't about color, it's about the color of money. I love that green'[75] – then filled the Sports Arena to listen to Stokely Carmichael, H. Rap Brown, Bobby Seale and James Forman adumbrate the unity program of SNCC and the Panthers. The Black Congress and the People's Tribunal (convened to try the LAPD for 'the murder of Gregory Clark') were other expressions of the same aspiration for unity and militancy.

But the combined efforts of the FBI's notorious COINTELPRO program and the LAPD's Public Disorder Intelligence Division (a super-Red Squad that until 1982 maintained surveillance on every suspicious group from the Panthers to the National Council of Churches) were concentrated upon destroying Los Angeles's Black Power vanguards. The February 1969 murders of Panther leaders Carter and Huggins on the UCLA campus by members of a rival nationalist group (which Panther veterans still insist was actually police-instigated) was followed a year later by the debut of LAPD's SWAT team in a day-long siege of the Panthers' Southcentral headquarters. Although a general massacre of the Panther cadre was narrowly averted by an angry community outpouring into the streets, the Party was effectively destroyed.

As even the *Times* recognized, the decimation of the Panthers led directly to a recrudescence of gangs in the early 1970s.[76] 'Crippin' ', the most extraordinary new gang phenomenon, was a bastard offspring of the Panthers' former charisma, filling the void left by the LAPD SWAT teams. There are various legends about the original Crips, but they agree on certain particulars. As Donald Bakeer, a teacher at Manual Arts High, explains in his self-published novel about the Crips, the first 'set' was incubated in the social wasteland created by the clearances for the Century Freeway – a traumatic removal of housing and destruction of neighborhood ties that was the equivalent of a natural disaster. His protagonist, a second-generation Crip, boasts to his 'homeboys' : 'My daddy was a member of the original 107 Hoover Crip Gang, the original Crips in Los Angeles, O.G. [original gangster] to the max'.[77] Secondly, as journalist Bob Baker has determined, the real 'O.G.' number one of the 107 Hoovers (who split away from an older gang called the Avenues) was a young man powerfully influenced by the Panthers in their late sixties heyday:

He was Raymond Washington, a Fremont High School student who had been too young to be a Black Panther but had soaked up some of the Panther rhetoric about community control of neighborhoods. After Washington was kicked out of Fremont, he wound up at Washington High, and something began to jell in the neighborhood where he lived, around 107th and Hoover streets.[78]

Although it is usually surmised that the name Crip is derived from the 107 Hoovers' 'crippled' style of walking, Bakeer was told by one 'O.G.' that it originally stood for 'Continuous Revolution in Progress'.[79] However apocryphal this translation may be, it best describes the phenomenal spread of Crip sets across the ghetto between 1970 and 1972. A 1972 gang map (see p. 301), released by the LAPD's 77th Street Division, shows a quiltwork of blue-ragged Crips, both Eastside and Westside, as well as miscellany of other gangs, some descended from the pre-Watts generation.[80] Under incessant Crip pressure, these independent gangs – the Brims, Bounty Hunters, Denver Lanes, Athens Park Gang, the Bishops, and, especially, the powerful Pirus – federated as the red-hankerchiefed Bloods. Particularly strong in Black communities peripheral to the Southcentral core, like Compton, Pacoima, Pasadena and Pomona, the Bloods have been primarily a defensive reaction-formation to the aggressive emergence of the Crips.[81]

It needs to be emphasized that this was not merely a gang revival, but a radical permutation of Black gang culture. The Crips, however perversely, inherited the Panther aura of fearlessness and transmitted the ideology of armed vanguardism (shorn of its program). In some instances, Crip insignia continued to denote Black Power, as during the Monrovia riots in 1972 or the L.A. Schools bussing crisis of 1977–9.[82] But too often Crippin' came to represent an escalation of intra-ghetto violence to *Clockwork Orange* levels (murder as a status symbol, and so on) that was unknown in the days of the Slausons and anathema to everything that the Panthers had stood for.

Moreover the Crips blended a penchant for ultra-violence with an overweening ambition to dominate the entire ghetto. Although, as Bakeer subtly sketches in his novel, Eastside versus Westside tensions persist, the Crips, as the Panthers before them, attempted to hegemonize an entire generation. In this regard, they achieved, like the contemporary 'Black P-Stone Nation' in Chicago, a 'managerial revolution' in gang organization. If they began as a teenage substitute for the fallen Panthers, they evolved through the 1970s into a hybrid of teen cult and proto-Mafia. At a time when economic opportunity was draining away from Southcentral Los Angeles, the Crips were becoming the power resource of last resort for thousands of abandoned youth.

EXPENDABLE YOUTH

> Gangs are never goin' to die out. You all goin' to get us jobs?
> *16-year-old Grape Street Crip*[83]

What would the Crips and Bloods say about the carnage if they could talk? It is, of course, a tactical absolute of 'anti-terrorism' – whether practiced in Belfast, Jerusalem or Los Angeles – to deny terrorism a public voice. Although terrorism is always portrayed precisely as inarticulate male-volence, authorities expend enormous energy to protect us from its 'ravings', even at the cost of censorship and restriction of free speech. Thus the LAPD has vehemently (and usually successfully) opposed attempts by social workers and community organizers to allow gang members to tell 'their side of the story'.

A major exception was in December 1972, just as Cripmania was first sweeping Southside schools in an epidemic of gang shootings and street fights. The Human Relations Conference, against the advice of the police, gave a platform to sixty Black gang leaders to present their grievances. To the astonishment of officials present, the 'mad dogs' outlined an eloquent and coherent set of demands: jobs, housing, better schools, recreation facilities and community control of local institutions.[84] It was a bravura demonstration that gang youth, however trapped in their own delusionary spirals of vendetta and self-destruction, clearly understood that they were the children of deferred dreams and defeated equality. Moreover as 'hard-core' Black and Chicano gang leaders have always affirmed, in the handful

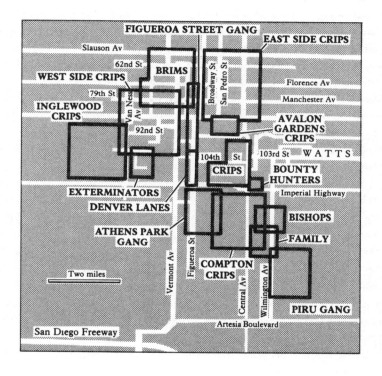

GANG TERRITORIES – 1972

of other instances over the last eighteen years when they have been allowed to speak, decent jobs are the price for negotiating a humane end to drug-dealing and gang violence.[85]

So, what has happened to the jobs? It is necessary to recall that the revolutionary rhetoric of the 1960s was sustained by the real promise of reformism. While the Panthers were mesmerizing the campuses, civil rights politics gained new momentum with the rise of the Bradley coalition of Blacks, Jews and Liberals. Moreover in the superheated summit of the Vietnam boom, young Black men at last began to find their way, in some substantial number, into factory and transportation jobs, while Black women thronged into the lower levels of the pink-collar workforce. And, for teenagers and the younger unemployed, the federal government supplied a seasonal quota of temporary 'weed-pulling' jobs and bogus training schemes to cool out the streets during the long summers.

But the illusion of economic progress was shortlived. By 1985 – the tenth anniversary of the Watts Rebellion and year two of the Bradley era – a special report by the *Times* found that the 'the Black ghetto is not a viable community . . . it is slowly dying'. In the face of double-digit unemployment (1975 was a depression year for Southland Blacks), overcrowded schools, high prices, and deteriorating housing, 'the fighting mood of the 1960s has been replaced by a sick apathy or angry frustration'. With rebellion deterred by the paramilitarization of the police and the destruction of the community's radical fringe, *Times* writer John Kendall described despair recycled as gang violence and Black-on-Black crime.[86]

Seen from a perspective fifteen years further on, it is clear that the *Times*, and other contemporary observers, did not fully appreciate the complexity of what was happening in Southcentral Los Angeles. Although the image of overall community demoralization was accurate enough, a sizeable minority was actually experiencing moderate upward mobility, while the condition of the majority was steadily worsening. In simplified terms, Los Angeles's Black community became more internally polarized as public-sector craftworkers, clericals and professionals successfully entrenched themselves within city, county and federal bureaucracies, while the semi-skilled working class in the private sector was decimated by the dual impact of job suburbanization and economic internationalization.

GANGS WILL NEVER DIE

Paradoxically it may be equally true that Black political leadership in Los Angeles County has sponsored significant economic advance and contributed to the community's benign neglect at the same time. Critics who accuse the Bradley administration of 'killing Southcentral L.A.' usually ignore its achievements in integrating the public workforce. It has been a dynamic Black public-sector job base (together with smaller-scale Black professional advances in the aerospace, financial and entertainment industries) that is responsible for the prosperity visible on the Black 'new Westside': the *nouveaux riches* hilltops of Ladera Heights and Baldwin Hills, and the tidy tractlands of suburban Inglewood and Carson.

At the same time, *community* economic development has been a total failure. As we have seen, the Bradley administration chose to accommodate the redevelopment agenda of the Central City Association, not the NAACP or the Mexican-American Political Association. Working-class Blacks in the flatlands – where nearly 40 per cent of families live below the poverty line – have faced relentless economic decline. While city resources (to the tune of $2 billion) have been absorbed in financing the corporate renaissance of Downtown, Southcentral L.A. has been markedly disadvantaged even in receipt of anti-poverty assistance, 'coming in far behind West Los Angeles and the Valley in access to vital human services and job-training funds'.[87] Black small businesses have withered for lack of credit or attention from the city, leaving behind only liquor stores and churches.

Most tragically, the unionized branch-plant economy toward which working-class Blacks (and Chicanos) had always looked for decent jobs collapsed. As the Los Angeles economy in the 1970s was 'unplugged' from the American industrial heartland and rewired to East Asia, non-Anglo workers have borne the brunt of adaptation and sacrifice. The 1978–82 wave of factory closings in the wake of Japanese import penetration and recession, which shuttered ten of the twelve largest non-aerospace plants in Southern California and displaced 75,000 blue-collar workers, erased the ephemeral gains won by blue-collar Blacks between 1965 and 1975. Where local warehouses and factories did not succumb to Asian competition, they fled instead to new industrial parks in the South Bay, northern Orange County or the Inland Empire – 321 firms since 1971.[88] An investigating committee of the California Legislature in 1982 confirmed the resulting economic destruction in Southcentral neighborhoods: unemployment rising by nearly 50 per cent since the early 1970s while community purchasing power fell by a third.[89]

If Eastside manufacturing employment made a spectacular recovery in the 1980s, it offered little opportunity for Blacks, as the new industry overwhelmingly consisted of minimum-wage sweatshops, super-exploiting immigrant Latino labor in the production of furniture or non-durables like clothes and toys. (Borrowing the terminology of Alain Lipietz, we might say that a 'Bloody Taylorism' now operates within the ruined shell of 'Fordism'.)[90] This extinction of industrial job opportunities has had profound gender as well as socioeconomic ramifications for the Black labor force. Young Black women have been partially able to compensate for community deindustrialization by shifting into lower-level information-processing jobs. Young Black working-class men, on the other hand, have seen their labor-market options (apart from military service) virtually collapse as the factory and truckdriving jobs that gave their fathers and older brothers a modicum of dignity have either been replaced by imports, or relocated to white areas far out on the galactic spiral-arms of the L.A. megalopolis – fifty to eighty miles away in San Bernardino or Riverside counties.

Equally, young Blacks have been largely excluded from the boom in suburban service employment. As we saw in chapter three, it is a stunning fact – emblematic of institutional racism on a far more rampant scale than usually admitted these days – that most of California's 1980s job and residential growth poles – southern Orange County, eastern Ventura County, northern San Diego County, Contra Costa County, and so on – have Black populations of 1 per cent or less. At the same time, young Blacks willing to compete for more centrally located, menial service jobs find themselves in a losing competition with new immigrants, not least because of clear employer opinions about labor 'docility'. As a result, unemployment amongst Black youth in Los Angeles County – despite unbroken regional growth and a new explosion of conspicuous consumption – remained at a staggering 45 per cent through the late 1980s.[91] A 1985 survey of public housing projects in the ghetto discovered that there were only 120 employed breadwinners out of 1,060 households in Nickerson Gardens, 70 out of 400 at Pueblo del Rio, and 100 out of 700 at Jordan Downs.[92] The scale of pent-up demand for decent manual employment was also vividly demonstrated a few years ago when *fifty thousand* predominantly Black and Chicano youth lined up for miles to apply for a few openings on the unionized longshore in San Pedro.

This deterioration in the labor-market position of young Black men is a major reason why the counter-economy of drug dealing and youth crime has burgeoned. But it is not the whole story. Correlated to the economic peripheralization of working-class Blacks has been the dramatic *juvenation of poverty* amongst all inner-city ethnic groups. Statewide, the percentage of children in poverty has doubled (from 11 per cent to 23 per cent) over the last generation. In Los Angeles County during the 1980s, a chilling 40 per cent of children either lived below, or hovered just above, the official poverty line. The poorest areas in the County, moreover, are invariably the youngest: of sixty-six census tracts (in 1980) with median family incomes under $10,000, over 70 per cent had a median age of only 20–24 years (the rest, 25–29).[93] As the political muscle of affluent homeowners continues to ensure residential segregation and the redistribution of tax resources upwards, inner-city youth have been the victims of a conscious policy of social disinvestment. The tacit expendability of Black and brown youth in the 'city of the angels' can be directly measured by the steady drainage of resources – with minimum outcry from elected officials – from the programs that serve the most urgent needs.

Most telling, perhaps, have been the successive attacks on youth employment schemes, beginning with the Nixon administration's decision, echoed by then Governor Reagan, to roll back Great Society community activism and redirect urban aid from the cities to the suburbs. The dismantling of the Neighborhood Youth Corps, followed under Reagan by the termination of the Comprehensive Employment and Training Act (CETA) and the evisceration of the Jobs Corps, were the landmarks in this retreat from the inner city. In Los Angeles the major, current source of public youth employment is the Los Angeles Summer Job Program – a typical 'fire insurance' scheme that is a pale shadow of its abolished federal predecessors. Ironically, at the very moment in 1987–8 when the klieg-light scrutiny of Hollywood and all the media was focused on illicit youth employment, the Summer Job Program was cut back by the City Council.[94]

Job alternatives for gang members have been almost nonexistent, despite widespread recognition that jobs are more potent deterrents to youth crime than STEP laws or long penitentiary sentences. As Charles Norman, the veteran director of Youth Gang Services, observed in 1981: 'You could pull 80 per cent of gang members, seventeen years old or younger, out of gangs, if you had jobs, job training and social alternatives.'[95] State Senate President Pro Tem David Roberti, the top Democrat from Hollywood, acknowledged eight years later that 'Proposition 13 had ripped inner-city neighborhoods apart', preventing Norman's strategic expenditures on gang prevention.[96] Finally, as the LAPD's budget crept above $400 million in 1988, the City Council begrudgingly approved a $500,000 pilot program to create one hundred jobs for 'high-risk' youth. In the vast escalation of hostilities since the mid 1980s, this pathetic program is the only 'carrot' that the City has actually offered to its estimated 50,000 gang youth.[97]

The school system, meanwhile, has been travelling backwards at high speed. At the state level, California's celebrated educational system has been in steep decline, with per capita student expenditure falling from ninth to thirty-third place, or merely a third of the per capita level of New York. The Los Angeles Unified School District, the nation's second largest serving 600,000 students, has classrooms more crowded than Mississippi's and a soaring dropout rate of 30–50 per cent in its inner-city high schools. The term 'Unified' is a misnomer, as for many years the District has operated de facto separate systems for Blacks, Latinos and whites. One result is that Black males from Southcentral are now three times more likely to end up in prison than at the University of California. As the NAACP has charged in a major lawsuit, segregation remains rampant and school quality is directly reflective of the socioeconomic levels of neighborhoods. Moreover, as NAACP attorney Joseph Duff has explained, racial isolation in schools has been ramified by historic rental discrimination against families with children:

Certain areas of the city with high-density, low-cost apartments and older, large single-family homes have become veritable 'children's ghettoes'. Public schools have been burdened by the concentration of school-age children in these family areas. The racial isolation has assumed an overlay of class isolation.[98]

Ill served by an overburdened and separate-but-unequal school system, low-income youth fare even worse after school. In Los Angeles County there are an estimated 250,000 to 350,000 'latch-key' kids between the ages of five and fourteen who have no adult supervision between the final school bell and their parents' return from work. In the meantime the Bradley administration, applying triage to city programs in the wake of fiscal austerity, has virtually abandoned public recreation. In 1987 it allocated a paltry $30,000 in recreational equipment for one hundred and fifty centers serving hundreds of thousands of poor children. It has also adopted the principle of apportioning its reduced park budget through a formula based on park size, while encouraging parks to operate as 'businesses' based on user fees. Since the wealthy areas of the city have disproportionate shares of park area and fee-generating facilities, this has entailed a regressive redistribution of park resources. The result is 'recreational apartheid' and a calamitous deterioration of public space in the inner city as parks become increasingly run down, unsupervised and dangerous.[99]

There has been desultory political mobilization against the hollowing out of the economic and social infrastructures of Southcentral or the pauperization of a generation of inner-city youth. Of the leadership generation of the Watts Rebellion only a handful have continued to raise hell about the fate of the community. Thus Assemblymember Maxine Waters and Watts Labor Action leader Ted Watkins did pressure the legislature to finally hold hearings on local plant closures and economic distress (no comparable City Council initiative was taken). Despite a harrowing accumulation of testimony, the legislature, so keen to succor law enforcement, did nothing to address the economic decline that was obviously fueling crime rates.

Bolder action has been advocated by the surviving cadre of Los Angeles's 1960s Black Power movement, particularly Michael Zinzun of the Committee Against Police Abuse and Anthony Thigpen of Jobs with Peace. But their dogged attempts to build precinct-level organization in the community and to develop a grassroots agenda of 'critical needs' have been repeatedly sabotaged by various power structures, including ostensibly 'liberal' Democrats. Thus the Jobs with Peace campaign for a citywide assessment of the impact of military spending on local communities was countered by a vicious propaganda barrage from the political consultants to the Westside 'Berman–Waxman–Levine' machine. Zinzun's efforts, meanwhile, to expose police brutality led to a savage, unprovoked beating by Pasadena police and the loss of an eye. It is no criticism of the courageous dedication of these inner-city organizers to point out the David and Goliath character of their struggle. Unlike Chicago in 1986, where economic devastation in the ghetto could be laid neatly at the door of white political supremacy, in Los Angeles the Bradley regime, with its inner circle of Southside ministers and cronies, has been a powerful deterrent to the coalescence of Black protest or electoral insurgency.

Without the mobilized counterweight of angry protest, Southcentral L.A. has been betrayed by virtually every level of government. In particular, the deafening public silence about youth unemployment and the juvenation of poverty has left many thousands of young street people with little alternative but to enlist in the crypto-Keynesian youth employment program operated by the cocaine cartels. Revisiting Watts nearly a generation after a famous pioneering study of its problems, UCLA industrial relations economist Paul Bullock discovered that the worsening conditions described by the *Times*'s 'Watts: 10 Years Later' team in 1975 had deteriorated still further, and that endemic unemployment was at the core of the community's despair. Bullock observed that the last rational option open to Watts youth – at least in the neoclassical sense of utility-maximizing economic behavior – was to sell drugs.[100]

THE POLITICAL ECONOMY OF CRACK

What's right? If you want something, you have the right to take it. If
you want to do something, you have the right to do it.
Bret Easton Ellis, Less Than Zero[101]

Since the late 1970s, every major sector of the Southern California economy, from tourism to apparel, has restructured around the increasing role of foreign trade and offshore investment. Southcentral L.A., as we have indicated, has been the main loser in this transformation, since Asian imports have closed factories without creating compensatory economic opportunities for local residents. The specific genius of the Crips has been their ability to insert themselves into a leading circuit of international trade. Through 'crack' they have discovered a vocation for the ghetto in L.A.'s new 'world city' economy.

Peddling the imported, high-profit rock stuff to a bipolar market of final consumers, including rich Westsiders as well as poor street people, the Crips have become as much lumpen capitalists as outlaw proletarians. If this has only underwritten their viciousness with a new competitive imperative, it has added to their charisma the weight of gold-braided neck chains and showy rings. In an age of narco-imperialism they have become modern analogues to the 'gunpowder states' of West Africa, those selfish, rogue chieftaincies who were middlemen in the eighteenth-century slave trade, prospering while the rest of Africa bled. The Latino Eastside gangs, by contrast, are still trying to catch up. Dealing largely in homegrown drugs, like PCP, amphetamines and marijuana, with relatively low turnover values in a market consisting almost entirely of other poor teenagers, they are unable to accumulate the fineries or weaponry of the Crips. They have yet to effectively join the world market.

The contemporary cocaine trade is a stunning example of what some political economists (after the MIT duo of Sabel and Piore) are now calling 'flexible accumulation', on a hemispheric scale. The rules of the game are to combine maximum financial control with flexible and interchangeable deployment of producers and sellers across variable national landscapes. At the primary producer end, of course, coca has been the major economic adaptation of the Andean economies to the bank-imposed 'debt depression' of the 1980s. Tens of thousands of peasants have migrated to 'coke rush' frontiers like the famous Huallaga Valley of Peru, where they increasingly enjoy the protection of the 'Inca-Maoists' of Sendero Luminoso against the Green Berets and the Peruvian Army. In the late 1980s, the Colombian overlords tried to ensure the continuity of their supply, as well as their ability to impose a buyer's price on peasant producers, by opening their own auxiliary coca plantations using wage labor. Like oil production, however, the strategic instance is the refining process, centralized in Colombian laboratories under the personal supervision of the Medellin Cartel (or its Cali-based rival).

In popular imagination the Medellin Cartel has replaced the Mafia as the symbol of a super-criminal conspiracy of almost occult power – indeed, Bush and Bennett often talk as if America is fighting a 'war of the worlds' against extra-terrestrial invaders. The reality, of course, has always been more prosaic. Washington wages war on the same invisible hand that it otherwise deifies. As *Fortune* pointed out a few years back, the Medellin group have always been distinguished by their 'businesslike mentality' and their success 'in turning cocaine trafficking into a well-managed multi-national industry'.[102] Eric Hobsbawm, an aficionado of bandits and imperialists, made the same point several years ago in a review:

Left to themselves and the principles of Adam Smith, the consortia of Medellin investors would no more see themselves as criminals than did the Dutch or English venturers into the Indies trade (including opium), who organized their speculative cargoes in much the same way . . . the trade rightly resents being called a mafia. . . . It is basically an ordinary business that has been criminalized – as Colombians see it – by a U.S. which cannot manage its own affairs.[103]

Like any 'ordinary business' in an initial sales boom, the cocaine trade had to contend with changing relations of supply and demand. Over-production, due both to the cartels' deliberate promotion of supply and to the peasants' desperate stampede toward a saleable staple, has been endemic since the mid 1980s. Despite the monopsonistic position of the cartels vis-à-vis the producers, the wholesale price of cocaine fell by half. This, in turn, dictated a transformation in sales strategy and market structure. The result was a switch from *haute cuisine* to fast food, as the Medellin Cartel, starting in 1981 or 1983 (accounts differ), designated Los Angeles as a proving-ground for the mass sales potential of rock cocaine or crack.

Shortly before its demise in 1989, the *Herald-Examiner* published a sensationalized overview of 'Cartel L.A.' that synthesized law enforcement viewpoints on the history and organization of the crack economy. According to this account, the Colombian cartels responded to the militarization of federal drug enforcement in south Florida after 1982 by rerouting cocaine through Mexico with the aid of the 'Guadalajara Mafia' run by Miguel Gallardo (the 'godfather' presumed to have ordered the torture-murder of DEA agent 'Kiki' Camarena in 1985). Upon its arrival in Southern California via couriers or light aircraft (the Drug Enforcement Authority claims there are 'over 100 clandestine airstrips' in the California desert), the cocaine – by 1988 estimated to total 450,000 pounds annually – is supposedly warehoused and processed for wholesale distribution by

Colombian nationals bound to the cartels by unbreakable omerta. Originally estimated to number a few hundred, the Colombians in 1989 suddenly became an 'invading army . . . thousands strong' organized into as many as '1,000 cells'. (An IRS official described cell workers as 'soldiers coming into this country who are doing their tours of duty and then getting out'.)[103] Alarmed by news of the 'invasion', nervous Southern California residents were put on the lookout for 'suspicious' Latin Americans, especially 'polite, well-dressed' families or individuals with penchants for quiet suburban neighborhoods.[105]

In any event, the financial turnover in L.A.'s rock and powder markets appears easier to estimate than the number of Cartel 'foot soldiers'. Los Angeles has been described by the Justice Department as 'an ocean of drug-tainted cash'. Between 1985 and 1987 (the real take-off years for crack) the 'cash surplus' in the Los Angeles branch of the Federal Reserve system increased 2,300 per cent to $3.8 billion – a sure index, according to federal experts, of the volume of illicit coke dollars.[106] In early 1989 a small army of Feds overwhelmed Downtown L.A.'s Jewelry Mart in 'Operation Polar Cap' – a spectacular attack on 'La Mina' ('the Gold Mine'), a billion-dollar per year money-laundering operation supposedly run on behalf of the Medellin Cartel by several dozen immigrant Armenian gold-dealers.[107] The disclosure of La Mina seemed to confirm earlier assertions by US Attorney (now federal judge) Robert Bonner that L.A. had surpassed Miami as 'the principal distribution center for the nation's cocaine supply' – a claim that the Justice Department officially recognized in August 1989.[108]

The vast, three-volume 'Dunn and Bradstreet Primer on the Pervasive-ness of Drugs in America' that Attorney General Thornburgh presented that month to drug czar William Bennett also proclaimed that L.A. drug gangs were firmly allied with the Medellin Cartel in a plot to flood American inner cities with crack. Quoting copiously from LAPD sources, the report pictured L.A. overrun by Colombians and the USA overrun by their Crip henchmen:

Los Angeles street gangs now dominate the rock cocaine trade in Los Angeles and elsewhere, due in part to their steady recourse to murderous violence to enforce territorial dealing supremacy, to deter cheating and to punish rival gang members . . . the LAPD has identified 47 cities, from Seattle to Kansas City to Baltimore, where Los Angeles street gang traffickers have appeared.[109]

Washington's official adoption of the LAPD's characterization of L.A. street gangs as highly organized mafias in cahoots with the Colombians (a view also embraced by the California attorney general's office) was challenged by two USC professors who had been carefully analyzing arrest records of crack dealers over the previous two years. In studying 741 cases in 'five gang-infested sections of Los Angeles County', they discovered that only 25 per cent of the alleged dealers were active gang members. Although acknowledging that the direct role of gangs might have substantially increased since their 1984–5 data, the USC team stood by their principal conclusions:

The explosion in cocaine sales was engaging a number of street gang members but was in no way dominated by gang involvement. The drug parameters simply overwhelmed the gang parameters. . . . the cohesiveness of the gangs themselves is very low. . . . To expect a group like that to take on Mafia characteristics seems very unlikely.[110]

Responding to this study, the LAPD's 'gang-drug czar', Deputy Chief Glenn Levant, admitted that 64 per cent of the seven thousand suspected dealers arrested through his Gang-Related Active Trafficker program were not identifiable as gang members. But he denied that the Department had 'over-stated the problem' since '36 per cent gang membership is very significant', and many, if not a majority, of the other arrestees were older ex-gang members.[111] But Levant's revision of the USC study – that is, a more signi-ficant direct participation of gang members and a large, if not dominant, role played by adult 'O.G.s' – still seemingly leaves in place the USC team's key finding that the gang role in drug distribution is too 'incoherent' to qualify for the 'organized crime network' badge that Levant's boss, Chief Gates, and most other law-enforcement officials want to pin on the Crips and Bloods.

All of which is to say that the Southcentral gangs are definitely in the drug business, but as small businessmen not crime corporations, and usually under the supervision of older dealers who, in turn, answer to a shadowy wholesale hierarchy of middlemen and cartel representatives. On the other hand, the very diffuseness of a crack trade organized through hundreds of competing gang sets and smalltime dealers, while it belies the demonic power that the gangbusters would attribute to it, also defies all efforts to deliver the decisive 'knockout' blow. In the ghetto itself there are hundreds of independent rock house franchises, each turning over (according to LAPD estimates) about $5000 per day ($25,000 on welfare and social security check days). The constant attrition of such outlets to LAPD raids (like the one Nancy Reagan used as a media picnic) has become an ordinary business cost. Moreover if Levant's estimate of 10,000 gang members making their livelihood from the drug trade is anywhere near correct, then crack really is the employer of last resort in the ghetto's devastated Eastside – the equivalent of several large auto plants or several hundred MacDonalds.[112]

Of course this is 'reindustrialization' through disease and the redistribution of poverty. When twenty-five-dollar rock hit the streets of L.A. in volume during 1984–5, hospital and police statistics registered the cataclysmic impact: doubling of emergency room admissions for cocaine trauma, 15 per cent of newborns in public hospitals diagnosed drug-addicted, quintupling of juvenile arrests for coke-dealing, and so on.[113] It is important to remember that crack is not simply cheap cocaine – the poor man's version of the glamor drug stuffed up the noses of the marina and country club crowd – but a far more lethal form. Whether or not it is actually the most addictive substance known to science, as originally claimed, it remains an absolute commodity enslaving its consumers, 'the most devastating of all the monster drugs to afflict any American adolescent generation thus far'.[114]

For this epidemic bred out of despair – which, like heroin, inevitably turns users into petty dealers – the only treatment on demand is jail. In Los Angeles County, where infant mortality is soaring and the County trauma-treatment network has collapsed, it is not surprising that medical care for crack addiction – which experts agree requires long-term treatment in a therapeutic community – is generally unavailable. Thus Skid Row, Downtown's nightmarish 'Nickle', has the largest single concentration of crack addicts – young and old – in the city, but not a single treatment facility. Wealthy Pasadena is fighting crack-based gang activity in its Northwest ghetto with its own version of the HAMMER, including humiliating strip-searches in the field and a drug-tenant eviction policy, without spending a single cent on drug rehabilitation.[115] The examples could be depressingly multiplied, as drug treatment is filed in the same bottom drawer of forgotten liberal nostrums as youth employment or gang counseling.

In the meantime gang members have become the Stoic philosophers of this cold new reality. The appearance of crack has given the Crip subculture a terrible, almost irresistible allure. Which is not simply to reduce the gang phenomenon, now or in the past, to mere economic determinism. Since the 1840s when tough young Irishmen invented the modern street gang in the slums of the Bowery, Five Points and Paradise Alley (making the Bowery Boys and the Dead Rabbits just as dreaded as the Crips and Bloods are today), gang bonding has been a family for the forgotten, a total solidarity (like national or religious fervor) closing out other empathies and transmuting self-hatred into tribal rage. But the Crips and Bloods – decked out in Gucci T-shirts and expensive Nike airshoes, ogling rock dealers driving by in BMWs – are also authentic creatures of the age of Reagan. Their world view, above all, is formed of an acute awareness of what is going down on the Westside, where gilded youth, practice the insolent indifference and avarice that are also forms of street violence. Across the spectrum of runaway youth consumerism and the impossible fantasies of personal potency and immunity, youth of all classes and colors are grasping at undeferred gratification – even if it paves the way to assured self-destruction.

There is little reason to believe that the crack economy or the new gang culture will stop growing, whatever the scale of repression, or stay confined to Southcentral Los Angeles. Although the epicenters remain in the ghetto zones of hardcore youth unemployment – like Watts–Willowbrook, the Athens district, or the Escher-like maze of the Crenshaw 'Jungle' – the gang mystique has spread (as Bakeer documents in *CRIPS*) into middle-class Black areas, where parents are close to panic, or vigilantism.

Meanwhile, as Southcentral itself undergoes an epochal (and surprisingly peaceful) ethnic transition from Black to new immigrant Latino (Mexican and Central American), the kids of the *mojados* look jealously at the power and notoriety of Cripdom.[116] In the absence of any movement towards social justice, the most explosive social contradiction in Los Angeles may become the blocked mobility of these children of the new immigrants. As a 1989 UCLA study revealed, poverty is increasing faster amongst Los Angeles Latinos, especially youth, than any other urban group in the United States.[117] While their parents may still measure the quality of life by old-country standards, the iron rations of Tijuana or Ciudad Guatemala, their children's self-image is shaped by the incessant stimuli of

L.A. consumer culture. Trapped in deadend low-wage employment, amid what must otherwise appear as a demi-paradise for white youth, they too are looking for shortcuts and magical paths to personal empowerment.

Thus they also enter the underground economy with guns blazing. Some of the Black gangs (especially the Eastside Crips) have accommodated the aspirations of the new immigrants by integrating Latino members (the police estimate at least 1,000 of these) or licensing crack-dealing franchises. In the MacArthur Park area, on the other hand, the upstart Salvadoreans of Mara Savatrucha have had to fight a bloody war against the established power of the 18th Street Gang – the largest and fastest growing Chicano gang which threatens to become the Crips of East L.A. But simultaneously in East L.A., and throughout all the barrios old and new, traditional gang topography is being radically redrawn by the emergence of a myriad of micro-gangs, more interested in drug sales territories than neighborhood turf in the old-fashioned sense.

Aside from the 230 Black and Latino gangs which the LAPD have identified in the Los Angeles area, there are also 81 Asian gangs, and their numbers are also rapidly growing. In Long Beach gangs of wild, parentless Cambodian boatchildren terrorize their elders and steal their hoarded gold. While the Filipino Satanas favor Chicano gang styles, the role-model of the Viet Crips (supposedly robbery specialists) is obvious. In Pasadena some Chinese high-school dropouts – unwilling to spend lifetimes as busboys and cooks – ambushed and killed a carload of crack DEA agents, before they too were cut down by a vengeful posse of nearly a hundred cops.[118]

These particular contradictions are rising fast, along a curve asymptotic with the mean ethos of the age. In a post-liberal society, with the gangplanks pulled up and compassion strictly rationed by the Federal deficit and the Jarvis Amendment, where a lynchmob demagogue like William Bennett reigns as 'drug czar' – is it any wonder that poor youths are hallucinating on their own desperado 'power trips'? In Los Angeles there are too many signs of approaching helter-skelter: everywhere in the inner city, even in the forgotten poor-white boondocks with their zombie populations of speed-freaks, gangs are multiplying at a terrifying rate, cops are becoming more arrogant and trigger-happy, and a whole generation is being shunted toward some impossible Armageddon.

INNER-CITY CROSSWORD
Temple-Beaudry district

NOTES

1. Story by Louis Sahagun and Carol McGraw, *Times*, 7 April 1989.
2. *Times*, 3 April 1988.
3. 'The commitment of the chief seemed to rub off on his officers, several of whom said arrests were being made for infractions that might normally be overlooked. In the east San Fernando Valley, a defiant 14-year-old wearing a Fred Flintstone T-shirt – and not much else – was booked on suspicion of indecent exposure after he 'mooned' a passing patrol car.' (Ibid.)
4. *Times*, 3 April and 15 May 1988; *Herald-Examiner*, 3 April 1988.
5. Mayor James Van Horn of Artesia quoted in Stanley Meisler, 'Nothing Works', *Los Angeles Times Magazine*, 7 May 1989.
6. *Times*, 6 April 1988.
7. Ibid., 27 May 1979; 4 November 1988.
8. Ibid., 29 February 1988; 4 May 1990.
9. Ibid., 12 April 1988; New York *Times*, 25 November 1988.
10. Ibid., 3 April 1988.
11. Ibid., 23 November 1978.
12. Ibid., 21 September and 6 October 1979; 2 June 1980.
13. Ibid., 28 March 1988. Fifteen people were reported to have died from the controversial police chokehold.
14. Ibid., 8 May 1988.
15. *Herald-Examiner*, 3 April 1988; *Times*, 6 April 1988.
16. Ibid., 14 January 1990.
17. Ibid., 10 April and 8 May 1988.
18. The LAPD seems to relish the upswing in inter-gang violence. In late 1986, eighteen months before GRATS and the HAMMER, Chief Gates lashed out at Community Youth Gang Services (CYGS) for trying to arrange a truce between forty local gangs. Steve Valdiva, the embattled director of the tiny agency, in turn struck back at the LAPD's uncompromising bellicosity and its characterization of all gang kids as 'stone killers'. (See Los Angeles *Sentinel*, 1 January 1987.)
19. Ibid., 5 April and 8 May 1988.
20. Joe Dominick, 'Police Power: Why No One Can Control the LAPD', *L.A. Weekly*, 16–22 February 1990; my intepretation of events here relies upon conversations (1988–89) with Michael Zinzun, the founder of the Coalition against Police Abuse, who expressed his dismay over the new reluctance of civil libertarians to defend the rights of Black youth.
21. Interviewed on CBS's 'Face the Nation' in 1985, Chief Gates called Mayor Goode of Philadelphia a '*hero*' for his bombing of the MOVE headquarters – an action that resulted in the incineration of a dozen men, women and children, as well as the destruction of a residential square-block.
22. *Times*, 5 and 6 January, 23 June, 26 July, 8 and 26 August, 2 September (chronology) 1989.
23. Ibid., 26 and 29 August, 2 September 1989; see also Dominick.
24. Ibid., 22 December 1988.
25. Ibid., 13 and 19 January 1989.
26. Ibid., 19 February 1989.
27. Ibid., op-ed, 2 May 1988.
28. Ibid., 5 January 1973.
29. Testimony, Charles Zunker, West Bureau CRASH and Maurice Malone, West Los Angeles Division, LAPD – in ACLU files.
30. The Inland Empire city of Fontana (the subject of chapter 7) also attempted to outlaw 'gang colors' until a profound legal mind pointed out that two-thirds of the American flag (i.e. the red and blue) would become illegal.

31. See 'People of the State of California vs. Playboy Gangster Crips, an unincorporated association, Does 1 through 300, inclusive. Complaint for Temporary Restraining Order and for Preliminary and Permanent Injunction to Abate Public Nuisance' – in ACLU files.

32. *Times*, 17 May 1988. While rejecting the 'overly broad' demands of Hahn's suit, the Superior Court did ratify a subsequent specification of the complaint to 23 named, 'hardcore gang individuals'.

33. Ibid., op-ed, 2 May 1988.

34. Ibid., 1 November 1987.

35. Ibid., 3 April 1988; see also Dominick. Reiner's merciless zeal against gang misdemeanors contrasts with his laxity toward possible police felonies. The Coalition for Police Accountability was formed in 1989 to dramatize the DA's failure to file charges in sixteen cases since 1985 involving Blacks or Latinos unlawfully killed by sheriffs or police. (Ibid., 12 July 1989.)

36. *Times*, 12 June, 22 August, and 7 September 1988. In August 1988 the US Attorney's office in Los Angeles also assigned DEA agents to a special anti-gang taskforce.

37. Ibid., 6 January and 21 April 1989. According to Lockyer, STEP was the *80th* piece of anti-gang legislation passed by the California Legislature.

38. Ibid., 2 and 10 May 1989.

39. Ibid., 31 May and 10 June 1989.

40. Ibid., 2 April 1988; 19 January and 23 February 1989; 23 January 1990. Kemp's war on drug families was prefigured by the 'tripod' program that former Councilmember Pat Russell and City Attorney Hahn invented to rid the maze-like apartment neighborhood in the Crenshaw area known as the 'Jungle' of gang-based drug-dealing. One leg of the 'Tripod' was landlord responsibility for the immediate eviction of anyone *arrested* for drug charges – a policy, like Kemp's, that not only punishes entire households but also throws away the constitutional pre-trial presumption of innocence. (See ibid., 12 February 1987.)

41. Ibid., 8 May 1988.

42. Jackson later was videotaped by network television while being abused by a Long Beach cop – an incident that led to a much-needed housecleaning in that notoriously racist department. Continuing to challenge L.A.-style apartheid in a variety of contexts, Jackson has become a Black folk hero.

43. Not that the average inner-city youth is ever likely to see the inside of any Southern California theme park – quite apart from racism, the average family of four admission to the five major centers is now $75. (See *Times*, Calendar, 19 June 1988; ACLU files for cases of discrimination.)

44. Ibid., 11 April 1990.

45. Interview with Carmelo Alvarez of *El Centro*; Douglas Sadownick, 'Tchaikovsky and the Gang', *Times*, Calendar, 19 June 1988; ibid., 12 April 1989.

46. Interview with Joan Howarth. One perverse byproduct of 'School Buy' is that new kids transferring into L.A. schools from out-of-town are now regularly ostracized as possible 'narks'.

47. *Times*, 2 February and 27 April 1988; interview with Howarth.

48. *Times*, 22 April 1990.

49. Ibid., 22 April and 3 May 1990.

50. Cf. Report of the Criminal Justice Research Program quoted in the Oakland *Tribune*, 3 March 1987; James Ridgeway, 'Prisons in Black', *Village Voice*, 19 September 1988; the Legislative Analyst's summary of the proposed New Prison Construction Bond Act of 1990 in the 1990 State Primary Ballot Pamphlet.

51. Miles Corwin, 'High-Tech Facility Ushers in New Era of State Prisons', *Times*, 1 May 1990.

52. Caldwell quoted in Ishmael Reed, 'Living at Ground Zero', *Image*, 13 March 1988, p. 15; Jackson quoted in *Times*, 18 May 1988.

53. Howarth interview, 16 March 1988.

54. *Times*, 12 June 1988.

55. Yaroslavsky questioned at public meeting, February 1988.

56. *Times*, 6 April 1988.

57. Ibid., 28 March 1990.

58. Ishmael Reed, pp. 12, 13, 15.

59. Interview by Ken Kelly in *San Francisco Focus*, March 1988, p. 100.

60. *Guardian* (New York), 18 May 1988.

61. *Eagle*, 20 March 1946 (Fremont), 25 July 1946 (Manual Arts), 30 January 1947 (Canoga Park), 20 March 1947 (Fremont), 25 September 1947 (Fremont), and 6 October 1949 (John Adams). It should be emphasized that this partial list includes only major incidents or 'riots'.

62. J.K. Obatala, 'The Sons of Watts', Los Angeles *Times*, *West Magazine*, 13 August 1972.

63. Quoted in Sophia Spalding, 'The Constable Blunders: Police Abuse in Los Angeles's Black and Latino Communities, 1945–1965', UCLA, Department of Urban Planning, 1989, unpublished, p. 7.

64. Joseph Woods, *The Progressives and the Police: Urban Reform and the Professionalization of the Los Angeles Police*, PhD thesis, Dept. of History, UCLA, 1973, p. 443.

65. Joe Dominick quotes Chief Parker warning a 1965 television audience: 'It is estimated that by 1970 45% of the metropolitan area of Los Angeles will be Negro; if you want any protection for your home and family . . . you're going to have to get in and support a strong police department. If you don't do that, come 1970, God help you.'

66. Spalding, p. 11.

67. Cf. Robert Conot, *Rivers of Blood, Years of Darkness*, New York 1967, pp. 114–19 (on 'junior criminal' theory); and *Frontier*, July 1958, pp. 5–7 (on Group Guidance); and October 1965, p. 9 (on Parker's elimination of gang counseling); Woods, pp. 494–5, 611(n 159).

68. Conot, pp. 97–8; California Advisory Committee to the United States Commission on Civil Rights, *Report on California: Police–Minority Group Relations in Los Angeles and the San Francisco Bay Area*, August 1963, pp. 3–19.

69. Ibid., p. 101; *Times*, 22 October 1972.

70. Obtala.

71. See Robert Fogelson, 'White on Black: Critique of the McCone Commission Report on the Los Angeles Riots', in Fogelson, ed., *Mass Violence in America*, New York 1969, pp. 120–21.

72. Conot, p. 244; the oral history project associated with 'Watts '65: To the Rebellion and Beyond' organized by the Southern California Library for Social Studies and Research is gathering new eye-witness testimony about the Rebellion.

73. *Times*, 19 March and 23 July 1972 (renewal of gang warfare in 1972 contrasted to post-Watts riot period). James O'Toole argues that until the Watts Rebellion politicized the young male gang leadership, 'there was no indigenous political activity within the ghetto except for the matriarch-preacher organizations'. He also claims that the Black vote was 'packaged and delivered from the outside' by middle-class Democratic activists loyal to Jesse Unruh. See *Watts and Woodstock: Identity and Culture in the United States and South Africa*, New York 1973, pp. 87, 89, 91.

74. Obatala; personal reminiscences.

75. Eazy-E quoted in *Times*, Calendar, 2 April 1989.

76. *Times*, 23 July 1972.

77. Donald Bakeer, *CRIPS: The Story of the L.A. Street Gang from 1971–1985*, xeroxed, Los Angeles 1987, pp. 12–13.

78. Bob Baker in the *Times*, 26 June 1988.

79. Ibid.

80. Ibid., 24 December 1972.

81. Ibid.

82. On the display of Crip insignia during the Monrovia riots, see ibid., (San Gabriel Valley edition), 2 April 1972. Seven months after the riots (during which one Black 17-year-old had his eye shot out by whites), a 13-year-old Black child was found hung in his cell in the city jail. (Ibid., 16 November 1972.)

83. Quoted in ibid., 10 April 1988.
84. Ibid., 15 December 1972.
85. For example, at the 1988 'End Barrio War' Conference sponsored by Father Luis Valbuena in Pacoima, 24 Valley gangs demanded less police harassment, and more job opportunity and youth recreation as a solution to increasing teenage violence. (see ibid., 7 December 1988.)
86. Ibid., 'Watts, 10 Years Later: A Special Report', 23 March 1975.
87. Ron Curran, 'Malign Neglect: The Roots of an Urban War Zone', *L.A. Weekly*, 30 December to 5 January 1989, p. 2. Also see the Economic Justice Policy Group, 'Policy Memorandum – Economic State of the City', presented to the City Council, 25 January 1990, p. 4.
88. See Mark Ridley-Thomas, 'California Commentary', *Times*, 29 January 1990. Ridley-Thomas argues that neither the 'office-based' nor 'shopping center-based' models of community redevelopment can compensate for a healthy industrial base.
89. California, Joint Committee on the State's Economy and the Senate Committee on Government Organization, *Problems and Opportunities for Job Development in Urban Areas of Persistent Unemployment*, Sacramento 1982, pp. 29, 50, 58, 94, 108, 111, 115.
90. For a typology of contemporary industrial regimes, see Alain Lipietz, *Mirages and Miracles*, London 1987.
91. This is the official estimate of the church-sponsored South Central Organizing Committee in 1988. For Watts, which has been more regularly surveyed than other areas of the community, youth joblessness (16–24 years old) has stayed near the 50 per cent mark since the early 1970s. (See data collected by UCLA's Institute of Industrial Relations)
92. *Times*, 16 May 1985. Hundreds of women in the projects who desperately wanted to work were unable to because of the absence of childcare.
93. 1983 L.A. Roundtable for Children; Policy Analysis for California Education, *The Conditions of Children in California*, Sacramento 1989.
94. *Times*, 19 April 1988; Paul Bullock, *Youth Training and Employment from the New Deal to the New Federalism*, Institute of Industrial Relations, UCLA, 1985, p. 78.
95. Quoted in ibid., 30 January 1981.
96. Ibid., 30 January 1989.
97. *Times*, 3 August 1988.
98. Ibid., 28 June, 18 October, and 25 November 1987; M.J. Wilcove, 'The Dilemma of L.A. Schools', *L.A. Weekly*, 6–12 November 1987.
99. Cf. *Times*, 20 March 1988; and Jack Foley, "Leisure Rights" Policies for Los Angeles Urban Impact Parks', paper presented to the People for Parks Conference, Griffith Park, 4 February 1989.
100. Cf. Paul Bullock, *Youth in the Labor Market*, PhD, UCLA, 1972; *Youth Training*; and interview, 1983 (Southern California Library for Social Research). U.C. Berkeley sociologist Troy Duster has estimated that Black youth unemployment nationally was *four times higher* in 1983 than in 1960. (See 'Social Implicatons of the 'New' Black Urban Underclass', *Black Scholar*, May–June 1988, p. 3.)
101. New York 1986, p.189.
102. Louis Kraar, 'The Drug Trade', *Fortune*, 20 June 1988, p. 29.
103. 'Murderous Colombia', *New York Review of Books*, 20 November 1986, p. 35.
104. 'Cartel L.A.' series, *Herald-Examiner*, 28 August to 1 September 1989. Also see the *Times*'s account of the 1989 Justice Department report (a 'Dun and Bradstreet primer') – 4 August 1989.
105. The *Herald-Examiner* reassured its readers that 'the 63,000 Colombians living in the Los Angeles area do not all work in cocaine distribution cells' – 'only 6,000'.
106. Ibid., 28 August 1987.
107. *Times*, 30 March 1989; Evan Maxwell 'Gold, Drugs and Clean Cash', *Los Angeles Times Magazine*, 18 February 1990.
108. *Times*, 15 May and 12 June 1988; 4 August 1989.

109. Ibid.
110. Malcolm Klein and Cheryl Maxson quoted in ibid., 8 September 1988.
111. Quoted in ibid.
112. Ibid. Earnings of the youthful employees of the illicit drug industry have been vastly exaggerated by the police and media, with the inadvertent or deliberate effect of discouraging employment schemes as a realistic alternative to repression. Judging from the most detailed study available (based on extensive surveys amongst the street trade in Washington DC), youth are more likely to make $700 per month, not per day as usually depicted. See Jack Katz, op-ed, ibid., 21 March 1990.
113. Ibid., 25 November 1984; 13 February 1989.
114. Novelist Claude Brown quoted in ibid., 17 May 1988.
115. Pasadena *Star-News*, 17 September 1989.
116. The Black population of Southcentral has fallen by 30% since 1980 as families flee crime and economic decay for Inglewood, the Inland Empire or even back to the South. The Latino population, on the other hand, has increased at least 200% (Mayan Indians now live in the Jordan Downs projects) and Black youth are suddenly minorities in the four major high schools. The old Slauson turf of Fremont High, for example, was 96% Black in 1980; it is now 71% Latino. (*Times*, 30 March 1990.)
117. See Paul Ong (project director), *The Widening Divide: Income Inequality and Poverty in Los Angeles*, UCLA, June 1989.
118. *Times*, 1 September 1988. Inter-ethnic gang warfare, surprisingly, remains rare in the gang-saturated Los Angeles inner city. One of the insidious deceits of the film *Colors* is its portrayal of a Black gang attacking Chicanos. Except for an outbreak in the Oakwood section of Venice in the late 1970s (which gang members blamed on the instigation of the LAPD), such a thing has never happened. On the other hand, antagonisms have mounted between Black youth and Asian adults. There have been bloody exchanges between Korean storekeepers and Black teenagers, and in May 1988 there was a pitched battle between Cambodians and local Bloods at the Pueblo del Rio housing project. The Bloods threw Molotov cocktails, while Cambodian men replied with fusillades from M1s and AK47s. (Ibid., 13 May 1988.)

CHAPTER SIX

NEW CONFESSIONS

Some teenagers were watching the Pope make a fast change in a fire station from his limousine to a more famous vehicle. As the white Popemobile sped away with its gold wheel rims flashing, they gasped 'Wow, just like Batman!' All along the route, vendors sold T-shirts boasting: 'I Gotta a Peek atta da Pope'. Initially this was no problem, as only thin crowds turned out in Anglo neighborhoods or Koreatown (where fundamentalist hecklers were lined up to denounce the Polish 'Antichrist'). But once the motorcade turned into the Westlake district, the largest Central-American neighborhood in the United States, the scene was dramatically different.

Suddenly the sidewalks were packed ten to fifteen deep with the faithful who had been waiting hours for his arrival. Refugees from the killing fields of El Salvador or Guatemala, the so-called 'foot people' of the Reagan era – many had borne witness, as lay activists or members of the *communidades de base*, to the persecution of the church of liberation in Central America. Now, from MacArthur Park to La Placita, in the tenement neighborhoods on the edge of the Los Angeles garment district, they were gathered in cheering crowds as dense and fervid as those he had encountered in his triumphal procession through the Polish-American neighborhoods of Chicago. While most Anglo Catholics stayed home in the suburbs, watching the spectacle on television, the Central American and Mexican immigrants flocked to his side while the bells tolled over the little church of Nuestra Senora La Reina de Los Angeles de Porciuncula.

A CATHOLIC RESTORATION?

The pueblo of the Queen of the Angels is becoming a Catholic town again. A century ago, in the great boom of the late 1880s, Catholic Los Angeles was submerged by a wave of Protestant immigration from the Midwest. By the turn of the century boosters were boasting that it was 'the ideal Protestant city', 'a bulwark against immigrant Papism'. Nearly 90 per cent of its office-holders were voluntarist Protestants; its religious life was dominated by fire-breathing fundamentalists like 'Fighting Bob' Schuler (a Ku Klux Klan supporter) and Aimée Semple McPherson. The so-called 'Fifth Great Revival' that created modern Pentecostalism began in a Downtown Los Angeles church, and each decade saw the emergence of new Southern

California inflections of Protestantism, from the Angelus Temple to the Crystal Cathedral. Every census from 1920 to 1960 recorded that Los Angeles had the highest proportion of native-born white Protestants of the largest American cities.[1]

Now the pendulum is swinging back. In the early 1980s the Archdiocese of Los Angeles surpassed Chicago to become the largest Catholic congregation in the USA. With an estimated 3.4 million parishioners (growing at 1,000 per week), the archdiocese accounts for at least 65 per cent of 'communicant members of all religions' in Los Angeles, Ventura and Santa Barbara counties (according to 1980 data). That is to say, there are more than twenty Catholics for each adherent of the next largest religious group (in Los Angeles County, the Church of Latter Day Saints). Indeed the archdiocese is larger than the *national* memberships of either the Episcopalians or Presbyterians, or, for that matter, any but four of America's national Protestant denominations.[2]

Moreover the 8,762 square mile, 3-county archdiocese, with its 300 parishes, 3,400 clerical and 12,000 lay employees, has a massive and far-reaching institutional presence, comparable to one of California's largest corporations or city governments. It administers the second largest school system in the state (after L.A. Unified) with 275 elementary schools and 71 high schools, enrolling 314,000 students. It also operates ten cemeteries and five colleges, as well as sixteen major hospitals treating more than a million patients per year. In addition the archdiocese is one of the state's largest landowners. Besides churches, rectories and parking lots, it controls, through one of its seven chartered corporations (Roman Catholic Archbishop, Inc.), more than 900 parcels of local real estate worth several billion dollars.[3]

More significant than sheer size, however, is the multifaceted strategic position of the archdiocese. The suburban church in Southern California has long been one of the Vatican's most difficult frontiers in the struggle between traditional moral dogma and modern individualism. Now the Los Angeles archdiocese is also a cutting edge in geo-political controversies over the 'Latin Americanization' of world and American Catholicism. The renaissance of Catholicism in Southern California is a byproduct of the irresistible demographics of Latino immigration and family size (what the Quebecois call 'the revenge of the cradle'). Over the last generation the

A MISSIONARY CHURCH

archdiocese has become nearly two-thirds Mexican and Central American in ethnic origin, with more than a million Latino Catholics added during the 1980s alone. Yet the archdiocese also retains hundreds of thousands of affluent Anglos. This dramatic mingling of the first and third worlds makes it a laboratory for the church's cautious experiments in ethnic accommodation and power-sharing. At the same time, it is also the major battlefield, north of the Rio Bravo, in an increasingly high-stake competition between Catholicism and aggressive Spanish-language evangelicalism.

In addition the archdiocese is a major force shaping the 'post-Anglo', poly-ethnic Los Angeles of the year 2000. Three aspects of its role are particularly important. First, there is the aggressive leadership of Archbishop Mahony. Only fifty-three years old, he is likely to remain in Saint Vibiana's Cathedral until his retirement in the year 2011. Although occasionally seen demonstrating against repression in Central America, his public persona is mainly identified with the moral backlash against gender and sexual equality. In blessing 'Operation Rescue' while denouncing 'safe sex', the ambitious Archbishop has become a rising star of the national Right to Life movement, as well as a favorite of Vatican hardliners. And, to the dismay of most of his early progressive supporters, the former champion of the farmworkers' union and first chairman of California's Agricultural Labor Relations Board, has also become an increasingly strident opponent of organized labor, turning a small-scale dispute over the unionization of Catholic gravediggers into a full-fledged confrontation with the statewide labor movement. Both his critics and admirers within the church now compare him to the late Cardinal McIntyre, whose autocratic regime suffocated the archdiocese during the Cold War years and led to the exodus of many liberal Catholics.

Secondly, a Catholic power structure – combining Mahony's spiritual authority with the economic clout of leading laymen – plays an important, if discreet, role in city politics and land-use decision-making. The *éminence grise* of Richard Riordan – investment banker, land developer, city commissioner, lawyer for the archdiocese, and intimate of Mahony – raises a number of especially intriguing questions about the traffic in influence between the hierarchy and the city's 'invisible government' of developers and bankers.

Thirdly, as the dominant organizer of community life in the city's barrios, the church unavoidably assumes a central role in the Latinos' search for power. It will be a major arbiter of social and political realignments between old and new status quos. Yet the church itself is a contested terrain between different strategies of empowerment. On the one hand, Mahony's 1987 'Latino Aid Plan', together with single-issue campaigns organized by episcopally approved community groups, offer gradualist and legalistic approaches to Latino advancement in church and society. On the other hand, Father Luis Olivares and his fellow Claretian and Jesuit priests Downtown represent Liberation Theology's 'preferential option for the poor', emphasizing direct action in favor of the oppressed, even when this defies secular law.

Although the debate between Mahony and Olivares is rooted in local circumstances, many Catholics believe that it reflects global stakes – what the late Penny Lernoux called 'the struggle for the soul of the contemporary church ... between the liberationists and the restorationists'.[4] Not surprisingly, a portrait of Zapata and a quotation from Sandino hang over Olivares's modest desk, while Pope John Paul II smiles over the Archbishop's elegant writing table. It is the interplay of these local and international dimensions – the simultaneous salience of neighborhood organizing and church geopolitics – that makes the archdiocese perhaps the most fascinating institution in Southern California.

A MISSION ON THE RIM OF THE WORLD

As the local branch of 'the oldest surviving complex organization in the world', the contemporary archdiocese needs to be first situated in its own, unique historical context.[5] The Catholic legacy of Los Angeles is preserved in the archives at Mission San Fernando del Rey, just outside the small city of the same name, a few blocks from where Richie Valens grew up. The archive is a building of unexpected opulence, containing not only musty baptismal ledgers and parish accounts, but also part of the great Doheny library and priceless ecclesiastical treasures, including heirlooms of the Mexican church brought out of the country during the 'Cristero Revolt' of the 1920s by its fleeing bishops. Saturated in a suprisingly baroque ambience, the archives have for many decades supported the labors of Monsignor Francis Weber, keeper of the keys to archdiocesan history.

Unfortunately the Monsignor's own efforts (which take up an entire shelf) consist mainly of voluminous, often repetitious, anecdotes. A protégé and defender of the late Cardinal McIntyre, and openly skeptical of the 'Latino orientation' of the present Archbishop, the Monsignor has devoted much of his life to sketching idealized vignettes of the early California church. Although the forced labor system of the original Franciscan missions was tantamount to slavery (as California Indian leaders have recently reminded the Church), Monsignor Weber – a leading crusader for the canonization of Father Serra – defends a vision of gentle padres and their happy neophytes. It is an image drawn not so much from his archives, as from the pages of Helen Hunt Jackson's famous 1880s novel, *Ramona*: a romance that generations of tourists and white Angelenos have confused with real history.

It is no accident that the church still relies upon the 'Mission Myth' as a buffer between itself and its past. Despite its precedence in the order of Southern California's colonization (indeed the small, secular pueblo of Los Angeles was founded by Bourbon bureaucrats to counter the growing danger of a Franciscan theocracy), the church has never become fully indigenous. To this day it retains a sense of being a missionary outpost ('on the rim of the Western World') with a hierarchy drawn from outside its majority communities. In the eighteenth and nineteenth centuries the California church (divided between north and south in 1853) was dominated by a Catalan dynasty: Serra (Mallorca), Alemany, Amat and Mora. In the twentieth century, from the appointment of Bishop Thomas Conaty in 1903 to the current regime of Archbishop Mahoney, the modern archdiocese has been led by Irishmen or their American descendants. No one of Mexican or Latin American origin has ever risen higher than the current auxiliary bishops, Juan Arzube (appointed 1971) and Armando X. Ochoa (1986).

Given their historic lack of power in the archdiocese, Latino parishioners have been long accustomed to variable doses of neglect, paternalism and accommodation. Archbishop John Cantwell (1917–47), a Limerick man like many of his priests, is officially celebrated for pioneering the modern mission to the Spanish-speaking. During the 1920s and early 1930s he provided refuge for the exiled Mexican episcopate (at one point thirty-six bishops and archbishops), and established fifty new parishes for Mexican immigrants. He inaugurated the annual Corpus Christi procession on the Eastside, from Our Lady of Guadalupe to La Soledad, that for many years rivaled Cinco de Mayo in community importance; he was the first North American churchman to make the pilgrimage to the shrine of the Virgin of Guadalupe. Yet his attitude to his half million Mexican parishioners was characterized by unwavering condescension ('the simple people of God') and entrenched hostility to the community's progressive and nationalist currents.[6]

In the 1920s the archdiocese became a major support base for the Cristero revolt: a church-instigated guerrilla movement of Catholic peasants in the central plateaus of Mexico. In a civil war without mercy on either side, Cristeros assassinated secular school teachers and blew up passenger trains, while troops of the 'Antichrist' (President Plutarcho Calles) executed priests and their peasant parishioners. The defeat of the Cristeros in 1928 only hardened Cantwell's antipathy to the revolutionary-nationalist Mexican state. Following another wave of clerical expulsions from Sonora in 1934, he organized the largest demonstration in Los Angeles history: a giant procession of 40,000 people, many of them Cristero refugees, chanting 'Viva Cristo Rey' and marching behind banners that denounced the 'atheistic regimes in Mexico City and Moscow'.[7]

Some contemporary critics smelled oil as well as incense in Cantwell's lobbying for US intervention on behalf of Mexican Catholics (Washington did move military forces to the border). The archdiocese's most generous endower – the builder of St. John's Seminary – was oil millionaire Edward Doheny, a papal count and the richest Catholic in Los Angeles. He is probably best remembered in American history for the $100,000 bribe that put ex-Secretary of the Interior Fall in jail during the Teapot Dome scandal in 1921. But Doheny was also the original wildcatter of the Tampico oil fields, and, together with his partner Harry Sinclair, the biggest individual foreign investor in Mexico. He had an obvious personal stake in a Cristero victory or a Marine landing.

Cantwell's politics were nothing if not consistent. Local Catholic Action rallies through the 1930s also applauded Franco and Mussolini, while the Legion of Decency denounced celluloid immorality in Hollywood.[8] The archdiocesan newspaper *Tydings* poured vitriol on the New Deal and red-baited local political progressives. As a result, Catholic

Los Angeles – already at the losing end of its *Kulturkampf* with hegemonic local Protestantism – isolated itself as well from New Dealers, intellectuals, the Jewish community and CIO trade unionists.

TRUE CONFESSIONS
OF CARDINAL McINTYRE

Hopes that Cantwell's backward-looking thirty-year reign would be followed by a liberal succession were dashed in 1948 when Pope Pius XII appointed Francis McIntyre to Los Angeles. Chancellor to the 'American Pope', New York's all-powerful Cardinal Spellman, McIntyre has been described by Spellman's biographer as 'a mean-spirited, vindictive man' who employed 'gestapo tactics' against pro-labor priests in the New York archdiocese. 'The train that carried McIntyre to the West Coast was cynically called "the Freedom Train" by New York priests who were glad to be rid of him.'[9]

Consecrated as Western America's first Cardinal in 1953, McIntyre used his rising power to witchhunt suspected liberals in the hierarchy. Thus when Bishop James Shannon of Minneapolis dared to criticize McCarthyism, McIntyre attacked him as 'an incipient heretic' and hounded him into resignation.[10] He also thoroughly 'Spellmanized' Los Angeles, silencing moderate voices and mobilizing the archdiocese against every liberal cause in Southern California. His paper, *Tydings*, became particularly notorious as a pulpit of McCarthyism with red-baiting fulminations drawn from the Hearst press and the fringes of the John Birch Society.[11]

As a holy cold warrior, however, McIntyre was only following in the well-trodden footsteps of Spellman and others. His individual genius was rather as an ecclesiastical entrepreneur who broke all records for school and church construction. Before the priesthood he had worked on Wall Street, and his business acumen, including his ruthlessness in labor relations, had been decisive in his meteoric rise in the New York chancery. In Los Angeles, at the height of the postwar suburban boom, when the incoming (mostly Anglo) Catholic population was 1,000 per week, McIntyre transformed his see into a huge development company – setting up seven major archdiocesan corporations and a dependent network of 'approved' contractors and vendors. He also successfully battled public education leaders to win tax exemption for his burgeoning parochical school system. It was this McIntyre – the spiritually hollow (he was dubbed 'His Emptiness' by his own priests) but financially shrewd and politically well-connected autocrat – whom John Gregory Dunne made the *éminence grise* of his novel about postwar Los Angeles Catholics, *True Confessions*.[12]

McIntyre's unbending authoritarianism went virtually unchallenged during the conformist 1950s. However, with the convocation of the Second Vatican Council in 1962, and John XXIII's program of modernization (*aggiornamento* or 'bringing up to date'), McIntyre – a diehard opponent of the reform process – found himself at the head of a gradually shrinking minority of conservative American bishops. Younger clergy, under the dual spell of Vatican II and the social protests of the 1960s, began to question McIntyre's autocracy and to confront his reactionary political positions.[13]

A particular source of contention was McIntyre's defense of L.A. Police Chief William Parker, a hated and feared figure in Black Los Angeles, but the apple of the Cardinal's eye. Parker was the most powerful Catholic in local government and incarnated the authoritarian virtues admired by McIntyre. When police racism was implicated in the Watts Rebellion of 1965, the Cardinal rallied to Parker, denouncing the rioters as 'inhuman, almost bestial'. *Tydings'* political columnist, George Kramer, added that reports of police abuse were only an 'old Communist canard'. This infuriated a young priest in a predominantly Black parish, Father William Dubay, who lashed out at McIntyre for his lifelong 'silence on racial injustice' and called upon the Pope to remove him. Although Dubay was immediately suspended, his views were echoed by an ad hoc group called Catholics United for Racial Equality (CURE).[14]

These were only opening skirmishes. In 1968 McIntyre split the archdiocese apart in a heavy-handed attempt to crush clerical liberalism. The highly esteemed teaching order of the Immaculate Heart of Mary had evolved in the middle sixties toward greater engagement in social issues, including the civil rights and anti-war movements. Although McIntyre initially focused his public condemnations against the Order's experiments with secular dress styles and new teaching methods, there was never any doubt that the real issue was their social activism. Cheered on by the political right, the Cardinal expelled the order from the archdiocesan schools. More than 25,000 outraged parishioners, in turn, signed a petition to the Pope requesting his intervention to protect the Order. Ultimately three hundred Immaculate Heart nuns – the majority of the Order – chose to become a lay community rather than accede to McIntyre's orders.

The purge of Immaculate Heart, as well as the archdiocese's entrenched opposition to Vatican II's liturgical and structural reforms, destroyed any common ground for compromise between McIntyre and progressive Catholics. As he became more isolated, the Cardinal – like the embattled dictator of a banana republic – resorted to increasingly paranoid surveillance and repression. Nolan Davis has described the tragic consequences: 'Scores of nuns and priests began to leave the religious life entirely, and an underground Church began to proliferate. Contributions to the established Church plummeted by 40 per cent.' McIntyre, who maintained an elaborate and highly effective spy network, fought back, sending priests and monsignors and others faithful to him in disguise into the homes of underground Catholics, armed with hidden tape recorders. Whenever a priest was caught conducting one of the liberalized masses, he was reported to the Cardinal. Scores of dissident priests and nuns were removed from their parishes, some exiled to McIntyre's favorite Siberia – Orange County. A visiting Italian Jesuit wrote to Rome that 'priests in Los Angeles . . . worked in an atmosphere of sheer terror'.[15]

Eventually a wing of the dissent overlapped with the Chicano power movement sweeping across California. As their turn came to protest the chancery's paternalism and neglect,[16] as well as its continuing support for the war in Vietnam, militant Eastside Catholics led by writer-lawyer Oscar Acosta (the celebrated 'Brown Buffalo') decided to confront McIntyre with non-violent, civil disobedience. On Christmas eve 1969, a hundred members of 'Católicos por la Raza' marched from Lafayette Park to the midnight mass at St. Basil's, 'McIntyre's $4 million "showcase" residence church on a ritzy stretch of Wilshire Boulevard'.[17] They were demanding an equal voice for Chicanos in the archdiocese, as well as full public disclosure of the chancery's financial wheeler-dealings. As the marchers commenced a prayer vigil on the steps they were attacked by off-duty sheriffs acting as McIntyre's ushers. In the general mêlée that followed, a police tactical alert was declared and the riot squad was called in. While 'the scene in the church vestibule was . . . of fist-swinging, pushing, screaming, and kicking', the Archbishop led the rest of the well-heeled congregation 'in singing *O Come, All Ye Faithful* in order to drown out the noise of protest'. In spite of mass arrests and police beatings, the protestors reappeared in greater numbers on Christmas Day with an angry picket line. For his part, McIntyre compared the demonstrators to 'the rabble at Christ's cruci- fixion', and, in an ultimate gesture of overweening paternalism, arranged a special mass of loyal Chicanos at the old church in the Plaza to pray for forgiveness for the demonstrators.[18]

But St. Basil's was strictly a pyrrhic victory for the Cardinal. The archdiocese was confused and demoralized from the succession of public quarrels and purges of oppositionists. McIntyre himself was in his mid- eighties and was no longer able to maintain his traditional fierce regimen. Above all the Vatican was weary of his intransigence and alarmed by the publicity given to the internecine struggles. Barely a month after the battle of St. Basil's, McIntyre bowed to pressure from Pope Paul VI and announced his retirement. His successor was Bishop Timothy Manning of Fresno.

THE QUIET MAN

A protégé of Archbishop Cantwell, the wiry, soft-brogued Manning, from Ballingeary, County Cork, had risen rapidly, becoming at thirty-six the youngest bishop in the USA in 1946. For the next quarter century, however, he languished under McIntyre's shadow, first as auxiliary, then as chan- cellor, until he received his own San Joaquin Valley diocese in 1967. His personality – usually described as 'moderate' or 'non-confrontational' – was a dramatic contrast to the imperious, intolerant McIntyre. Moreover, un- like his predecessor, Manning had genuine sympathy for dissidents, derived from his childhood experiences of Black-and-Tan brutality during Ireland's war of independence. One of his first acts as Archbishop was to support the right of young Catholics to become conscientious objectors against the war in Vietnam – something that had been anathema to McIntyre.

Manning came to power with a program of reforms aimed to undo the damage of McIntyre's last years and to win back the confidence of inner-city parishes and clergy. In direct repudiation of McIntyre's celebrity lifestyle, he moved his residence out of the Wilshire Boulevard area and back to St. Vibiana's Cathedral on Skid Row. He encouraged the archdiocese to catch up with Vatican II reforms by establishing a consultative priests' senate, and made a gesture toward ecumenicism (which McIntyre had derided) by becoming active in the Interreligious Council of Southern California headed by Rabbi Alfred Wolf.

Most importantly he began to redress the benign neglect of South-central and Eastside parishes. He levied a light tax on suburban parishes to pay for long-overdue improvements and repairs on inner-city churches and schools. Modifying McIntyre's previous insistence on compulsory 'Americanization', he introduced bilingual classes into parochial schools on the Eastside, popularized the liturgy with Spanish-language masses, and integrated the coverage of *Tydings* with new attention to Black and Latino affairs. On 9 February 1971, he nominated Ecuador-born Juan Arzurbe as Los Angeles's first (auxiliary) bishop of Latino origin.

Yet *anciens régimes* are not so easily, or peacefully, transformed. Despite the Los Angeles *Times*'s claim (in early 1972) that Manning had already 'revitalized the Church in Southern California, becoming renowned as one of the most socially progressive Catholic officials in America', the reality was somewhat different.[19] Unlike the Scrooge-like McIntyre who signed every check, Manning (elevated to Cardinal in 1973) had no aptitude for administration or finance. Bureaucratic authority in the archdiocese as a result devolved onto his conservative vicar-general, Monsignor Benjamin Hawkes, who exercised 'sweeping power' as a kind of 'shadow Cardinal'.[20] Most importantly, despite his tax on the suburbs and the appointment of a Latino auxiliary, Manning was unable to stop the hemorrhage of inner-city Catholics – both Black and Latino – that had begun during the 1960s.

The real issue remained empowerment versus paternalism. Eastside Catholics wanted something more substantial than mariachi masses. But Manning's own romanticized view of Irish–Mexican relations made it difficult for him to appreciate the urgency of Latino demands within the church. In a famous speech at McIntyre's installation in 1948, he had evoked instead a 'Celto-Californian' religious synthesis – a 'blend of green and brown, rain and sunshine, a perfect mating of two traditions of faith'.[21] He clung to this personal version of the 'Mission Myth' for the next forty years; since the fusion of cultures was 'perfect', he saw no incongruity in the continuation of Celtic leadership over an archdiocese that in the last year of his reign was nearly 70 per cent Latino. Despite the tactical appointment of Arzurbe, he inveighed vehemently against the 'theory that you have to have ethnic leaders' and controversially appointed a white as episcopal vicar to Los Angeles's Black community. Even faced with dramatic evidence of the success of Protestant evangelicalism on the Eastside, he confidently reassured an interviewer that 'all Latinos are really Catholic'. Yet on unguarded occasions the Cardinal would admit that he still thought of Los Angeles 'as a foreign mission . . . the rim of the Western World'.[22]

At once indecisive and paternalistic, Manning oversaw an interregnum (or 'low-key hiatus' in the words of his *Times* obituary),[23] not a real transition. Perhaps his greatest mistake was in failing to create consultative structures for his rapidly growing Latino parishes. One of the key Vatican II reforms most opposed by McIntyre had been the establishment of parish councils to implement the new goal of 'shared responsibility'. After five years of Manning's 'reforms', Los Angeles still lagged in last place amongst the large archdioceses with councils in only 12 per cent of local parishes as contrasted to 72 per cent nationally. And amongst the minority of parishes with councils, there was widespread criticism of their unrepresentative and sycophantic character.[24]

The laggard pace of Latino advancement sowed anger within the archdiocese and throughout the Southwest. In 1970 Latino priests formed PADRES (translated from Spanish as 'United Priests for Religious, Educational and Social Causes') to lobby for greater attention to Latino issues. When Bishop Leo Maher of San Diego announced in 1978 the formation of a new, predominantly Chicano diocese encompassing Riverside and San Bernardino counties, expectations were raised that one of three Southern California Latino auxiliaries – Juan Arzurbe or Manuel Moreno from Los Angeles, or Gil Chavez from San Diego (acting vicar for San Bernardino) – would be selected. Gossip heavily favored Arzurbe, the most senior of the Latino auxiliaries, whom Manning had elevated on the same day in 1971 as Bishop William Johnson – since 1976 the head of the spinoff diocese of Orange County.

Rome's decision, in consultation with Cardinal Manning, to award the new diocese instead to Philip Straling, an Anglo who spoke only halting Spanish, sparked an explosion. An *encuentro* of PADRES and Las Hermanas (Sisters) near Las Cruces, New Mexico, one hundred and fifty Latino clergy, including Archbishop Robert Sanchez of Santa Fe and Bishop Patricio Flores of El Paso, sent a letter to the Vatican's apostolic delegate in Washington, Archbishop Jean Jadot, protesting the Straling appointment 'as an insult to the Hispanic community of California and the country'. In the Inland Empire a series of mass demonstrations, organized by Armando Navarro of the Congress for United Communities, expressed 'anguish, indignation and outrage' – a sentiment echoed by such distinguished rally speakers as Cesar Chavez, State Senator Ruben Ayala and Bishop Chavez. At a conclave of the California hierarchy in Redlands in November, fifteen Latino lay representatives met with Cardinal Manning and several bishops. They demanded Latino bishops for majority Latino dioceses, with candidates drawn from the (more progressive) religious orders as well as the ordinary clergy, and lay participation in the nomination process. Maria Guillen, one of the Latino delegates (from St. Edward's Parish in Corona) later described the prelates' response as 'evasive, defensive, resistant, vague and trite . . . the ugly head of racism has won out.'[25]

Meanwhile throughout the parochial school system Latino and Black parents were complaining about the chancery's refusal to act against racist or physically abusive administrators and teachers. In 1982, three years before Manning's retirement, the long-festering Catholic school crisis exploded in Pico Riviera. Seventy-seven parents, calling themselves 'Parents for Christian Justice', filed a $3-million suit against the principal of St. Hilary's Elementary, Sister Urban Maureen Molitar, and the archdiocese, alleging systematic discrimination and physical/emotional abuse against Mexican students. They claimed that their children had been punched, had had their mouths taped shut for entire days, had been shoved headfirst into walls, had been hoisted into the air by their cheeks, and had been called 'liars, animals, stupid, unteachable' and so on. Petitions to higher authorities, including Cardinal Manning himself, had been ignored, and as a result more than an eighth of the student body had been withdrawn by their parents.[26]

Alienated Latino Catholics did not typically join protest groups like 'Catolicos por la Raza' or sue the archdiocese, instead they voted quietly with their feet. Surveys conducted by the Hispanic secretariat for the US Catholic Conference revealed a mass exodus of Latinos in the 1970s; perhaps a fifth of Spanish-surname Catholics in Los Angeles converted to

THE PENTECOSTAL CHALLENGE
Montebello

other religions during the decade. (Nationally a tenth of Latino Catholics were 'lost' in the 1970s and 1980s, something that Catholic sociologist Andrew Greeley has characterized as 'an ecclesiastical failure of unprecedented proportions'.)[27] The winners were evangelical sects – particularly the Assemblies of God and the Billy-Graham-style Latinos Para Cristo – who offered unhappy Spanish-speaking Catholics a more individuated and emotionally intense religious experience, and whose ministers – in contrast to most Catholic parishes – were themselves Latinos. Although, as we shall see, the church now claims to be addressing the roots of Latino disaffection, the conversion rate of the evangelicals amongst newly arrived Spanish-speaking immigrants remains very high (15–25 per cent), and some Catholic bishops have warned that the church could lose up to half of its Latino members over the next generation.[28]

THE MAHONY ENIGMA

One of the prelates who met with protestors in Redlands in 1978 was the young auxiliary bishop of Fresno, Roger Mahony. Growing up in the still semi-rural San Fernando Valley of the 1940s and 1950s, Mahony practiced Spanish with his father's poultry-plant workers. Later, armed with a degree in social work from Catholic University in Washington, DC, he became secretary to the US Catholic Bishops' Ad Hoc Committee on Farm Labor, serving as their eyes and ears during the heroic early days of the United Farmworkers' crusade in the San Joaquin Valley. His bilingualism and expertise on social conditions in the Valley – at a time when California elites, political and religious, were feeling the pressure of Latino demands, catapulted him into the ecclesiastical fast track. Closely associated with Archbishop Manning from the late 1960s, he became successively the director of charities and social work in Fresno, auxiliary bishop (1975), first chair of the state's Agricultural Labor Relations Board (1975), and then bishop of Stockton (1980). Having risen to having his own see at age forty-two it was rumored that Mahony could even have a shot at an urban diocese like San Diego or Sacramento before he was fifty.

When in 1985 public rumors of Manning's retirement became rife, there was widespread speculation that Rome would finally address Latino petitions and appoint either Archbishop Sanchez of Santa Fe or Archbishop Flores of San Antonio as the Cardinal's successor. Since Manning's accession fifteen years earlier, the archdiocese, despite the separation of Orange County, had doubled in size from 1.5 million to 3 million, with the bulk of the increase coming from Spanish-speaking immigrants.[29] A dramatic realignment of church leadership to reflect Latino demographics seemed long overdue. When, instead, Manning retired in early 1986 and the Vatican announced the appointment of Mahony as the youngest archbishop in North America (at age forty-nine), Latino disappointment, which might otherwise have erupted in another exodus or wave of protest, was partially ameliorated by the new prelate's reputation.

Although he was another Celt in the same old ethno-dynastic succession, Mahony was also a fluent Spanish-speaker whose entire career had involved ministering to *campesinos* and the Latino working classes. Having marched with Cesar Chavez, he was also reputed to be a strong defender of immigrant rights, who had repeatedly stood up to the INS. A leader in the Bishops' Committee for the Spanish-speaking, he was felt to have a sophisticated and sympathetic overview of the situation of Latino Catholics. Moreover, in dramatic contrast to the McIntyre tradition, Mahony was an outspoken proponent of nuclear disarmament who played a leading role in the dissemination of the American bishops' famous 1983 pastoral letter on peace. Unsurprisingly, some observers, within the church as well as without, thought they saw in Mahony (as others had in Cardinal Wojtyla a decade before) the arrival of an innovative spirit, liberal if not radical on the big social questions.

In fact Mahony arrived not only as a former peacenik, but equally as an outspoken doctrinal conservative and papal monarchist. Avowing that church dogma was 'simply not negotiable', he had clamped a tight lid on teaching and discussion within his Stockton diocese. 'Outside' religious speakers of any kind were forbidden except with his express approval. Soon after becoming Archbishop of Los Angeles, he parroted the calumnies against academic freedom at American Catholic universities being spread by Cardinal Ratzinger, the head of the Vatican's latter-day Inquisition. Singling out a distinguished moral theologian who had challenged Vatican strictures on artificial birth control, Mahony claimed that Father Charles Curran of the Catholic University had been 'over-influenced . . . by the reigning ethos of academic freedom. It therefore becomes more necessary than ever for the church to have firm authority structures.' On another occasion Penny Lernoux reported that Mahony advised American Catholics that they 'could dissent if they kept the matter to themselves or told only a few close friends. Public dissent by people who wanted to modify the church's teaching was prohibited.'[30]

Evidence suggests that Mahony's appointment was a complex move in a Vatican strategy to reshape the American hierarchy. Thomas Reese, a Jesuit sociologist studying the American episcopate, has described how since 1980 with the purge of apostolic delegate Jadot (blamed for too many liberal nominations) the Vatican has reclaimed control of the selection process. The body of the American hierarchy is no longer consulted as a matter of course; 'many church observers' felt that Mahony was expressly selected to bolster a 'conservative' bloc of recent appointments that includes Cardinals Law of Boston and O'Connor of New York (both 1984), as well as Cardinal Bevilacqua of Philadelphia (1987). According to Reese, Mahony was sponsored by Archbishop Justin Rigali, originally from Los Angeles, who as president of the Vatican's diplomatic school and speechwriter for the Pope, has had a powerful behind-the-scenes influence on appointments to the American hierarchy. Predictably the Roman support that elevated Mahony to St. Vibiana's Cathedral in Los Angeles has also ensured his nomination to prestigious pontifical bodies, including the Synod of Bishops and the Vatican councils on peace and migrants. On the other hand, the American bishops – identifying Mahony with the Vatican bureaucracy and the theological crackdown – have twice rebuffed his aspirations for NCCB office (in 1986 and 1989).[31]

It would be nonetheless misleading to suggest that Mahony is a mere lackey of the Vatican or a McIntyre redux (although their similar penchants for authoritarian management are often compared these days). Ideological cross-currents in the contemporary church are far more complex than they were in the 1950s. Wojtyla's rabid anti-communism, for instance, goes hand-in-hand with denunciations of free enterprise that would have scandalized McIntyre or Spellman as 'Marxist'. And unlike several Roman clones whom Rigali and Ratzinger parachuted into the ranks of the American bishops during the 1980s, Mahony, though a papal loyalist, is a completely homegrown product of the US hierarchy. If he has been resented at times for supporting Roman hardliners in their attacks on American doctrinal liberals he has also been admired for his untiring energy on pastoral taskforces, including peace, international affairs (of which he was elected chair) and the 'right to life'.

Yet, in summing up the qualities visible at the time of his appointment in 1985, it would be too easy to say that Mahony was a 'social liberal and doctrinal conservative' (a formula commonly used to characterize Catholic politics these days). On a scale of 'liberalism' – where many American bishops now stand to the left of the Democratic Party on crucial issues of peace and economic justice – Mahony leaned to the right, closer to old guardists like Cardinal Law of Boston than to Vatican II progressives like Archbishop Weakland of Milwaukee. Even his 'very liberal' stances on labor and immigration had been nuanced by his emphases on respect for authority and moderation of protest. Although he frequently criticized immigration officials, he insisted on compliance with the law and opposed the strategy of 'sanctuary'. A long-time supporter of the farmworkers, he became increasingly critical of their tactics after his appointment to the Agricultural Labor Relations Board (ALRB) by Jerry Brown, and, despite the endorsement of the Bishops Committee on the Spanish-speaking, he opposed the 1975 grape and lettuce boycott.[32] A shrewd and sophisticated politican, moving acrobatically between Vatican, NCCB and secular power structures, Mahony in 1985 (like Wojtyla in 1978) was an enigma awaiting better definition.

THE LATINO AID PLAN

In a single broad stroke, a year after moving into St. Vibiana's Cathedral, Archbishop Mahony attempted to redress the accumulated grievances of his Eastside parishes. His 'Latino Aid Plan', announced in May 1986, was heralded as a dramatic reorientation from the archdiocese's traditional Anglo power-centers towards its new Latino majority. Combining an ambitious program of evangelization with social activism, while subtly preserving the underlying tradition of paternalism, the Aid Plan registered not only a new dynamism in the chancery after the drift of the Manning years, but also a potential quantum leap in the church's role in the political and social life of Los Angeles's largest ethnic sector. Yet it was a leap made only after cautious trial-and-error experimentation in Eastside parishes during the last half of the Manning episcopate.

This prelude to Mahony's Plan requires a brief accounting. Under the careful supervision of Auxiliary Bishop Arzurbe, Eastside parishes had been allowed to introduce more culturally accessible rituals and catechisms. Small, intense evangelical study groups promoting a 'conversion experience' – *cursillos de Cristiandad* – had been imported from Spain (where they had animated the fascist Catholic Action movement) and spread rapidly through the Southwest. The *cursillos*, as well as the tremendously popular Marriage Encounter retreats, offered Latino Catholics (in the words of a Chicano Jesuit) 'unabashedly affective' religious community as 'a counter-balance to a more somber, even cold, kind of Catholicism of northern origins that has dominated North American Catholicism'. The popularity of the *cursillos*, in turn, paved the way for official acceptance of the bible-thumping, tent-shaking revivalism of the Charismatic Renewal movement in the 1970s. Nervously sanctioned by Manning and Arzurbe, the new movement was opposed by many old-line priests who considered its practices shockingly 'un-Catholic'.[33]

Charismatism was a deliberate and far-reaching adaptation of Catholic liturgy to Pentecostal emphases on scripture, personal devotion, and ectastic celebration. Although the Charismatic movement in the 1970s and early 1980s swept through Anglo as well as Latino parishes, its spiritual epicenter was East Los Angeles and the estimated 60,000 Latino Charismatics participating in 140 Spanish-speaking 'prayer communities'. An ex-Assembly of God minister, Marilyn Kramer (who converted to Catholicism in 1972), founded Charisma in Missions – an East L.A.-based group fighting on the religious frontline against the Spanish-language evangelicals. A *Times* reporter, covering one of the group's giant monthly gatherings at the old Olympic Auditorium, was struck most by the similarity to traditional fundamentalism. 'Except for the manner in which communion is administered', an Eastside Charismatic revival 'could easily be mistaken for a Pentecostal service': participants 'clap their hands and sway while in song, they cry while praying with uplifted hands, they shout out hallelujahs during the sermon and occasionally they speak in the tongues of the holy spirit'.[34]

The success of Charismatism, which roused thousands of dormant or borderline Latino Catholics, encouraged the chancery to allow Eastside

THE EASTSIDE HEARTLAND

parishes to organize around community issues as well. Like many other big-city archdioceses, Los Angeles already had some experience with the Industrial Areas Foundation (IAF) model of parish/community self-help. The IAF is the national outgrowth of organizer Saul Alinsky's famous Chicago neighborhood movements (Back of the Yards, the Woodlawn Organization), built in alliance with Cardinal Stritch during the 1940s and 1950s, often using young priests as community organizers. The Community Services Organization – an earlier Alinksyite formation – had played a significant role in East Los Angeles since the 1950s, training organizers (notably Cesar Chavez and Dolores Huerta), fighting discrimination and registering voters.[35]

A new layer of IAF-style community organizations emerged in the 1970s after the National Conference of Catholic Bishops, reacting to Nixon's rollback of the War on Poverty, decided to subsidize self-help movements of the urban and rural poor. As the bishops rescued or restarted local anti-poverty organizations across the country, they also built an important new political infrastructure for the church in the inner cities. Perhaps the most impressive of these new groups was San Antonio's Communities Organized for Public Service (COPS). Unlike most previous 'Alinskyite' groups, it was built monolithically on the existing parish structure with little pretense of autonomy from the Catholic church. With support from the bishops' Campaign for Human Development and the IAF, COPS conducted highly successful voter registration drives, challenged the local chamber of commerce's promotion of the city as a sweatshop paradise, and fought to channel federal bloc grant money directly to neighborhoods.

Sent by Manning to observe COPS firsthand, Arzurbe returned an enthusiast. Here, he claimed, was a perfect strategy for re-integrating alienated Eastside parishes while strengthening Catholic social values and Chicano political clout at the same time. With initial participation from twenty parishes (especially Father Luis Olivares's La Soledad), and under the direction of an IAF veteran from Chicago, Peter Martinez, the fledging United Neighborhood Organization (UNO) began evening and weekend training workshops for its initial cadre of one hundred and fifty grassroots leaders.

Like similar groups across the country influenced by Alinsky's ideas, UNO was an expression of a peculiar radical-conservative philosophy: 'radical' in the sense that it focused on grassroots mobilization, organized dramatic confrontations with power structures, and eschewed formal deals or electoral endorsements; 'conservative' in its general avoidance of coalition-building with progressive groups, its apotheosis of 'family values' (in common with Charismatism) and its selection of only 'winnable issues' one at a time from an agenda that emphasized Catholic moralism (opposition to family planning counseling in high schools, for example) as much as community empowerment and economic survival. Moreover, as many frustrated organizers who have attempted to work with UNO or its sister organizations have complained, its self-image of grassroots democracy is sometimes belied by the behind-the-scenes machinations of IAF advisors and church leadership.[36]

Thanks primarily to the energy of Olivares and his parish members, UNO took off spectacularly in 1977–8 with a high-profile campaign against discriminatory auto insurance rates on the Eastside – a neighborhood 'survival issue' in a city with inadequate public transport. Mass demonstrations and aggressive political lobbying prompted a Federal Trade Commission investigation and a substantial reduction of local auto insurance rates. Buoyed by this success, UNO – claiming over 90,000 affiliated families by early 1980 – launched new campaigns to win housing rehabilitation funds, build new supermarkets and improve Eastside schools. In a typical mobilization, right out of the Alinsky textbook, 1,300 UNO members packed a school board meeting in June 1980, protesting poor educational quality and incompetent administration in local schools. In a heated shouting match, UNO President Gloria Chavez commandeered control of the meeting, forcing board members to answer only yes or no to carefully prepared questions from the audience, while keeping a scoreboard tally of their responses.

Confrontations like this one, whether or not they produced immediate results, were always powerful morale builders for both UNO and the church. According to an enthusiastic Bishop Arzurbe, the first cycle of UNO actions

produced a tremendous unity of lay people, priests and sisters that we've never had before. This has brought many people back to active church participation, because they've felt that for the first time we were not telling them something they had to do, but were asking them, 'What are your concerns, what are your needs?'.[37]

Although neither Charismatism or UNO by themselves could mitigate the stagnation of the Manning years, or make up for the bitter legacy of McIntyre, their local success emboldened Mahony in his dramatic debut before his Eastside flock. The day after his installation, he launched the most ambitious polling of the Catholic grassroots ever attempted in the USA. For the first time, ordinary Latino, as well as Anglo, Catholics were invited to participate in setting goals for the archdiocese. Over the course of a year, 70,000 people attended parish assemblies or regional convocations, while 320,000 answered questionnaires (in Spanish as well as English) on the archdiocese's 'mission'. One result, ratified by an archdiocese-wide convocation in November 1986, was a new focus on providing counseling and social services to troubled youth and deprived families.

The poll was followed by the 'Latino Aid Plan', carefully hatched with the support of UNO, hundreds of whose members had participated in preliminary Eastside assemblies. Admitting that 'ever growing numbers of Hispanics [had been] marginated [sic] and alienated from the church', the archbishop claimed that 'no other diocese in the nation has a plan for Hispanics so definite, so concrete, so comprehensive'. The proposals included taskforces to deal with gang violence and the housing problems of undocumented immigrants; daycare centers for latchkey children and more Latino youth ministers for Eastside parishes; opening parochial schools at night for English and citizenship classes; and a sweeping plan of evangelization that included sending volunteers to every Latino household in the archdiocese.[38]

The rally that kicked off the Aid Plan (*Celebracion '86*) was itself an unprecedented recognition of the new social weight of Latinos within the archdiocese, as well as an extraordinary personal spotlight for the archbishop. The largest all-Latino crowd in L.A. history packed into Dodger Stadium to cheer videotaped blessings from the Pope and ranchero music from Mexican superstar Lola Beltran. As 50,000 admirers chanted 'Rogelio! Rogelio!', Mahony dramatically entered the infield with a colorful escort of mounted *charros*. Evoking the parable of the loaves and fishes, the archbishop offered to nourish the 'spiritual hunger' of his Latino parishioners. 'Many of you have left your homes to be here. Many of you have even left your countries. Now Los Angeles is your home, the Catholic Church is your home, and I am your pastor.'[39]

To give even greater weight to the 'Latino Aid Plan', Mahony announced in December the Vatican's approval of his nomination of Monsignor Amando X. Ochoa of Sacred Heart Church, Lincoln Heights as auxiliary bishop for the San Fernando Valley. Within a new structure of regionally delegated auxiliaries, two of the five bishops were now Latino (Ochoa and Arzurbe – San Fernando and San Gabriel valleys), and one was Black (Carl Fisher – the Harbor region). In little more than a year, Mahony seemed to have unleashed archdiocesan perestroika, involving tens of thousands of grassroots Catholics in the formation of goals, institutionalizing UNO-type community activism as official policy, and, most radically, demonstrating his 'preferential option' for the Spanish-speaking inner city. Indeed the *Times* and other media pointed to the anxiety of 'rich Catholics', like wealthy autodealer Robert A. Smith, who worried that their new archbishop had 'tunnel vision' in the direction of Latino poor and might shun the archdiocese's former Anglo power-brokers.[40]

Yet the Latino Aid Plan was not nearly as radical or far-reaching as it appeared on first sight. Closely examined, it promised parish consultation, but stopped far short of institutional innovations like the networks of 'base communities' that Bishop Straling was creating in San Bernardino and that the National Pastoral Plan for Hispanic Ministry (which Mahony helped to draft) advocated in 1987 as primary 'instruments of evangelization' for the Spanish-speaking.[41] Nor did the Aid Plan squarely confront the 'crisis of vocation' – or clerical labor-power shortage – that has made it so difficult for the archdiocese to replace aging Anglo priests in inner-city parishes with younger Latinos or Blacks. Los Angeles has the highest ratio of Catholics per priest in the country (2,151 contrasted to 835 in New York), with no sign of abating the shortfall. Unless ways are found to attract more Latinos into seminaries, a strange, new ethnic mismatch may result as refugee Vietnamese or Chinese clergy replace retiring Irish priests in predominantly Latino parishes.[42]

Most telling, the Aid Plan, despite its rhetoric, has failed to redistribute power. The reorganization of the archdiocese in 1985–6 in fact only further centralized the archbishop's control. 'Consultation', together with what a disgruntled observer characterized as the 'papal-Maoism' of the Dodger Stadium rally, masked Mahony's relentless reassemblage of the authority enjoyed by McIntyre in his 1950s prime. To begin with, Mahony reclaimed the personal control over archdiocesan finances that Manning had yielded to Monsignor Benjamin Hawkes, the 'shadow cardinal' who died shortly after his retirement by Mahony in 1986. In Los Angeles, as in a few other localities, the archbishop, not the archdiocese, is the legal owner of all church assets – a fact that assures a hands-on executive like McIntyre or Mahony extraordinary financial power over his parishes, staff and contractors.

At the same time Mahony was reestablishing a monolithic chain of command. Although he was widely praised for organizing a chancery cabinet and defining geographical constituencies for his auxiliaries, his managerial style does not involve power-sharing or the devolution of decision-making. His subordinates are universally regarded as mild-mannered, obedient lieutenants, seldom outspoken in public or private.[43] The archbishop, on the other hand, is a forceful politician and an autocratic boss who clearly relishes his ability to wield power without 'red tape' or checks and balances.[44] In independent interviews, two priests from opposing ideological viewpoints – one a 'liberationist', the other a 'conservative' – both equated Mahony's use of power and his domination of subordinates with McIntyre's. As one sarcastically commented: 'The old regime is dead. Long live the old regime.'[45]

A TROUBLESOME PRIEST

A flashback to the 1987 Papal tour: Stopping briefly at St. Vibiana's Cathedral Downtown, before rushing off to Universal City to chide Lew Wasserman and one hundred and fifty other media executives for eroding moral values, the Pope says a few words in English to the predominantly Latino crowd. There is palpable disappointment that he has failed to speak Spanish, and some members of the press corps, surprised by the poor Anglo turnout for the Pope, wonder out loud whether he understood the significance of the ethnic transition in Los Angeles Catholicism.

Just in case there was any confusion in the Holy Father's mind, Father Luis Olivares, the radical pastor of La Reina de Los Angeles (or La Placita, as it is commonly called), had put the Papal visit in context a few days earlier in a *Times* op-ed piece. 'Whether by design or happenstance,' Olivares

OUR LADY QUEEN OF ANGELS
La Placita

pointed out that the Pope's visit spotlighted the 'mutually important relationship between Latinos and the church' at a time when the Latino community in the Los Angeles archdiocese (led by UNO and its sister organizations) was mobilizing around crucial minimum wage and immigration struggles. Quoting from recent statements by both John Paul and Mahony that expressed solidarity with the poor and undocumented, Olivares argued that while it was an 'unrealistic expectation' to believe either would yield to 'majority rule' on issues like divorce or abortion, their attitudes toward social justice would determine the future of Latinos within the church:

If Latinos can see in the person of Pope John Paul II a sign that the church really cares about the issues that affect their lives, and that he is willing to place the power of the church on the line, there is no doubt that Latinos will assume their rightful roles of leadership and responsibility in the church they so love.[46]

If on this occasion Father Olivares was subtle in his polemic – alternately praising and cautioning his spiritual superiors – he had already become renowned for blunt statements that caused seismic distress in the publicity-sensitive Los Angeles chancery. Just a year before the Pope's visit, he had declared that 'if it is expedient for the church's survival to align itself with the rich and powerful, I'd go as far as to say that the church should not survive.'[47]

Since assuming the pastorate of La Placita (a Claretian mission) in 1981, Olivares had made the old plaza church the city's major base of liberationist social practice, as well as a bustling civic center for refugee Central Americans. No parish in the country has a larger or more destitute congregation. On a typical Sunday 12,000 regular parishioners attend the day-long schedule of masses, which often spill into the courtyard, while another 100,000 or so 'constituents' visit La Placita occasionally for weddings and quinceañeras, ethnic fiestas and processions, family counseling and political meetings. Publicly contemptuous of laws that 'criminalize the poor', Olivares has opened his doors as a sanctuary to undocumented immigrants and political refugees, allowed hundreds of homeless men to sleep on his pews every night, and declared the church grounds a 'zone of safety' for harassed street vendors. A longtime thorn in the side of immigration officials, Downtown merchants and the LAPD, Father Olivares by 1987 had also become chief gadfly to Archbishop Mahony's 'centrist', top-down approach to the problems of the Spanish-speaking city-within-a-city.[48]

Listening to Olivares playfully address his assistant, Father Michael Kennedy, in perfect revolutionary etiquette as 'mi commandante', it is hard to imagine that La Placita's pastor was once a fast-track clerical bureaucrat in the mode of the ambitious 'Monsignor' in Dunne's *True Confessions*. Yet, rising out of the San Antonio barrio, through Anglo-run schools and seminaries, to become corporate treasurer for the Claretian Missionaires (an order working primarily in US Latino communities), Olivares had been preoccupied with portfolio management and fundraising amongst rich Anglo Catholics. As in the case of Mahony, it was an encounter with Cesar Chavez's striking farmworkers that brought 'a complete turn-around' in his life. But, whereas Mahony was launched upward into the hierarchy as a result of his mediating role in Valley labor strife, Olivares was brought down to earth and 'conscientized'. In 1974–5 he was active in the same UFW grape boycott that Mahony opposed. In the late 1970s, as we have seen, he was a dynamic force in getting UNO off the ground in East Los Angeles and making his La Soledad parish one of its most militant chapters.

Meanwhile the crisis in Central America, especially the increasingly frontline roles of the Guatemalan and Salvadorean clergy in the struggle for social justice, was beginning to make a profound impact on the conservative Los Angeles archdiocese. *Tydings*, for example, after generations of raving against communism and revolutionary nationalism, sharply rebuked the incoming Reagan administration in March 1981 for its proposed aid package to the Salvadorean junta.[49] Traditional cold war demonology – so fundamental to archdiocesan discipline in the era of McIntyre – began to disintegrate. In this context, Olivares and his Claretian and Jesuit 'commandantes' became the most important transmission belt between the radical church in Central America and Latinos in the Los Angeles archdiocese. Olivares visited Salvadorean refugee camps in Honduras, organized vigils for the martyred Archbishop Romero (who became his special hero), supported the protests of the burgeoning non-intervention movement, and in 1984, despite right-wing death threats, hosted a controversial breakfast at La Placita for Daniel Ortega.

Then, in December 1985, Olivares and his pastors institutionalized their defiance of the Reagan administration's immigration and foreign policies by dedicating La Placita as the first sanctuary church in the archdiocese and declaring it off limits to INS agents. In increasingly virulent public exchanges with the INS's regional director, Howard Ezell, Olivares was accused of 'promoting lawlessness' and trying to 'turn America . . . into a third-world country'. Ezell, in turn, was lambasted for 'playing on anti-immigrant mood in the country and feeding the fire of prejudice and racism'.[50]

Although Archbishop Mahony made little effort to conceal his contempt for Ezell, he staunchly refused to endorse Olivares's sanctuary initiative. Indeed, to an extent that few outsiders understood at the time, the archdiocese was being polarized by the chancery's cooperation with the enforcement of the Immigration Reform and Control Act (IRCA) during 1986–8. Although Mahony, like other bishops, officially endorsed a church 'balancing act' – helping to implement the IRCA amnesty provision while defending the rights of those excluded from its coverage – chancery resources were one-sidedly devoted to processing amnesty applications. There was, in fact, growing alarm within the immigrant communities that the Immigration and Citizenship Division of Catholic Charities was operating as a de facto arm of the INS. When ICD director Elizabeth Krisnis brazenly brought an INS official as her guest to a meeting of an immigrant rights coalition, the other members were rightly appalled. Linda Wong, the highly respected representative of the Mexican-American Legal Defense and Education Fund (MALDEF), was led to characterize Catholic Charities as a 'reluctant member' of the coalition, widely regarded as a 'fossilized institution . . . resistant to change'.[51]

Olivares, a tribune of immigrant rights in a parish full of undocumented workers, had opposed IRCA from the very beginning, faulting the National Conference of Catholic Bishops for not blocking its enactment. ('The bishops could have stopped the law and they didn't.')[52] He further criticized the local Catholic Charities for underestimating the number of applicants and failing to counsel them on how to protect themselves from the law's punitive, 'family-busting' provisions. As nearly half of the church-processed applications for amnesty were disqualified by the INS, Olivares mobilized concerned clergy 'to close the gap between what the church says and what it sometimes does not do'.[53] Pledging 'strong, concerted actions' to extend amnesty to all, or break the back of the law, La Placita moved into open civil disobedience. At a news conference in Lincoln Heights, Olivares disclosed that he was already breaking the law by hiring undocumented workers, and urged others to do the same.

> The Lord's command is clear. In the Book of Leviticus, God says, 'When aliens reside with you in your land . . . you shall treat them no differently than the natives born among you.' In the light of the Gospel call to justice, we find ourselves unable to comply with the current regulations regarding the hiring of undocumented workers. Today we stand with these people . . . to feed, clothe and house those rejected by the law.[54]

During the next year La Placita organized repeated acts of defiance. In December 1987, on the second anniversary of the declaration of sanctuary, Olivares and Kennedy were joined by San Diego's militant auxiliary bishop, Giberto Chavez, in a ceremony to reiterate their opposition to IRCA and to US military aid to El Salvador. As the parish renewed its commitment to shelter the undocumented, three hundred members signed pledges of non-cooperation with the IRS – what Chavez called 'a sign of real love'. Later that spring, on the eve of the amnesty filing deadline, hundreds of demonstrators wearing black armbands gathered at La Placita 'in mourning because this government is denying them the right to work'. Then in September, Olivares and Kennedy, joined by Father Gregory Boyle from Mission Dolores in Boyle Heights (which had become the archdiocese's second official sanctuary), published an op-ed piece in the *Times* challenging the government to arrest them. 'When laws trample human rights, they must not be obeyed . . . to the extent that we openly aid, abet and harbor the undocumented, we indeed are breaking the law. The gospel would have us do no other.'[55]

INS regional director Ezell was apoplectic. He raged at the priests in the press, ordered a criminal investigation of their confessed violations, and even suggested that they were to blame for an earlier incident when irate Salvadorean refugees, whose amnesty petitions had been rejected, broke some windows in the federal building Downtown. Then, as a barbed demonstration of Ezell's attitude toward the sanctuary status of churches, INS agents burst into a mass in an Orange County church, roughly arresting worshippers without immigration papers.

Mahony was put on the spot. Seldom, if ever, in modern American history had any federal agency so arrogantly violated the dignity of the Catholic mass (especially ironic in light of the church's central, collaborative role in the national implementation of IRCA). On the other hand, the civil rights movement of the undocumented poor that Olivares was building raised the specter of 'dual power' in the archdiocese, a grassroots church of liberation emerging side by side with the highly centralized chancery. Faced with intolerable challenges to his authority, Mahony first joined with Orange County's (normally right-wing) Bishop McFarland to force a public apology from Ezell (who was wounded by the political backlash to the raid). Then, in carefully chosen words, Mahony announced that every member of the archdiocese was restrained to obey the law of the land (strictures which the archbishop would later ignore in his own incitations on behalf of 'Operation Rescue'). Referring specifically to the three defiant priests (whose popular support had just been demonstrated by a week-long solidarity fast conducted by their parishioners), he added: 'I have met with them and reviewed their policies and their actions, and I have instructed them that as members of the Archdiocese of Los Angeles they are required to follow the policies and directives of the Archdiocese.' He also 'strongly discouraged' other inner-city parishes from joining the sanctuary movement.[56]

Olivares, placed in a position analogous to many Latin American churchmen upbraided by the Vatican for their radical stands, did the typically Latin American thing. He acknowledged the authority of Mahony and, without blinking, continued to break the immigration law in full view of the INS. By his sheer ethical and political consistency in fighting for the rights of the undocumented poor, Olivares was implicitly challenging the credibility of Mahony's Latin Aid Plan. Was the Plan truly devoted to Latino empowerment and the 'preferential option for the poor', or just to the containment of the evangelical threat? Faced with the deteriorating position of immigrants excluded from amnesty, would the archdiocese assume leadership in their struggle for economic and political rights? If finally forced to choose, would the Archbishop exile Olivares or join him in his fight against an unjust law?

UNHOLY ALLIANCES

Over the course of the next year, from the late summer of 1988 through the fall of 1989, the archbishop's actions crushed the hopes of those who, four years earlier, had believed he would be a champion of social justice. Unexpectedly the crisis erupted, not over the punishment of Olivares as many had anticipated, but over the hoary issue of union representation amongst the archdiocese's own workers.

Although the Catholic church has supported the conservative wing of the American trade-union movement since the 1890s, its own labor record is notorious. Considered as a single institution (although in law it is composed of myriad individual corporations) the church is the nation's largest private employer of teachers, hospital workers, housekeepers, and, in general, of low-wage service workers. It has been the rule, rather than the exception, for individual dioceses to operate as open shops, even while giving lip service to the ideal of unionism. As we noted earlier, one of McIntyre's duties during his earlier career as chancellor to Cardinal Spellman was to bust organizing campaigns; indeed his breaking of a New York gravediggers' strike became a dark legend in that archdiocese.[57]

Mahony, in contrast, was welcomed to Los Angeles as an old friend of labor and crusader for the rights of the unorganized (even if there were ambiguities in his record of support for the farmworkers). At the 1986 Catholic Labor Day breakfast, for example, he lectured eloquently to the leadership of the Los Angeles County Federation of Labor on the need to devote more resources to organizing low-wage groups like domestic workers. The next year, in the course of a spirited campaign that temporarily alloyed the energies of La Placita, UNO, the chancery and some of the more progressive unions, the archbishop joined Senator Edward Kennedy at a Shrine Auditorium rally to demand a dramatic hike in the minimum wage. 'No wage should be so low that it denies to a family the basics for a decent human existence.'[58]

Mahony was still basking in the moral afterglow of this campaign when organizers of the Amalgamated Clothing and Textile Workers Union informed him (in July 1988) that 120 of 140 gravediggers employed by the archdiocese had signed union representation cards. The gravediggers – mostly immigrants from Mexico and Central America – were exasperated by low wages ($6–7.85 per hour in contrast to $15 per hour in the archdiocese of San Francisco) as well as by recent 'takebacks' of their life insurance coverage and Christmas bonuses. The organizers believed that the gravediggers' plight was a legacy of the *ancien régime* that had escaped

Mahony's attention, and they assured workers that the chancery would negotiate in good faith.

Instead, to their consternation, Mahony disdained the representation cards in the haughty manner of a McIntyre. 'I've been around unions long enough to know how you get people to sign cards. You have a big rally, serve a lot of food and drink and get people to sign cards.'[59] Although he publicly conceded the union's right to test the workers' sympathies in a secret ballot representation election, his attorneys immediately challenged the NLRB's jurisdiction over church employees and cautioned the Board against 'illegal' entanglement in religious affairs. The Reaganized NLRB, already engaged in a broad retreat from regulating non-profit sectors, accepted the archdiocese's specious argument that gravediggers were 'religious workers' like theologians and bishops.

Although the California Mediation Service conducted an election in February, the removal of Wagner Act protections allowed Mahony to engage in intimidation that would have been illegal under NLRB auspices. He bribed the gravediggers with 'merit raises', cajoled them to form a *Catholic* employees' association (aka company union), and, for good measure, threatened that 'all of your wages, benefits and working conditions . . . could be lost, changed or diminished during negotiations'. The chancery even hired an infamous union-buster, Carlos Restropo (winner of the County Federation of Labor's 'No Heart Award'), to circulate leaflets 'stating that a vote against the union was a vote for the archbishop'.[60]

Despite anti-union innuendo and open threat of victimization, a majority of the gravediggers ratified the Amalgamated's mandate in the February representation election. Although union organizers looked forward to amicable negotiations, Mahony rejected the vote's legitimacy in a tantrum more becoming of a Valley lettuce grower or Southern textile magnate than the supposed pastor of Los Angeles's Latino poor. Denouncing 'personal attacks on my integrity', he accused the union of 'extremely hostile, strident, anti-Catholic rhetoric' and of creating 'an atmosphere of threats and intimidation'. Vowing to set aside the election in third-party arbitration, Mahony turned his wrath upon three gravediggers who were believed to be the original instigators of the organizing campaign. Despite the fact that one of them, Zacarias Gonzales, had worked for the archdiocese for nearly thirty years, they received curt notices stating: 'You are being discharged for conduct that is inconsistent with the work and mission of the sacred ministry of Catholic cemeteries.' Amalgamated organizer Christina Vasquez, who had repeatedly tried to break the ice with Mahony, gasped at these 'reprisals against poor people'.[61]

The victimization of the three union militants focused the attention of the entire labor movement upon the widening implications of the archdiocese's anti-union stance. Up to this point, nervous county and state labor leaders had watched the escalating conflict from the sidelines, incredulous that Mahony would risk their friendship over a few underpaid gravediggers. Now, John Henning, executive secretary of the California Federation of Labor (whose son, Patrick, was the president of the Catholic Labor Institute), was forced to remind the archbishop that it was his 'moral duty ... to recognize and bargain with the union of the workers' choice'. William Robertson, secretary of the County Federation of Labor, whose conciliatory phone calls to the chancery had gone unreturned in the weeks after the election, wrote that the Federation 'does not want war with Mahony. . . . But the attitude of the archdiocese now seems to rival that of the Merchants and Manufacturers Association in its cold disdain for the laboring man and woman.' The frigidity of Mahony's disdain, or at least the immobility of his pride, was confirmed a few months later when he broke two generations of tradition and refused to attend the Catholic Labor Institute's annual Labor Day breakfast and mass. In an extraordinary letter to Peter Henning he characterized the Institute (whom he had lectured, just two years before, on the need to organize the working poor) as 'a travesty ... a hostile anti-Catholic union ... so fully unacceptable that there is no redeeming value of any kind to be found.'[62]

Although union leaders over the next six months spoke frequently of the need for a 'healing process', Mahony spurned their olive branches. When third-party arbitrators accepted by the archdiocese upheld the February pro-union election result, the chancery repudiated their 'illogical reasoning' and the archbishop 'vowed never work with the union'.[63] True to his word, he broke off negotiations and launched a new pressure campaign to change the minds of the pro-union gravediggers. Intimidated by the realization that Mahony could not be compelled under law to bargain with them, a majority of the gravediggers capitulated to the archdiocese in a second representation election in February 1990.

The matter, of course, does not end with the gravediggers. As Harry Bernstein, the *Times*'s veteran labor reporter, has pointed out, 'Mahony's conduct as the archbishop of the largest Catholic archdiocese in the nation gives a sort of blessing to anti-union forces'.[64] Moreover the archbishop clearly intends to keep the entire archdiocese 'a union-free environment', instituting 'employee advisory councils' as virtual company unions for his low-wage 'coworkers in the church's programs, apostolates and ministries'.[65] Flabbergasted progressive Catholics, meanwhile, have grasped at different explanations for Mahony's sudden antipathy to the labor movement. If some blame his vanity, others are inclined to attribute his intransigence to the growing influence of a 'million-dollar club' of wealthy, conservative donors, functioning as his informal lay cabinet.

The existence of such an inner circle was revealed by the archbishop himself during 1989, in the course of defending the propriety of accepting a $400,000 jet-powered helicopter as a gift. Mahony answered criticism that the money would have been better spent aiding refugees and the home-less poor by stating that no archdiocesan funds had been involved. The funding, he said, came from 'men who have given at least a million dollars each to the archdiocese in the last year, in some cases, more than a million'. Although individual donors went unnamed, the archbishop revealed that his 'close friend' and advisor, Richard Riordan, had been the organizer of the initiative.

By all accounts, Riordan is heir to the kind of lay preeminence in the archdiocese once enjoyed by oil magnate Doheny during Cantwell's regime, or by corporate attorney Joe Scott during the McIntyre years.[66] A power-broker *par excellence*, who moves like a spider through virtually every elite circuit in Los Angeles, Riordan might well be a character invented by John Gregory Dunne. A securities attorney and investment banker, he has also won fame as a leverage buyout operator (principally in the supermarket industry) and 'as one of the shrewdest land speculators in Downtown Los Angeles'. In a famous exposé of behind-the-scenes deals between City Hall and developers, *Herald-Examiner* writer Tony Castro revealed how Riordan's spectacular profit-taking from a sale to the Community Redevelopment Agency was shortly followed by a $300,000 interest-free loan to the 1982 gubernatorial campaign of Mayor Bradley (who later appointed Riordan to the Recreation and Parks Commission). Castro emphasized the apparent incongruity of Riordan – 'very much a Reagan Republican' – becoming 'the largest contributor' to liberal-Democrat Bradley.[67]

At first glance it may seem equally odd that one of the first acts of 'social liberal' Mahony in his reorganization of the chancery in 1978 was to retain the eminently Republican firm of Riordan & McKinzie.[68] But the alliance of Riordan and Mahony has had many mutually strategic benefits. Riordan's promotion to the apex of lay influence within the archdiocese, as well as his intimate access to the often remote archbishop, are valuable currencies in his many fields of enterprise. In turn, the archbishop – struggling to replenish the archdiocese's donor base in the post-Hawkins period, as well as to aid the financially stricken Vatican – was inducted into Riordan's fast-track world of LBO operators, Downtown developers, and junkbond raiders.

Riordan and Mahony have also shared in the past a mutual enthusiasm for 'Bird-hunting'. The full story remains to be told of Mahony's behind-the-scenes contribution to the juridical counter-revolution in California during the 1980s that deposed the liberal Supreme Court majority headed by Chief Justice Rose Bird. At the very least it is well known that Mahony despised Bird for her role in the Supreme Court's rulings on abortion, as well as for supposed 'emotional instability' in her previous career as state agricultural commissioner. While still in Stockton, he shocked Brown administration officials by openly excoriating the Chief Justice. Riordan, for his part, spearheaded (together with agribusiness) the successful recall of Bird and fellow liberal justices, Grodin and Reynoso, bringing to the bench the present conservative, pro-capital-punishment majority led by 'Maximum Malcolm' Lucas.

Mere congruity between the affinities (or *bêtes noires*) of Mahony and Riordan, however, should not be inflated into conspiracy. If Riordan's ascendency within the archdiocese is suggestive of a renewal of a lay power structure around the chancery (shades, once again, of *True Confessions*), its actual lineaments and influence are poorly understood (even by church progressives). Suffice it to say that, having deliberately alienated the Los Angeles labor movement, the archbishop chose to highlight his relations with Riordan and other millionaire Catholic patrons. At the same time, he was also making equally fateful choices about other moral priorities for the archdiocese.

MAHONY JOINS THE 'CLINIC BUSTERS'

During 1989 the chancery was challenged to take stands across a range of controversial issues. Not only was it confronted with demands for union recognition from its own employees, it was also besieged by passionate appeals for increased interventions on behalf of the undocumented poor and AIDS victims. While Mahony was denouncing the unions as 'anti-Catholic', Olivares and his co-workers had been grappling with a new level of social emergency in the inner city. Just as predicted, immigration 'reform' had only driven unamnestied workers further into a 'black economy' of super-exploited homework, streetvending, day labor, and homelessness. At the beginning of the year La Placita and Mission Dolores joined with immigrant rights groups to defend laborers arrested in street-corner sweeps by the LAPD and suburban police departments. Later in March, Fathers Kennedy and Boyle (Olivares's two Jesuit 'commandantes') held a press conference to reveal dramatic testimony about unenforced labor codes, child labor, and ubiquitous sub-minimum wage employment (they even gave employers' names and addresses). They warned that as the economic situation of the poor worsened, crack addiction and street violence would only escalate. In La Placita's consistent view, solidarity with the poor had to be the urgent, overriding concern of the archdiocese.[69]

At the same time parish clergy and Catholic layworkers were awakening to the imminent threat of AIDS in the inner city. With the greatest concentrations of poverty and drug abuse in the state, Southcentral and East Los Angeles were targeted as likely centers for rapid, potentially catastrophic spread of the virus. Because of its cultural and institutional centrality in the lives of Spanish-speakers, the archdiocese was viewed by public health workers as an educational frontline in the battle against the epidemic. Many sisters and parish priests, including Carl Fisher, the Black auxiliary bishop for the Harbor–Southcentral region, had welcomed the American bishops' December 1987 statement that gave 'implicit permission' to discuss the role of condoms as a safeguard against AIDS, thus allowing church agencies to participate in the general mobilization co-ordinated by the surgeon-general.

Mahony, however, was not prepared to endorse La Placita's emphasis on the emergency of the poor, nor to tolerate the participation of archdiocesan agencies in the last-ditch fight to prevent an AIDS holocaust in Los Angeles's poor neighborhoods. In a decisive definition of his priorities, he chose fetuses and Vatican orthodoxy (and, thus presumably, Vatican favor) over the right-to-life crises of the undocumented immigrants and AIDS victims. Together with other conservatives in the hierarchy (including Bishops Maher of San Diego and McFarlane of Orange County), Mahony took advantage of the apparent *dénouement* of *Roe vs. Wade* to launch a Catholic *jihad*, whose main targets were 'permissive' Catholic politicians and liberal laity. Although superficially it appeared that Mahony and other conservative prelates were only responding to the grassroots right-to-life movement, the Vatican had long been urging the American hierarchy to take the initiative on behalf of moral monolithicity. The waxing offensive of the anti-abortion movement during the summer of 1989 provided an irresistible pretext for the hardliners to assert leadership, and, by focusing on an issue above debate in the hierarchy, to inflect the entire agenda of the NCCB. Indeed, in exactly the same spirit in which he had denied Father Curran's right to free speech, Mahony on 2 June notified Catholic public officials in his three-county archdiocese that 'there is no such thing as a Catholic, "pro-choice" elected or appointed official.' As Catholics, politicians ('Democrats and Republicans, liberals and conservatives') did not have freedom of opinion, but only the 'moral imperative' to work for the repeal of laws permitting abortion. Although a few Catholic elected officials, including State Senator Diane Watson from Southcentral Los Angeles, challenged the archbishop's intimidating assault on their constitutional obligation 'to act free of personal religious bias', most maintained an embarrassed silence.[70]

Having preemptively made it more difficult for Catholic politicians to endorse pro-choice (although refraining from the direct sanctions later invoked by San Diego's Bishop Maher), Mahony carried his case to the public through the press. In an op-ed piece for the *Times* later that month, he urged readers 'to reflect on this fact: that the number of deaths caused by abortion every year in this country is the equivalent of losing a city the size of Detroit to a nuclear attack.'[71] According to the archbishop, it was therefore as immoral for a majority to attempt to legislate the 'right to choose' as to demand the right to drop an annual atomic bomb on a defenseless minority.

Casuistry became conspiracy a few months later, when the archbishop joined with Randall Terry to promote the blockade of Los Angeles and Orange County family planning and women's health clinics. Taking the pulpit at an Operation Rescue rally in Anaheim, alongside other fundamentalists and moral majoritarians, Mahony exhorted 5,000 latter-day Cristeros to escalate their crusade to stop the functioning of local abortion clinics. 'In the face of the manifest injustice of legalized abortions which destroy more than 1.5 million lives each year, resorting to civil disobedience is not a surprising response.'[72] Although he had previously refused to attend the Sanctuary dedication at La Placita, or to endorse the civil disobedience of Father Olivares, the archbishop now sat by Terry's side, lavishing praise on the 'spiritual courage' of the clinic-busters (whom he compared to the civil rights pioneers of the 1960s). Although no one could doubt Mahony's genuine fervor (or his sincere belief in the equation between abortion and nuclear war), cynics within the archdiocese did point out that while solidarity with Olivares won few points in the Vatican, blessing the banners of Operation Rescue undoubtedly racked up white stars on Roman scorecards.

Suspicion that the right-to-life bandwagon was also a Trojan horse for Vatican 'anti-Americanists' was further fueled by Mahony's parallel role as point man for Cardinal Ratzinger in the furor over the NCCB's 1987 letter on the AIDS epidemic. Echoing the Vatican grand inquisitor's criticisms of the statement, Mahony had censored the version issued in Los Angeles to prohibit the dissemination of the surgeon general's recommendations about 'safe sex'. Under pressure from Rome, the NCCB in 1988 commissioned an expanded position paper on AIDS; Mahony was appointed chair of the drafting committee. Adopted in November 1989, 'Called to Compassion: A Response to the HIV/AIDS Crisis' condemned the use of condoms as 'promoting behavior which is morally unacceptable'. By closing off the 'tolerance' option that had allowed church agencies to explain the prophylactic role of condoms, Mahony effectively withdrew the American church from the national public health effort. 'Safe sex', the archbishop asserted, was 'both a lie and a fraud'.[73]

In Los Angeles, where younger inner-city populations are at special risk, outraged healthworkers derided Mahony's 'Latino AIDS plan'. An Episcopal cleric, the Rev. Albert Ogle, who had worked with the archbishop to found the Interfaith AIDS Council of Southern California, pictured the tragic consequences in Latino neighborhoods:

The reality is that young people in our parishes are being infected by the virus and will get sick and die and infect others because the church has painted itself in a corner over birth control. . . . The Catholic church is killing young people and that is not a pro-life stance.

Auxiliary Bishop Carl Fisher seemed to agree with Ogle. In an anguished dissent from Mahony – even more courageous in face of the archbishop's zero tolerance for doctrinal disagreement – Fisher explained: 'I work in the Long Beach area with persons who are dying from AIDS in some nine hospices. I do not believe that withholding information . . . is going to help in the curtailment in the spread of AIDS.'[74]

THE FORGOTTEN ONES

In full view of a cop sipping coffee in a nearby black-and-white cruiser, a group of hungry Salvadorean kids forage through a bin of spoiled vegetables next to the old Seventh Street Market. While an elderly white wino shouts abuse, they dissect the rubbish with the skill of surgeons. Some edible carrots and turnips are salvaged, and as the gang retreats, one of them kicks a wilted lettuce head very precisely through the doorway of a Central Avenue bar. The others cheer. Point for El Salvador.

Like thousands of Central American and Mexican teenagers who have arrived in Los Angeles in the wake of the 1987 immigration reform, they have found neither work nor shelter. Sleeping in abandoned buildings, parks, under bridges, even in the storm drains that feed the Los Angeles River, these *olvidados*, or forgotten ones, pool their street skills to survive in a city that many claim is even tougher, and definitely more hard-hearted, than Mexico, D.F. or San Salvador. Some, friendless and hungry, succumb to the temptations of crack-dealing and teenage prostitution that thrive in the MacArthur Park area. Many others cling to the lifeline thrown to them by the bespectacled priest with the funny *tejano* accent. At La Placita, and almost nowhere else in this *pinche lugar*, there is sleep, dignity and solidarity.

But the rumor which has spread through the barrios since September is that Olivares is leaving. Indeed, just before Halloween, he explained that, as part of the established rotation policy of the Claretian Order, he will be reassigned in the new year. 'I have no complaints, I knew very clearly this was coming. . . . My only concern is what's going to happen to the ministry for undocumented immigrants and refugees who have come to see La Placita as sometimes their only recourse.'[75] It is a class act, but almost no one familiar with the archdiocese really believes that Olivares is simply being 'rotated'. The more likely reason is that Mahony had a few words with the new superior of the Claretian Order – something along the lines, perhaps, of Henry II's complaint about Thomas à Becket.[76]

But Olivares – ever the organizer, not the mourner – is primarily concerned with La Placita's survival as a community of resistance. In front of the media (including the *L.A. Weekly*'s Reuben Martinez), as well as his parishioners, he rehearses an almost Socratic dialogue: 'If this ministry dies, I really must say that it was mainly my fault, because I did not establish it on a strong grassroots basis.'[77] In a different conversation, Father Michael Kennedy, the Jesuit at La Placita, speaks of the failure, not only of the chancery and the rich Anglo parishes, but also of the UNO heartlands of East L.A., to respond to the survival crisis of the new immigrants. Only La Placita and Father Boyle's Mission Dolores have opened their doors to the homeless: 'One of our lessons is that only the poor help the poor in this archdiocese.'[78]

Pessimism about UNO's role is widespread at La Placita, despite the historic role of Olivares in its formation. It is rumored that only five of the original twenty-seven East Los Angeles parishes remain active in the organization, and that grassroots participation has steadily atrophied as organizers assume more bureaucratic roles. Although UNO's younger sisters – EVO, VOICE, and SCOC – have involved tens of thousands of new supporters in the San Gabriel and San Fernando valleys, as well as South-central Los Angeles, they have focused on a rather narrow range of moral and law-enforcement issues: more police patrols, sterner drug law enforcement, restriction of liquor sales, clean-up of junked cars, banning of outdoor 'graffiti museums' ('an invitation to gangs'), prohibition of contraception counseling in high schools and so on.[79] The four IAF groups have tended to downplay the cutting-edge social justice demands (minimum wage, insurance, healthcare, and so on) of previous years, as well as

THE FORGOTTEN ONES

reducing their direct outreach to poorer, new immigrant constituencies. A recent IAF-organized march against gang violence – supported by the LAPD, a supermarket chain and several radio stations – did not include a single placard or banner referring to youth unemployment or poverty.

It is unclear whether this transformation of UNO and its sisters into more conservative, law-and-order movements is attributable to pressures from the chancery, or, alternatively, the reflection of a tendential polarization within the Latino community itself, between the new immigrants and the older, homeowning Chicano lower middle classes. In any event, it has become more difficult to imagine rekindling the kind of broad populist insurgency around inner-city 'critical needs' that the minimum wage coalition of 1987 had seemed to prefigure.

Meanwhile, in liberal church circles outside La Placita – amongst the religious orders, Catholic academics and parish laity – there is widespread conviction that the chancery is adrift and that the Latino Aid Plan of 1986 has floundered. Some claim that Mahony's permanent distraction with NCCB and Vatican politics has plunged the chancery into a profound crisis of direction. Others bemoan the absence of staff and resources to address the youth needs of the inner city, one of the supposed priorities set by the 1985 consultation process. All recognize that the exile of Olivares is probably a fatal blow to any hope for a detente or *modus vivendi* between St. Vibiana's and the project of a liberationist ministry to the city's immigrant poor.[80] Caught in the crossfire of the global struggle over the future of the church (an institution more resistant than the Kremlin to the supposedly democratic spirit of the times), they fear that the archdiocese under Mahony may be headed backwards – to the intolerance and ultramontane rigidity of the McIntyre era.

NOTES

1. Cf. Mathew Ellenberger, 'The "Middle Westerner" in the *Day of the Locust*: an Examination of Their History in Los Angeles and Their Role in Nathanael West's Novel', *Southern California Journal*, Fall 1983, p. 236; and Gregory Singleton, 'Religion in the City of the Angels: American Protestant Culture and Urbanization: Los Angeles, 1850–1930', PhD thesis, History, UCLA 1976, pp. 5, 143, 161, 180, 213, 253, and 307. See also Sandra Frankiel, *California's Spiritual Frontiers*, Berkeley 1987.

2. *The Official Catholic Directory 1990*, Wilmette, Il. 1989; *California Almanac*, 1988–9 edition, Novato 1987; Bernard Quinn, et al., *Churches and Church Membership in the United States 1980*, Atlanta 1982. The US Census does not collect data on religious affiliation, so that estimates of church adherence, as well as definitions of membership, vary widely.

3. *Times*, 6 August 1983, 7 July 1985, and 17 February 1985; Nolan Davis, 'The Archbishop in Motion', *Times – West Magazine*, 12 March 1972.

4. Penny Lernoux, *People of God: The Struggle for World Catholicism*, New York 1989.

5. Thomas Reese, *Archbishop: Inside the Power Structure of the American Catholic Church*, New York 1989, p. vi.

6. The archdiocese's failure to nurture Mexican hopes for educational and occupational mobility alienated the emerging Mexican-American intelligentsia of the 1930s. By contrast, Protestant churches, above all the Methodists, won prestige for their policy of training Mexican youth for non-agricultural occupations and providing scarce college scholarships. See Singleton, pp. 173–4; and Carlos Muñoz, *The Chicano Generation*, London 1989, chapter 1.

7. *Tydings*, 14 December 1934.

8. Legion of Decency boycotts in the 1930s forced studio moguls to reach public and private accommodations with the hierarchy, which in the postwar period extended censorship into political as well as sexual areas (e.g. the banning of Chaplin's *Monsieur Verdeux*, as 'unAmerican'). Making a virtue of necessity, Louis B. Mayer of MGM not only negotiated censorship problems with Cardinal Spellman but became his friend and ardent admirer ('a large portrait of Spellman in his red vestments was the first sight that greeted visitors to Mayer's library'). See Neal Gabler, *An Empire of Their Own: How the Jews Invented Hollywood*, New York 1988, pp. 285–6.

9. John Cooney, *The American Pope*, New York 1984, pp. 78–9, 88–9, 321.

10. See Davis.

11. See Davis; obituary, *Times*, 17 July 1979.

12. John Gregory Dunne, *True Confessions*, New York 1980. 'McIntyre was an enigma. He spent long stretches on his knees obviously praying fervently, but when he stood up, the grace he had tried to summon drained out of him.' (Cooney, p. 78.)

13. McIntyre opposed the popularization of the liturgy, particularly the vernacular mass. As he put it, 'active participation [of the congregation] is frequently a distraction'. (James Hennesey, S.J., *American Catholics*, Oxford 1981, p. 312.)

14. Cf. Davis, and Robert Conot, *Rivers of Blood, Years of Darkness*, New York 1967, pp. 106–7.

15. See Davis.

16. The Jesuits' top expert on California Latinos, Father Allen Figueroa Deck, faults the archdiocese in the postwar period under McIntyre for abandoning the 'national parish' – the foreign-language and ethnically specific congregations previously common amongst European immigrants – in favor of Americanization. 'Little or nothing has been written on the abandonment of the national parish just when the Hispanic presence was becoming strong . . .' (*The Second Wave: Hispanic Ministry and the Evangelization of Cultures*, New York, Paulist Press 1989, pp. 58–9.)

17. *Times*, 26 December 1969.

18. See Davis.

19. Ibid.

20. Reese. p. 109.

21. *Days of Change, Years of Challenge: The Homilies, Addresses and Talks of Cardinal Timothy Manning*, Los Angeles 1987, p. 29.

22. *Times*, 29 August 1975, 7 July and 23 August 1985, and Davis.

23. Manning obituary, *Times*, 24 June 1989.

24. *Times*, 29 August 1975, 8 August 1983.

25. *Times*, 24 August, 18 September, 11 November 1978. Bishop Straling has since worked overtime to win the support of his diocese. Amongst Southern California bishops, he took the lead in promoting *communidades eclesiales de base* as supports to Latino church participation. According to the *Times*: 'Latino activists say the diocese of San Bernardino has become a showplace of base communities – non-territorial parishes governed by lay ministers. The diocese is also known for its leadership training of Latino lay workers and its advocacy of peace and justice causes.' (20 May l985; see also 21 January 1984.)
26. *Times*, 6 May 1982.
27. Andrew Greeley, 'Defection Among Hispanics', *America*, 30 July 1988, p. 62. Greeley emphasizes the particular success of the evangelicals in appealing to the Latino 'upwardly mobile middle class for whom the Protestant denomination provides both a way of becoming acceptably American and a support community in which they are comfortable as they break with their old religious heritage'. He adds that in leaving their old religion behind, Latino Protestant converts also tend to abandon the Democratic Party (ibid.). (See also Richard Rodriguez, 'A Continental Shift', *Times*, 13 August 1989.)
28. *Times*, 6 May 1982, 21 November 1987.
29. Nationally Latinos have become not only the largest Catholic ethnic groups, but by 2000 (if immigration patterns persist and Protestant proselytism does not increase) they will be an absolute majority. Evangelicals, on the other hand, maintain that up to 80 per cent of Latinos have no active relationship with the church. (*Times*, 2 February 1980, 20 May 1985; Los Angeles *Business Journal*, 1 May 1989.)
30. *Times*, 15 August 1986. In the same period Mahony also joined with conservative Cardinal Law of Boston to oppose tenure at CUA for Father James Provost, one of the country's 'most respected canon lawyers' – see Lernoux, p. 240 and *Times*, 17 October 1986.
31. Reese, p. 30; also see the account of Rigali's current power in the Religious News Service's review of the Reese book (*Times*, 22 July 1989).
32. Mahony was reported to be 'surprised' by the negative reaction within the church to his opposition to the boycott. His call for a 'truce between all parties' was ignored. (*Times*, 28 August 1975.)
33. See Allen Figueroa Deck, S.J. (Society of Jesus), *Second Wave: Hispanic Ministry and the Evangelization of Cultures*, New York, Paulist Press 1989, pp. 67–9; also speech by Bishop Raymond Pena, 'Opening the Door to Life in the Church', *Origins*, NC documentary service, vol. 19, no. 12 (17 August 1989).
34. *Times* 8 August 1983; also Deck, p. 69.
35. For a brief history of CSO and its founder, Fred Ross (the director of the government migrant camp in *Grapes of Wrath*), see Sanford Horwitt, *Let Them Call Me Rebel: Saul Alinksy, His Life and Legacy*, New York 1989, pp. 229–35, 262–3, and 520–22. CSO effectively collapsed when Chavez and Huerta resigned in 1962 to organize farmworkers in the San Joaquin Valley.
36. Although none was as ambitious as UNO, a number of other interesting social experiments in the archdiocese emerged during the late 1970s. In Pacoima – a Black and Latino area of the San Fernando Valley – six low-income parishes banded together in 'Meet Each Need with Dignity' (MEND) to organize social work and self-help – a model that was replicated by the Holy Cross Center in the Central-Avalon area. At the same time, religious orders and seminarians were moving back into Los Angeles's inner city, both as 'missionaries' (as in the case of the Society of the Divine Word in Latino Boyle Heights) and as social workers.
37. Neal Pierce, 'Power to Hispanics', *Times*, 17 May 1979; and ibid., 11 October 1978 and 11 June 1980.
38. *Times*, 28 May 1986; and Frank del Olmo, 'Latino Community, With Church's Help, Is on Move', ibid., 12 June 1986.
39. *Times*, 28 May and 12 June 1986.
40. Ibid., 17 February 1986.

41. Ibid., 21 November 1987
42. Ibid., 1 March 1989.
43. Ibid., 14 January 1988.
44. 'There is something to be said for a hierarchical system' (Mahony). See Paul Ciotti, 'The Plugged-In Archbishop', *Los Angeles Times Magazine*, 17 December 1989.
45. Under canon law bishops are virtually monarchical vis-à-vis their dioceses. Combining legislative, judicial and executive powers, they are advised by, but free to ignore, priests' senates and pastoral councils. See Reese.
46. Luis Olivares, 'Pope Can Reach Latinos If He Shows the Church Cares . . . , *Times*, 14 September 1987.
47. Ibid., 7 July 1986.
48. *Times*, 7 July 1986 and 19 June 1989. Olivares has continued a long tradition. During the mass deportations of Mexican workers in the 1930s La Placita was often a refuge, and on several occasions was raided by the police.
49. See *Tydings*, 7 March 1981. Sister Mayeski, chair of theology at Loyola Marymount (Los Angeles's major Catholic university), is approvingly quoted: 'The Latin American bishops and missionaries are educating us that the world is not divided into two camps with Communism on one side, and capitalism and Christianity on the other.'
50. *Times*, 7 July 1986.
51. Ibid., 12 January 1987.
52. Ibid.
53. *Daily News*, 29 April 1988; *Times*, 1 December 1987, 4 May 1988.
54. Ibid.
55. *In These Times* (Chicago), 9–15 November 1988.
56. Ibid.; Reuben Martinez, *L.A. Weekly*, 22–28 December 1989.
57. Cooney, p. 321.
58. 1987 wage rally.
59. *Times*, 8 October 1988.
60. Ibid., 17 March and 4 April, 1989.
61. Ibid.
62. Ibid., 28 June 1989.
63. Mahony letter to the *Times*, 28 January 1990; and Ciotti, p. 54.
64. 19 December 1989.
65. Mahony, ibid.
66. See Scott obituary, *Tydings*, 28 March 1958, p. 7.
67. Tony Castro, 'How Politics Built Downtown', *Herald-Examiner*, 10 March 1985.
68. *Times*, 13 June 1986. William Wardlaw oversees archdiocesan legal affairs for Riordan and McKinzie.
69. Ibid., 13 and 15 January, 18 and 25 February, and 24 March 1989.
70. Ibid., 11 October 1989.
71. Ibid., 2 and 22 June 1989.
72. *Herald-Examiner*, 12 August 1989.
73. *Times*, 4 and 13 November; 5 December 1989.
74. Ibid.
75. Olivares's quote.
76. A suspicion partly confirmed by Olivares when he conceded that his Claretian superior '*believes* that Mahony wants him out' and, therefore, refused Olivares's petition for an extension of his term. (See Dave McCombs, 'The Final Days of Father Olivares', *Downtown News*, 12 March 1990.)
77. Martinez, *Weekly* (author's manuscript).
78. Interview, September 1989.

79. Assemblywoman Maxine Waters, state chair of the 1988 Jackson campaign, has condemned UNO-SCOC efforts to give police wide-ranging wiretapping powers. She blamed the groups' white IAF organizers in particular. The proposal, Waters implied, resulted from naivety on the part of white organizers. 'Sometimes we in the minority community have to educate white folks on certain things,' she said, explaining that police abuse of greater wiretapping powers was inevitable and would undoubtedly be directed at minority communities first and foremost. (Ruben Castenada, 'Community Organizers Bring New Clout to Urban poor', *California Journal*, January 1988, p. 25.)

80. In July 1990 La Placita was saddened by the revelation that Father Olivares was gravely sick with AIDS, apparently contracted from a blood transfusion several years before in El Salvador.

CHAPTER SEVEN

JUNKYARD OF DREAMS

Mental geographies betray class prejudice. In the trendy-chic *L.A. Weekly*'s 'Best of Los Angeles' guide, one of the 'Ten Best of the Best' is the Robertson Boulevard off-ramp of the Santa Monica Freeway near Beverly Hills: where the air starts to clear of smog and the true heaven of the Westside begins. In Yuppie deli-map consciousness, landscapes tend to compress logarithmically as soon as one leaves the terrain of luxury lifestyles. Thus Fairfax is the near Eastside, while Downtown is the far horizon, surrounded by dimly known zones of ethnic restaurants. Even if the Westsider is vaguely familar with the old concentrations of Wasp wealth marooned in Pasadena, Claremont or Redlands, the eastbound San Bernardino Freeway (the I-10) – traversed at warp speed with the windows rolled up against the smog and dust – is merely the high road to Palm Springs and the Arizona Desert. The 'Inland Empire' of western San Bernardino and Riverside counties is little more than a blur.

One of the few modern writers to venture thither, Joan Didion, on her way to a San Bernardino murder trial, found the landscape 'curious and unnatural':

The lemon groves are sunken, down a three- or four-foot retaining wall, so that one looks directly into their dense foliage, too lush, unsettlingly glossy, the greenery of nightmare; the fallen eucalyptus bark is too dusty, a place for snakes to breed. The stones look not like natural stones but like the rubble of some unmentioned catastrophe. [1]

Rising from the geological and social detritus that has accumulated at the foot of the Cajon Pass sixty miles east of Los Angeles, the city of Fontana is the principal byproduct of this 'unmentioned catastrophe'. A gritty blue-collar town, well known to line-haul truckers everywhere, with rusting blast furnaces and outlaw motorcycle gangs (the birthplace of the Hell's Angels in 1946), it is the regional antipode to the sumptuary belts of West L.A. or Orange County. 'Designer living' here means a Peterbilt with a custom sleeper or a full-chrome Harley hog. A loud, brawling mosaic of working-class cultures – Black, Italian, hillbilly, Slovene and Chicano – Fontana has long endured an unsavory reputation in the eyes of San Bernardino County's moral crusaders and middle-class boosters.

But Fontana is more than merely the 'roughest town in the county'. Its indissoluble toughness of character is the product of an extraordinary, deeply emblematic local history. Over the course of the seventy-five years since its founding, Fontana has been both junkyard and utopia for successive tropes of a changing California dream. The millions of tourists and commuters who annually pass by Fontana on I-10, occasionally peeking into the shabbiness of its backyards and derelict orchards, can little imagine the hopes and visions shipwrecked here.

In its original, early-twentieth-century incarnation, Fontana was the modernized Jeffersonian idyll: an arcadian community of small chicken ranchers and citrus growers living self-sufficiently in their electrified bungalows. Then in 1942 the community was abruptly reshaped to accommodate the dream of a Rooseveltian industrial revolution in the West. The Promethean energies of Henry Kaiser turned Fontana overnight into a mighty forge for war, the only integrated steel complex on the Pacific Slope. In the early 1980s, with equally brutal swiftness, the milltown was shuttered and its workers and machines reduced to scrap. Yet phoenix-like, a third Fontana – the 'affordable suburb' – has arisen from the ruins of Kaisertown. In the new economic geometry of the Southern California 'metrosea', where increasing masses commute three or more hours daily to reconcile paychecks with mortgages, Fontana – and its sister communities of San Bernardino County's 'West End' – are the new dormitories of Southern California's burgeoning workforces.

If violent instability in local landscape and culture is taken to be constitutive of Southern California's peculiar social ontology, then Fontana epitomizes the region. It is an imagined community, twice invented and promoted, then turned inside-out to become once again a visionary green field. Its repeated restructurings have traumatically registered the shifting interaction of regional and international, manufacturing and real-estate, capitalism. Yet – despite the claims of some theorists of the 'hyperreal ' or the 'depthless present' – the past is not completely erasable, even in Southern California. Steelmaking in the shadow of the San Bernardinos – the transposed culture of Pennsylvania millworkers on a horticultural semi-utopia on the edge of the desert – have left human residues that defy the most determined efforts of current developers to repackage Fontana as a vacant lot. To this extent the Fontana story provides a parable: it is about the fate of those suburbanized California working classes who cling to their tarnished dreams at the far edge of the L.A. galaxy.

PHANTOM ORCHARD

FONTANA FARMS

It was just the type of place they often had talked of. Ten acres of level
land . . . rich, fertile. On it were 200 fine walnut trees, young, but
sturdy. And on four sides was a beautiful fringe of tall, graceful
eucalypti, through which they glimpsed the lofty crests of the
San Bernardinos.
'It would be wonderful, if we just had money enough', said she. 'At
least,' said he, 'we have enough to make a start. We can pay down
what we can spare and stay in the city for a while. There'll be enough
to put up a little garage house, and we'll have a place of our own to
come to weekends and holidays'.
And so, much sooner than they had hoped, their dream of a place all
their own, out in the country, came true. Every weekend, every
holiday, found them on their Fontana farm, planting things, cultivating
their walnut trees, watching things grow. And their farm returned their
affection in full measure. Never did the walnut trees thrive so. Never
did berry bushes and fruit trees do better. Each week they carried back
with them some of the products of their farm.
Then there came a day when they could build the farm home they
always had planned. A roomy, rambling house, with a world of
windows. A broad green lawn, and trees in front, and at the back
equipment for 2,000 chickens, a rabbitry for 240 full-blooded New
Zealand Whites, and, just for the fun of it, pens for Muscovy and
Peking ducks, turkeys . . .
And so, the first of the year, they moved in. Each week brings an egg
check of $40 to $50 or more. There is a ready market for every rabbit
they can produce. The walnut trees will be in production soon, and in
full bearing they will add another $2,000 per year net to the profits of
the place. In all Fontana there's no farm that's finer, no couple that is
happier, and it's proved so easy . . . after they found their Fontana
farm.
Fontana Farms ad, 1930[2]

Fontana Farms was the brainchild of A.B. Miller, San Bernardino contractor
and agriculturalist. All but forgotten today, Miller was one of the hero-
builders of a unique civilization of affluent agricultural colonies in what was
once known as the 'Valley of the South',[3] stretching from Pomona to
Redlands. Like the more widely known George Chaffey, whose Ontario
colony had decisive influence on the technology of Zionist settlement in

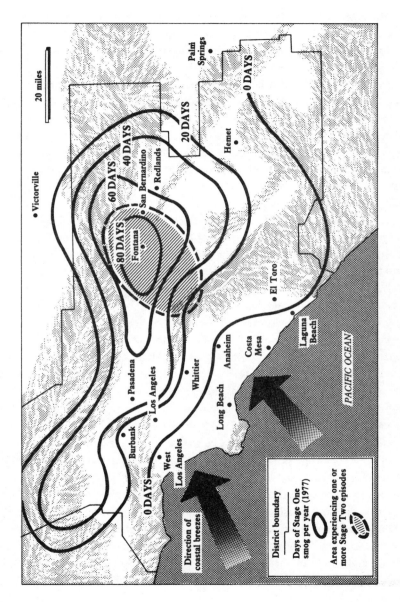

20 miles

Palm
Springs

0 DAYS

20 DAYS

40 DAYS

Hemet

60 DAYS

San Bernardino
Redlands

80 DAYS

Fontana

Victorville

El Toro

Laguna
Beach

Pasadena

Los Angeles

Whittier

Anaheim

Costa
Mesa

Burbank

Long Beach

PACIFIC OCEAN

West
Los Angeles

0 DAYS

Direction of
coastal breezes

District boundary

Days of Stage One
smog per year (1977)

Area experiencing one or
more Stage Two episodes

FONTANA, CAPITAL OF THE SMOG BELT

Palestine, Miller was a visionary entrepreneur of hydroelectric power, irrigated horticulture, cooperative marketing, and planned community development. Which is to say, he was a brilliant real-estate promoter who fully grasped the combination of advertising and infrastructure required to alchemize the dusty plains of the San Bernardinos into gold. If Chaffey, along with L.A. water titan William Mulholland, far surpassed the hydraulic accomplishments of Miller, the latter was unique in the thorough planning and complementary agricultural diversity that made Fontana such a striking realization of the petty-bourgeois ideal of withdrawal into Jeffersonian autonomy. Only the failed Socialist utopia of Llano del Rio, in the Mojave Desert north of Los Angeles, aspired to a more ambitious integration of civility and self-sufficiency.

In 1906 Miller, flush with construction profits from the new Imperial Valley, took over the failed promotion of the Semi-Tropic Land and Water Company: twenty-eight square miles of boulder-strewn plain west of San Bernardino. Incessantly raked by dust storms and dessicating Santa Ana winds, the alluvial Fontana–Cucamonga fan for the most part retained the same forlorn aspect – greasewood, sage and scattered wild plum trees – that had greeted the original Mormon colonists sent by Brigham Young in 1851 to establish San Bernardino as Deseret's window on the Pacific. Raising capital from prominent Los Angeles bankers, Miller undertook the construction of a vast irrigation system (tapping the snows of Mount Baldy via Lytle Creek) and the planting of half a million eucalyptus saplings as windbreaks. By 1913 his Fontana Company was ready to begin laying out a townsite between Foothill Boulevard (an old wagon road soon to become part of famous US 66) and the Santa Fe tracks. At the inaugural barbecue, Miller's friend and sponsor, Pacific Electric Railroad President Paul Shoup, promised that his Red Cars would soon bring thousands of daytrippers and prospective homesteaders to see the future at work in Fontana.[4]

Other famous irrigation colonies of the day – Pasadena, Ontario, Redlands, and so on – thrived by franchising citrus growing as an investment haven for wealthy, sun-seeking Easterners. The cooperative, 'Sunkist' model (later so influential in shaping Herbert Hoover's vision of self-organized capitalism) provided newcomers with a network of production services, a coordinated labor pool and a national marketing organization with a common trademark.[5] On the other hand, the arcadian life of a Southern

California orange, lemon or avocado grower required substantial startup capital (at least $40,000 in 1919) and outside income to sustain the operator until his trees became fruit-bearing.[6] Ready access to capital was also necessary to tide growers over between the seasons, and periodically to absorb the costs of crop-killing frosts. Seduced by the siren song of fabulous profits in the foothills, thousands of undercapitalized citrus ranchers lost their life savings in a few seasons.[7]

Miller's concept of Fontana was presented as an alternative to aristocratic citrus colonies like Redlands as well as to the more speculative settlements in the eastern San Gabriel Valley. Fontana was envisioned as an unprecedented combination of industrialized plantation (Fontana Farms) and Jeffersonian smallholdings (subdivided by Fontana Land Company). Fontana Farms was a futuristic example of vertically integrated, scientifically managed, corporate agriculture. Its primary input was the City of Los Angeles's garbage which, from 1921 to 1950, it received in daily gondola car shipments by rail. (The garbage contract was so lucrative that Miller was forced to make large payoffs to corrupt city councilmen – igniting a 1931 municipal scandal.) The five or six hundred daily tons of garbage fattened the sixty thousand hogs that made Fontana Farms the largest such operation in the world. When the hogs reached full weight they were shipped back to Los Angeles for slaughter, recycled garbage thus providing perhaps a quarter of the region's ham and bacon. The coincident accumulation of manure was no less valued: it was either utilized as fertilizer for Miller's citrus grove (also the world's largest) or peddled to neighboring ranchers. Fontana Farms even made a small profit reselling the silverware it reclaimed from restaurant garbage.[8]

Meanwhile the Fontana Company was busy subdividing the rest of the Miller empire into model small farms. With an enthusiasm for mass marketing and production that clearly prefigured Henry Kaiser's, Miller aimed his promotion at precisely that middling mass of would-be rural escapists who had previously been cannon-fodder for Southern California's most ill-fated land and oil speculations. His 'affordable' Fontana farm idyll, by contrast, was designed to be assembled on lay away with combinations of small semi-annual installments and lots of sweat equity. For bare land prices of $300–500 (for the minimum 2.5 acre 'starter farm' in 1930), the prospective Fontanan was offered a choice of bearing grapevines or walnut trees (corporate Fontana Farms maintained a vast nursery of a million saplings). Starting with 'vacation farming' on weekends (Los Angeles was only an hour away by automobile or Red Car), the purchaser could gradually add on living quarters, which the Fontana Farms Company offered in a complete range from weekend cabins to the ultimate 'charming, redtile Spanish Colonial farmhouse'. Examples of these are still widely visible throughout Fontana.

What was supposed to make the whole endeavor ingeniously self-financing, however, was Miller's formula of combining tree crops (walnuts and mixed citrus) or vineyards with poultry, supported by cheap inputs from Fontana Farms' industrial economies of scale (fertilizer, saplings, water and power). Colonists were urged to install chicken coops as soon as possible to generate reliable incomes. This famous 'Partnership of Hens and Oranges' was intended to stabilize the small tree rancher through the vagaries of frost and cashflow, while simultaneously guaranteeing the Fontana Company its installment payments. Ideally, it was supposed to allow the retired couple with a modest pension, the young family with rustic inclinations, or the hardworking immigrant, the means to achieve a citrus-belt lifestyle formerly accessible only to the well-to-do.[9]

Miller's dream sold well, even through the early years of the Depression. By 1930 the Fontana Company had subdivided more than three thousand homesteads, half occupied by full-time settlers, some of them immigrants from Hungary, Yugoslavia and Italy. The ten pioneer poultry plants of 1919 had grown to nine hundred, making the district the premier poultry center of the West. Fontana Farms, meanwhile, had expanded to a full-time workforce of five hundred Mexican and Japanese laborers – comparable to the largest cotton plantations in the Mississippi Delta. In the early thirties Miller joined forces with the Swift dynasty from Chicago to buy out the historic Miller (no relation) and Lux cattle empire in the San Joaquin Valley. His rising stature in California agriculture, together with his contributions to making it into a genuine 'agribusiness', were acknowledged by Republican Governor Rolph, who appointed Miller president of the State Agricultural Society, and, ex officio, a regent of the University of California.

Even if Fontana Farms was ultimately little more than a real-estate promotion cleverly, and extravagantly, packaged as semi-utopia, it retains considerable historical importance as the most striking Southern California

FONTANA FARMS

example of the 'back to the land' movement in the inter-war years. Originally a yeoman's version of the irrigation colony ideal (exemplified by both Chaffey's Ontario and the Socialists' Llano del Rio), Fontana grew to share many of the qualities of Frank Lloyd Wright's 'Broadacres' project and the 1930s anti-urban experiments. Skimming through old advertising brochures for Fontana Farms, one is struck by the ideological congruence – however inadvertent – between Miller's declared aims and the Henry Georgian program which Giorgi Ciucci has claimed infused Wright's Broadacres: 'labor-saving electrification, the right of the average citizen to the land, the integration of the city and the countryside, cooperation rather than government, and the opportunity for all to be capitalists'. If, as Ciucci sarcastically observes, 'Wright's ideal city would be realized only in the grotesque and preposterous form of Disneyland and Disney World',[10] Miller's more practical version of the Broadacre ideal had a brief, but real tenure. All the more ironic, then, that pastoral Fontana Farms would be upstaged, and eventually uprooted, by Henry Kaiser's 'satanic mill'.

MIRACLE MAN

The 'Miracle Man' Comes to Fontana.
1942 headline[11]

In 1946, after two years of criss-crossing all the old forty-eight states ('my ideal day was to spend all morning with the First National Bank and the afternoon with the CIO'), John Gunther published *Inside USA* – his vast (979-page), Whitmanesque snapshot of the domestic political scene on the threshold of the postwar era.[12] For Gunther, the most popular journalist of his generation, World War Two was comparable to the Revolution or the Civil War as a watershed of American character. From the standpoint of an onrushing 'American Century', he was concerned to distinguish the pro-gressive from the reactionary, the visionary from the backward-looking. Although later journalists, albeit only by team effort, eventually duplicated the scale of his canvas (that is, the entire US political universe), none has ever matched the astuteness or piquancy of his characterizations of an entire generation of public figures. Unsurprisingly, in the gutter bottom of national political life, Gunther identified the representatives of Mississippi, the Hague machine of New Jersey, and other avatars of domestic fascism. Conversely, at the very pinnacle of his new American pantheon, rising above even Governors Warren and Stassen (perennial Gunther favorites), was 'the most important industrialist in the United States . . . the builder of Richmond and Fontana', Henry J. Kaiser.[13]

Forty-five years later, with the mighty Kaiser empire now dismantled, Gunther's panegyric to Kaiser (he was given an entire chapter to himself) requires some explanation.[14] In essence, Gunther, like many contemporary observers, saw Kaiser as the exemplary incarnation of the Rooseveltian synthesis of free enterprise and enlightened state intervention. Kaiser of the 1930s and 1940s is heroically entrepreneurial – Gunther compares him to nineteenth-century empire-builders like the Central Pacific's 'Big Four' – yet, unlike the old-fashioned 'railroad corsairs', Kaiser 'has great social consciousness and conscience'. A lifelong registered Republican, he avidly supports the New Deal. 'As to labor Kaiser's friendly relations are well known. He wants to be able to calculate his costs to the last inch, and he never budges without a labor contract.'[15] Although his early background was as a small-town salesman, lacking any formal training in engineering or manufacturing, Kaiser by the mid 1940s had become the great problem-solving magician of the war economy: mass-producing Liberty ships in four days and achieving other productivist feats worthy of Edison or Ford. Even better than Ford himself (who represented an earlier era of authoritarian engineer-capitalism), Kaiser personified the spirit of the war-generated high-productivity, high-wage economy that later economic historians would refer to as 'Fordism'. But 'Kaiserism' would have been a more apt name for the postwar social contract between labor and management:

Production in the last analysis depends on the will of labor to produce . . . you can't have healthy and viable industry without, first, a healthy labor movement, and second, social insurance, community health, hospitalization plans, and decent housing. 'To break a union is to break yourself.' The 'Kaiser Credo'[16]

Kaiser was also a hero of the West. Denounced by Wall Street as the 'economic Antichrist' and 'coddled New Deal pet', he was welcomed west of the Rockies as a self-made frontier capitalist who, against incredible odds, had triumphed over William Jennings Bryan's 'cross of gold'.[17] To Western economic nationalists, like A.G. Mezerik, Kaiser was a 'new kind of industrialist', an incarnation of the 'trust-busting Second New Deal' and a pioneer of the 'independent industrialization of the West'.[18] In fact, Kaiser, accumulating a small fortune in the corrupt street-paving business during the auto-crazy 1920s, was transformed into an industrial giant during the 1930s by virtue of strategic (and sometimes secretive) business and political alliances. In the late 1920s, Kaiser became a favorite of the legendary Amadeo Giannini, founder of the Bank of Italy (later, Bank of America) and the West's major independent financier.[19] With Giannini backing, Kaiser assumed de facto leadership over the coalition of construction companies building Hoover Dam and became the Six Companies' Washington lobbyist. In the capital Kaiser hired consummate New Deal 'fixer' Tommy Corcoran to represent his interests in the White House, while cultivating his own special relationship to powerful Interior Secretary Harold Ickes.[20]

Most importantly, Kaiser, together with Giannini and other local allies, were able to recognize the extraordinary 'window of opportunity' for Western economic development opened up by the political crisis of the 'First' New Deal in 1935–6. To be fair, it was actually Herbert Hoover, the first president from California, who had launched the industrialization of the Pacific Slope by authorizing construction of both the Hoover Dam and the Golden Gate Bridge. But the big chance for Western (and Southern) businessmen came in the interregnum between the Banking Act of 1935 and the beginning of Lendlease, when relations between the White House and Wall Street reached their twentieth-century nadir. As Eastern finance capital (including many key supporters of FDR in 1933) turned against the New Deal, Kaiser and Giannini, together with Texas oil independents and Mormon bankers (led by Six Companies partner and new Federal Reserve chairman Mariner Eccles), politically and financially shored up the Roosevelt administration, preventing the insurgent labor movement from dominating the national Democratic Party.[21] In his epic *Age of Roosevelt*, Arthur Schlesinger describes the convergence of interests that supported the 'Second' ('anti-trust') New Deal of the late 1930s:

It included representatives of the 'new money' of the South and West, like Jesse Jones, Henry J. Kaiser and A.P. Giannini, who . . . were in revolt against the *rentier* mentality of New York and wanted government to force down interest rates and even supply capital for local development. It included representatives of new industries, like communications and electronics [including Hollywood]. ... It included representatives of business particularly dependent on consumer demand, like Sears Roebuck. And it included speculators like Joseph P. Kennedy, who invested in both new regions and new industries.[22]

The modern 'Sunbelt' was largely born out of the political rewards of this Second New Deal coalition. Billions of dollars in federal aid (representing *net* tax transfers from the rest of the country) laid down an industrial infrastructure in California, Washington and Texas. And nearly $110 million in major construction contracts – including the Bay Bridge, the naval base on Mare Island, and Bonneville, Grand Coulee, and Shasta dams – fueled the breakneck expansion of the Kaiser Company. Long before Pearl Harbor, Kaiser was already discussing with Giannini and a select group of Western industrialists (Donald Douglas, Stephen Bechtel, and John McCone) strategies for maximizing the role of local capital in a war economy. Recognizing that a Pacific War would make unprecedented demands on the under-industrialized California economy, Kaiser proposed to adapt Detroit's assembly-line methods to revolutionize the construction of merchant shipping. Although critics initially scoffed at the idea that a mere 'sand and gravel man' could master the art of shipbuilding, Kaiser, with the support of his high-level New Deal connections, became the biggest shipbuilder in American history. In four years his giant Richmond, Portland and Vancouver (Washington) yards launched a third of the American merchant navy (80 per cent of 'Liberty Ships') as well as fifty 'baby flat-top' aircraft carriers: nearly 1,500 vessels in all.[23]

In Richmond, where 747 ships were built, Kaiser was able to create a social and technological template for postwar capitalism. To simplify welding, huge deckhouses were assembled upside-down and then hoisted into place, helping reduce the traditional six-month shipbuilding cycle to a week. In the absence of a skilled labor force, Kaiser 'trained something like three hundred thousand welders [at Richmond alone] out of soda jerks and housewives'.[24] But his real genius was the systematic attention he focused on maintaining labor at high productivity with minimum time lost to sickness or turnover – the nightmares of other military contractors. Back in 1938, while trying to meet deadlines on the Grand Coulee, Kaiser experimented with transforming indirect medical costs into a direct, calculable industrial input by subscribing his workers to the pre-paid health plan pioneered by Dr Sidney Garfield. This Permanente Health Plan – to be the most enduring part of the Kaiser legacy – was adapted with union collaboration to the massive Richmond workforce, together with active company intervention to construct war housing, organize recreation and rationalize overloaded public transport (Kaiser imported cars from the old Sixth Avenue El in New York).[25]

But Kaiser's Richmond shipyards had a critical bottleneck: a persistent shortage of steel plate. An industrial colony of the East, the West Coast had always imported steel at high markups ($6–$20 per ton); now, in the midst of a superheated war economy, the Eastern mills could not supply, nor could the railroads transport, enough of this high-cost steel to meet the demands of Pacific shipyards. Although US Steel's Benjamin Fairless claimed that 'abstract economic justice no more demands that the Pacific Coast have a great steel industry than that New York grow its own oranges',[26] the war shortage prompted the corporation to propose a new integrated (ore to steel) mill on a Utah coalfield. Arguing, however, that the postwar Western market would not justify the extra capacity added by the mill, US Steel demanded that the Defense Production Corporation pay the cost of construction.

Kaiser countered with his own, characteristically audacious proposal to borrow the money from the government to build on his own account a tidewater steel complex in the Los Angeles area, using Boulder (Hoover) Dam power. From the outset this was treated by all sides as a Western declaration of independence from Big Steel, provoking rage in Pittsburgh in equal measure to the enthusiasm it generated in California. In the event, Washington tried to satisfy all sides by allowing US Steel to operate the government-built mill in Geneva, Utah, while loaning $110 million to Kaiser via the Reconstruction Finance Corporation.[27] The War Department, however, whether acting from post-Pearl Harbor hysteria, or secretly lobbied by Big Steel (as Mezerik believed), insisted that the Kaiser facility had to be located at least fifty miles inland, 'away from possible Japanese air attack'.[28] This locational constraint was widely thought to preclude postwar conversion of the facility to competitive production. Rule-of-thumb wisdom held that an integrated complex could only operate at a profit if dependence on rail transport was confined to one 'leg' of its logistical 'tripod' of iron ore, coking coal and steel product. A Southern California tidewater plant was accorded but a slim chance of survival in the postwar market; an inland location, dependent upon coal and iron rail shipments from hundreds of miles away, was considered an economic impossibility.[29]

But Kaiser believed that 'problems were only opportunities with their work clothes on', and refused to be daunted. He calculated that radical economies in steel-making and mining technology, together with the vast promise of the postwar California market (drastically underestimated by Big Steel), would allow him to convert profitably to peacetime production. Accepting the War Department's disadvantageous conditions, he sent his engineers in search of a suitable inland location. They quickly fixed their sights on Fontana.

THE DE LUXE WAR BABY

From Pigs to Pig Iron!
Fontana Steel Will Build a New World!
Kaiser Slogans, 1940s[30]

In that Indian summer before Pearl Harbor, Fontana's destiny seemed fixed forever on hogs, eggs and citrus. While locals debated the hot prospects in the annual 'Hen Derby' or fretted over rising mortality on 'Death Alley' (Valley Boulevard), Fontana Farms publicists were boasting that the 1940 Census 'Proves Fontana, Top Agricultural Community in the United States!'[31] A.B. Miller, now in partnership with giant Swift and Company, waxed more powerful than ever in state agribusiness circles and conservative Inland Empire politics. Then, with chilling punctuality, death struck down Fontana's founders: Miller (April 1941), followed within months by leading businessman Charles Hoffman, water system founder William Stale, and Fontana Farms Citrus Director J.A. McGregor.[32]

With the passing of the pioneer generation, and the growing awareness that California would soon become the staging ground for a vast Pacific war, boosters in spring 1941 began a xenophobic promotion of Fontana as an ideal location for war industry. Miller's Fontana Farms successor, R.E. Boyle, joined local supervisor C.E. Grier and congressman Henry Sheppard, in cajoling Fontanans into accepting that their 'patriotic duty . . . based on real American principles' was to create the new 'Partnership of Agriculture and [War] Industry'.[33] But six months of aggressive advertising and patriotic bombast yielded not a single munitions plant or aircraft factory. Instead, the hysteria that followed Pearl Harbor, when Japanese aircraft were daily 'sighted' over Long Beach and Hollywood, prompted a sudden rush for 'safe', inland residences. In the early weeks of 1942 Fontana Farms was selling two ranches per day to anxious refugees from Los Angeles.[34] Even supervisor Grier, chief advocate of the military industrialization of the Inland Empire, was forced to admit that Fontana would contribute 'in great measure to winning the war by the productivity of its poultry'.[35] Then came the great bolt from Kaiser headquarters in Oakland.[36]

Prevented from building at tidewater, Kaiser was attracted to Fontana for two different reasons. On the one hand, his engineers and their military counterparts added up the ready-made advantages of Miller's infrastructural investments: cheap power from Lytle Creek (now augmented by Boulder Dam), excellent rail connections near two major railyards (San Bernardino and Colton), and, most importantly in a semi-desert, an autonomous, low-cost water supply.[37] The weak claims of local government over the unincorporated Fontana area were also considered an asset. San Bernardino was a 'poor rural county' with an unusually large relief load, and Kaiser clearly preferred to deal with, and if necessary, overawe and intimidate, its unsophisticated officials, desperate for any type of industrial investment, than face more powerful and self-confident public bureaucracies elsewhere.

On the other hand, Kaiser was personally captivated by Miller's utopia. As in Richmond, he placed social engineering on par with the priorities of production engineering, figuring that hens and citrus might mitigate the class struggle.

He saw advantages to building in a rural community. Workers at the steel mill had the opportunity to raise chickens on the side or plant gardens. Kaiser believed these 'hobby farms' created a more relaxed atmosphere and the workers would be more content. It was something that could not be found in the Eastern steel towns [and, therefore, a comparative advantage].[38]

On the first anniversary of A.B. Miller's interment, Kaiser broke ground on a former Miller ranch a few miles west of Fontana township, his

THE MIRACLE MAN COMETH

bulldozers literally chasing the hogs away.[39] Under the supervision of veterans of Grand Coulee and Richmond, the construction shock-brigades made breathtaking progress. By 30 December 1942 the acrid smell of coke smoke hung over the citrus groves, and, as local radio announcer Chet Huntley officiated, Mrs Henry J. Kaiser threw the switch that fired the giant, 1,200-ton blast furnace named in her honor ('Big Bess'). An even more elaborate ceremony in May 1943 celebrated the tapping of the first steel. Surrounded by Hollywood stars and top military brass, Kaiser – with typical bravado – announced that Fontana was the beginning of the 'Pacific Era' and 'a great industrial empire for the West'. Fleets of diesel trucks began the long shuttle of Fontana-made plate to the steel-hungry shipyards of Richmond and San Pedro.[40]

The vast, mile-square plant – Southern California's 'de luxe war baby'[41] – seemed to erupt out of the earth before Fontanans had a chance to weigh the impact on their small rural society. Perhaps because of the rapidity of the transition, or because of patriotic consensus, there was no recorded protest against the plant construction. Kaiser spokesmen reassured residents that the plant 'could be erected in the middle of an orange grove and operated continuously without the slightest damage to trees'.[42] By the end of the first year, however, disturbing evidence to the contrary had become obvious. The coking coal first employed at Fontana had high sulfur content, producing acidic vapors that withered saplings and burnt the leaves off trees. Ranchers across from the mill picked grapefruit from their trees for the last time in the fall of 1942.[43] This was the beginning of the end of Miller's Eden, as well as the start of a regional pollution problem of major proportions.

While Fontanans were watching their trees die, Kaiser was shattering the illusion of starry-eyed San Bernardino County supervisors that the plant would be an enormous tax windfall. Assessed at normal rates in July 1943, the Company rejected the County's bill out of hand, warning that they 'might be forced to close the plant'. Although reporters scoffed at the obviously absurd threat to shutter the brand-new, $110 million mill, over-awed supervisors obediently reduced the assessment to a small fraction of the original.[44] Their concession set a precedent that allowed Kaiser officials to protest any prospective tax increase as undercutting the economic viability of the plant. As a result, San Bernardino County saw its major potential tax resource evolve into a net tax liability (a fact that helps explain official apathy to the plant's closure a generation later).

As the experts had foreseen, the major difficulty in producing steel in Fontana was the organization of raw material supply. Kaiser could purchase limestone and dolomite flux from local quarries, but it had no alternative but to develop its own network of captive mines to source iron and coal. Although geologists reassured Kaiser that the nearby Mojave Desert contained enough iron ore within a three-hundred-mile radius to supply the plant for several centuries, exploitation of the richest deposits required costly investments in rail-laying and mining technology. Initially Fontana was supplied with ore from the Vulcan Mine near Kelso; after the war, the company developed the great Eagle Mountain complex in Riverside County with its own rail line and mining workforce of 500. Coking coal – the most difficult supply variable – had to be imported 800 miles from Price, Utah (in 1960 Kaiser Fontana switched to new mines in New Mexico). Overall, Fontana was refining low-cost iron ore with the nation's highest cost coal: an equation that left its furnace costs well above other integrated mills (including US Steel's coalfield plant in Utah).[45]

Despite the burden of these supply costs, Kaiser by 1944 was making steel more efficiently than anyone had expected to build ships in greater tonnage than anyone had dreamt possible. He was also smelting aluminum, assembling bombers, mixing concrete, even producing the incendiary 'goop' with which the Army Air Corps was systematically immolating Tokyo and Osaka. At the pinnacle of his popularity, he was widely rumored to be Roosevelt's favorite choice for a fourth-term running-mate. Meanwhile, his alliance with the New Deal had catapulted the Kaiser companies to the top rank of privately-owned firms, and, unlike the California aircraft industry, his operations were totally independent of Wall Street and Eastern banks. (When he was not borrowing government money, his old ally Giannini made available the Bank of America's largest single line of credit.)[46] Buoyed by the successes of his shipyards and steel and aluminum mills, Kaiser surveyed a bold, coordinated expansion into postwar markets for medical care, appliances, housing, aircraft and automobiles. In his wartime speeches, Kaiser was fond of adding a fifth 'freedom' to Roosevelt's original four: 'the freedom of abundance'.[47]

He recognized, with singular prescience, that the conjuncture of rising union power (which he supported) and wartime productivity advances were finally going to unleash the mass consumer revolution that the New Deal had long promised. He also calculated that the pent-up demand for housing and cars, fueled by the fantastic volume of wartime forced savings, created an explosive market situation in which independent entrepreneurs like himself might find the opportunity of the century to compete with the Fortune 500. Everything depended on the speed of reconversion/retooling and the ability to offer the kind of streamlined products that Americans had been dreaming about since the 1939 New York World's Fair.

With characteristic hubris, Henry J. attempted to expand into all markets simultaneously. His venture into experimental aviation was short-lived, when he abandoned to the obsessive Howard Hughes the further development of their prototype super-transport, the notorious 'Spruce Goose'.[48] In the field of mass-produced housing, on the other hand, Kaiser had substantial success. For two decades he had been building homes for his dam and shipyard workers, even master-planning entire communities. He had also been discussing the national housing crisis with such seminal thinkers as Norman Bel Geddes, the designer of the famous Futurama exhibit at the 1939 World's Fair. Shortly after V-J Day Kaiser dramatically announced a 'housing revolution': 'America's answer to the so-called accomplishments of Communists and Fascists'. Creating 'a nearly 100 mile plant-to-site assembly line' in Southern California (where he predicted that immigration would reach a million per year in the immediate postwar period), he launched construction of ten thousand pre-fabricated homes in the Westchester, North Hollywood and Panorama City areas. Defying an acute shortage of ordinary building materiel, Kaiser engineers innovated with fiberglass board, steel, aluminum siding, and sheet gypsum, while 'appplying Richmond methods' to train armies of construction workers whom Kaiser promptly unionized.[49]

But Kaiser Homes, however important in demonstrating the feasibility of postwar 'merchant homebuilding', were only a sideshow for their master. Henry J.'s real ambition was to challenge the Eastern corporate establishment on its own turf. Unfortunately, he chose to fight Detroit and Pittsburgh at the same time. 'Tilting at the most dangerous and dramatic of American windmills',[50] he launched Kaiser-Frazer Motors in a giant reconverted bomber plant in Willow Run, Michigan. Simultaneously, he brought Fontana steel into direct competition with Big Steel for control of Western markets.

Only one capitalist from the West had ever attempted such a brazen invasion of the East: Giannini in the late 1920s. For the impudence of

staking a seat on Wall Street, Giannini was temporarily deposed in his own
house, as J.P. Morgan mounted a retaliatory raid on Transamerica, the
Giannini bank holding company.[51] (As a Morgan director told Giannini:
'Right or wrong, you do as you're told down here'.)[52] It was poetic justice,
therefore, that Giannini was allied to Kaiser's postwar schemes, introducing
him to Joseph Frazer, the rebel Detroit capitalist, as well as supporting the
campaign to refinance Fontana steel.

The 'debacle' of Kaiser-Frazer has been recently retold in Mark Foster's
scholarly biography of Henry J. Fearing postwar layoffs as well as an anti-
union backlash by the major automakers, the United Auto Workers had
begged Kaiser to convert the Willow Run assembly lines (scheduled for
closure after V-J Day) to auto production. Teamed up with Frazer, the
former head of Willys-Overland, and cheered on by the unions, Kaiser and
his engineers tried to duplicate the miracle of Richmond. Within a year of
taking over Willow Run, they had built 100,000 cars and recruited an impressive national network of dealerships. The 1947 Kaiser-Frazer shock-
wave rattled nerves in the executive suites of Dearborn Park and the
Chrysler Building. But, endemically undercapitalized in face of the auto
majors' billion-dollar plant expansions and model-changes, the new
company sank deep into the red. In the meantime Giannini had died, Wall
Street had boycotted Kaiser's offerings, and Frazier had resigned. After the
failure of a last-ditch remodeling in 1954–5, Willow Run was sold off to
General Motors and the dies were shipped to South America where Kaiser-
body cars were still being assembled as late as the 1970s. Although Kaiser
continued for another decade to build Jeeps at his Willys-Overland subsidiary in Toledo, the Western invasion of Detroit was over.[53]

Fontana, by contrast, was an untrammeled success, despite bitter
opposition from Big Steel and comparable financial problems to Kaiser-
Frazer's. In the immediate reconversion period of steel shortages and
turbulent industrial relations (1945–6), Kaiser's friendship with the CIO
exempted Fontana from the bitter national steel strike. Expanding into new
product markets, especially construction, Kaiser Steel strained at capacity
during the steel drought, even briefly exporting to Europe. But, once the
steel strike was settled and capacity had began to adjust to demand,
Fontana's inherent logistical and financial problems seemed to signal
doom.[54]

Fortunately, Kaiser metallurgists produced the kind of technical break-through at Fontana that eluded the design teams at Willow Run. Just as Henry J. had brashly promised, his engineers offset their high coal costs by radically reducing coke loads and increasing blast furnace efficiency. Similarly at Eagle Mountain, Kaiser mining engineers pioneered new eco-nomies in ore extraction, reducing their iron costs even further below Eastern averages. By the mid 1950s Fontana was an international bench-mark of advanced steelmaking, keenly studied by steelmasters from Japan and other high raw-material-cost countries.[55]

A more intractable problem was repaying the Reconstruction Finance Corporation (RFC) loan that had built Fontana. With Congress recaptured by the Republicans in 1946, and his New Deal allies leaving the Truman Admini-stration in droves, Kaiser was politically isolated. Under fire in Congress for alleged profiteering on his wartime shipbuilding contracts (a calumny, he charged, that was spread by his Eastern corporate enemies), he was unable to persuade the RFC to discount or refinance any of his 1942 loan. Despite liberal support (the *New Republic* denounced the RFC for betraying the West's 'attempts to build its own steel mills and free itself from control by the East'), and innumerable resolutions from chambers of commerce, Kaiser had exhausted his political IOUs. To rub salt in his wounds, the War Assets Administration auctioned the Geneva, Utah, mill to US Steel (the *lowest* bidder) for a mere twenty-five cents on the dollar of its cost.[56]

If steel demand had softened at this precarious point, Fontana might have floundered. Instead a big transcontinental gas pipeline deal provided Kaiser Steel with invaluable collateral, while the sudden outbreak of the Korean War revived the West Coast shipbuilding industry. Following the advice of the Giannini family (who also extended Fontana's credit), Kaiser made his steel operations public. The Los Angeles business elite, led by *Times* heir Norman Chandler (who became a Kaiser Steel director) and old friend John McCone, rallied to the initial stock offering, allowing Henry J. to retire the RFC loan in 1950.[57]

With increased access to private capital, and with a Southern California market booming beyond all expectations, Kaiser Steel expanded and diversified. Two postwar expansions added a second blast furnace as well as new tinplate, strip and pipe mills; a revolutionary pellatizing plant was installed at Eagle Mountain; and in 1959 Governor Brown joined Henry J.

for the dedication of a state-of-the-art basic oxygen furnace. With a work-force of eight thousand, and plans on the drawing board for doubling capacity, Kaiser Steel was a national midget, but a regional giant. In 1962, in a move that 'was a big step in the direction of eliminating that historic phrase "prices slightly higher west of the Rockies" ', Kaiser Steel sharply reduced its prices. Eastern steel was virtually driven from the market, leaving Fontana, together with US Steel at Geneva, to co-monopolize the Pacific Slope.[58]

Equally reassuring, Kaiser Steel seemed to continue in the forefront of enlightened industrial relations. Although, unlike in 1946, Fontana was closed down during the long 1959 steel strike, it broke ranks with Big Steel to embrace the United Steel Workers' proposals for a gains-sharing plan to integrate technological change into the collective bargaining framework. First a tripartite committee, with a public member, was established to study conflicts between local work rules and the introduction of automation. Then in 1963 the company and union, with considerable ceremony, forma-lized the landmark Long Range Sharing Plan (loosely based on the so-called 'Scanlon plan'), whose complex formulae and provisions were supposed to fairly compensate workers for accepting rapid productivity advance. The Plan, whose original backers had included the elite of academic industrial relations specialists and two future Secretaries of Labor (Goldberg and Dunlop), became the Kennedy Administration's prototype for New Frontier-era collective bargaining, and was soon cited as such in every industrial relations textbook.[59]

This was the golden age of Kaiser Steel, Fontana – flagship of the West's postwar smokestack economy. Neither the captain on the deck, nor the crew below, could see the economic icebergs ahead.

HOLOCAUST IN FONTANA

Whites from the South compose the majority of the population of
Fontana. They have brought to that community their backward
community mores, their hate-mongering religious cults . . .
O'Day Short, murdered by Fontana vigilantes, 1946[60]

For hundreds of Dustbowl refugees from the Southwest, still working in the orchards at the beginning of World War Two, Kaiser Steel was the happy ending to the Grapes of Wrath. Construction of the mill drained the San Bernardino Valley of workers, creating an agricultural labor shortage that was not relieved until the coming of the *braceros* in 1943. Kaiser originally believed that he could apply his Richmond methods to shaping the Fontana workforce: leaving the construction crews in place and 'training them in ten days to make steel' under the guidance of experts hired from the East. But he underestimated the craft knowledge and folklore, only communicated through hereditary communities of steelworkers, that were essential to making steel. Urgent appeals, therefore, were circulated through the steel valleys of Pennsylvania, Ohio and West Virginia, recruiting draft-exempt steel specialists for Fontana.[61]

The impact of five thousand steelworkers and their families on local rusticity was predictably shattering. The available housing stock in Fontana and western San Bernardino County (also coveted by incoming military families) was quickly saturated. With few zoning ordinances to control the anarchy, temporary and substandard shelters of every kind sprouted up in Fontana and neighboring districts like Rialto, Bloomington and Cucamonga. Most of the original blast furnace crew was housed in a gerry-built trailer park known affectionately as 'Kaiserville'. Later arrivals were often forced to live out of their cars. The old Fontana Farms colonists came under great pressure to sell to developers and speculators. Others converted their chicken coops to shacks and rented them to single workers – a primitive housing form that was still common through the 1950s.[62]

Although areas of Fontana retained their Millerian charm, especially the redtiled village center along Sierra with its art-deco theater and prosperous stores, boisterous, often rowdy, juke joints and roadhouses created a different ambience along Arrow Highway and Foothill Boulevard. Neighboring Rialto – presumably the location of Eddie Mars's casino in Chandler's *The Big Sleep* – acquired a notorious reputation as a wide-open gambling center and L.A. mob hangout (a reputation which it has recovered in the 1990s as the capital of the Inland Empire's crack gangs). Meanwhile the ceaseless truck traffic from the mill, together with the town's adjacency to Route 66 (and, today, to Interstates 10 and 15), made Fontana a major regional trucking center, with bustling twenty-four-hour fuel stops and cafes on its outskirts.[63]

Boomtown Fontana of the 1940s ceased to be a coherent community or cultural fabric. Instead it was a colorful but dissonant *bricolage* of Sunkist growers, Slovene chicken ranchers, gamblers, mobsters, over-the-road truckers, industrialized Okies, *braceros*, the Army Air Corps (at nearby bases), and transplanted steelworkers and their families. It was also a racial frontier where Black families tried to stake out their own modest claims to a ranch home or a job in the mill. Although, as the war in the Pacific was ending, there was an optimistic aura of sunshine and prosperity in the western San Bernardino Valley, there were also increasing undertones of bigotry and racial hysteria. Finally, just before Christmas eve 1945, there was atrocity. The brutal murder (and its subsequent official cover-up) of O'Day Short, his wife and two small children, indelibly stamped Fontana – at least in the eyes of Black Californians – as being violently below the Mason-Dixon line.

Ironically Fontana had been one of the few locations in the Citrus Belt where Blacks had been allowed to establish communities. Every week during the 1940s, the *Eagle* – Los Angeles's progressive Black paper – carried prominent ads for 'sunny, fruitful lots in the Fontana area'.[64] For pent-up residents of the overcrowded Central Avenue ghetto, prevented by restrictive covenants ('L.A. Jim Crow') from moving into suburban areas like the San Fernando Valley, Fontana must have been alluring. Moreover, Kaiser's Richmond shipyards were the biggest employer of Black labor on the coast, and there was widespread hope that his new steel plant would be an equally color-blind employer. The reality in Fontana was that Blacks were segregated in their own tracts – a kind of citrus ghetto – on the rocky floodplain above Baseline Avenue in vaguely delineated 'north Fontana'. Meanwhile in the mill, Blacks and Chicanos were confined to the dirtiest departments – coke ovens and blast furnaces (a situation unchanged until the early 1970s).

O'Day Short, already well known in Los Angeles as a civil rights activist, was the first to challenge Fontana's residential segregation by buying land in town (on Randall Street) in fall 1945. Short's move coincided with the Ku Klux Klan's resurgence throughout Southern California, as white supremacists mobilized to confront militant returning Black and Chicano servicemen. In early December, Short was visited by 'vigilantes', probably Klansmen, who ordered him to move or risk harm to his family. Short stood his ground, reporting the threats to the FBI and the county sheriff, as well as alerting the Black press in Los Angeles. Instead of providing protection, sheriff's deputies warned Short to leave before any 'disagreeableness' happened to his family. The Fontana Chamber of Commerce, anxious to keep Blacks above Baseline, offered to buy Short out. He refused.[65]

A few days later, on 16 December, the Short house was consumed in an inferno of 'unusual intensity'. Neighbors reported hearing an explosion, then seeing 'blobs of fire' on the ground and the family running from their home with clothes ablaze. Short's wife and small children died almost immediately; unaware of their deaths, he lingered on for two weeks in agony. According to one account, Short finally died after being brutally informed by the district attorney of his family's fate. (The D.A. was later criticized for breaking the hospital's policy of shielding Short from further trauma.)[66]

The local press gave the tragedy unusually low-key coverage, quoting the D.A.'s opinion that the fire was an accident.[67] That a coroner's inquest was held at all (on 3 April 1945) was apparently due to pressure from the NAACP and the Black press. 'Contrary to standard practice in such cases', District Attorney Jerome Kavanaugh refused to allow witnesses to testify about the vigilante threats to the Short family. Instead Kavanaugh read into the record the interview he had conducted with Short in the hospital, 'in which the sick man repeatedly said he was too ill and upset to make a statement, but yielded to steady pressure and suggestion by finally saying that the fire seemed accidental "as far as he was concerned" '. Fontana fire officials, conceding they had no actual evidence, speculated that the holocaust might have been the result of a kerosene-lamp explosion. The coroner's jury, deprived of background about the vigilante threats, accordingly ruled that the Shorts had died from 'a fire of unknown origin'. The sheriff declined an arson investigation.[68]

The Black community in Fontana – many of whom 'themselves had been admonished by deputy sheriff "Tex" Carlson to advise the Shorts to get out' – were 'unanimous in rejecting the "accident" theory'. Fontana's most famous Black resident, Shelton Brooks (composer of the *Darktown Strutter's Ball*), demanded a full-scale arson investigation. J. Robert Smith, crusading publisher of the *Tri-Country Bulletin*, the Black paper serving the Inland Empire, decried an official cover-up of 'mass murder' – a charge echoed by Short's friends, Joseph and Charlotta Bass, publishers of the Los Angeles *Eagle*.[69]

The case became a brief national *cause célèbre* after the Los Angeles NAACP, led by Lorenzo Bowdoin, hired renowned arson expert, Paul T. Wolfe, to sift through the evidence. Noting that the supposed cause of the fire, the kerosene lamp, had actually been recovered intact, he found compelling evidence that the Short home had been deliberately soaked in quantities of coal oil to produce an explosive blaze of maximum ferocity. He concluded that 'beyond a shadow of a doubt the fire was of an incendiary origin'. In the meantime, the *Tri-County Bulletin* discovered that the original sheriff's report on the fire had 'mysteriously' disappeared from its file, while the *Eagle* raised fundamental doubts about Short's purported testimony to D.A. Kavanaugh. Mass demonstrations were held in San Bernardino and Los Angeles, as scores of trade-union locals, progressive Jewish organizations, and civil-rights groups endorsed the NAACP's call for a special investigation of 'lynch terror in Fontana' by California's liberal attorney general Robert Kenny (another Gunther favorite). Catholic Interracial Council leader Dan Marshall pointed out that 'murder is the logical result of discrimination', while Communist leader Pettis Perry described the Short case as 'the most disgraceful that has ever occurred in California'.[70]

But it was hard to keep the Short holocaust in focus. Attorney General Kenny succeeded in temporarily banning the Ku Klux Klan in California, but made no attempt to reopen investigation into the Short case or expose the official whitewash by San Bernardino officials. The Los Angeles NAACP, spearhead of the campaign, quickly became preoccupied with the renewed struggle against housing discrimination in Southcentral Los Angeles.[71] The Trotskyist Socialist Workers' Party continued its own sectarian campaign through the spring of 1946, but used the Short case primarily to polemicize against Kenny (Democratic nominee for governor) and his Communist supporters.[72] In the end, as protest faded, the vigilantes won the day: Blacks stayed north of Baseline (and in the coke ovens) for another generation, and the fate of the Short family, likely victims of white supremacy, was officially forgotten.[73]

However, early postwar Fontana found it difficult to avoid notoriety. If the press downplayed the Short case, it sensationalized the murder trial of Gwendelyn Wallis – a local policeman's wife who confessed to shooting her husband's mistress, a pretty young Fontana schoolteacher named Ruby Clark. At a time when countless Hollywood films in the Joan Crawford vein were beginning to sermonize against wartime morals and gender equality, the Wallis trial became a lightning rod for contending values. Girls argued with their mothers, husbands fought with wives, marriages reportedly even broke up, over Gwendelyn's justification for killing Ruby: that she was a 'scheming, single, working woman'. Her surprise acquittal in March 1946 was greeted across the country with both anger and celebration. At the courthouse in San Bernardino she was 'mobbed by sympathetic women' – mostly long-suffering housewives like herself, who had become her adoring fans in the course of this real-life soap opera.[74]

Finally, to permanently reinforce the new Fontana's wild image, 1946 was also the year that the original nucleus of the Hell's Angels began to coalesce in the area. According to legend, the founders were demobbed bomber crewmen, right out of the pages of Heller's *Catch 22*, who rejected the return to staid civilian lives. Whatever the true story, the Fontana-based gang were surely participants in the infamous Hollister (July 1947) and Riverside (July 1948) motorcycle riots that were immortalized by Brando in *The Wild One* ('the bike rider's answer to the *Sun Also Rises*').[75] When the beleaguered American Motorcycle Association denounced an 'outlaw one per cent', the proto-Angels made that label their badge of honor. At a 'One-Percenters' convention in Fontana in 1950 the Hell's Angels were formally organized; the 'Fontana-Berdoo' chapter became the 'mother' chapter with exclusive authority to charter new branches. The founding philosophy of the group was succinctly explained by a Fontana member: 'We're bastards to the world, and they're bastards to us.'

Although 'Berdoo' continued through the 1960s as the nominal capital of outlaw motorcycledom, power within the Angels shifted increasingly toward the ultra-violent Oakland chapter led by Sonny Barger, who also launched the group into big-time narcotics dealing.[76] As Hunter Thompson put it, 'the Berdoo Angels made the classic Dick Nixon mistake of "peaking" too early'. There are two different versions of the story of their decline. According to 'Freewheelin' Frank', the acidhead Nazi secretary of the San Francisco chapter, 'Berdoo' was ruined by the seduction of the movie industry and a lawyer-huckster named Jeremiah Castelman who convinced them that they would become rich selling Hell's Angels T-shirts.[77]

In the other version of the story, they were driven off the streets by police repression. After the lurid publicity of a rape and two violent brawls, the Berdoo Angels became the *bête noire* of LAPD Chief William Parker, who organized a posse of law enforcement agencies to crush the chapter. Establishing police checkpoints on favorite motorcycle itineraries like the Pacific Coast Highway and the Ridge Route, he generated 'such relentless heat that those few who insisted on wearing the colors [Angel jackets] were forced to act more like refugees than outlaws, and the chapter's reputation withered accordingly'. By 1964, when Thompson was slumming with the Oakland chapter, Fontana – 'heartland of the Berdoo chapter's turf' – had been essentially pacified. Local Angels 'couldn't even muster a quorum' for an outlaw motorcycle scene in a Sal Mineo movie: 'some were in jail, others had quit and many of the best specimens had gone north to Oakland'.[78] Despite its eclipse, however, the Berdoo chapter never collapsed. A generation after Thompson's account, mother Angels are still bunkered in their Fontana redoubt, raising enough hell to force the cancellation of a major motorcycle show in Downtown Los Angeles (in February 1990) after a violent collision with another gang.[79]

MILLTOWN DAYS

For Abel to win the nomination at Fontana, the public relations pivot of the McDonald administration, would be a definite psychological victory. *John Herling*[80]

After the turbulent, sometimes violent, transitions of the 1940s, Fontana settled down into the routines of a young milltown. The Korean War boom enlarged the Kaiser workforce by almost 50 per cent and stimulated a new immigration from the East that reinforced the social weight of traditional steelworker families. The company devoted new resources to organizing the leisure time of its employees, while the union took a more active role in the community. The complex craft subcultures of the plant intersected with ethnic self-organization to generate competing cliques and differential pathways for mobility. At the same time, the familar sociology of plant-community interaction was overlaid by lifestyles peculiar to Fontana's Millerian heritage and its location on the borders of metropolitan Los Angeles and the Mojave Desert. Although locals continued to joke that

Fontana was just Aliquippa with sunshine, it was evolving into a *sui generis* working-class community.

This is not to deny that there was a lot of Aliquippa (or Johnstown or East Pittsburgh) in Fontana. Mon Valley immigrants ended up as the dominant force in United Steel Workers Local 2869. Dino Papavero, for instance, who was president of the local in the early 1970s, moved out from Aliquippa in 1946 because his father was worried about a postwar slump at Jones and Laughlin. It was widely believed amongst Pennsylvania steelworkers that Kaiser, in booming California, was recession-proof. John Piazza – Papavero's vice-president and current leader of the Fontana School Board – first came to San Bernardino County (from Johnstown, PA) as one of Patton's 'tank jockeys' training for the Sahara in the Mojave. While hitchhiking Route 66 to the Hollywood USO he was intrigued by a billboard boasting of the opening of Kaiser Steel. After the war, he found himself trapped in an apparently hopeless cycle of layoff and rehiring at Bethlehem which seemed to preclude any advancement up the seniority ladder. Together with other Johnstowners, he headed out to Fontana – initially living in one of the converted chicken coops – because Kaiser advertised itself as a frontier of opportunity for younger workers.[81]

These young Mon Valley immigrants quickly discovered that mobility within the plant or union in Fontana, as in Aliquippa or Johnstown, depended upon the mobilization of ethnic and work-group loyalties. The oldest and most visible of local ethnicities were the Slovenes. Their community core – a group of Ohio coal miners who had amassed small savings – had come to Fontana in the 1920s as chicken ranchers, establishing a prosperous branch of the Slovene National Benevolent Society, a large meeting hall and retirement home. Some of their children worked in the mill. Although only informally organized, the 'Roadrunners' from West Virginia and the Okies constituted distinctive subcultures within both the plant and the community. But it was the local Sons of Italy chapter – attracting streetwise and ambitious young steelworkers like Papavero and Piazza – that ultimately generated a whole cadre of union leaders during the 1960s and 1970s.

Although the Southern California District of the USW in the 1950s and early 1960s, under Director Charles Smith and his henchman, Billy Brunton, was a loyalist stronghold of international president Donald McDonald, Local 2869 with its Mon Valley transplants became a hotbed of

DREAM HOUSE

discontent. Many Kaiser workers resented Smith's and Brunton's proconsular powers and ability to bargain over their heads in a situation where Local 2869 was far and away the largest unit in the District. In 1957 the rank and file dramatically registered their dissent by electing Tom Flaherty, local spokesman for the national anti-McDonald movement (the Dues Protest Committee), as president of 2869. After several wildcat strikes, the Kaiser management demanded that McDonald intervene to force the local 'to discharge its contractual obligations'. Obligingly the international imposed an 'administratorship' on 2869 and deposed Flaherty and his followers.[82]

Although 'law and order' were now officially restored within Fontana by the international's police action, the opposition was simply driven underground. By 1963–4 the older dues protesters (led by Joe and Minnie Luksich) had been joined by younger workers embittered by the wage inequalities generated by the new 'fruits of progress' plan. To rub salt in rank-and-file wounds, the Committee of Nine who administered the plan virtually ignored Local 2869 and Fontana, preferring to conduct their deliberations in the more congenial setting of a Palm Springs resort. As a result, 'the situation deteriorated so badly in the summer of 1964 that the members picketed the union hall. Their signs read: "USWA Unfair to Organized Labor" and "Equal Pay for Equal Work".' At this point, Ronald Bitoni, former chairman of the plant grievance committee, began to unify the different opposition factions around the national insurgency of I.W. Abel, a dissident official supported by Walter Reuther. In his history of the successful Abel campaign, John Herling described Fontana as both the 'gem of McDonald's achievement in labor–management cooperation' and the Achilles heel of his power in the West. On election day, 9 February 1965, tens of thousands of pro-Abel steelworkers in the oppositional heartland of the Ohio and Monogahela valleys nervously watched to see how Fontana, two thousands miles away, would vote. Abel's commanding 2,782 to 1,965 victory within Local 2869 announced the end of the *ancien régime*.[83] But at the same time it warned of profound rank-and-file discontent with the 'textbook' gains-sharing model. Within a few years many Kaiser unionists would be as alienated from the 'reformist' administration of Abel as they had been from the absolutism of McDonald.

While Local 2869 was fighting to increase local control over the gains-sharing plan, the relationship between the company and the town was evolving in a very curious way. Despite the stereotype of being a Kaiser 'company town', Fontana was no such thing. When Fontana incorporated in 1952, the mill was left outside the city limits in its own, low-tax 'county island'. Not contributing directly to the town's budget, Kaiser lacked the despotic fiscal clout that Eastern steelmakers conventionally exercised over their captive local governments. Nor did a majority of Kaiser management ever live in the Fontana area. Unlike Bethlehem or Johnstown, no corporate suburb or country-club district projected the social and political power of management into the community. Managers, instead, commuted from gentile redtile towns like Redlands, Riverside and Ontario. The dominating presence in Fontana was, rather, the huge union hall on Sierra. Local merchants and professionals were left in relatively unmediated dependence upon the goodwill of their blue-collar customers and neighbors. Although never directly controlled by labor, Fontana government, as a result, tended to remain on the friendly side of the union.

Yet while eschewing direct control, the Company still played an ubiquitous role in communal life. The location of the mill, far from big city lights, stimulated the organization of leisure time around the workplace. Kaiser's 1950s–60s personnel director, Vernon Peake, managed one of the most extensive corporate recreation programs west of the Mississippi. The internal structure of plant society was vividly reproduced in the composition of Kaiser's six bowling leagues during the kegling craze of the 1950s. While Hot Metal battled Cold Roll in the no-nonsense Steelers League, white-collar Bulb Snatchers traded spares with Pencil Pushers in the Fontana League, and Slick Chicks edged Pinettes in the Girls' (sic) League. Like other steel towns, Fontana prided itself on Friday night 'smokers', and there were usually half a dozen pros and scores of amateurs training in the mill's boxing club. 'Roadrunners' and Okies were especially active in the plant's various hunting and gun clubs, while others joined the popular fishing club.[84]

But blue-collar Fontana also enjoyed recreations that were usually management prerogatives in the more rigid caste order of Eastern steel towns. Golf was popular in some production departments, and leading union activists were frequently seen on the fairways. Other steelworkers took up tennis, joined the toastmasters, became rockhounds, rehearsed with the excellent local drama society, or even moonlighted as stuntmen in

Hollywood. Others raced stockcars, dragsters and motorcycles, or simply spent weekends plowing up the Mojave in their dune buggies.[85] Whatever the avocation, the point was that Fontana tended to see itself differently – as more egalitarian and openminded (at least for white workers) – than the steel cultures left behind in the valleys of the Ohio.

DRIVIN' BIG BESS DOWN

The Fontana plant has the potential to be competitive with any in the world. *(1980)*
You can't melt steel in the middle of a residential valley profitably. *(1981)*
Elliot Schneider, steel industry 'expert' [86]

Like every decline and fall, Kaiser Steel's was an accumulation of ironies. One was that the future began to slip away from Fontana, not in the midst of a recession, but at the height of the Vietnam boom. Kaiser was forced out of a rapidly expanding market. Another irony was that, although Kaiser executives in the last days would complain bitterly that Washington had abandoned them in the face of Japanese competition, the company had collaborated avidly with that very same competition in a vain attempt to restructure itself as a steel resource supplier. Kaiser was literally hoisted on its own corporate petard.

After firing up its first Basic Oxygen Furnace (BOF) in 1959, Kaiser Steel neglected plant modernization for almost fifteen years. Having wrested the West from Pittsburgh, it ceased looking over its shoulder at the competition. In the meantime Asian and European steelmakers were rapidly moving ahead with a technological revolution that included full conversion to BOF and the introduction of continuous casting. Kaiser fought the Japanese, its erstwhile protégés and main competitors (whose original plants Kaiser-made 'goop' had incinerated in 1945), with Pearl-Harbor era technology that included obsolete open-hearth furnaces, old-fashioned slab casting, thirty-five-year-old blast furnaces, and dinosaur, over-polluting coke ovens. Although Kaiser protested that the Japanese steel industry enjoyed 'unfair' state subsidies, this hardly explains why its own investment program (the company was in the black until 1969) failed to

BIG BESS, 1990

sustain technological modernization. If Kaiser Steel squandered its once formidable technical leadership, it was because, unlike the more single-minded Japanese, it purposely diverted its cashflow into alternative accumulation strategies.

In truth, Fontana and the other fifty-odd Kaiser enterprises were an unwieldy legacy. After Henry J.'s retirement to Hawaii in the mid 1950s, Kaiser Industries evolved as a family holding company with decreasing hands-on affinity for the world of production. Orthodox financial management, not heroic technical problem-solving, became the order of the day. From this basically rentier perspective, Kaiser Aluminum, with its consistently high profit margins, became the family's darling. Kaiser Industries' long-range planning focused on how to complement aluminum sales to the Pacific Basin with other primary product exports. When, in the early 1960s, the Japanese demand for steel began to soar (as a result of the first stages of a 'Fordist', home-market-led expansion), Kaiser Industries (the major shareholder in Kaiser Steel) was more concerned about sourcing this demand with raw materials than with the future implications of expanded Japanese capacity for international competition. Specifically for Kaiser Steel this entailed a fateful diversion of its plant modernization budget to purchase export-oriented iron ranges in Australia and coal mines in British Columbia. Eagle Mountain was also expensively remodeled, with an elaborate pellatizing plant added to process iron ore for export to Japan. Thus, years before US Steel's notorious acquisition of Marathon Oil with funds coerced from its basic steel workforce in the name of 'modernization', Kaiser Steel was restructuring itself, with diverted capital improvements, to export resources to its principal competitor, while allowing its own industrial plant to become obsolete.[87]

The Vietnam War – which jump-started the Japanese export offensive – dramatically transformed economic relationships around the Pacific Rim. In 1965 Japanese steel imports claimed a tenth of the US West Coast market; by the war's end, a decade later, nearly half the steel in California was Asian-made and the state was officially included in the Japanese steel industry's definition of 'home market'. Kaiser Steel made large profits exporting iron and coal to the Japanese only to see these raw materials shot back at them in the form of Toyotas and I-beams for skyscrapers. Together with US Steel's Geneva mill (still entirely open-hearth since USS's plant modernization had been concentrated in the East), Kaiser Fontana could supply barely half of Western demand, and they were constrained from adding capacity because of their technological inability to compete at cost with the foreign steel. Thus the Japanese, and increasingly the Koreans and the Europeans as well, were able to confiscate all the Vietnam-boom growth in Western steel demand. The so-called 'trigger price mechanism', adopted by the Carter administration at Big Steel's urging, only worsened the situation on the West Coast. Trigger prices were too low to prevent Japanese imports and, because they were calibrated higher in the East, they actually encouraged EEC producers to dump steel in California.[88]

In the meantime Kaiser's vaunted labor peace was beginning to erode. Over the years relations between workers and managers had calcified at the shop level – a situation that was exacerbated by the recruitment of truculent managers from Big Steel during the 1970s. At the same time the incredibly complex formulae of the Long Range Sharing Plan continued to generate pay inequalities that had already sparked protest in 1964–5. Workers retaining membership in the older incentive scheme were winning pay increases at a dramatically higher rate than participants in the general savings scheme (a trend which also aggravated inter-generational tension within the union). Likewise LRSP remuneration seemed arbitrarily detached from individual productivity efforts.[89]

Faced with a new wave of rank-and-file discontent, the recently elected president of Local 2869, Dino Papavero, called a strike vote in February 1972. The resulting 43-day walkout was the first 'local issues' strike – apart from the two 1957 wildcats – in the plant's history. Papavero, who clearly visualized the import threat, hoped that the strike would be a safety-valve, releasing accumulating tensions and paving the way for a new labor–management detente. With the encouragement of the company, he launched a plant-wide 'quality circle' movement in a last-ditch effort to raise productivity to competitive levels. Although workers cooperated in hundreds of improvements, management appeared to go along for a free ride, refusing to implement the broad capital modernization program that was necessary to save the plant. Moreover there was the traditional dissonance between Local 2869's priorities and the International's goals. USW Regional Director George White – as always, concerned about the impact of Kaiser innovations upon Big Steel – opposed the workrule-weakening precedent of the quality circles. He was supported, moreover, by Fontana rank-and-filers embittered by the long walkout and fearful of the loss of hardwon seniority rights and clearcut job boundaries. In 1976 Papavero, the main advocate of cooperativism in the historic spirit of the LRSP, was defeated by a more confrontationist slate.[90]

The year 1976 was indeed one of bad omens. Steel profits had entirely collapsed and Kaiser Steel's net earnings were exclusively sustained by profits from resource exports. The long delayed modernization program, aiming at full conversion to BOF and continuous casting, was finally launched, only to immediately encounter complaints about the plant's role as chief regional polluter. Since the 1960s Fontana had emerged as the literal epicenter of air pollution in Southern California, and Kaiser Steel's huge plume of acrid smoke became indissolubly linked in the public mind with the smog crisis in the Inland Empire.[91] (See map, p. 379.)

The actual situation was considerably more complex: aerial photographs taken by Kaiser during the 1972 strike, when the plant was entirely shut down, showed no abatement in air pollution.[92] Moreover many ex-steelworkers still vehemently believe that the Kaiser pollution scare was purposely manufactured by developers who regarded the plant – smog-spewing or not – as a huge negative externality to residential construction in the Cucamonga–Fontana area. As San Bernardino County's West End fell under the 'urban shadow' of Los Angeles and Orange County, developable property values came into increasing conflict with the paycheck role of the mill as leading local employer. Inevitably the pollution debate reflected these divergent material interests. While developers became strange bed-partners with environmentalists in demanding a huge cleanup at Fontana, the Kaiser workforce joined with its management to protest the costs of abatement. As one ex-steelworker put it, 'Hell, that smoke was our prosperity.'[93]

In the event, Kaiser was forced to sign a consent decree with the Southern California Air Pollution Control Board that mandated $127 million dollars for pollution reduction. This was more than half of the modernization budget.[94] Partly as a result – from 1975 to 1979 while 'modernization' was being implemented – the union was forced to accept painful triage. Capacity was ruthlessly pared as older facilities were scrapped, including the open hearth, the cold weld, pipe and cold roll mills, and, finally, the original BOF. The inefficient and polluting coke ovens, on the other hand, were deemed too expensive to replace and were left intact. Fontana, in quiet anguish, began to bleed away its future. Four thousand younger workers – sons, brothers, and a few daughters – were laid off by seniority. With the company reassuring them that the new technology would restore price competitiveness, Local 2869 accepted partial decimation as a necessary sacrifice to save the plant and the community of steelworkers.[95]

When, at last, the new Kaiser Steel chief, Mark Anthony, launched the modernized facilities in an elaborate ceremony on 9 February 1979, he proclaimed the company's 'rededication to making steel in the West'.[96] But the new technology – including BOF 2, the continuous caster and state-of-the-art emission controls – proved cruelly disappointing. Startup costs were staggeringly over budget, and pollution from the antiquated coke ovens continued to embroil the plant in battles with local and federal air quality control agencies. In the face of this deteriorating situation, and with the vaunted modernization program near shambles, Anthony was removed and Edgar Kaiser, Jr. personally took the helm, advised by experts from his family's investment bankers, First Boston. Although company publicists extolled the return of 'Kaiser magic' to active management, most workers were skeptical.[97] Henry J.'s grandson was widely viewed as a 'playboy', more interested in his toys, like the Denver Broncos, than in saving California's ailing steel industry.[98]

Mistrust became rampant as the Kaiser family's real strategy was gradually revealed. Years later Edgar Jr. confessed to an interviewer that, despite all the promises to the contrary, he had been sent to Fontana in 1979 by his father as a liquidator:

We were both in tears. I knew what it meant. Nobody else saw it, but I knew what I had to do . . . break up a lot of Steel. I sold off a lot of divisions of Steel. My first day on the job was the prodigal son returning. I had to go out after 30 per cent of the workforce at Fontana. . . . It sure wasn't fun.[99]

The Kaiser family had in fact been engaged in negotiations with Nippon Kokan KK, the world's fifth largest steelmaker.[100] The Kaisers wanted the Japanese to take over Fontana while they restructured Kaiser Steel as Nippon Kokan's resource supplier. This was, perhaps, the inevitable consequence of the company's long-term bias towards resources rather than steel products. But to Oakland's consternation Nippon Kokan did not take the bait as expected. Instead, following detailed technical inspections of Fontana by its engineering teams, the Japanese giant politely declined Kaiser's offer.[101]

As Kaiser Steel ran out of cash and its stock plummeted on the exchanges, a second merger deal was hastily confected and put on offer to Dallas-based LTV. The negotiations collapsed in the face of the Volcker–Reagan recession which plunged the US steel industry into its worst crisis since 1930.[102] On the West Coast, as explained in chapter five, local branch-plant manufacture was swept away by a typhoon of Asian imports. At the very moment when Fontana's fate depended on an iron will to survive – as during Henry J.'s fight to pay off the RFC loan after World War Two – the Kaiser heirs reached for the financial ripcord. The cherished goal of a resource-oriented restructuring was abandoned in favor of a staged liquidation of Kaiser Steel.

In order to keep Fontana temporarily afloat as an attraction to potential buyers, and to drive stock values up to assuage panicky stockholders, the Kaisers sold off the Australian ore reserves, the British Columbia coal mines, and the Liberian ore shipping subsidiary.[103] Edgar Jr. withdrew as CEO in 1981 after, as promised, 'breaking up a lot of Steel'.[104] The new managerial team, after a few months of bravado about a 'crusade' to save the blast furnaces, stunned the survivors of previous cutbacks with the announcement that ore mining at Eagle Mountain and primary steelmaking at Fontana would be phased out, while the modernized fabrication facilities were put up for sale. Barely two years after their ceremonious 'rededication', BOF 2 and the continuous caster were being written off as scrap, a $231 million loss.[105]

Local 2869 mustered for a last stand, as best it could, but it had tragically few friends or resources. A desperate move to trade wage and work-rule concessions for job-protection guarantees was cold-shouldered by the company before being vetoed altogether by the international.[106] As horrified members watched another two thousand pink slips being readied, the Local clutched at the final straw of an employee buyout, an 'ESOP'.[107] British Steel, long interested in finding a stable market on the West Coast for its unfabricated steel slabs, signaled that it was ready to consider a liaison with a restructured Fontana mill under ESOP ownership. Local 2869 retained the Kelson Group as advisors and sent representatives to Sacramento to lobby Governor Brown and the Democratic leadership.[108] In the event, however, Kaiser's intransigence about the ESOP frightened off British Steel, while government intervention on behalf of Fontana – or, for that matter, of any of California's floundering heavy industrial plants – was ruled out by Jerry Brown's new *entente cordiale* with the California Business Roundtable.

Meanwhile, San Bernardino County leaders were divided over the implications of the closure of Kaiser Steel. Having boasted for years that Kaiser pumped nearly a billion dollars annually into the local economy, they were anxious about the loss of so many paychecks. But apprehension was balanced by delight at the thought of rising real-estate values and the removal of the county's principal environmental stigma. As a result, with the exception of pro-union Democratic Congressman George Miller, the local elites and politicos sat on their hands.

In the face of this inertia in the local power structure, Local 2869's only remaining hope might have been a militant community-labor mobilization against shutdowns that allied Fontana with similarly threatened factories and communities, like Bethlehem–Maywood, General Motors–South Gate, or US Steel–Torrance.[109] Unfortunately there was no tradition of communication or mutual support between Southern California's big smokestack workforces. Moreover the international unions and the county federations of labor tended to oppose any rank-and-file or local union initiative that threatened their prerogatives. When the rudiments of such a united front – the Coalition Against Plant Closures – finally emerged in 1983 it was too little and too late to save Fontana. At best, some of the survivors managed to float a life raft: the Steelworkers' Oldtimers Foundation, which has helped unionists deal with the bitter aftermaths at Fontana and Bethlehem.

THE UNSCRUPULOUS SUITORS

> How Kaiser Steel arrived at this sorry state is an American tragedy.
> *Forbes*[110]

While Local 2869 was fruitlessly searching for friends in high places, Kaiser Steel was like Ulysses' wife Penelope: haplessly pursued by a hundred

unscrupulous suitors. Despite the reluctance of other steelmakers to assimilate Fontana to their operations, there was no shortage of corporate
predators eager to stripmine the company's financial reserves. Following
the sale of the offshore mineral properties, the company was temporarily
awash in liquidity – by one estimate, almost one-half billion dollars.[111]
Many Wall Street analysts believed that the plant was undervalued. With
shrewd management, they guessed that the modernized core could be
reconfigured as a profitable 'minimill', fabricating imported slabs or local
scrap.[112]

While the new CEO (the sixth in seven years), Stephen Girard, feuded
with the Kaiser family over the terms of sale, desperate unionists and
stockholders looked toward San Francisco investor Stanley Hiller, who was
rumored to represent billionaire speculators Daniel Ludwig and Gaith
Pharaon. Hiller's offer of $52 per share appeased the Kaiser family, but
Girard, trying to retain control over a cash hoard still estimated at $430
million, broke off negotiations. The Kaisers, backed by the union (which
believed it could interest the Hiller group in its ESOP concept), rallied other
large stockholders to override Girard.[113] By March 1982, however, when
Girard resumed talks with Hiller, the write-down costs of phased-out steel
facilities, originally estimated at $150 million, were admitted to be nearly
$530 million, including $112 million in employee termination costs. The
contingent liabilities in health and benefits for the laid-off workforce
seemed especially to overawe the Hiller group, who, to the consternation
of unionists and stockholders, abruptly retreated from the field on 11
March.[114]

The company promptly moved to claim tax write-offs by auctioning its
primary steelmaking equipment for scrap: a final blow that killed any hope
of an ESOP-based resurrection.[115] In late October 1983 the last heat of
Eagle Mountain iron ore was smelted into steel; for another month a
skeleton crew of 800 (out of a workforce that once numbered 9,000) cold-
rolled the remaining slabs into coils, sheets and plate. At 4 p.m. on Saturday,
31 December, Kaiser Steel Fontana died.[116]

While thousands of Kaiser workers and their families mourned the
sinking of California's industrial flagship, sharks in grey flannel suits circled
around the undervalued assets of Kaiser Steel, no longer hemorrhaging $12
million per month in operating deficits. The first to strike was corporate

raider Irwin Jacobs of Minneapolis – known in the trade as 'Irv the Liquidator' – who had become the leading shareholder after the withdrawal of Hiller.[117] Scared that he would simply 'gut' the company, Kaiser Steel management swung behind the rival bid of Oklahoma investor J.A. Frates. Then, as *Forbes* later reported, 'Monty Rial suddenly appeared, uninvited and unknown', swaggering like a corporate Butch Cassidy, and brandishing the high-powered law firm of Wachtell, Lipton, Rosen and Katz. Posing as a coal baron from Colorado (though his holdings had never actually produced a ton of coal), Rial dealt himself into the Kaiser Steel takeover game by boasting that he could profitably restructure the company around its billion tons of high-grade coal reserves in Utah and New Mexico.

What Jacobs and Frates didn't realize, or bother to find out, was that Rial was simply bluffing. While laying siege to Kaiser's half billion dollar equity, Rial's 'Perma Group' was itself less liquid than some of the Fontana bars in which the ex-steelworkers groused. According to *Forbes*, the 'Perma Group couldn't even pay its copying bills. A local copy shop was pursuing the company to collect a past-due $1,200, which Perma paid in twelve monthly installments.' No matter: an impressed and incredibly gullible Frates admitted Rial ('it rhymes with smile') as a fifty–fifty partner. In February 1984 they outbid Jacobs to take control of Kaiser Steel, offering $162 million in cash and $218 million in preferred stock.

The most viable sections of the Fontana plant were immediately sold off – for $110 million (exactly the amount that Kaiser had borrowed from the RFC in 1942) – to a remarkable consortium that included a Long Beach businessman, Japan's giant Kawasaki Steel, and Brazil's Campanhia Vale Rio Doce Ltd. In a mindbending demonstration of how the new globalized economy works, California Steel Industries (as the consortium calls itself) employs a deunionized remnant of the Kaiser workforce under Japanese and British supervision to roll and fabricate steel slabs imported from Brazil to compete in the local market against Korean imports. Derelict Eagle Mountain, whose iron ores are five thousand miles closer to Fontana than Brazil's, has meanwhile been proposed as a giant dump for the non-degradable solid waste being produced by the burgeoning suburbia of the Inland Empire.

While Fontanans were trying to absorb these strange economic dialectics, Rial – the guy who couldn't pay his xerox bill ten months before

– was wresting control of the company from Frates (and transferring its headquarters to Colorado). His method of financing the takeover was ingenious: he sold to Kaiser Steel, at incredibly inflated prices, additional coal reserves which he owned and which it scarcely needed. The impact of the two back-to-back leveraged buyouts was little short of devastating. The original half-billion-dollar cash hoard was reduced to $500,000 as the raiders ran away with their spoils.[118] Moreover the company was hopelessly saddled with new, and utterly unnecessary, debt. As the rest of the business press was celebrating the contribution of corporate raiders to making the economy 'leaner and greener', two *Forbes* journalists saw a different moral in the story of Frates and Rial looting Kaiser Steel without spending a penny of their own money:

Frates staged a classic, no-money-down, 1980s takeover. Kaiser Steel changed hands for $380 million. Where did the money come from? Not from the pockets of the people doing the takeover. The Frates Group used $100 million borrowed from Citibank and $62 million of Kaiser's own cash to pay $22 a share to Kaiser's stockholders, and gave them $30 [face value] of preferred stock for the rest of the price. Thus, for $162 million that wasn't his and $218 million of paper in the form of Kaiser Steel preferred, Frates took over the company. Naturally, Frates took millions of dollars in fees and expenses, so his net cash investment was less than nothing.

[To buy out Frates] Rial traded illiquid assets to Kaiser for land and cash. . . . Kaiser shelled out $78 million for the same Perma assets Frates valued 18 months earlier at only $65 million. What's more, because the SPS [coal contract] was valued at only $12.2 million this time around, the value of Rial's coal properties must have risen to $65.8 million – a 65% increase. . . . When the dust settled Frates had $20 million of cash, a $5 million near-cash receivable . . . and $15 million of Kaiser land. . . . Rial hasn't stinted himself, however. He took $2.4 million in salary last year.[119]

Rial's swashbuckling depredations finally provoked a backlash from Kaiser Steel's preferred stockholders who allied themselves with Bruce Hendry, the famous scrapdealer in distressed companies (he had previously picked over the remains of Erie-Lackawanna and Wickes).[120] Forcing Rial aside as CEO in 1987, Hendry proposed to rescue the stockholders' equity at the expense of the ex-Kaiser workforce. Borrowing a leaf from Frank Lorenzo, Hendry plunged Kaiser Steel into a chapter-eleven proceeding in order to liquidate worker entitlements.

'LIKE TOKYO IN 1945'
Ruins of Kaiser Steel, 1990

During the shutdown in 1983, workers had taken some solace in the assurance that cash-rich Kaiser, unlike some bankrupted Eastern steelmakers, would always be able to honor its obligations. Now, four years later, six thousand outraged former employees watched as Hendry cancelled their medical coverage and pension supplements, while transferring part of the burden of their pension funding to the federal Pension Benefit Guarantee Corporation. In order to deflect worker anger, he also initiated lawsuits to recover the $325 million in Kaiser reserves allegedly 'stolen' by Frates and Rial through their buyouts.[121] At the moment of writing, three years further on, most of the benefits remain unrecovered, the various lawsuits have disappeared in a judicial logjam, and thousands of ex-steelworkers and their families have endured further, unexpected hardships.

THE MIRAGE OF REDEVELOPMENT

Nothing Is As Nice As Developing Fontana
Current official slogan

Fontana Headed For Economic Catastrophe
Headline, 1987[122]

Even as the 'Reagan Boom' was taking off in 1983, steel towns were still dying across the country, from Geneva (Utah) to Lackawanna (New York), Fairfield (Alabama) to Youngstown (Ohio). Aliquippa, from which so many Fontanans had emigrated in the 1940s and 1950s, was amongst the hardest hit. The shutdown of the immense, seven-mile-long Jones and Laughlin (LTV) complex, and the lay-off of twenty thousand workers, was the equivalent of a nuclear disaster. A third of the population fled; of those left behind, more than half were still jobless four years after the closure. The Salvation Army became the town's leading employer. A 1986 study of three hundred Aliquippa families revealed that 59 per cent had difficulty feeding themselves, 49 per cent were behind in their utility bills, and 61 per cent could not afford to see a doctor.[123]

Driving through the Valley on Thanksgiving Day 1988, on the way to lay a wreath at the union martyrs' monument in Homestead, I found little improvement or new hope. For miles along the Ohio River the sides of the great mill had been stripped away by demolition crews, exposing the rusting entrails of pipework and machinery. Downtown Aliquippa, tightly wedged in its abrupt valley, was boarded up and as empty as any Western ghost town. At the old main gate, through which ten thousand Aliquippans had once daily streamed to work, a forlorn lean-to and some fading picket signs announced 'Fort Justice', the site of a futile, two-year vigil by local unionists to save the plant from demolition.

By any standard Fontana should have suffered the same fate as Aliquippa. Studies in the early and late 1970s confirmed that almost half of the town worked for Kaiser and nearly three-quarters drew paychecks dependent upon the mill.[124] Yet when the final shutdown came in December 1983, Fontana was a boom-, not a ghost-town. Side by side with the defeated milltown, a new community of middle-class commuters was rapidly taking shape. In the last years of the plant's life the population began to explode: doubling from 35,000 to 70,000 between 1980 and 1987, with predictions of 100,000–150,000 by the year 2000. In an interview with the *Times* as the last slabs were being rolled out at Kaiser, Fontana's Mayor Simon exulted about the city's new-found prosperity as the housing frontier of Southern California. 'Nobody expected what's been happening here. When Kaiser closed, everybody thought the town was going to go kaput, but that hasn't happened.'[125]

The recycling of Fontana had begun in the mid 1970s after a clique of local landowners and city officials, led by City Manager Jack Ratelle, recognized that residential redevelopment was a lucrative alternative to continued dependence upon the waning fortunes of Kaiser Steel and its blue-collar workforce. Unlike Aliquippa they had the dual advantages of being the periphery of a booming regional economy and having access to an extraordinary tool of community restructuring – California's redevelopment law. Created by a liberal legislature in the late 1940s to allow cities to build public housing in blighted areas, the law had become totally perverted by the 1970s. Not only was it being employed for massive 'poor removal' in downtown San Francisco and Los Angeles, but 'blight' was now so generously interpreted that wealthy cities and industrial enclaves – from Palm Springs to City of Industry – were using the law to build luxury department stores, convention centers, and championship golf courses with 'tax increments' withheld from general fund uses.

Fontana's particular riff on these redevelopment strategies was its creation of an open, some would say 'golden', door for developers. Ratelle and the other city fathers fretted about their ability to compete with Rancho Cucamonga to the west – a 'greenfield' city concocted out of several thinly populated, agricultural townships. In order to eventually become like Orange County, they started out by acting like Puerto Rico. To compensate for gritty Fontana's 'image problem', and to give it a comparative advantage in the Inland Empire's landrush, they bent redevelopment law to offer 'creative financing' for large-scale developers: tax-increment and tax-exempt bonds, waiver of city fees, massive tax rebates, and, unique to Fontana, direct equity participation by the redevelopment agency. Application and inspection processes were drastically streamlined to accelerate groundbreaking in the city that aspired to become the 'developer's best friend'.

Fontana's pioneer redevelopment project was an expensive – many would say, unnecessary – facelift of Sierra Avenue begun in 1975. David Wiener, whom the local paper likes to call the 'dean of Fontana developers', was given tax-exempt financing and sales-tax rebates to construct four new shopping complexes. A little later the Fontana Redevelopment Agency (FRA) began to uproot vineyards south of Interstate 10 to build the South-west Industrial Park. But the big Orange County and West L.A.-based developers, already heavily involved in Ontario and Rancho Cucamonga, refused to consider Fontana until it was clear that Kaiser Steel was doomed and that the milltown onus could be removed.

Fontana's first megaproject, initiated in 1981, was the Village of Southridge, located in the Jurupa Hills redevelopment area south of I-10 and projected for a build-out of nine thousand homes by the year 2000. Creative Communities, the Huntington Beach-based developers of Southridge, seduced Fontana's civic leaders by giving them a tour of Irvine, the famous master-planned city in southern Orange County. They convinced the starstruck Fontanans that a simulacrum of Irvine could be developed in Fontana's own south end if the city were willing to provide adequate infrastructure and financing. As Mayor Simon later recalled, 'the city fathers wanted the project so bad that they could taste it'. Accordingly, with visions of Fontana-as-Irvine dancing before their eyes, they signed a far-reaching agreement with Creative Communities that pledged the FRA to reimburse most of the infrastructural costs normally borne by developers.[126]

In 1982, one year after the groundbreaking in Southridge, Fontana annexed a huge triangle of boulder-strewn fields north of the city, abutting Interstate 15 (then under construction). The completion of I-15 through western San Bernardino and Riverside and northern San Diego counties has created one of the nation's most dynamic growth corridors. (One of the corridor's boomtowns is 'Ranch California', a 100,000-acre project originated by Kaiser Development Co. in Temecula.) Three hundred thousand new residents are expected in western San Bernardino County alone.[127] Fontana, sitting at the strategic intersection of I-15 and I-10 (the San Bernardino Freeway), has superb linkages to this rapidly expanding commutershed. The North Fontana Project Area, which incorporates the old Fontana 'ghetto' (an area of ironically exploding land values), is the largest redevelopment project in California (fourteen square miles), encompassing a series of prospective master-planned communities. Largest is the upscale Village of Heritage, directly competitive with Rancho Cucamonga's Terra Vista, and Victoria, which is being developed by BD Partners of West Los Angeles (Richard Barclay and Joseph Dilorio), with heavy equity participation from FRA. Heritage will provide four thousand of the eighteen thousand new homes that the FRA wants to add in North Fontana over the next generation.[128]

By the time the demolition crews had got around to dismantling Big Bess, Fontana's leaders had managed to put 20,000 new homes in the $60,000-and-up range on the drawing boards in Southridge and North Fontana.[129] Within four years of Kaiser Steel's closure, raw land prices in Fontana had doubled.[130] This remarkable achievement garnered national accolades and much talk of a paradigmatic 'Fontana miracle'. The Los Angeles *Times*, for example, downplayed the impact of the Kaiser shutdown and resulting 15 per cent local unemployment (which it misreported as 9 per cent) in order to emphasize the city's 'bright future' under its redevelopment strategy.[131] Journalists uncritically reproduced city officials' claims that Fontana would soon be wealthy from its soaring tax bases and profits on its equity position in different developments. Just as Kaiser industrial relations had once been studied as a textbook model, now Fontana's resilience was presented as laboratory confirmation of the Reagan administration's claim that deindustrialization was only a temporary and marginal cost in the transition to postindustrial prosperity based on services, finance and real estate.

The first symptom that all was really not so well in Fontana *redux* was the sharp increase in white supremacist agitation and racial violence after the layoffs at the mill. During the course of 1983 the local Ku Klux Klan – about two dozen strong – crawled out from under their rock and began distributing leaflets in the high schools, holding public rallies and even offering to 'assist' the Fontana police. The Klan revival seems to have exercised a certain charisma upon a periphery of skinhead youth. In a savage October 1984 attack, a twenty-year-old Black man, Sazon Davis, was left paralyzed from the chest down after being beaten by three skinheads on Sierra Avenue – Fontana's main street. The Black community was further outraged – shades of O'Day Short – when the San Bernardino County district attorney refused to prosecute the white youth, one of whose mothers was the dispatcher for the Fontana police. (The reaction of Fontana development director Neil Stone to this local precursor of Howard Beach was to moan 'image has been our main problem'.)[132]

Worse problems lay soon ahead. By Christmas 1986 the Fontana bubble had burst. City Finance Director Edwin Leukemeyer resigned in face of charges that he had embezzled public funds and sold off city-owned vehicles to his friends and relatives. Within six months the stream of resignations and indictments prompted one paper to claim that 'police detectives and auditors [are] almost as common a sight in City Hall as file clerks'.[133] Amongst the new casualties – a list that included the city treasurer, the motor pool director, the redevelopment director, and the development director – was City Manager and ex officio FRA chief Jack Ratelle, the chief architect of the 'third Fontana'. The city council forced Ratelle to resign after published reports of gratuities from leading developers made his position untenable.[134]

Demoralization in Fontana City Hall was turned into panic in August 1987 by the release of an independent audit of the city by the regional office of Arthur Young. The Young report was devastating: the FRA was in a 'chaotic state of disarray' and the city was on the edge of bankruptcy.[135]

The Young analysts discovered that the FRA had pawned Fontana's future in order to seduce developers. With 60 per cent of its tax base located in redevelopment areas, and obligated as payments or rebates to developers, the city could not afford to meet the needs of its expanding population. No tax revenue was left over to pay for the additional load that the new suburban population placed on its schools or public services.

Southridge alone, which Ratelle had always portrayed as a municipal gold mine, threatened to drive the city into bankruptcy as the FRA faced $10,000 per day in new interest charges accumulating on the unreimbursed principal which it owed Creative Communities. Official estimates of the total tax revenue that will be absorbed in debt service to Southridge run as high as *$750 million* by 2026 when the agreement expires.[136] It is unlikely that the principal will ever be repaid. Like a miniature Mexico or Bolivia, Fontana is a debtor nation held in thrall to its Orange County and West L.A. creditor-developers. With its suburban property tax streams diverted to debt service, the city has had both to impose austerity (in the form of over-crowded schools and degraded services) and (as in Southridge) special fee assessments on unhappy new arrivals. The alternative of raising additional city income from existing commerce is excluded by the FRA's profligate rebates of sales taxes and municipal fees to the owners of the new shopping centers.

The release of the Young report (which also included sensationalist details of financial mismanagement and the destruction of records in City Hall) emboldened local journalists to muckrake through the FRA's records, untangling the circumstances of the agency's incredible profligacy. Mark Gutglueck of the *Herald-News* eventually exposed in detail how various redevelopment schemes had pauperized the city.[137] The older mom-and-dad businesses along Sierra Avenue, for instance, were starved of redevelop-ment funds by FRA policies that favored chain-store 'K-Martization'. Thus the FRA, in a typical example, gave tax-exempt financing and a $750,000 tax rebate to induce National Lumber to move into one of David Weiner's new shopping centers, itself financed by tax givebacks. The net result for the city was a large tax deficit and the closure of Ole's Hardware, an oldtime Fontana institution.[138]

Likewise, in the case of Southridge, Gutglueck revealed how City Manager Ratelle and redevelopment lawyer Timothy Sabo (accused in the Young report of raking off excessive fees) overrode the strong objections of the city attorney to provide Creative Communities (later Ten-Ninety Ltd.) with whatever they demanded: hiked-up interest rates on FRA's obligation, forgiveness for their failure to build schools on time per contract, and so on. Moreover, the developers were repeatedly allowed to modify the community's specific plan, successively reducing the quality of housing and local amenities. The developers, in turn, pampered officials (like planning chief Neil Stone) with 'finders fees', gratuities and the use of a lakeside resort, while Southridge – which Mayor Simon liked to call 'the Beverly Hills of Fontana' – evolved into misery.[139] One planner who worked there has described it as 'rabbit hutches with two-car garages, without adequate schools or public services'.[140] Not surprisingly the Young report and the Gutglueck revelations fueled a revolt by embittered Southridge residents who demanded a moratorium on further growth, the recall of the council majority, and a system of district elections.[141]

Given the enormity of Fontana's suddenly exposed problems – the venality of its officials, its Andean-sized debt and the lien on its tax base until the next millennium, its underfunding of essential services, a growing mismatch between housing and jobs, and so on, the voter revolt was strangely muffled. Closure of Kaiser had dispersed much of the political base once organized by Local 2869, while the new commuter citizens had little time or focus for civic engagement. As a result the growth coalition – minus a few leaders in jail or exile – handily dispersed its challengers.[142] The Southridge-instigated recall campaign was easily defeated, while the demand for a growth moratorium was harmlessly converted into a 45-day temporary freeze on building permits. The council did scale back a few development plans in North Fontana, and gave lip service to the Young report's two hundred recommendations. But the most symptomatic reaction to the crisis came from Mayor Simon (then under investigation for making unlawful personal investments in one of the redevelopment areas), who simply urged Fontanans 'to just keep smiling'.[143]

Since then the city fathers have tried to escape bankruptcy by tacking their sails to various, sometimes countervailing, winds. Like the rubes they are, they have ended up buying back into schemes virtually identical to those that Bolivianized Fontana in the early 1980s.

First, they have searched high and low for some commercial *deus ex machina* to generate a compensatory tax flow for their fiscal deficit. Mayor

SOUTHRIDGE TURNED FONTANA INTO BOLIVIA

Simon's own pet-rock scheme – contrived during a Canadian vacation from his legal problems – was to induce a multi-billion-dollar investor to build the California version of the Edmonton supermall in Fontana.[144] In the absence of responses from Donald Trump or the Sultan of Brunei, the city teamed up instead with Alexander Haagen, Southern California's major mall builder, in a scheme to build a combination mall-entertainment complex in South Fontana. Just like Southridge, Haagen's Fontana Empire Center (scheduled for completion in 1995) was sold to local officials in a blaze of Orange County imagery: 'Fontana's answer to the South Coast Plaza'. Lest any of the Fontanans stop to ponder the absurdity of a Sears-anchored mall competing with the nation's wealthiest regional center anchored by Gucchi and Neiman-Marcus, Haagen anesthetized opposition by generously donating to all ten candidates vying for the two vacant seats on the council.[145] (Recently Haagen has started to backtrack on his original promises, proposing to develop one-half of the mall site for luxury homes instead of commerce.)[146]

Meanwhile, Fontana leaders have tried to scrub the city clean of its blue-collar, 'felony flats' image by drastically limiting the development of apartments and low-income units.[147] The revised Fontana masterplan even de-emphasizes 'starter homes' – the meat and potatoes of the previous plan – to favor more expensive 'move-up' or second homes.[148] Salesmen of Fontana's 'new look', however, were immediately embarrassed by a re-crudescence of the old Fontana in 1988. Millions of television viewers nationwide watched as celebrants of Martin Luther King's birthday had to be escorted down Sierra Avenue by a hundred and twenty police as acrid little knots of Fontana Klansmen shouted 'Long live the Klan. Long live the white boys.' Subsequent 'Death to the Klan' counter-rallies by the Jewish Defense League contributed yet more unwanted notoriety.[149]

The campaign for an upscaled Fontana also collided with plans for a reindustrialized Fontana. With an unerring sense for courting contradiction, as one group of Fontana planners was trying to increase residential exclusivity, another was simultaneously kicking out the jambs for break-neck factory and warehouse construction. Offering contractors the state's fastest track for industrial development, they guarantee building starts six days after application, rather than the nine months normal elsewhere.[150] As angry homeowners have pointed out, combining poorly monitored industrial development – much of it highly toxic – with dense residential development is like mixing oil with water. This point was vividly illustrated in 1988 when more than 1,500 Southridge residents had to be evacuated after a nearby chemical spill.[151]

The final irony, however, is Fontana's ardent courtship of Kaiser Steel's residuum: Kaiser Resources. Left with a mile-long slag mountain and seven hundred acres of polluted wasteland, KR in partnership with Lusk-Ontario Industries has maneuvered brilliantly to get Fontana to foot the bill for the clean-up. By coyly flirting with Ontario and Rancho Cucamonga, then suddenly throwing kisses to advocates of independent cityhood for Fontana's unincorporated westside ('Rancho Vista'), KR drove Fontana officials into a jealous frenzy. As a result, debt-hobbled Fontana is offering a memorandum of understanding to KR and Lusk that would guarantee $190 million in public funds to renovate the ex-Kaiser Steel site. In particular Fontana would help clean up the still spreading plume of soil and groundwater contamination that is the legacy of forty years of steelmaking, and which has replaced the smoke-cloud from Kaiser's coke ovens as the symbol of environmental distress in San Bernardino County. KR and Lusk, in turn, would accept annexation by Fontana and agree to develop a high-tech industrial park. But a centerpiece of KR's plan is a perverse environmental joke: importing Silicon Valley's toxic waste for processing in Kaiser Steel's still extant treatment facility.[152]

SO WHAT'S LEFT?

It's tacky, very, very tacky. But, maybe I should be grateful. People tell me it used to be worse. *New Fontana commuter-resident*[153]

Eat shit and die.
Reaction of old Fontana 'homeboy'

After so many schemes, scandals, and sudden upheavals, what is Fontana today? Begin, arbitrarily, with its Wild West, unincorporated fringe. Follow the fire-engine-red Kenworth K600A 'Anteater' pulling its shackled double reefers into the lot of 'Trucktown' off the Cherry Street exit of I-10, just south of the Kaiser ghost plant. There are more than one-hundred-and-twenty independent trucking companies based in the Fontana area, and this is their central fuel stop and oasis. Around midnight Trucktown really bustles and rigs are often backed up to the Interstate waiting for a fuel-stop or parking berth. The biggest truckstop in the country is just a few miles further west in Ontario, but drivers resent Union 76's private police force and stale pie.

Cherry Avenue is clearly, as they say, 'west of the Pecos', and it is easier to make deals of all kinds here. Inside the cafe the counter is occupied by an apparition of Lee's Army after Appomattox: lean, bearded, hollow-eyed and taciturn. There is more animation in the booths. Owner-operators wrestle with logbooks and second-driver problems; husband-wife teams have family arguments; brokers with questionable loads wrangle for haulers; outlaw bikers peddle old ladies and 'Black Molly' (speed). The Cherry Avenue fringe has always accommodated illicit but popular activities. Until its recent closure by the Highway Patrol, the adjacent rest area on I-10 functioned as a girls-and-dope drive-in for morning commuters in Toyotas and tourists in Winnebagos.

Now the entire Fontana periphery (including the incorporated north-side and Rialto as well as the Cherry Street area) has become the Huallaga Valley of Southern California. Long the 'speed capital of the world', its meth labs have recently diversified into the mass manufacture of 'ice' (crystal, smokable speed) and 'croak' (a smokable combination of speed and crack). For the most part this is grassroots narco-patriotism: drug addiction made-in-America by small-town good old boys and distributed throughout the heartland by a vast network of motorcycle gangs and outlaw truckers. From the standpoint of free enterprise economics it is also a textbook example of small entrepreneurs filling the void left by the collapse of a dinosaur heavy industry. Speed not steel is now probably Fontana's major export.

Which is not to deny that a lot of steel is still being hauled out of Fontana even if Big Bess herself was long ago melted for scrap. The multi-national hybrid of California Steel Industries, just up Cherry Avenue, continues to roll Brazilian slabs into a variety of products for local markets (although the Japanese, and increasingly the Koreans, dominate the big-ticket structural items). The United Steel Workers recently attempted to organize CSI but the campaign ended in disaster. Whether out of fear of

DEATH ALLEY
Valley Boulevard

losing their jobs again, or in resentment against the international's failure to come to their aid eight years earlier, the ex-Local 2869 men at CSI resoundingly voted the union down (88 per cent to 12 per cent).

The former primary steelworks itself looks like Dresden, Hiroshima or, perhaps the most fitting image, Tokyo in April 1945 after three months of concentrated fire-bombing with Kaiser-made 'goop' had burnt the city down to the ferroconcrete stumps of its major buildings. The wreckers long ago picked the plant clean of any salvageable metal – some of which, reincarnated in Toyotas and Hyundais, zooms by on I-10. Meanwhile, the towering smokestacks, once visible for thirty miles, are collapsed into rubble, while only the skeletal concrete cores of the blast furnaces remain. Around the heavily guarded perimeter, Kaiser Resources leases land to a series of 'mom-and-dad' scrapyards, who, having run out of Kaiser wreckage, are now happily crushing and shredding derelict automobiles. The whole scene looks like *Mad Max*: a post-apocalyptic society of industrial scavengers and metal vultures.

Across the road lie shadows of Fontana Farms. A ghostly vintage chicken ranch is overgrown with weeds but otherwise kept intact by its octogenarian owner who recalls the great plague of Newcastle's disease in 1971 that killed millions of Fontana hens. A few miles away in South Fontana a handful of chicken ranchers have managed to hang on and modernize their operations. Near the corner of Jarupa and Popper stands an astounding automatic chicken plant that works by conveyors belts, where one man can easily tend 250,000 hens. But the resulting accumulation of chicken manure is so vast that it has to be pushed around the ranch by bulldozers. Nearby commuter homeowners – no longer beguiled by the romance of chicken shit – are circulating petitions to close down this successful survival of the Millerian age. When the last trace of the chickens, pigs and orchards have been removed, Fontana's remaining link to its agrarian past will be its thousands of dogs. We are not talking about manicured suburban house dogs, but old-fashioned yard dogs: snarling, half-rabid, dopey, friendly, shaggy, monstrous and ridiculous Fontana dogs.

Fontana probably also has more wrecked cars per capita than anywhere else on the planet. The nearby Southern California Auto Auction is considered by some aficionados to be the eighth wonder of the world. More

THE LOST ELEPHANTS

impressive to me is the vast number of dismantled or moribund cars deliberately strewn in people's yards like family heirlooms. I suppose it is a sight that blights Fontana's new image, but the junkyard sensibility can grow on you after a while (at least it has on me). The Fontana area – or rather the parts of it that are not named 'Heritage' or 'Eagle Pointe Executive Homes' – is a landscape of randomly scattered, generally uncollectable (and ungentrifiable) debris: ranging from Didion's creepy boulders to the rusting smudge-pots in phantom orchards, to the Burma-Shave-era motel names (like 'Ken-Tuck-U-In') on Foothill Boulevard. Even crime in Fontana has a random surreality about it. There is, for instance, the maniac who has murdered hundreds of eucalyptus trees, or Bobby Gene Stile ('Doctor Feldon'), the king of obscene phone calls, who has confessed to fifty thousand dirty phone conversations over the last twenty-three years.

'Doctor Feldon' had, perhaps, wandered too far and too freely in the fleshpots of Fontana's Valley Boulevard (still, as in 1941, 'death alley'). Just east of Cherry Avenue the boulevard is a boring repetition of adult bookstores and used truck dealerships. Closer to Sierra, however, there is a gathering sense of a *mise en scène* by a downhome Fellini. On one corner a hardluck cowboy is trying to sell his well-worn Stetson hat to the patriarch of a family of road gipsies – or are they Okies circa 1990? – who pile out of their converted Crown bus home. They have just left the Saturday swap meet at the nearby Belair Drive-In. Inside a lobster-faced desert 'flea' from Quartzite is haggling with a trio of super-bag-ladies from the San Fernando Valley over the value of some 'depression' glass saucers and an antique commode. Some local kids with 'Guns and Roses' gang-bang T-shirts are listening to another grizzled desert type – this one looking like Death Valley Scotty – describe his recent encounter with aliens. A Jehovah's Witness in a maroon blazer kibbitzs uncomprehendingly.

A block away is an even more improbable sight: a circus wrecking yard. Scattered amid the broken bumper cars and ferris wheel seats are nostalgic bits and pieces of Southern California's famous extinct amusement parks (in the pre-Disney days when admission was free or $1): the Pike, Belmont Shores, Pacific Ocean Park, and so on. Suddenly rearing up from the back of a flatbed trailer are the fabled stone elephants and pouncing lions that once stood at the gates of Selig Zoo in Eastlake (Lincoln) Park, where they had enthralled generations of Eastside kids. I tried to imagine how a native of Manhattan would feel, suddenly discovering the New York Public Library's stone lions discarded in a New Jersey wrecking yard. I suppose the Selig lions might be Southern California's summary, unsentimental judgement on the value of its lost childhood. The past generations are like so much debris to be swept away by the developers' bulldozers. In which case it is only appropriate that they should end up here, in Fontana – the junkyard of dreams.

NOTES

1. Joan Didion, *Slouching Towards Bethlehem*, New York 1968, p. 5. Her reaction to the Fontana area was a symptomatic premonition of her very revulsion to the landscape of El Salvador twenty years later.
2. '. . . and then they found Fontana Farms' – 1930 advertising brochure in Fontana Historical Society collection. Fontana Farms Company was headquartered at 631 S. Spring St. in Downtown Los Angeles.
3. At least this was the name given by geographers to the intermontane basin which includes the Pomona, Chino and San Bernardino valleys, as well as the Riverside Basin and the great Cucamonga Fan. (See David W. Lantis, *California: Land of Contrast*, Belmont, Calif. 1963, p. 226.) The current appellation of 'Inland Empire' loosely encompasses the Perris Valley and the San Jacinto Basin as well.
4. See Karen Frantz, 'History of Rural Fontana and the Decline of Agriculture', typescript, no date, in Fontana Public Library.
5. See Richard Lillard, 'Agricultural Statesman: Charles C. Teague of Santa Paula', *California History*, March 1986.
6. By 1895 Riverside was supposedly 'the richest city per capita' in the United States. See Vincent Moses, 'Machines in the Garden: A Citrus Monopoly in Riverside, 1900–31', *California History*, Spring 1982.
7. See Charles Teague, *Fifty Years a Rancher*, Santa Paula (private printing) 1944.
8. See Silver Anniversary issue, *Fontana Herald-News*, 10 June 1938.
9. Frantz. According to Mr Barnhold, who still lives in his 1927 Fontana Farms bungalow just east of Cherry Street: 'One thousand chickens and two-and-a-half acres did not make a good living. Miller's propaganda was untrue, and many Fontanans had a hard, uphill struggle to survive the Depression especially.' (Interview, June 1989)
10. Giorgio Ciucci, 'The City in Agrarian Ideology and Frank Lloyd Wright: Origins and Development of Broadacres', in Ciucci, et al., *The American City: From the Civil War to the New Deal*, Cambridge, Mass. 1979, pp. 358, 375.
11. *Fontana Herald-News*, 31 July 1942.
12. *Inside USA*, New York 1946, p. xiv.
13. Ibid., p. 68.
14. By the 1951 revised edition of *Inside USA*, however, Gunther's infatuation with Kaiser had clearly waned, and the Kaiser chapter was abridged into a short subsection.
15. Quotes from 'Life and Works of Henry Kaiser', ibid., pp. 64, 70.

16. Ibid., p. 70. On the other hand, Kaiser became a patron of labor only *after* he had become a leading beneficiary of lucrative New Deal contracts. Earlier, during the construction of Hoover Dam, he and his partners had systematically violated labor standards and health and safety regulations. When, after a series of appalling industrial accidents and deaths from heat prostration, the dam workers struck under IWW leadership in 1931, they were crushed by the Six Companies. See Joseph Stevens, *Hoover Dam: An American Adventure*, Norman 1988, pp. 69–78.

17. Gunther, p. 64.

18. A.G. Mezerik, *The Revolt of the South and West*, New York 1946, p. 280.

19. A major disappointment of Mark Foster's recent biography of Kaiser (*Henry J. Kaiser: Builder in the Modern American West*, Austin 1989) is its failure to shed new light upon the Kaiser–Giannini relationship.

20. Ibid., pp. 58–9.

21. Cf. Marquis and Bessie James, *Biography of a Bank: The Story of Bank of America*, New York 1954, pp. 389–92; Arthur Schlesinger, *The Age of Roosevelt: The Politics of Upheaval*, Cambridge, Mass. 1960, pp. 121, 297, 411. In 1934 Giannini made a last-minute intervention on FDR's behalf to buy out Upton Sinclair's radical bid for governor on the Democratic ticket. (See Russell Posner, 'A. P. Giannini and the 1934 Campaign in California', *Journal of California History* 34, 2, 1957.) Although unsuccessful in coopting Sinclair, Giannini went on to play a crucial role in winning California for Roosevelt in 1936. His support for the New Deal, however, waned after 1938 as he perceived the consolidation of the power of a 'Jewish cabal' led by his old enemy Eugene Meyer and Secretary of Treasury Morgenthau. See Julian Dana, *J.P. Giannini: Giant in the West*, New York 1947, pp. 315–17, 322–3.

22. Schlesinger, p. 411.

23. Gunther, pp. 71–2; Foster, Chapter 5, 'Patriot in Pinstripes – Shipbuilding', pp. 68–89.

24. Gunther, p. 71.

25. The Kaiser model of the expanded or complex wage agreement, including a medical component (cheapened by an economy of scale), was a potent influence upon the collective bargaining system ultimately hammered out by the CIO unions and the major industrial employers in the late 1940s.

26. Quoted in Mezerik, p 265.

27. Gerald Nash is quite mistaken, of course, in asserting that Fontana was built 'largely at government expense'. (See *The American West Transformed: The Impact of the Second World War*, Bloomington, Ind. 1985, p. 28.)

28. Ibid., p. 264.

29. See the discussion in John E. Coffman, 'The Infrastructure of Kaiser Steel Fontana: an Analysis of the Effects of Technical Change on Raw Material Logistics', MA thesis, Department of Geography, UCLA, Los Angeles 1969, pp. 1–2, 5, 25–9.

30. Frantz, p. 25; *Fontana Herald-News*, 7 January 1943.

31. Ibid., 14 and 21 January 1941.

32. Ibid., 18 April (Miller obituary), 16 May and 19 September 1941.

33. Ibid., 6 June 1941.

34. Ibid., 29 May 1958 (recollections of the war years).

35. Ibid., 2 and 30 January 1942. The critical role of poultry in the national defense had been avidly discussed by Fontanans the previous fall. (See ibid., 19 September 1941.)

36. The 'bolt' appeared in local papers on 6 March 1942 (see ibid.).

37. Frantz, p. 26.

38. Ibid.

39. *Fontana Herald-News*, 3 and 10 April 1942.

40. Cf. *Business Week*, 21 November 1942; *Fontana Herald-News*, 30 December 1942, 7 and 14 January 1943. Cal-Ship in San Pedro was operated by Kaiser's old partners, Stephen Bechtel and John McCone (the future CIA chief).

41. Gunther, p. 72.
42. Ibid., 3 April 1942.
43. Interview with Barnhold family, early residents of the Cherry Street area across from the Kaiser plant. See also Frantz, p. 27.
44. *Fontana Herald-News*, 22 July 1943.
45. *Steel Magazine*, 25 September 1944. On the other hand, Kaiser Steel in its early years was able to take advantage of the informal tariff barrier erected around California by the railroad's exorbitant shipping rates and Pittsburgh's own monopoly surtax.
46. James and James, p. 468.
47. See Henry J. Kaiser Jr.'s exposition of his father's views in *Fontana Herald-News*, 10 December 1942.
48. See Foster, pp. 1–2, 179–82.
49. *Fontana Herald-News*, 26 February and 19 September 1946; Foster, pp. 132–4.
50. Gunther (1951 revised edn), p. 47.
51. See Book Four, 'Transamerican Titan', in Julian Dana, *A.P. Giannini: Giant in the West*, New York 1947.
52. Dana, p. 163.
53. Cf. Gunther, pp. 73–74; and Foster, pp. 142–64.
54. *Iron Age*, 7 October 1948.
55. Cf. Coffman; J.S. Ess, 'Kaiser Steel – Fontana', *Iron and Steel Engineer* 31, February 1954; and C. Langdon White, 'Is the West Making the Grade in the Steel Industry?', *Stanford Business Research Series* 8, 1956.
56. Ibid., pp. 102–3; and Mezerik, p. 266.
57. Ibid., pp. 103–5; James and James, pp. 493–4; and Robert Gottlieb and Irene Wolt, *Thinking Big: The Story of the Los Angeles Times*, New York 1977, p. 244.
58. Cf. Neil Morgan, *Westward Tilt: The American West Today*, New York 1963, p. 29; and Kaiser Steel Company, *Annual Reports*, 1959 and 1965.
59. For history of agreement, see William Aussieker, 'The Decline of Labor-Management Cooperation: The Kaiser Long-Range Sharing Plan', IRRA, *35th Annual Proceedings*, pp. 403–9. For typical textbook celebrations of the Plan, see James Heney, ed., *Creative Collective Bargaining*, Englewood Cliffs, N.J. 1965; and Herbert Bltiz, ed., *Labor-Management Contracts and Technological Change*, New York 1969.
60. Quoted in *Eagle*, 20 December 1945.
61. Frantz, pp. 27–30; *Fontana Herald-News*, 12 August 1943.
62. Interviews with pioneer Barnhold family, steelworker veterans, John Piazza and Dino Papavero, and my own family (residents of Fontana from 1941 to 1949). Also see *Fontana Herald-News*, 31 December 1942, and 22 July and 12 August 1943; as well as the recollections in the 29 May 1955 issue.
63. Ibid.
64. See virtually any issue of the *Eagle* on file at the Southern California Library for Social Research.
65. Cf. *Eagle*, 20 December 1945; Charlotta Bass, *Forty Years: Memoirs from the Pages of a Newspaper*, Los Angeles (privately printed) 1960, pp. 135–6; and *The Militant*, 2 February 1946.
66. Bass, ibid.; *The Militant*, 2 February and 23 March 1946.
67. *Herald-News*, 3 January 1946.
68. *Eagle*, 3 January 1946; *Daily World*, 2 January 1946.
69. Bass, ibid.; *Eagle*, 17 and 31 January 1946; *The Militant*, 2 February 1946.
70. *Daily World*, 6 and 14 February 1946; *Eagle*, 7 February 1946; *The Militant*, 11 February 1946.

71. The period from V-J Day 1945 to Fall 1946 witnessed a rising arc of white resistance to civil rights in Los Angeles: riots by white high-school students, unwarranted police shootings, cross burnings at USC, a judicial verdict in support of restrictive covenants, and, on 7 May 1946, a Klan bombing of a Black home in Southcentral. See the *Eagle* file; and Bass.

72. *The Militant*, 23 March 1946.

73. However the civil rights fight in Fontana continued. For example, in early 1949 ministers of the local AME church sued a Fontana cafe for lunch-counter discrimination. (See *Eagle*, 13 January 1949.)

74. See *Herald-News*, 14 March 1946.

75. Hunter Thompson, *Hell's Angels: A Strange and Terrible Saga*, New York 1966, p. 90.

76. For an insider's account of the Oakland chapter's rise, see George Wethern (with Vincent Colnett), *A Wayward Angel*, New York 1978.

77. Frank Reynolds (as told to Michael McClure), *Freewheelin' Frank*, New York 1967, pp. 7, 110–11.

78. Thompson, pp. 59–62. Thompson makes an interesting case that the harassment tactics used against the Berdoo Angels were the precedent for police 'street cleaning' efforts against the 1960s peace movement (p. 60).

79. Los Angeles *Times*, 15 February 1990.

80. John Herling, *Right to Challenge: People and Power in the Steelworkers Union*, New York 1972, p. 207.

81. Interviews with Dino Papavero and John Piazza, Steelworkers' Oldtimers Foundation, Fontana, May 1989.

82. John Herling, pp. 198–212.

83. Ibid., pp. 207–11, 265–6, 280. The essence of Local 2869 alienation was summarized by a McDonald supporter: 'Dissatisfaction developed because of the wage discrepancy between those who were paid under the sharing plan and those under the incentive plan [older workers]. Added to this, the Committee of Nine had not consulted the local union leadership. . . . All the local leadership got was a decision handed down to them by the big boys on top.' (p. 212)

84. From a cuttings album of the Kaiser Personnel Department in the 1950s, retrieved from trash during the plant dismantling in 1985 by Dino Papavero. Most historical records of plant society were wantonly discarded.

85. Ibid.

86. *Times*, 6 September 1980 and 4 November 1981.

87. KSC *Annual Report*, 1961, 1963, 1964, 1966, and 1971.

88. Cf. retrospective analysis in KSC (Form 10–K) *Annual Report* 1980; and *Times*, 31 July 1977, 24 April 1978, 9 February 1979.

89. See Aussieker, pp. 403–9.

90. Interview with Dino Papavero, May 1989; also see Aussieker, pp. 405–6; *Times*, 2 February 1972, 28 March 1972.

91. KSC *Annual Report*, 1976, 1977; *Times*, 25 December 1976.

92. 'And the Smog Stayed On', pamphlet issued by Kaiser Steel, 1972.

93. 'Bill', in discussion at Steelworkers' Oldtimers Foundation, Fontana, May 1989. See also *Times*, 30 May 1978.

94. KSC (Form 10–K) *Annual Report* 1980.

95. *Times*, 6 and 10 September 1980.

96. *Times*, 9 February 1979.

97. *Times*, 27 September 1979.

98. Interview with Papavero and Piazza, May 1989.

99. Interviewed in *Times*, 4 August 1985.

100. KSC *Annual Report* 1979.

101. KSC (Form 10–K) *Annual Report* 1980; *Times*, 24 October and 22 November 1979.

102. Cf. KSC; and *Times*, September 1980.

103. *Times*, 2 June 1979.

104. KSC *Annual Report* 1981.

105. *Times*, 4 November 1981.

106. *Times*, 27 August 1980 and 13 February 1982.

107. The ESOP (Employee Stock Ownership Plan) divided Local 2869 into bitterly opposed factions with president Frank Anglin in favor and Ralph Shoutes leading the opposition. The last Local election was narrowly won by Anglin in April 1982. (Fontana *Herald-News*, 8 April 1982.)

108. See Aussieker, p. 408; *Times*, 14 August 1982.

109. In the Volcker–Reagan recession of 1979–1983 nearly 20,000 jobs were lost in California's steel and iron products sector, and the state membership of the United Steel Workers fell by 41%. See Anne Lawrence, 'Organizations in Crisis: Labor Union Responses to Plant Closures in California Manufacturing, 1979–83', Dept. of Geography, University of California, Berkeley 1985, pp. 55–7.

110. Allan Sloan and Peter Fuhrman, 'An American tragedy', *Forbes*, 20 October 1986.

111. On the accumulation of this cash hoard, see *Times*, 18 October 1979, 6 September 1980, 4 November 1981.

112. Ibid.

113. *Times*, 5 February 1982.

114. *Times*, 16 March 1982.

115. The *People's World*, 7 January 1984, marveled at the tax laws that make it so 'profitable' to scrap the plant. 'Net profits from the destruction of the only basic "integrated works" in the West may exceed all the profits made on the corporation's activities since the end of World War Two.'

116. *Herald-News*, 2 January 1984; *Times*, 4 August 1985.

117. *Times*, 27 May 1983.

118. *Sun*, 18 January 1988.

119. Sloan and Fuhrman, pp. 32–3; see also *Times*, 25 September 1987.

120. *Times*, 9 February 1987.

121. *Times*, 27 January, 9 and 13 February 1987, 10 and 31 August 1988. Ex-Local 2869 President Frank Anglin expressed the following opinion of Hendry's management: 'I haven't seen him do anything but lose money' (*Sun*, 18 January 1988).

122. *Sun*, 19 August 1987.

123. See 'Horse Dies in One-Horse Steel Town', *Times*, 1 September 1986.

124. *Times*, 30 January 1971; 23 June 1978 (Urbanomics Research Associates study); and 1 September 1985. 3,200 Kaiser workers lived in Fontana (population 21,000), 2,600 in Rialto/San Bernardino, and 3,200 in the rest of the Inland Empire.

125. *Times*, 15 August 1985.

126. See Joe Bridgman, 'Southridge Village: Milestone or Millstone for Fontana?', *Sun*, 16 February 1986.

127. *San Bernardino County General Plan Update*, 1988.

128. *Times*, 1 September 1985; *Sun*, 23 January 1986.

129. Cf. 'Southridge Village Specific Plan', FRA, n.d.

130. *Times*, 25 September 1988.

131. *Times*, 30 December 1983.

132. *Times*, 15 August 1985.

133. *Times*, 24 June 1987.

134. *Herald-News*, 14 December 1987.

135. Arthur Young International, Inland Empire Office, *Management Audit of the City of Fontana*, six volumes, 18 August 1987 (public copy of volume one in Fontana Library); *Sun*, 19 August 1987; and *Herald-News*, 19 August 1987.

136. *Sun*, 16 February 1986; debt estimate updated, 5 September 1987. In fact the FRA was so 'informal' in dealings with developers that it never bothered to accurately record or report its burgeoning debt. As the Arthur Young auditors noted: 'Although the Redevelopment Agency is highly leveraged, a definitive assessment on the exact amount of its obligations has not been made. . . . a determination of the Agency's total financial obligation has been frustrated by a lack of adequate record-keeping and file maintenance in the Agency, resulting in missing documents that are essential in quantifying the dollar amounts committed by the Agency to various developers.' (p. II–7)

137. *Herald-News*, 15 September, 26 and 29 October 1987.

138. Ibid., 26 and 29 October 1987. See also *Sun*, 17 August 1986.

139. Ibid., 15 September 1987; also the *Sun*, 16 February 1986.

140. Interview with 'P.C.', former Fontana planner, September 1989. It is questionable whether Southridge will ever be finished; phase three is officially described as 'in limbo'. (See *Herald-News*, 9 January 1990.)

141. The Fontana School Board also sued because of the developers' failure to build desperately needed schools.

142. The dissipation of the union political base was emphasized by John Piazza, May 1989.

143. *Sun*, 18 September 1987.

144. Ibid., 13 August 1987.

145. *Herald-News*, 1 November 1988.

146. Ibid., 9 January 1990.

147. On 'image' see *Sun*, 13 August 1978.

148. *Herald-News*, 8 December 1987; 26 October 1988.

149. Ibid.

150. Ibid., 24 August 1988.

151. Ibid., 26 October and 13 December 1988.

152. Cf. *Herald-News*, 3 November 1988; 11 January and 19 April 1989; and 16 January 1990.

153. *Times*, 6 August 1989.

INDEX